Mass Politics in Tough Times

Mass Politics in Tough Times

Opinions, Votes, and Protest in the Great Recession

Edited by

NANCY BERMEO

and

LARRY M. BARTELS

OXFORD
UNIVERSITY PRESS

OXFORD
UNIVERSITY PRESS

Oxford University Press is a department of the University of Oxford.
It furthers the University's objective of excellence in research, scholarship,
and education by publishing worldwide.

Oxford New York
Auckland Cape Town Dar es Salaam Hong Kong Karachi
Kuala Lumpur Madrid Melbourne Mexico City Nairobi
New Delhi Shanghai Taipei Toronto

With offices in
Argentina Austria Brazil Chile Czech Republic France Greece
Guatemala Hungary Italy Japan Poland Portugal Singapore
South Korea Switzerland Thailand Turkey Ukraine Vietnam

Oxford is a registered trademark of Oxford University Press
in the UK and certain other countries.

Published in the United States of America by
Oxford University Press
198 Madison Avenue, New York, NY 10016

Library of Congress Cataloging-in-Publication Data
Mass Politics in Tough Times : Opinions, Votes and Protest in the Great Recession /
edited by Nancy Bermeo and Larry M. Bartels.
pages cm
Includes bibliographical references and index.
ISBN 978–0–19–935750–5 (hardback)—ISBN 978–0–19–935751–2 (paperback)
1. Political participation—United States—History—21st century. 2. Political
participation—Europe—History—21st century. 3. Global Financial Crisis, 2008–2009.
I. Bermeo, Nancy Gina, 1951– II. Bartels, Larry M., 1956–
JK1764.M375 2014
323'.042—dc23
2013028226

Contents

About the Contributors

CHRISTOPHER J. ANDERSON is Professor of Government at Cornell University. His research focuses on inequality and legitimacy in the European Union and the OECD countries. He has written on such issues as the popularity of governments, the legitimacy of political institutions, and the link between welfare states and citizen behavior.

LARRY M. BARTELS holds the May Werthan Shayne Chair of Public Policy and Social Science at Vanderbilt University. He has written extensively on public opinion, electoral politics, and American democracy, including *Unequal Democracy: The Political Economy of the New Gilded Age* and *Presidential Primaries and the Dynamics of Public Choice.*

MARK R. BEISSINGER is the Henry W. Putnam Professor of Politics at Princeton University and Director of the Princeton Institute for International and Regional Studies (PIIRS). His main fields of research have been protest movements, nationalism, and revolutions, with special reference to the former Soviet Union and the postcommunist states.

NANCY BERMEO is the Nuffield Professor of Comparative Politics at Oxford University. She writes on regime change, institutional design, and the effects of systemic shocks on political behavior and institutions. Her publications include *Ordinary People in Extraordinary Times: The Role of the Citizenry in the Breakdown of Democracy* and, most recently, *Coping with Crisis: Government Reactions to the Great Recession* (ed. with Jonas Pontusson).

KATHERINE J. CRAMER is Professor of Political Science at the University of Wisconsin-Madison. Her work focuses on public opinion, political communication, civic engagement, and deliberative democracy. She is the author of *Talking About Race: Community Dialogues and the Politics of Difference* and *Talking About Politics: Informal Groups and Social Identity* *in American Life* and coauthor of *Democracy at Risk: How Political Choices Have Undermined Citizenship and What We Can Do About It.*

RAFAELA DANCYGIER is Assistant Professor in the Department of Politics and the Woodrow Wilson School at Princeton University. Her broad research interests are in comparative politics, with a focus on the implications of ethnic diversity in advanced democracies. Her work has examined the domestic consequences of international immigration, the political incorporation and electoral representation of immigrant-origin minorities, and the determinants of ethnic conflict. She is the author of *Immigration and Conflict in Europe* and has published in the *American Journal of Political Science, the Journal of Politics, Comparative Politics, World Politics,* and edited volumes.

MICHAEL DONNELLY is a Max Weber Fellow at the European University Institute. He received his Ph.D. in Politics and Social Policy from Princeton University in 2013. He studies comparative political behavior, European politics, and quantitative methods, focusing on issues at the intersection of group identities and political economy. He is currently working on a book manuscript titled "Identity and Interests: Voter Heuristics and Support for Redistributive Policies." His research has appeared in the *Journal of Politics*.

RAYMOND M. DUCH is an Official Fellow at Nuffield College, Oxford University, where he directs the Nuffield Centre for Experimental Social Sciences (CESS). He is the coauthor of *The Economic Vote: How Political and Economic Institutions Condition Election Results*, which demonstrates, from analysis of more than three hundred public opinion surveys, how citizens hold political parties accountable for economic outcomes. More recently, Duch has turned to experiments in order to identify the information shortcuts that individuals deploy for attributing responsibility for collective decision making, such as those made in multiparty governing coalition governments.

JASON D. HECHT is a Ph.D. candidate in the Department of Government at Cornell University and was a Visiting Scholar in Politics at the University of Oxford from 2012 to 2013. His dissertation explores how the onset of recessions affects public concern for income inequality in Europe and the United States. More broadly, his research investigates how economic, political, and social contexts shape individuals' behavior and attitudes.

SARA B. HOBOLT is Professor and Sutherland Chair in European Institutions at the London School of Economics and Political Science. She has previously held posts at the University of Oxford and the University of

Michigan and has published extensively on public opinion, elections, and European Union politics. Her book *Europe in Question: Referendums on European Integration* (Oxford University Press, 2009) was awarded the Best Book prize by the European Union Studies Association.

HANSPETER KRIESI currently holds the Stein Rokkan Chair in Comparative Politics at the European University Institute in Florence. He previously taught at the universities of Amsterdam, Geneva, and Zurich. His wide-ranging research interests include the study of direct democracy, social movements, political parties, interest groups, public opinion, the public sphere, and the media. He was the director of a Swiss national research program, Challenges to Democracy in the 21st Century, from 2005 to 2012.

PATRICK LEBLOND is Associate Professor in the Graduate School of Public and International Affairs at the University of Ottawa as well as Research Associate at CIRANO (Montreal). He has published extensively on financial and monetary integration, banking regulation, international trade, and business-government relations. Prior to moving to Ottawa, he taught international business at HEC Montreal and worked in accounting and business consulting.

NONNA MAYER is Research Director at the Centre National de la Recherche Scientifique of France and the Centre d'Études Européennes of Sciences Po, Paris. Her fields of expertise are electoral sociology, racism, anti-Semitism, and political participation. Her current research explores the electoral impact of social precariousness in a context of crisis.

IÑAKI SAGARZAZU is a Lecturer in Comparative Politics at the University of Glasgow. He obtained his Ph.D. from the University of Houston and was a Postdoctoral Research Fellow at Nuffield College, Oxford University. His research mainly focuses on how parties communicate with voters and how voters perceive these messages. His work has been published in journals such as the *American Journal of Political Science, Latin American Politics and Society,* and *European Union Politics.*

GWENDOLYN SASSE is a Professorial Fellow in Politics at Nuffield College, and University Reader in the Department of Politics and International Relations and the School of Interdisciplinary Area Studies, Oxford University. Her research interests include postcommunist transitions, comparative democratization, ethnic conflict, and the political behavior of migrants. Her most recent book, *The Crimea Question: Identity, Transition, and Conflict,* won the Alexander Nove Prize awarded by the British Association for Slavonic and East European Studies.

STUART SOROKA is Associate Professor and William Dawson Scholar in the Department of Political Science at McGill University, Montreal. He is a member of the Centre for the Study of Democratic Citizenship, and a co-investigator of the Canadian Election Study. Much of his work focuses on the sources and/or structure of public preferences for policy, and on the relationships between public policy, public opinion, and mass media. His most recent books include *Degrees of Democracy: Politics, Public Opinion and Policy* (with Christopher Wlezien) and *Negativity in Democratic Policy: Causes and Consequences* (forthcoming).

CHRISTOPHER WLEZIEN is Hogg Professor of Government at the University of Texas at Austin. He has published widely on elections, public opinion, and public policy. His books include *Degrees of Democracy, Who Gets Represented?* and *The Timeline of Presidential Elections*. He was founding coeditor of the *Journal of Elections, Public Opinion and Parties* and currently is associate editor of *Public Opinion Quarterly* and *Parliamentary Affairs*.

Mass Politics in Tough Times

1

Mass Politics in Tough Times

Nancy Bermeo and Larry M. Bartels

THE GREAT DEPRESSION of the 1930s stressed—and in some cases shattered—political systems around the world. In the United States, the Republican Party, which had governed for most of the previous seven decades and won three straight presidential elections by double-digit margins, was swept from power for twenty years. Voters in the Canadian prairie province of Saskatchewan elected the first avowedly socialist government in the history of North America, while the adjacent prairie province of Alberta elected a brand new party led by a radio preacher promising free money. And in Germany, economic distress fueled the rise of the Nazis and the collapse of the Weimar Republic.

The Great Recession of 2008–9 inspired much talk of historical parallels to the Great Depression era. It was often—and plausibly—characterized as "the most serious economic calamity of our lifetimes" (Treas 2010, 3). Like the Great Depression, it began when a garden-variety recession triggered a financial crisis on Wall Street, which quickly spread to other sectors and countries (Romer 1993). The dramatic election of Barack Obama as U.S. president in the midst of the crisis heightened the parallel, bringing inevitable comparisons with Franklin Roosevelt's election in 1932. *Time* magazine published a cover photograph of the president-elect altered to resemble FDR, with iconic fedora and cigarette holder, and a title proclaiming "The *New* New Deal."[1]

In his final press conference before leaving office, Obama's predecessor, George W. Bush, conceded "I chunked aside some of my free market principles when I was told by chief economic advisers that the situation we were facing could be worse than the Great Depression."[2] Prominent economist Paul Krugman (2009) rushed out an updated version of his decade-old book *The Return of Depression Economics*.

Of course, the Great Recession turned out to be quite different from the Great Depression in a variety of important ways. In economic terms, the dizzying financial meltdown of late 2008 was controlled, and the resulting global recession was less deep and less prolonged than in the 1930s. Although the political ramifications of the crisis are still evolving, they too appear a good deal less momentous than those of the Great Depression era—at least for now.

Those political ramifications are the focus of the essays collected in this volume. We cannot know if the Great Recession will be followed by even worse calamities in the future, but we can and should take stock of how people reacted to the onset of recession and to government attempts to cope with the crisis in its immediate aftermath.[3] The research reported in this book focuses on only the first phase in what has turned out to be a continuing and multifaceted economic crisis; but the reactions analyzed here are the foundation of whatever lies ahead.

How did ordinary people react to the economic crisis? Did they change their political opinions? Did they alter their voting behavior? Did they take to the streets and protest? Insofar as the crisis did cause changes in political beliefs and behavior, what explains the scope and direction of those changes? This volume addresses these questions with evidence from the United States and nearly thirty other democracies in Europe and Asia. We focus on relatively wealthy democracies because these are the countries where the crisis was first felt, but our project is otherwise broad in both scope and methods.

The scope of our interests is reflected in the organization of the volume. We begin with essays on how the economic crisis was subjectively understood by ordinary people, with one chapter covering Western Europe and another focused specifically on Wisconsin in the United States. We then move on, in a second section, to assess how the crisis affected people's opinions about key political issues, with chapters focusing on inequality and redistribution, the euro, and immigration. Our third section considers how the crisis affected voting behavior—with one chapter on ideology and retrospection in the OECD countries, another on reactions to the crisis across income groups in Germany and the United Kingdom, and a third on how the crisis affected working-class support for the far right in France. In our final section, we focus on how the crisis affected the course and content of mass protest. It begins with a study of politics and protest in Western and Eastern Europe and ends with a comparative study of protest in post-communist countries.

Our project relies on multiple methods. Collectively, and often individually, our authors draw their evidence from both aggregate statistical data and qualitative and quantitative case studies. Aggregate studies allow us to trace general patterns and to uncover similarities and differences among affluent democracies. Country-level analyses help us understand and explain similarities and differences in reactions. Together, multimethod comparisons allow us to put the United States and other individual cases in comparative perspective.

What general patterns of mass political response to the Great Recession might we expect? Much of our academic literature suggests that popular reactions to economic crisis will be both dramatic and consequential (Lindvall 2012). Scholars teach us that voters should punish incumbents at the polls (Powell and Whitten 1993; Anderson et al. 2004; van der Brug, van der Eijk, and Franklin 2007; Duch and Stevenson 2008); that insecurity should make polities vulnerable to xenophobia, extremism and democratic collapse (McLaren 2003; Lipset 1959; Huntington 1991; Przeworski and Limongi 1993, Gasiorowski 1995; Bernhard, Nordstrom, and Reenock 2001); and finally, that protest should rise because of heightened grievance levels and changed opportunity structures (Taylor-Gooby 2013; Richards and Gelleny 2006, 795; Tarrow 1994). Even scholars who caution us about exaggerating the long-term political effects of economic crises note that "economic distress" carries "combustible potential" (Achen and Bartels 2005, 34).

The findings reported in this volume conform only partially to these generalizations. Voters did punish incumbents, as predicted; but contrary to expectations, the combustible potential of the Great Recession was realized in only a few of the countries we studied. This observation constitutes the first of our volume's two major themes: *in most countries, popular reactions to the Great Recession were surprisingly muted and moderate.* Though our authors were not constrained by any single vision of what the economic crisis might yield, each of our chapters furnishes evidence of moderation. None suggests an ideological sea change or even significant partisan realignments. Nearly all point instead to impressive continuities with the past.

This thematic convergence is especially surprising given the broad range of countries figuring in our analyses. The ordinary people whose political behavior we examined live in societies with varied sorts of democratic institutions and dissimilar types of market economies. Moreover, they experienced the Great Recession in dramatically different ways. Some weathered relatively brief economic downturns, while others experienced a significant economic crisis that is still ongoing, and for some of them growing worse.

Popular reactions to the Great Recession certainly reflected the depth and duration of each country's crisis, but only within limited parameters. The depth of a country's economic crisis and the severity of popular reactions to it were sometimes mismatched. In the time period of our study, massive swings of opinion, significant growth in extremism, and sustained political mobilization were the exception rather than the rule. Hungary, Latvia, Greece, and Iceland stand out as rare cases in which political conflict transcended ordinary bounds.

Our analysis of these exceptional cases yields the second theme of our project: *dramatic political reactions to the Great Recession were associated less with the direct economic repercussions of the crisis than with government initiatives to cope with those repercussions.* Radical reactions were less likely to be triggered directly by declining growth or escalating unemployment than by the austerity and bailout programs that policy makers adopted in response to crisis trends. Austerity programs alone were never, however, a sufficient cause for dramatic political reactions. Radical changes in behavior required institutional and ideational support, and in the period we studied, these coincided rarely and often fleetingly.

This introductory chapter develops both these themes and offers a more contextualized and focused summary of our authors' findings. It should be clear from the outset that these findings bear directly on real-world politics. In good times and in bad, votes, opinion, and protest are the very stuff of democratic government. In democracies, policy outcomes are supposed to reflect the preferences of citizens (Dahl 1971; Rehm 2011). Without votes, polls, and collective action, leaders have no means to gauge either the public's policy preferences or their own chances of holding on to power. Though the reactions we trace are critical to scholarly debates, their real importance lies in what they teach us about how ordinary people in developed democracies react to economic crisis. Since both elites and citizens often view current crises through the lens of past crises, we begin by putting the Great Recession in historical perspective.

The Great Recession in Historical Perspective

Figure 1.1 charts the basic course of the Great Recession in OECD countries, showing quarter-by-quarter trends in GDP growth and consumer confidence from 2007 through 2011. Quarterly growth in real GDP (denoted by the bars in the figure) declined steadily through 2008 and into the first quarter of 2009; the cumulative decline in real GDP through four quarters of negative

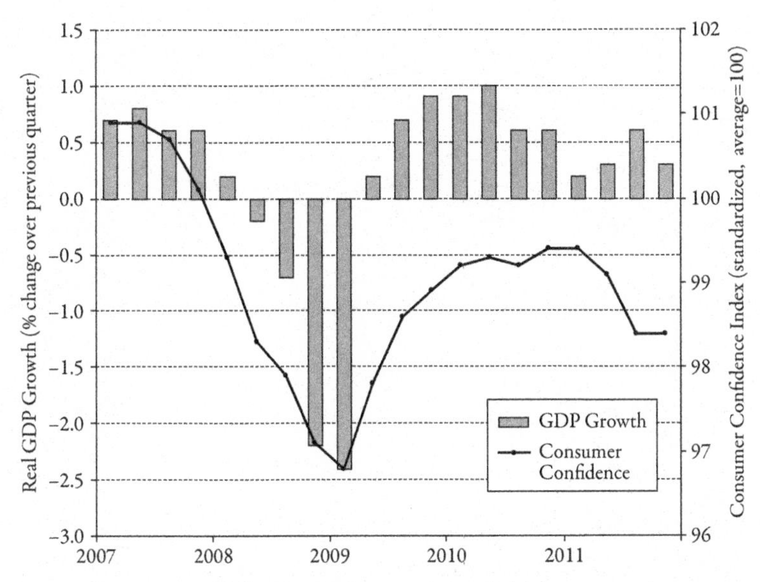

FIGURE 1.1 The Course of the Great Recession in OECD Countries, 2007–2011.

growth was more than 5 percent, with the bulk of that decline concentrated in the six months following the collapse of the U.S. investment bank Lehman Brothers in September 2008.[4] Positive growth resumed rather abruptly in the spring of 2009, but at a modest pace, and it was not until 2011 that the OECD economies regained the level of real economic output they had enjoyed three years earlier.

Surveys of consumer confidence tracked a roughly parallel decline and rebound (denoted by the solid line in Figure 1.1).[5] However, the revival of consumer confidence lagged well behind the corresponding rebound in real economic growth. Even after several quarters of fairly steady growth, consumers at the end of 2010 remained considerably less confident about the state of the economy than they were in 2007, and a resumption of slower growth in 2011 erased almost half of the rebound in confidence that occurred in 2009 and 2010.

Although Figure 1.1 captures the main outlines of the Great Recession as a global event, it is important to recognize that the crisis played out quite differently by region, and even in adjacent countries. The annual fluctuations in level of real GDP per capita shown in Figure 1.2 provide a sense of the varying economic trends in several parts of the developed world. Ireland's real GDP declined by more than 10 percent from its peak in late 2007, and had barely begun to recover by the end of 2011. Greece's real GDP declined

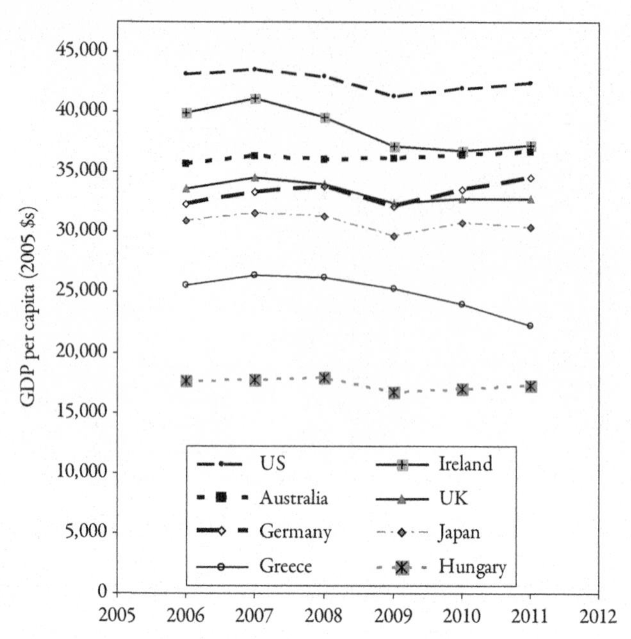

FIGURE 1.2 Economic Growth in the Great Recession, Selected Countries.
Source: OECD.

by more than 15 percent over the same period, with accelerating losses every year. In contrast, Germany rebounded quickly, exceeding its 2008 GDP figure by 2011.

By way of comparison, Figure 1.3 shows trends in real GDP per capita over the course of the Great Depression in some of the same countries represented in Figure 1.2. As in the Great Recession, there was a good deal of cross-national variation in the timing and magnitude of the economic collapse following the U.S. stock market crash of 1929. Real GDP in the United States and Canada fell by more than 30 percent between 1929 and 1933—a collapse twice as severe as in Greece from 2007 through 2011. Both countries experienced substantial and fairly steady rebounds through the rest of the 1930s, ending the decade with about the same level of economic output they had a dozen years earlier. Britain experienced a briefer and milder decline—similar in magnitude and duration to the one it would experience seventy-eight years later—followed by several years of fairly steady growth. In France, an initial decline much worse than in the Great Recession led to years of slow growth, while in Ireland and Greece economic output was virtually constant throughout the late 1920s and 1930s. For these cases, the Great Recession was actually worse than the Great Depression in terms of GDP decline.

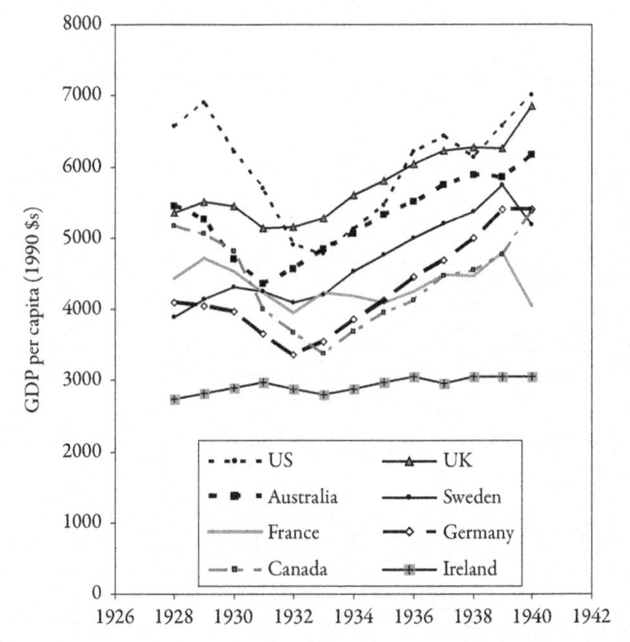

FIGURE 1.3 Economic Growth in the Great Depression, Selected Countries.
Source: Angus Maddison, *The World Economy: Economic Statistics* Paris: OECD, 2004.

Another useful point of comparison is the Long Recession, the prolonged period of economic stagnation that much of the developed world experienced in the 1970s and early 1980s. Figure 1.4 summarizes economic trends for this third period and shows that there were few declines in real GDP paralleling those in the Great Recession. The most severe downturns among OECD countries—in the United States in 1974–75, in Sweden in 1977–78, and in the UK in 1980–81—produced declines in real output of only 2 or 3 percent.

The more relevant parallel between the two recessions may lie in the marked rise in unemployment that accompanied both downturns. The Long Recession was so named because growth slowed for a decade or more in the aftermath of the 1973 oil shock. As growth slowed, the rate of unemployment more than doubled in the United States (peaking in 1982) and nearly tripled in the EU (rising through 1982 and beyond). The depth of the unemployment crisis varied across countries, as it does today, hitting Spain, Ireland, and Portugal especially hard. In Greece, however, unemployment dropped during the Long Recession, so by this measure too, the current Greek crisis is worse than its predecessors (Cameron 2001). Whether the

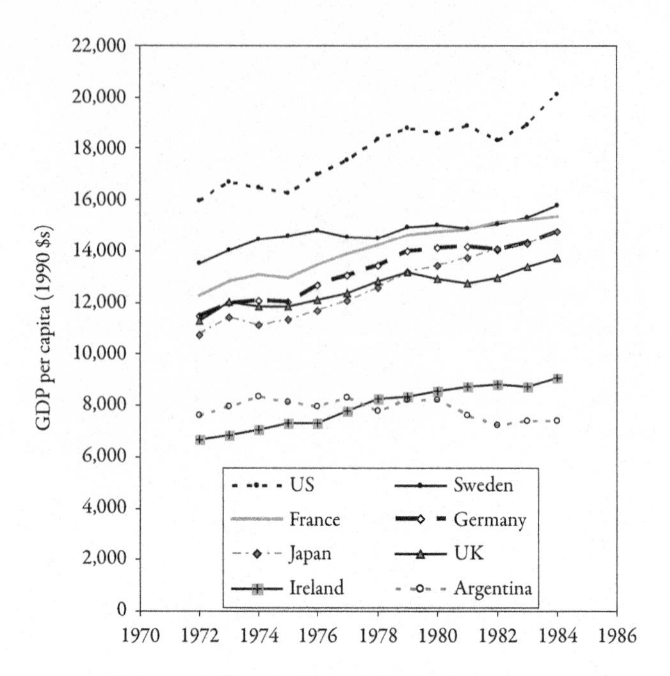

FIGURE 1.4 Economic Growth in the Long Recession, Selected Countries.
Source: Angus Maddison, *The World Economy: Economic Statistics* Paris: OECD, 2004.

Great Recession, the related sovereign debt crisis in Europe, and austerity policies around the globe will produce a comparable decade of slow growth and high unemployment remains to be seen—but credible observers are predicting precisely this.

Continuity in Policy Preferences and Ideologies

There are surely parallels between the Great Recession and past economic crises, but they are only partial. The differences between events may help explain why popular reactions to the current crisis are not as dramatic as many expected. Yet the patterns emerging between 2007 and 2012 are clear: with few exceptions, the Great Recession did not cause striking changes in people's political perceptions and behavior. Where changes did occur, they were often of short duration.

Three of our chapters examine shifts in specific policy preferences in a variety of countries over the course of the Great Recession, and each provides evidence of surprising continuity. Stuart Soroka and Christopher

Wlezien analyze how the Great Recession has affected public opinion toward income inequality, redistribution, and welfare spending in Britain (Chapter 4). They find that the median voter in Britain has been moving rightward since the early 1990s, and that the Great Recession has done little to reverse the rightward trend. Though they show a statistically significant increase in support for redistribution between 2008 and 2011, they note that it is very small in magnitude. And even though they show that support for welfare spending increased among citizens concerned with income inequality in 2010, they find an equal and opposite *decrease* in support for welfare spending in 2009. Finally, they illustrate that, although the British are well aware of rising levels of income inequality, the recession has caused no significant shift in opinion about the income gap. Overall, their results suggest that the recession has not boosted radicalization or even caused an obvious leftward trend.

Soroka and Wlezien's findings regarding Britain are echoed in a variety of other countries. Figure 1.5 maps shifts in public support for reducing economic inequality between 2006 and 2010 in twenty countries represented in the European Social Surveys (ESS) project.[6] There is a good deal of cross-national variation—from Denmark, where the balance of opinion was only slightly favorable toward the notion that "the government should take measures to reduce differences in income levels," to Greece, Hungary, and Portugal, where most survey respondents strongly agreed with that proposition. However, there is rather little evidence here of significant changes in opinion over the course of the Great Recession. Moreover, where noticeable shifts in opinion did occur, they were almost as likely to reflect *declining* support for mitigating economic inequality (for example, in Greece, Poland, and Norway) as *increasing* support for redistribution (in Ireland, Slovenia, and Portugal).

Sara Hobolt and Patrick Leblond analyze how the recession has affected support for the euro, and though they discover some predictable changes, they also find surprising continuities (Chapter 5). Studying more than a decade of survey data for seventeen European countries, they find that support for the euro has declined in countries outside the eurozone and in "euro hopefuls." Yet they show that for the latter, the crisis has only reinforced the decline in support that began in 2001. In addition to highlighting that the effects of crisis are sometimes only reinforcing, Hobolt and Leblond also reveal that the effects of crisis are limited. In the eurozone itself, they unearth the "surprising" finding that two-thirds of respondents still favored the euro at the height

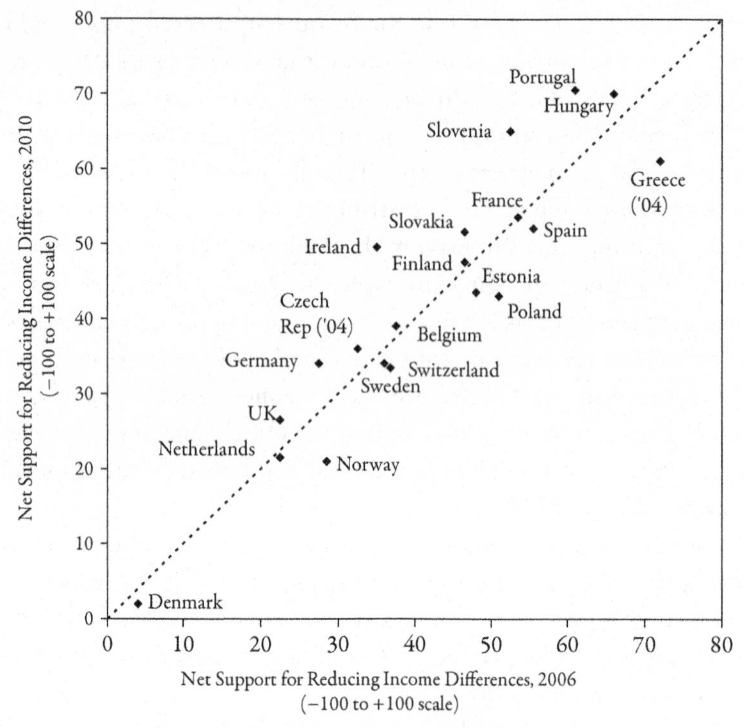

FIGURE 1.5 Shifts in Support for Reducing Income Differences, 2006–2010.

of the crisis. They also find that though some regions felt and feel the crisis more deeply, support for the euro does not vary regionally within the eurozone. The backlash against the euro that many expected in the traumatized GIIPS has not materialized.

Overall, their results suggest that the effect of the Great Recession on support for the euro has been modest. In keeping with our theme about continuity, they find that "support for the euro has remained high and stable within the eurozone throughout the crisis."

Rafaela Dancygier and Michael Donnelly examine the recession's effects on a very different set of political attitudes—but they, too, find some surprising patterns of stability. Dancygier and Donnelly ask how the Great Recession has affected Europeans' attitudes toward immigration (Chapter 6). They show that sector of employment is an important and thus far neglected explanatory variable. Though they find only small changes in attitudes on average, they find that Europeans in economic sectors with a large proportion of foreign-born workers *do* evaluate the economic effects of immigration more negatively if their sector is hit hard by the crisis. However, they also find that when the "economy is doing well, sectoral patterns have little impact" and thus that the effects may not be permanent. They also find that the crisis has had no significant effect on people's views about the *cultural* impact of immigration even when the immigrant group is ethnically and racially distinct from the native population. Overall, they find that "predictions of extreme xenophobia are not borne out in the data." The attitudinal effects of the Great Recession seem to be sectorally specific and limited to the economic realm.

Looking back to studies of the 1970s, we find literature that presages both the modest effects found by our authors and our theme that popular responses to economic crisis may involve a surprising degree of political continuity. In a book-length study of the political impact of unemployment, Kay Schlozman and Sidney Verba (1979, 351) found that "the effects of unemployment are severe but narrowly focused, manifest in ways that are proximate to the joblessness itself." They found no tendency for unemployment to produce "general disenchantment with American life, wholesale changes in social ideology, or adoption of radical policy positions" (349). Challenging widespread assumptions linking economic distress with substantial shifts in attitude and behavior, they concluded, "Political activity is more a function of beliefs about politics than of specific personal experiences" and that "political beliefs" in turn are less a function of personal experiences than of "general social beliefs" (330, 332).

Lane Kenworthy and Lindsay Owens's broader and more recent survey of opinion data over the past four decades also found surprising continuities, suggesting that "recent economic recessions have had real but mostly temporary effects on American attitudes on key economic, political, and social issues" (2011, 198). They found "no indication of any increase in support for policies that enhance opportunity, support for the poor, or support for redistribution" and that "economic downturns, including the Great Recession, have had surprisingly little impact on Americans' views of government, even in the short run" (216–217, 204).

Narrower but more detailed studies interviewing people in the United States before, during, and after the crisis phase of the Great Recession also illustrate modest and fleeting change. Comparing responses from July 2007 and April 2009, Yotam Margalit (2013) found that fewer than 12 percent of those interviewed changed their pre-crisis positions on support for "an increase in the funding of government programs for helping the poor and the unemployed." Those who actually became unemployed during this period did increase their support for "helping the poor and the unemployed," but the increase was of modest magnitude and short duration; only 59 percent of those who lost their jobs during the course of Margalit's panel study supported increased funding of these programs, as compared with 47 percent of those who kept their jobs. Moreover, the modest change in opinion proved transitory: only 49 percent of those who became reemployed during the course of the study supported increased spending on programs for the poor and unemployed—a figure only 2 percentage points higher than for people who remained employed throughout the recession.

Lindsay Owens and David Pedulla (2013) examined changes in preferences for redistribution from 2006 to 2010 among people who lost their jobs or suffered significant income losses.[7] They, too, found generally modest effects of personal economic dislocations on political views. Only 33 percent of those who became unemployed between 2008 and 2010 expressed greater support for redistribution, compared with 23 percent of those who remained employed full-time; and only 27 percent of those who reported significant income losses expressed greater support for redistribution, compared with 23 percent of those who reported no income loss.

The findings in our opening chapters and these specific findings from the United States are indicative of a much more general pattern of muted popular response to the Great Recession. At the level of broad ideology, Figure 1.6 summarizes the shifting balance of ideological views over the course of the Great Recession in the twenty countries represented in the ESS. The horizontal axis maps the average left-right self-placement of survey respondents in each country in 2006, before the economic crisis began, while the vertical axis maps the corresponding average placement in 2010.[8] Countries above the diagonal line shifted to the right over this four-year period, while those below the diagonal line shifted to the left. However, the magnitude of the shift was in almost every case quite modest; only one (in Hungary) exceeded half a point on the ten-point ideological scale.

There is certainly no evidence in these data of any general ideological shift in response to the Great Recession. The average change in average self-placement across all twenty countries was +.04, an almost imperceptible shift on the ten-point scale. Nor is there any evidence of consistent responses to especially severe economic crises. Among the countries that were hardest hit, Hungary moved significantly to the right (continuing a trend dating back to 2004), but Greece and Ireland moved significantly to the left. These shifts underline the contingency of political responses to economic distress noted by Larry Bartels in Chapter 7; Hungary's shift to the right reflected a repudiation of the left-wing incumbent Socialist Party (MSZP), while

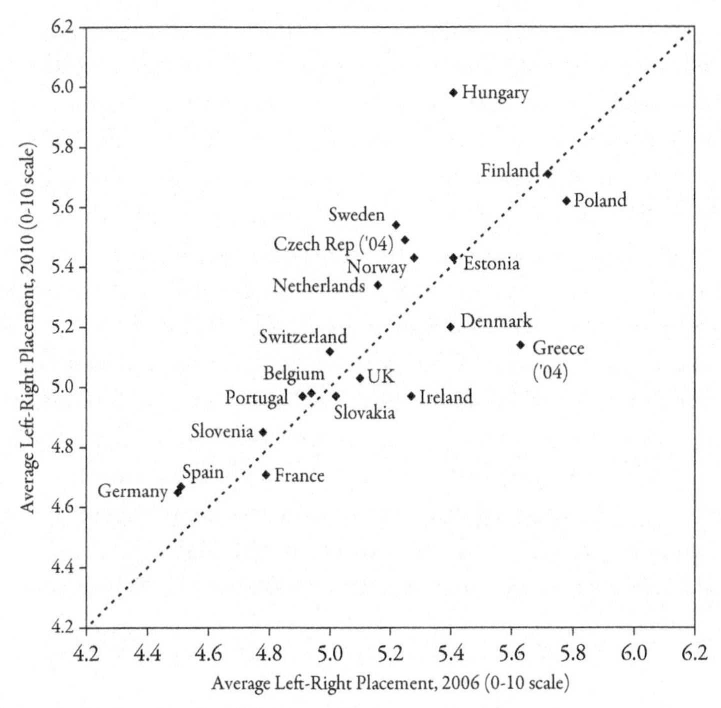

FIGURE 1.6 Shifts in Citizens' Ideological Views, 2006–2010.

Greece's shift to the left reflected a repudiation of the right-wing incumbent New Democracy Party. Expectations that the Great Recession would mean a dramatic move leftward or rightward across democracies in general have not been met. The apparently contrarian ideological shifts we see instead are consistent with considerable historical evidence suggesting that public opinion is much more likely to react *against* perceived shifts in policy than to reinforce them (Stimson 1998; Erikson, MacKuen, and Stimson 2002).

Assessments of Politicians and Policy Responses

Though ideologies and broad policy preferences were not dramatically affected by the Great Recession, there is more evidence of change in public views regarding political leaders and the specific policy measures adopted in response to the crisis. This pattern, too, seems consistent with Schlozman and Verba's emphasis (1979, 351) on opinion change that is "narrowly focused" and "proximate" rather than broadly ideological. And it underlines the extent to which ordinary citizens "tend to reward or punish incumbent governments based on simple assessments of immediate success or failure" (Bartels 2013).

A summer 2009 BBC World Service Poll shed useful light on citizens' assessments of the performance of political leaders in addressing the crisis, because it asked similar questions about the performance of various national and international figures in seven countries.[9] Specifically, respondents were asked, "How satisfied or dissatisfied are you with what the following groups of people are doing to address the current financial crisis?" The objects of evaluation included economic actors (major banks, international companies), national leaders, and the leaders of the United States and the European Union. Responses to these items are summarized in Table 1.1.

Generally, people in all of these countries were quite dissatisfied with the efforts of major banks and international companies—the private actors at the heart of the financial crisis. This dissatisfaction suggests that blaming economic actors may have been a promising political strategy. Political leaders fared relatively well in comparison, depending mostly on how hard their economies were hit. Thus in Japan, where real GDP contracted by more than 7 percent in the six months preceding the survey, people were quite

Table 1.1 Satisfaction with Efforts to Address the Financial Crisis, 2009.

	National Leaders	United States	European Union	International Companies	Major Banks
Australia	+20	+17	+10	−26	−33
Canada	+6	+19	+16	−20	−15
France	−32	+7	−11	−48	−60
Germany	−21	+18	−10	−47	−66
Japan	−44	−20	−16	−18	−36
United Kingdom	−26	+8	−12	−21	−52
United States	−6	−6	+2	−22	−43

"How satisfied or dissatisfied are you with what the following groups of people are doing to address the current financial crisis?

- The leaders of [country]
- The leaders of the United States
- Leaders of the European Union
- Executives of international companies
- Executives of major banks"

Net satisfaction ranges from +100 ("very satisfied") to −100 ("very dissatisfied").
Source: BBC World Service Poll conducted by GlobeScan, June–August 2009.

dissatisfied with their national leaders (and everyone else); but in Australia, where the recession was exceptionally mild, most people were satisfied with their leaders' response to the crisis. Interestingly, all three of the European countries represented in the survey showed similar patterns of public dissatisfaction, with rather negative assessments of their own national political leaders, modestly negative ratings of the leaders of the European Union, and modestly positive ratings of U.S. leaders.

The impact of crisis severity on popular assessments of political leaders also appears in a changing level of trust in politicians. Figure 1.7 draws once again on data from the ESS to document changes in trust in politicians across twenty European countries from 2006 to 2010. These changes were, on the whole, a good deal larger than the corresponding changes in redistributive preferences and general ideological stances summarized in Figures 1.5 and 1.6, respectively. They were also more one-sided: although a few countries (Hungary, Sweden, Poland, and Norway) did record significant *increases* in trust over this period, there were many more instances of significant *declines* in trust. In Greece, the average level of trust in politicians declined from 3.59 to 1.35 on the 0-to-10 scale.[10] Slovenia, Slovakia, Spain, and Ireland also recorded declines in trust

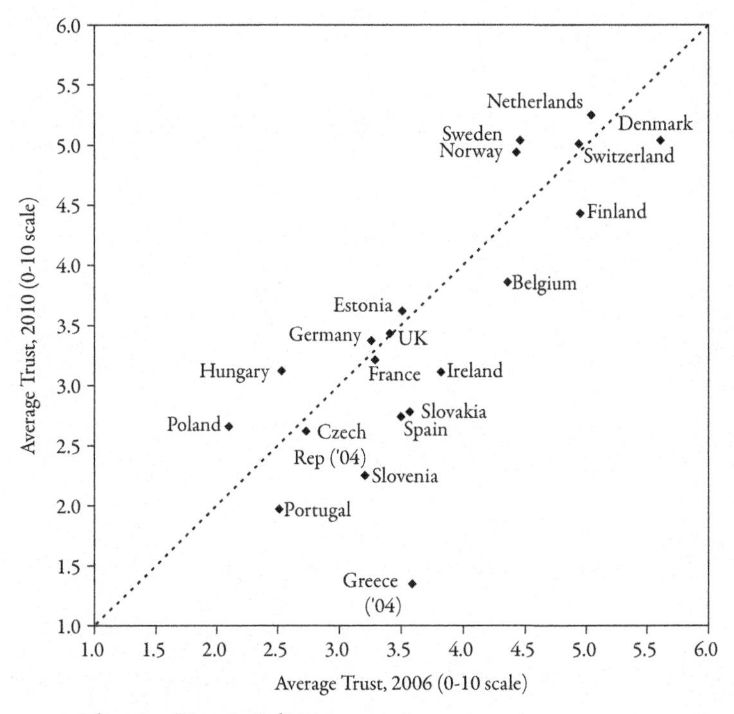

FIGURE 1.7 Changing Trust in Politicians, 2006–2010.

larger in magnitude than the largest increases in the ESS data. It is probably no coincidence that most of these substantial declines occurred in countries that experienced especially large economic shocks over this period.

If the severity of economic shocks contributed to declining trust in politicians, the slowness of the subsequent economic recovery seems to have contributed to declining enthusiasm for the specific policies adopted by those politicians to address the crisis. A 2006 survey on the role of government conducted in thirty-three countries by the International Social Survey Programme provides a useful "baseline" measure of public attitudes regarding economic policies before the onset of the crisis.[11] As part of a battery of questions inviting citizens to assess "some things the government might do for the economy," they were asked whether they favored or opposed "cuts in government spending" and "financing projects to create new jobs." Figure 1.8 summarizes responses to these two questions in each country.

These data suggest that there was substantial public support for both types of government action before the onset of the Great Recession.

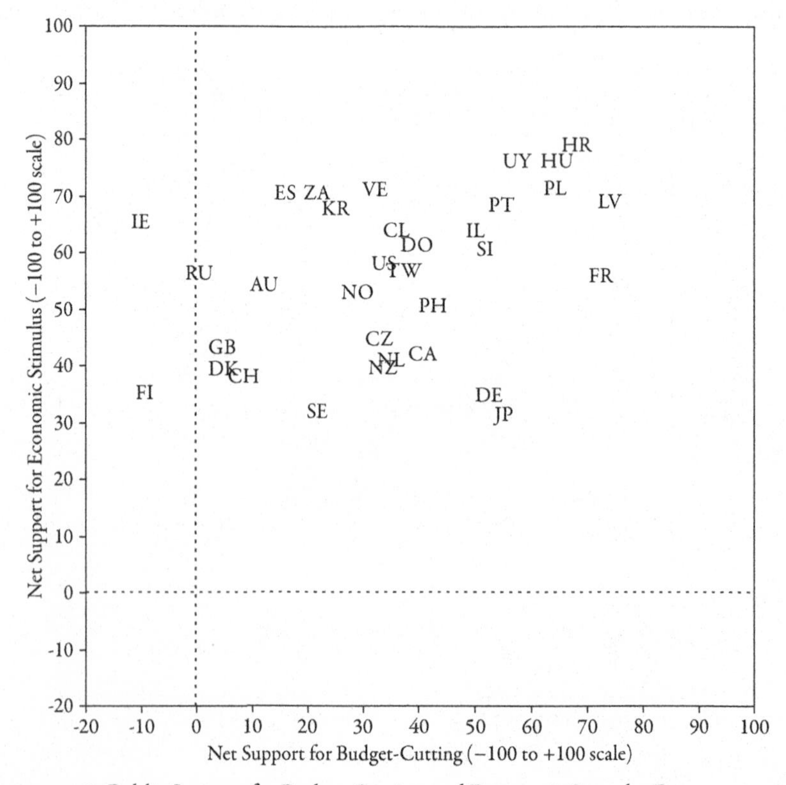

FIGURE 1.8 Public Support for Budget Cutting and Economic Stimulus Programs, 2006.

A plurality of citizens in almost every country supported "cuts in government spending"; and most citizens in *every* country supported government "financing projects to create new jobs," by pluralities ranging from 30 percent to 80 percent. In general, there was surprisingly little connection between levels of public support for these two seemingly contrasting economic policies.[12] As a result, it would seem that governments had a good deal of popular latitude to respond to the economic crisis using whatever policy approaches they preferred.

However, this popular latitude does not seem to have lasted long. The summer 2009 BBC World Service Poll measured public support in a variety of countries for three of the most salient policies adopted in the wake of the Great Recession: "giving financial support to banks in trouble," "increasing government regulation and oversight of the national economy," and "significantly increasing government spending to stimulate the economy." Table 1.2 reports the results from seven affluent democracies included in the survey—Australia, Canada, France, Germany, Japan, the United Kingdom, and the United States. Financial support to troubled banks was strongly opposed in Germany, the United States, and France. Citizens in Australia and Canada were also opposed to helping banks, but strongly supportive of increasing both government regulation and government spending. However, public support for these approaches was quite mixed in the other countries, with balances in most cases quite close to the midpoint of the favor-oppose scale.

In a follow-up survey conducted the next summer, the same pollsters asked about the same three possible government responses to the crisis. Strikingly, levels of public support for aiding troubled banks and for increasing government spending had declined over the intervening year in every one of the six countries included in both surveys—by an average of 16 to 18 points. Having experienced varying doses of these policies, and seeing no dramatic improvement in tangible economic conditions as a result, most citizens were in no mood for counterfactual arguments that, as one U.S. study put it, "the comprehensive policy responses saved the economy from another depression" (Blinder and Zandi 2010, 10). Changes in support for increasing government regulation were more mixed, with similarly large declines in Australia and the United States balanced by *rising* support in Germany and France.[13]

The 2010 BBC World Service Poll also included an additional policy option: "taking steps to reduce the government's budget deficit and debt, by cutting some spending or increasing some taxes." That option was distinctly more popular than any of the original three, with at least a slight positive

Table 1.2 Public Support for Government Actions, 2009 and 2010.

	Financial Support to Troubled Banks	Increasing Government Regulation	Increasing Government Spending	Reducing Government Deficit/debt
Australia				
2009	−10	+24	+30	—
2010	−14	+2	+16	+14
Canada				
2009	−18	+22	+26	—
2010	−50	+24	+3	+6
France				
2009	−26	+28	−12	—
2010	−39	+39	−29	+2
Germany				
2009	−44	+1	−8	—
2010	−61	+22	−27	+6
Japan				
2009	−6	0	+8	—
Spain				
2010	−28	−6	−8	−7
United Kingdom				
2009	+3	+10	+14	—
2010	−26	+6	+10	+17
United States				
2009	−31	−1	−6	—
2010	−42	−18	−22	+14

"In our current economic conditions, do you favor or oppose the [country] government doing each of the following?

- Giving financial support to banks in trouble
- Increasing government regulation and oversight of the national economy
- Significantly increasing government spending to stimulate the economy
- Taking steps to reduce the government's budget deficit and debt, by cutting some spending or increasing some taxes"

Net support ranges from +100 ("strongly favor") to −100 ("strongly oppose")
Source: BBC World Service Polls conducted by GlobeScan, June-August 2009 and June-September 2010.

balance of opinion in every country except Spain (which was not included in the 2009 survey). Even in Spain, reducing debt was essentially tied with increasing spending and increasing regulation as the "least opposed" policy option. In the United States, it was by far the most popular of the four policy options. These data reveal surprisingly widespread public support for deficit reduction in the midst of a severe economic downturn.

Lest the policy implications of this sentiment be unclear, the 2010 survey also asked respondents *which* of two possible approaches to deficit reduction they would "prefer to see the government focus on more": "cutting spending on government services, including ones you use" or "increasing taxes." Offered this choice, the clear preference in every country was for cutting spending over raising taxes. In the United States, respondents preferred cutting spending by an overwhelming 64–23 margin. It is tempting to interpret this public support for budget cutting as a reflection of Americans' deep-seated suspicion (at least in the abstract) of big government. However, the public sentiment in favor of budget cutting seems to have been widely shared throughout the developed world. The average margin in the six other countries represented in Table 1.1 was 64–21. In Spain and France, the percentages favoring higher taxes were in single digits. Thus public opinion seems to have been remarkably supportive of austerity as a policy response to the economic crisis—at least, before it was really tried in most of these countries.

Although the specific questions and countries included in the BBC World Service Polls are different from those in the ISSP survey, a comparison of the results suggests that public support for stimulus spending declined dramatically between 2006 and 2009, and then dropped further by 2010. The most plausible interpretation of these shifts in public opinion is that citizens saw their governments implementing stimulus programs without producing much in the way of immediate economic improvement. By comparison, public support for budget cutting seems to have been rather more stable between 2006 and 2010—presumably because most countries had not yet implemented major austerity programs during that period. Will public support for budget cutting survive significant cuts in actual spending? This will probably depend on whether those cuts *seem* to lead to vigorous growth and job creation.

Elections: Punishing Incumbents

Whatever the duration of popular support for budget cutting, our analyses suggest that the Great Recession's effects on elections were much more dramatic than its effects on policy preferences. Larry Bartels's study of legislative elections in twenty-eight OECD countries in the period between 2007 and 2011 (Chapter 7) makes the point. He finds that voters consistently punished incumbents for bad economic conditions regardless of ruling party ideology. Voters "generally rewarded their governments when their economies thrived and punished their governments when economic growth slowed." Real GDP growth in the quarters immediately preceding the election was the most powerful predictor of incumbent party vote share: long-term growth rate and cross-national comparison had no significant effect on vote share, suggesting that electorates meted out punishment with little regard for global economic circumstances or subtle assessments of responsibility. Just as the retrospective voting literature would predict, facing voters in "the midst of an economic downturn" proved to be "hazardous."

Hanspeter Kriesi in Chapter 10 also shows that the Great Recession had a substantial effect on election outcomes. Drawing on evidence from elections of varied sorts in thirty countries in Central Eastern and Western Europe, he too finds that incumbents were punished for poor performance and argues that punishment was most severe in majoritarian countries, where responsibilities could be most "clearly attributed to the government." He illustrates that the party of the chief executive in majoritarian countries lost approximately 5 percent more than the chief executive's party in consensus democracies. Parties holding cabinet seats in poorly performing coalition governments were also punished at the polls, though to a lesser extent.

Though Bartels and Kriesi both show that the Great Recession had a dramatic effect on the electoral fate of incumbent parties, neither makes the case that the parties replacing the incumbents were more extremist or indeed of any consistent ideological hue. In this respect, their essays reinforce the conclusion that the Great Recession has not provoked radical change thus far. Bartels illustrates that the crisis did not produce a swing to the left or the right in legislative elections. On average, left-wing incumbents lost more votes than right-wing incumbents, but this was mostly because left-wing governments presided over deeper recessions and not because of ideological voting.

Kriesi finds no consistent ideological shift in the heterogeneous set of elections in his study, either. In Central Eastern Europe generally, incumbents were replaced by new parties that were essentially the functional equivalents of established opposition parties in Western Europe. In Hungary, the radical right did benefit from the crisis, but in the rest of Central Eastern Europe "the new populist right generally tended to *lose* votes in the aftermath of the crisis." In Western Europe, incumbents were almost always replaced by mainstream opposition parties. Though the new populist right "benefited from the predicament of governing parties in post-crisis elections," it expanded only in consensus democracies where electoral access was not constrained. Throughout the continent, extremist parties fell far short of winning a plurality, much less a majority.

Nonna Mayer's study of the National Front (Chapter 9) provides an in-depth analysis of both the expansion and the limitations of the extreme right vote in France. Tracing the National Front's support in local, national, and EU elections from 1988 to 2012, Mayer shows that the party garnered an historic high of 17.9 percent of the vote in the first round of the 2012 presidential elections. She notes that the Great Recession contributed to the party's electoral gains, but in keeping with the theme of continuity emerging in our other chapters, she shows that the "current economic crisis has mainly amplified a preexisting electoral trend." Male workers have been vulnerable to right-wing extremist appeals because of structural trends that began decades ago. Women became vulnerable to the party's appeal more recently—as they increasingly took on precarious, unskilled service sector jobs—but this too "began long before 2008."

In addition to highlighting continuities across time, Mayer illustrates "the very modest scope of the electorate's move to extremism." Even under the leadership of Marine Le Pen, the party has not expanded beyond its original base among unskilled workers. And even though a record number of unskilled workers voted for the far right in 2012, the change was modest: the first round presidential vote was only 1 percentage point above the tally in 2002, and the party did not reach historic highs in legislative, regional, or EU elections. In all French elections between 2008 and 2012, the vast majority of voters—even the vast majority of working-class voters—chose centrist parties at the polls.

If the disadvantaged did not move massively rightward during the Great Recession, why did they also not swing massively to the left? Given that the crisis was so clearly associated with the misdeeds of the financial sector, and that it emerged after years of increasing economic inequality, this is precisely what many hoped for and others feared. Ray Duch and Iñaki Sagarzazu offer helpful insights on this puzzle in their study of rich and poor voters in parliamentary elections in Germany and the UK (Chapter 8). Looking at the first post-crisis elections in each country, they found "no evidence that the economic vote of [either] the rich [or the] poor would favor redistributive responses to the economic shocks generated by the financial crisis."

Getting at the causal root of this observation, Duch and Sagarzazu found evidence that poor voters gave personal financial conditions little weight in their voting decisions. Whereas personal financial conditions were reasonably important for the rich, the poor voted largely on how they saw the national economy and not on the basis of their own economic conditions. Since the poor are, by definition, most in need of redistributive policies, this behavior eroded the constituency for an openly redistributive leftist agenda. These findings are in keeping with longstanding patterns of sociotropic voting found in the United States (Bartels 2005) and with the research cited above on the effects of the current recession on public opinion. Economically disadvantaged voters were not especially likely to back redistribution before the Great Recession, and the crisis had not done much to change that fact—at least by 2010.

More generally, centrifugal movement of voters toward extremist parties in the wake of the Great Recession has been rare. A notable exception is Greece, where electoral support for radical parties on both the left and the right escalated substantially—and more or less symmetrically—between 2009 and 2012, leaving the various centrist parties with only a narrow majority of the total vote. Another exception is Hungary, where the right-wing populist Fidesz won elections in 2010 alongside the new, far-right Jobbik Party, which garnered nearly 17 percent of the vote. However, voters in other countries have mostly continued to support centrist political leaders and technocrats, despite hard times. For example, Spain's most popular noncentrist party, the IU, won only 7 percent of the vote in 2011 (compared to 5 percent in 2004 and 4 percent in 2008). Portugal's mainstream parties won more than 90 percent of the vote in 2011. In Ireland, no significant extremist parties have emerged, and electoral support for more mainstream leftist alternatives—Sinn Fein and the Green Party—held steady at 12 percent in 2007 and 2011, up only 2 percent from 2002. Voters in these and other countries have certainly punished specific incumbents for presiding over economic distress, but they have shown little impulse to reject conventional parties more generally.

Movement Politics and Protest

Beyond voting, hundreds of thousands of ordinary people took to the streets and raised their voices in protest in the aftermath of the financial crisis. Two of our chapters focus on how the recession affected protest behavior. Kriesi's Chapter 10 highlights the fact that early crisis-era protests in Europe were usually triggered by austerity measures and not, strictly speaking, by the recession itself. Supplementing his electoral analysis with case studies of Iceland, Ireland, Hungary, and Latvia, he demonstrates strong causal links among budget deficits, austerity packages, incumbent electoral losses, and mass protest.

He also shows how many protests were outgrowths of previous mobilizations against government corruption and how protest everywhere was instrumentalized by opposition parties. Protests were always the product of local histories and local institutions, and as such they were not a simple function of the intensity of any nation's economic decline.

In Chapter 11, Mark Beissinger and Gwendolyn Sasse analyze patterns of protest in post-communist Europe. Using an original database detailing major protests and incidents of mass violence in eighteen states, they confirm Kriesi's view that crisis-era protests were overwhelmingly sparked by austerity measures and not by the recession itself. They show conclusively that protest against economic austerity dwarfed other forms of economic protest, mobilizing 71 percent of all protest participants in the region in 2009 and 80 percent in 2010. In keeping with the theme that the Great Recession has not provoked ideological radicalization, they find that protest thus far has been "largely defensive." Indeed, only 2 percent of total protests in 2010 aimed at obtaining new benefits.

In keeping with the theme that reactions to the crisis have been surprisingly moderate, Beissinger and Sasse show that there was actually "a general decline in protest activity in the post-communist region—irrespective of whether one measures protest by the number of events, protest days, or participants." The decline in protests started before the recession—and the recession, once again, had no effect on the preexisting trend. One of the few trends that changed during the recession regarded ethnic and nationalist protests; but, contradicting the presumed association between crisis and increased xenophobia, ethnic and nationalist protests actually "declined sharply." Economic protests increased, but only as a proportion of total protests. The absolute number of economic protest events "remained at roughly the same level" as before the Great Recession. Surprisingly, both "the duration of economic protests and the overall number of people who participated in them" dropped sharply.

In keeping with the theme that reactions to the crisis varied independently of the intensity of the economic downturn, Beissinger and Sasse illustrate that people in Ukraine, Estonia, Hungary, and Latvia experienced similarly deep economic crises, but that Ukrainians and Estonians engaged in very little protest. Kriesi's case study of Ireland provides another example in which a severe downturn provoked only a moderate and short-lived response.

Explaining Muted Reactions

Why has the Great Recession not provoked more immoderate response? Christopher Anderson and Jason Hecht's study of economic mood in eleven

European countries between 1985 and 2011 (Chapter 2) offers a variety of leads. First, their findings expose an explanation that does not work. Their data illustrate that the public's reaction was not a function of unawareness. They show that "publics across Europe felt...the recession" even before governments officially named it as such; and that economic mood dipped significantly during the course of the Great Recession, reaching a twenty-five-year low.

A second set of findings offers insight regarding an explanation that does work. In keeping with our general theme of continuity, Anderson and Hecht conclude that citizens respond similarly to economic conditions in crisis and non-crisis periods, and find no evidence that the recession caused a "fundamental reorientation of public opinion about the economy." However, they also find that "European publics became more sensitive to macroeconomic outcomes during the crisis" than prior to its onset. Increased sensitivity meant that "in those countries that weathered the crisis well, publics soon went back to business as usual" and that shifts in mood and priorities were short-lived. Thus, in countries with a quick recovery, such as Germany, Belgium, Denmark, and the Netherlands, the opportunity for dramatic reaction was limited.

How might moderation in countries with a slower recovery be explained? Anderson and Hecht's findings offer insights on this question as well. Examining the effects of welfare spending on people's subjective experience of the crisis, they find that the connection between the real and the perceived economy was weaker in countries with more developed systems social protection. They conclude that "welfare states and their associated programs" may cushion crisis effects. Thus, extensive social protection schemes may help explain moderate reactions, even in states where recovery was slow.

Anderson and Hecht's emphasis on the significance of "welfare states as buffers" is handsomely justified by evidence on the varying personal fallout from the Great Recession across Europe. Successive waves of the ESS fielded in 2006, 2008, and 2010 included two distinct questions tapping respondents' feelings about the economy. One asked, "On the whole how satisfied are you with the present state of the economy in [your country]?" Responses to that question shifted substantially over the course of the crisis, generally tracking trends in economic perceptions derived from other sources, including those analyzed by Anderson and Hecht and by Duch and Sagarzazu. The other question asked more specifically about people's own economic circumstances: "How do you feel about your household's income nowadays?"[14] Significantly, responses to the question about household income were much stabler, and generally much less negative. Survey respondents were certainly well aware of the crisis, but they were surprisingly sanguine about its impact on their own day-to-day lives. Figure 1.9 shows the responses, from the same countries represented in Figure 1.2.

In most of these countries (and many others included in the ESS but not shown in Figure 1.9), there was little or no decline in people's comfort with their own household income over the course of the Great Recession. Indeed, all five countries Anderson and Hecht classify as "extensive welfare states" experienced at least a slight *increase* in average comfort with household income between 2006 and 2010.[15] The prevalence and effectiveness of modern welfare states in these countries may provide much of the explanation for their modest political responses to the Great Recession.

The apparent disconnect in many countries between people's perceptions of national economic conditions on one hand and their own economic circumstances on the other may be of considerable significance in accounting for the relative modesty of political responses to the economic crisis. A major recession may be seen as an indication of faulty political management, warranting punishment of the incumbent government at the polls; but if people's own day-to-day lives are mostly unaffected, they may be quite unlikely to take to the streets or rethink their basic views about politics and policy, much less to reject the fundamental legitimacy of the political order.

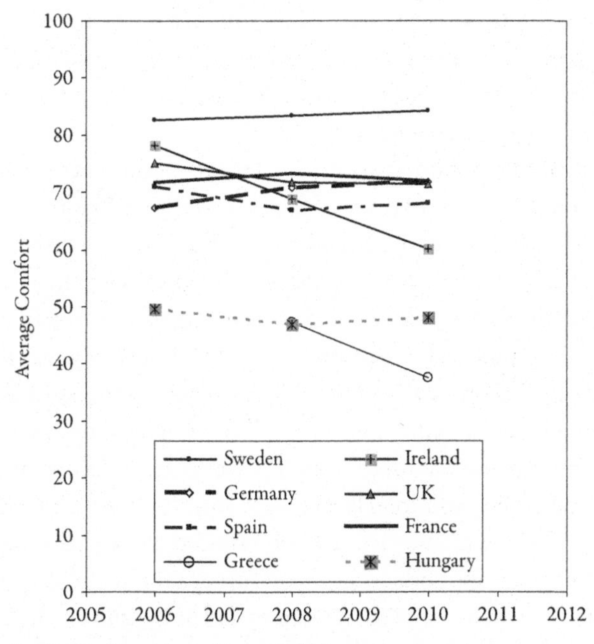

FIGURE 1.9 Public Feeling About Household Income, 2006–2010.

People's day-to-day circumstances were less insulated from the economic crisis in the countries Anderson and Hecht characterized as having less extensive systems of social protection. Indeed, in every one of these countries, respondents experienced a *decline* in average comfort, ranging from slight to substantial.[16] Anderson and Hecht find that the contemporaneous effects of economic variables are significantly more pronounced in countries with less extensive systems of social protection. The most striking examples are Greece (at least after 2008) and Ireland, where the crisis produced substantial erosion in ordinary people's sense of personal economic well-being. The absence of ample social protection schemes—and the dismantling of some that already existed—may help explain why reactions to the crisis in Greece have been notably less moderate than elsewhere.

Although preexisting welfare states were clearly important in mitigating the impact of the Great Recession, governments also adopted a variety of extraordinary policy responses (Bermeo and Pontusson 2012). Insofar as these measures reduced the severity of the recession, they also tended to limit its political impact. In the United States, for example, the six months following the collapse of Lehman Brothers in September 2008 saw a "stunning range of initiatives" improvised by the Federal Reserve, the Treasury Department, and the Obama White House to stabilize the financial system and stimulate the economy. By one estimate (Blinder and Zandi 2010, table 4), these initiatives boosted real GDP by 4.9 percent in 2009 and by 6.6 percent in 2010. Bartels (Chapter 7) estimates that these economic gains bolstered the incumbent Democrats in the 2010 midterm election, even though the stimulus measures themselves were politically unpopular.

Although a long period of painfully slow economic recovery consumed President Obama's entire first term, this was nothing like the "Depression 2.0" that Fed chairman Ben Bernanke and other policy makers feared. Of course, the millions of people who had lost their jobs or their homes were unlikely to be cheered by the fact that things might have been much worse. However, from a political perspective, one of the most remarkable features of the Great Recession in the United States is the starkness of the division between casualties and noncombatants. While victims of the economic crisis in Greece, France, and Britain took to the streets, the millions of Americans hit by unemployment and foreclosure were almost invisible in public space. The Occupy Wall Street movement was mobilized by neither group (Tarrow 2012). A majority of respondents in a 2010 survey said they *did not know* "anyone who has had their home foreclosed or fallen behind in their mortgage payments in the past year."[17] For most Americans, a few months of genuine panic faded fairly quickly into the more familiar economic strain of recession and slow recovery.

In Chapter 3, Katherine Cramer offers additional leads on popular reactions to the Great Recession in her study of Wisconsin, a state that saw substantial popular mobilization after Tea Party Governor Scott Walker introduced an austerity budget in 2011. Using evidence from a participant observation study running from May 2007 to June 2011, Cramer shows us both what makes people available for mobilization and what restrains the mobilization that does take place. Focusing on the question of how ordinary people "make sense of economic conditions," she explains that the people she studied attributed the economic crisis, and economic problems more generally, not to Wall Street or to corporations but to "big government" and to "public employees." Thus, despite their modest means, and the fact that many held union jobs themselves, the mostly rural citizens in Cramer's study were unavailable for mobilization by the left—even the moderate left. They were mobilized instead by the conservative right, precisely because they had come to see the public sector–private sector divide as substantially more salient than divisions based on income or class.

In Wisconsin, as in France, the advances made by the radical right were based on longstanding trends: Cramer illustrates that the resentment of government and government workers predated the recession by many years. But she also illustrates that political entrepreneurs were limited in the extent to which they could exploit this resentment after the crisis erupted. A first limit to extremist reactions came from cross-cutting cleavages. Marital and other personal connections with public sector employees led even citizens with a deep level of resentment to moderate their behavior (if not their ideas). A shared union identity trumped the private sector vs. public sector divide when it came to supporting the right-wing governor's proposal to limit collective bargaining.

A second factor that tempered the reactions to the Great Recession derived from sharp regional differences in the pace and nature of economic decline. Statistically, a recession is defined as a national event involving a sustained decline in aggregate national production figures. But people in rural Wisconsin had seen their local economy deteriorating for many years. For them, the Great Recession was less an "economic shock" than the simple naming of an ongoing, long-term process they knew all too well. Predictably, people's availability for immoderate mobilization was lessened by a widespread sense of resignation. Beissinger and Sasse noted a somewhat similar phenomenon in Ukraine.

Accounting for the Exceptions: Immoderate Responses to Austerity

Moderate reactions to the Great Recession were not, of course, universal. Our chapters highlight several cases in which ordinary people reacted immoderately. In Iceland, as Kriesi explains, people across the social spectrum mobilized en masse when a banking crisis brought on by rampant financial speculation hit the country in the third quarter of 2008. Bank nationalizations, an IMF austerity package, and a 70 percent currency devaluation led to the storming of parliament in January 2009 and to a historically unprecedented level of political violence. Though a majority of people backed established parties when early elections were called in April 2009, several new protest parties attracted substantial support and unsettled the once-stable party system. Massive and sometimes violent economic protests erupted in Latvia, too. More than fifty thousand people participated in over a dozen demonstrations, including one, on January 13, that marked the country's worst violence since 1991.

Hungary's politics in 2008–2011 were especially unsettled. Its economic protests were among the most numerous and violent in the post-communist region, according to Beissinger and Sasse, and it stood out, as mentioned above, in spawning the far-right Jobbik Party.

Greece also represents a setting where ordinary people reacted to economic crisis more dramatically. Mass protests have been mounted repeatedly, violence against property and people has become commonplace, and, as mentioned above, centrist parties have eroded and given way to what looks like a classically polarized party system.

What distinguishes these cases from those with less dramatic responses? What, in other words, are the conditions under which the combustible potential of the Great Recession was realized? Not surprisingly, all of these cases were especially hard hit by the economic crisis. Yet the severity of a country's economic crisis did not predict popular political reactions in any simple way. Beissinger and Sasse find "considerable variation in the extent to which economic pain translated into economic protest" in post-communist regimes, and their observation appears to hold elsewhere as well. The crisis in Ireland, for example, was among the worst in Europe; but, as Kriesi notes, Ireland's draconian austerity programs were eventually accepted with "surprising stoicism" and Irish voters initiated no major changes in the party system.

So if even a severe economic downturn is not sufficient to provoke a radical response, what else is required? Though the question deserves much more attention than we can give it here, our authors provide a number of important leads for further investigation. Two factors seem to have made radical responses to significant downturns more likely. The first is a trigger that enables ordinary people to link economic hardship directly to the actions of incumbent political elites. This triggering mechanism lies at the root of our observation that radical reactions are prompted more by austerity than by economic decline itself. Beissinger and Sasse show that in the post-communist countries adoption of an IMF standby agreement increased the likelihood of protest dramatically (by up to 84 percent). They show that "protest against austerity measures (cuts in pay, benefits, or services) came to dominate protest agendas, . . . mobilizing 71 percent of all protest participants in the region in 2009 and 80 percent in 2010." Kriesi's analysis confirms that the connection between protest and the adoption of austerity programs is generalizable to other, very different sorts of European states. Cramer draws a similar observation from her study of Wisconsin. Though she deliberately focuses on individuals who backed austerity rather than on the many who opposed it, she reminds us that "conditions are ripe for political mobilization" when people can attribute the cause of economic decline to specific political actors, organizations, or social groups.

The adoption of austerity plans makes the attribution of blame much simpler, and thus more likely. Because austerity programs are the subject of public debate in legislatures and in the media, they provide a much more salient focal point for mobilization than the release of statistics on economic growth or unemployment. And even though politicians may sometimes escape blame for poor economic performance if citizens attribute economic distress to global factors beyond domestic political control (Alcañiz and Hellwig 2010), the more obvious connection between austerity and the political actors who impose it makes a government's response to economic crisis a natural lightning rod for popular discontent.

Of course, austerity programs do not always trigger radical reactions. The second factor required for a radical reaction—at the ballot box or in the streets—is a political capacity for mobilization. Our chapters offer a number of leads regarding the contextual factors that boost the capacity for mobilization, and here too, similarities across different sorts of polities emerge.

Kriesi's research draws our attention to the "close interaction" between "conventional politics and contentious mobilization in the streets" and shows that sustained radical reactions depended on the "support of allies within the established institutional structures." The support of established public sector unions was key in all the immoderate cases. Kriesi argues that public sector unions (and unions more generally) played a pivotal role in Iceland, Latvia, Hungary, and Southern Europe. Beissinger and Sasse also find that public sector unions "provided the mobilizing capacity for generating large and sustained protest campaigns," and show that post-communist "countries with high levels of public sector employment experienced greater protest." Public sector unions have been pivotal to mobilization in Greece as well. Ireland is the exception that proves the rule. After early mobilization initiatives similar to those emerging elsewhere, Ireland's public sector unions agreed to a temporary ban on strikes in March 2010. Protest in general has dropped dramatically, suggesting that both mobilization and demobilization are greatly affected by labor organizations and labor leadership.[18]

Beyond labor organizations, formal institutional structures such as dual executives and referenda gave a boost to radical reactions too. In both Latvia and Iceland, mobilizers benefited greatly from the support of the country's president. Mobilizers also benefited from popular support garnered during referenda in Iceland, Hungary, and Latvia. Other things being equal, mobilizing agents probably benefit from multiple channels of access to representation.

But the conventional institutional structures most closely and consistently associated with radical reactions were political parties. Kriesi counts political parties among his pivotal "mobilizing agents" and shows how opposition parties and even defecting coalition partners encouraged economic protests for electoral purposes. Similarly, Beissinger and Sasse highlight the "key role" that political parties played in high protest cases and conclude that large-scale mass protest is unlikely "without parties mobilizing" along the cleavages exacerbated by the crisis itself. They conclude that "significant or sustained waves of protest" did not emerge where parties lacked "the credibility or desire to mobilize citizens around the issues of economic pain" and point to Ukraine and Estonia to make their argument.

The mention of credibility brings us to the role that ideational factors played in boosting mobilization capacity and in distinguishing high-mobilization cases. Beissinger and Sasse find that the "countries that were most vulnerable to high levels of economic protest" were those in which "huge expectations" had been generated by EU integration and the massive economic and political reform that went along with it. Countries where governments "lacked public trust or a reputation for effectiveness" prior to the crisis, were also "more likely to see sustained and significant protest." Ultimately Beissinger and Sasse suggest that mobilization depends most importantly on whether ordinary people believe that protest will pay off. They conclude that "if citizens are disillusioned" and do not believe "that collective action might be an effective remedy to their plight," then significant or sustained waves of protest will prove impossible, even if other enabling conditions are present.

Disillusion figures prominently in Kriesi's analysis, too. He asserts that "eventually, protest may subside...because the discontented population...loses faith in the effectiveness of protest or because it is forced to acknowledge the constraints" imposed on government. He uses Ireland, where the population grew resigned to austerity in the face of unyielding EU and IMF pressures, to illustrate his point.

A "Great Recession Era"?

It would be obtusely literal to think of the Great Recession as having ended in June 2009, the date chosen (more than a year later) by the National Bureau of Economic Research as marking the beginning of economic recovery in the United States. As Figure 1.2 makes clear, many countries continued to experience slow growth—and some experienced substantial further economic decline—in the years following the official end of the recession. In much of Europe, the difficulties of recovery have been compounded by a sovereign debt crisis exacerbated by the financial crisis of 2008.

The economic fallout from the Great Recession is entirely consistent with the fallout from previous financial crises: these events have generally had "a deep and lasting effect on asset prices, output, and employment" (Reinhart and Rogoff 2009, 238). Alarmingly, economists are now suggesting that longer-term shifts in demography, education, globalization, the environment, and accumulated debt could result in decades of low economic growth (Gordon 2012). If these forecasts are correct, the economic crisis of 2008–9 may come to be seen as the beginning of a "Great Recession Era" (akin to the Great Depression Era) defined less by the recession itself than by its economic and political legacy: an extended period of slow growth, overhanging debt, fiscal austerity, and struggles to reform national and international institutions to deal with these challenges.

The research reported in this volume sheds important light on the responses of ordinary citizens to the initial economic shock of the Great Recession and to the measures adopted by political leaders to address that shock. But what of the future? As of this writing, in the spring of 2013, many of the countries we have studied face the prospect of persistent slow growth, staggering unemployment and continued austerity measures. Will ordinary people react to these troubling conditions with rage, or with resignation? Will the pattern we have discerned of "surprisingly muted and moderate" popular reactions give way to more dramatic political shifts?

Of course, it is too soon to tell for sure. But for the time being, the evolving politics of the Great Recession mostly seem to fit the general patterns of political behaviour highlighted in this volume. Demonstrations and political protest may be on the rise, but these events are overwhelmingly related to the expansion and deepening of austerity programs. Moreover, political moderation seems to be quite resilient, at least so far. Incumbents continue to get punished for poor economic performance at the polls, but mainstream political parties have still not been challenged successfully in national elections, even in Europe's most troubled economies. In Portugal and Spain, center-right parties remain in firm control of government after being swept into power in 2011. In Greece, the 2012 elections yielded a center-right government in coalition with parties of the center and center-left. Current opinion polls suggest that the ruling party is actually rising in popularity and overtaking the leftist Syriza (Reuters UK 2013). In Italy, the February 2013 national elections also yielded a government controlled by a grand coalition of mainstream parties and technocrats. The protest party that garnered more than 20 percent of the vote in national elections and huge amounts of media attention was soon routed in local elections and is thought to be disintegrating (BBC News 2013 May 28). Even in Bulgaria, where massive protests drove a corrupt government from power in February 2013, April elections brought the only extremist party of note (Attack), a mere 5 percent of the national vote.

Some observers of the current scene look to the streets and to extremist parties and warn of political crises comparable to those of the 1930s. But direct comparisons with the Great Depression are likely to prove misleading. First, most of the people who fill the streets today seem intent on deepening democracy rather than destroying it. Second, today's would-be spoilers are hampered by the absence of any plausible alternative to capitalist democracy. Communism and fascism both offered credible alternatives during the Great Depression (for capitalists and laborers alike), but both have lost their luster—and no widely credible ideological substitute has emerged to take their place.

Third, and precisely because of the experience of depression and war, democratic governments have formed powerful international organizations that aim to advance political and economic stability and protect formal democracy itself. NATO and the European Union have, and use, resources to sanction anti-democratic actors—an option unavailable in the 1930s.

Finally, in the United States and elsewhere, most ordinary people had to face the Great Depression without a social safety net. Eight decades later, rich democracies—even in liberal market economies—have greatly expanded the welfare programs that buffer citizens from economic calamities. As we have seen, these safety net programs seem to have worked very much as intended, mitigating households' economic distress despite the severity of the recession. Ironically, much of the popular mobilization we see today harnesses widespread opposition to cuts in welfare programs that barely existed at the time of the Great Crash in 1929.

For all these reasons, rage in the wake of the Great Recession is unlikely to reach a level comparable to that of the 1930s. And we must remember that, even in the 1930s, only a minority of citizens embraced anti-democratic options anyway; democracies did not die at the hands of their voters (Bermeo 2003). Today, further cuts in safety nets may lead to increased popular resistance and the decline in trust may gradually extend from specific incumbent politicians to mainstream leaders and parties in general. Yet the economic crisis we have focused on here differs from the Great Depression in both depth and context. With a very different stimulus, we should expect a different political response.

For the United States and most of the richer European democracies, the Great Recession was simply much less severe than the Great Depression. The rise in unemployment was much smaller, the peak-to-trough drop in GDP was much more modest, and the time to recovery was much shorter. The Great Depression had less dire effects in Ireland and the Southern European countries, primarily because of their lower levels of development. For these countries, the economic crisis sparked by the Great Recession was, by some criteria, actually worse than the Great Depression. Its aftermath is proving to be worse as well, notably with respect to youth unemployment. Yet even in Europe's south, several crucially important contextual differences limit the applicability of Depression-era parallels.

First, the political crises that erupted during the Great Depression were rooted not simply in economic turmoil but also in the massive dislocations brought on by World War I, the Russian Revolution, and the collapse of the Ottoman Empire. The nationalist veterans, politicized refugees and military figures who played such pivotal roles in the mobilizations of the 1930s, have no counterparts today. Moreover, the countries we have focused on here are sufficiently rich—and sufficiently integrated, both economically and politically—to ensure that the "combustible potential" of economic distress remains largely contained.

As we write, there are signs that containment is already under way. The IMF began to caution against drastic austerity measures in early 2013, noting that the negative effects on employment had been underestimated and that fiscal consolidation should be "slow and steady" (Blanchard and Leigh 2013; BBC News, January 24, 2013). The EU now seeks to include a €6 billion Youth Employment Initiative in its next budget and recommends that no fewer than nine member states "strengthen social safety nets" to protect the 120 million people who "are now at risk of poverty or social exclusion" (Barroso 2013). The EU has also granted several countries extra time to meet their deficit targets. In 2012, it allowed Greece, Portugal, and Spain one-year extensions. In 2013, Portugal got a second extension, Belgium and the Netherlands got single-year extensions, and France, Spain, Poland, and Slovenia secured two-year delays (Rehn 2013).

Whether the softening of EU austerity policy will actually dampen political rage or boost economic growth remains to be seen. For now, even the framing of the policy change seems ambiguous. Though EU President Barroso insisted that the changes were made "on purely economic grounds, rather than for political reasons" (BBC, May 29, 2013), he announced the reforms insisting that a "successful crisis strategy has to... have the necessary political and social support" (Barroso 2013), implying that public opinion may still be an important consideration in current policy making. As our collection illustrates, preferences certainly matter for the legitimacy of the EU and for the continuity of leadership in individual democracies.

If changing policies do not yield quick results and we do turn out to be in a "Great Recession Era," it will probably look and feel less like the Great Depression Era than like the Long Recession of the 1970s and early 1980s. This was a period in which conservatives in many countries successfully exploited economic stagnation to reinforce popular fears of big government and resentment of its beneficiaries. It was also a period in which political scientists noted that hard times made people less generous (Alt 1979). Thomas Edsall, who chronicled the politics of the 1970s and 1980s in the United States (Edsall and Edsall 1991), has recently argued that the current "age of austerity" will likewise prove to be a boon to conservatives, who are strategically advantaged in "a dog-eat-dog political competition over diminishing resources" (Edsall 2012).

It is true that public support for government budget cutting was surprisingly strong even before the Great Recession, and as we saw in Table 1.1 it remained strong in 2010, two years into the crisis—not just in liberal market economies such as the United States, Australia, and the United Kingdom but also in Germany and France. However, public support for budget cutting in the abstract is seldom matched by public support for real cuts in significant government programs, and those cuts were just beginning to be implemented in 2010. Thus it remains to be seen whether major long-term retrenchments in welfare states will prove to be politically feasible.

Much will probably depend on the nature and apparent impact of austerity programs. Austerity budgeting can take a variety of forms. Certain states, such as Estonia, have managed to cut spending while conserving popular programs and the act of cutting spending seems to matter less for resistance than the nature of the groups who are affected (Taylor-Gooby 2013). In any case, economies in several countries are beginning to bounce back from austerity programs and grow again; Ireland, Latvia, Iceland, and Estonia are counterweights to the Greek example of a crushing, apparently self-defeating austerity regime. Where austerity comes to be seen—rightly or wrongly—as a formula for renewed economic vitality, it will probably be tolerated. Where it is seen as an impediment to growth, and especially job creation, resistance may grow. The role of the media and public intellectuals may be pivotal here.

In these respects and others, the political story of the Great Recession remains unfinished. Nevertheless, the interim reports collected in this volume handsomely illustrate both the strong continuities with the past evident in popular responses to the crisis and the potential impact of those responses on the shape of politics and government for years to come.

*The authors thank the John Fell Fund, Nuffield College and Princeton's Institute for International and Regional Studies for funding and Andrew Shipley for indexing.

Notes

1. http://www.time.com/time/covers/0,16641,20081124,00.html.
2. http://www.foxnews.com/politics/2009/01/12/raw-data-transcript-bushs-white-house-press-conference/.
3. We examine how governments reacted to the crisis in a companion volume titled *Coping with Crisis: Government Reactions to the Great Recession* (Bermeo and Pontusson 2012).
4. "Quarterly National Accounts: Quarterly Growth Rates of Real GDP, Change over Previous Quarter," OECD (http://stats.oecd.org).
5. "Composite Leading Indicators (MEI): OECD Standardized Consumer Confidence Indicator (CCI), Amplitude Adjusted (Long Term Average = 100)," OECD (http://stats.oecd.org). We have averaged the monthly data for each quarter.
6. Information about the study design and the data employed in our calculations is available from the ESS website, http://www.europeansocialsurvey.org/.
7. Owens and Pedulla's data came from the General Social Survey 2006–2008–2010 and 2008–2010–2012 panel studies. The redistribution question asked, "Some people think that the government in Washington ought to reduce the income

differences between the rich and the poor, perhaps by raising the taxes of wealthy families or by giving income assistance to the poor. Others think that the government should not concern itself with reducing this income difference between the rich and the poor.... What score between 1 and 7 comes closest to the way you feel?"

8. In the Czech Republic and Greece, our comparison is with 2004 because there was no 2006 European Social Survey in those countries.
9. http://www.globescan.com/news_archives/bbc2009_globalPoll-04/.
10. Because Greece was not included in the 2006 European Social Survey, the 3.59 figure is based on 2004 data. The corresponding average level of trust in 2008 was 2.46.
11. Study information and data are available from the ISSP website, http://www.issp.org/.
12. Citizens in Germany and Japan were more enthusiastic about budget cutting than about economic stimulus (putting them in the lower-right quadrant of Figure 1.8). Citizens in Finland, Denmark, and Great Britain favored economic stimulus programs but were evenly divided on the merits of budget cutting (putting them in the lower-left quadrant of the figure). The Irish and Spaniards were similarly divided about budget cutting, but even more strongly supportive of government financing of projects to create jobs (putting them in the upper-left quadrant), while the Portuguese and Hungarians, among others, were highly enthusiastic about both (putting them in the upper-right quadrant). Examining distributions of opinion *within* countries reveals rather more evidence of awareness that these were potentially competing policy alternatives. In most countries, the average views of partisan subgroups lined up more or less sensibly, with left-of-center parties above and to the left of right-of-center parties in the policy space defined by Figure 1.8. The partisan gaps were larger in the United States (Democrat versus Republican) and Britain (Labour and Liberal versus Conservative) than in Germany, Spain, or (especially) Portugal. However, even the largest partisan differences were dwarfed by cross-national differences in level of support for each of these policy options.
13. http://www.globescan.com/news_archives/bbc2010_economics/.
14. The survey response options were "very difficult on present income," "difficult on present income," "coping on present income," and "living comfortably on present income." In Figure 1.9, we translate these responses to range from 0 (for "very difficult") to 100 (for "living comfortably").
15. Anderson and Hecht's five "extensive welfare states"—Belgium, Denmark, France, Germany, and the Netherlands—saw changes in average comfort level ranging from +.1 to +4.4 on our 100-point scale.
16. Changes in average comfort level in Greece, Ireland, Portugal, Spain, and the United Kingdom ranged from −1.6 to −18.2 on our 100-point scale. (Anderson and Hecht's sixth example of a less extensive welfare state, Italy, is not represented in the ESS data.)

17. "Do you know anyone who has had their home foreclosed or fallen behind in their mortgage payments in the past year?" Yes, 36 percent; no, 54 percent; not sure, 9 percent. YouGov/Polimetrix survey, October 2010.
18. The ban will last until 2014. Union leader Jack O'Connor's justification for cooperation with the government provides a vivid illustration of the complexity of public sector worker calculations: "Is it better," he asked, "to fight on in the knowledge that we are still living in a ruined economy and that any action we take will be depicted as an attack on the citizens of the country?" The Services, Industrial, Professional and Technical Union (SIPTU) March 31 agreement with Ireland's Labour Relations Commission, reported April 13, 2010.

References

Achen, Christopher H., and Larry M. Bartels. 2005. "Partisan Hearts and Gall Bladders: Retrospection and Realignment in the Wake of the Great Depression." Paper prepared for the Annual Meeting of the Midwest Political Science Association, Chicago, April 7–9.

Alt, James E. 1979. *The Politics of Economic Decline.* Cambridge: Cambridge University Press.

Alcañiz, Isabella, and Timothy Hellwig. 2010. "Who's to Blame? The Distribution of Responsibility in Developing Democracies." *British Journal of Political Science 41*, 389–411.

Anderson, Christopher J., Silvia M. Mendes, Yuliya V. Tverdova, and Kim Haklin. 2004. "Endogenous Economic Voting: Evidence from the 1997 British Election." *Electoral Studies* 23(4): 683–708.

Barroso, José Manuel Durão. 2013. "Statement by President Barroso on the Country-specific Recommendations Package 2013." May 29, http://europa.eu/rapid/press-release_SPEECH-13-473_en.htm. Accessed June 1, 2013.

Bartels, Larry M. 2005. "Homer Gets a Tax-Cut: Inequality and Public Policy in the American Mind." *Perspectives on Politics* 3: 15–31.

Bartels, Larry M. 2013. "Political Effects of the Great Recession." *Annals of the American Academy of Political and Social Science, 650*(1): 47–75.

BBC. 2013. "IMF's Olivier Blanchard." January 24, www.bbc.co.uk/news/business-21175407. Accessed June 1, 2013.

BBC. 2013. "European Countries to Be Allowed to Ease Austerity." May 29, www.bbc.co.uk/news/business. Accessed June 1, 2013.

BBC News. 2013. "Election Setback for Grillo Protest Party in Italy." May 28, http://www.bbc.co.uk/news/world-europe-22690165. Accessed June 1, 2013.

Bermeo, Nancy. 2003. *Ordinary People in Extraordinary Times: The Citizenry and the Breakdown of Democracy*. Princeton, NJ: Princeton University Press.

Bermeo, Nancy, and Jonas Pontusson. 2012. *Coping with Crisis: Government Reactions to the Great Recession*. New York: Russell Sage Foundation.

Bernhard, Michael, Timothy Nordstrom, and Christopher Reenock. 2001. "Economic Performance, Institutional Intermediation, and Democratic Survival." *Journal of Politics 63*(3): 775–803.

Blanchard, Olivier, and Daniel Leigh. 2013. "Growth Forecast Errors and Fiscal Multipliers." IMF Working Paper, January 3.

Blinder, Alan S., and Mark Zandi. 2010. "How the Great Recession Was Brought to an End." Princeton University and Moody's Analytics, July 27 (http://www.Economy.com/mark-zandi/documents/End-of-Great-Recession.pdf).

Cameron, David. 2001. "Unemployment, Job Creation and Economic and Monetary Union." In Nancy Bermeo ed., *Unemployment in the New Europe*. New York: Cambridge University Press.

Dahl, Robert. 1971. *Polyarchy: Participation and Opposition*. New Haven: Yale University Press.

Duch, Raymond M., and Randy Stevenson. 2008. *The Economic Vote: How Political and Economic Institutions Condition Election Results*. Cambridge: Cambridge University Press.

Edsall, Thomas Byrne. 2012. *The Age of Austerity: How Scarcity Will Remake American Politics*. New York: Doubleday.

Edsall, Thomas Byrne, with Mary D. Edsall. 1991. *Chain Reaction: The Impact of Race, Rights, and Taxes on American Politics*. New York: Norton.

Erikson, Robert S., Michael B. MacKuen, and James A. Stimson. 2002. *The Macro Polity*. New York: Cambridge University Press.

Gasiorowski, Mark. 1995. "Economic Crisis and Political Regime Change: An Event History Analysis." *American Political Science Review 89*(4): 882–897.

Gordon, Robert J. 2012. "Is U.S. Economic Growth Over? Faltering Innovation Confronts the Six Headwinds." *National Bureau of Economic Research Working Paper 18315* (http://www.nber.org/papers/w18315.pdf).

Huntington, Samuel. 1991. *The Third Wave*. Norman: University of Oklahoma Press.

Kenworthy, Lane, and Lindsay A. Owens. 2011. "The Surprisingly Weak Effect of Recessions on Public Opinion." In David B. Grusky, Bruce Western, and Christopher Wimer, eds., *The Great Recession*. New York: Russell Sage Foundation.

Krugman, Paul. 2009. *The Return of Depression Economics and the Crisis of 2008*. New York: Norton.

Lindvall, Johannes. 2012. "Economic Crises as Political Opportunities." In *Crises as Political Opportunities*, Matts Benner ed. Cheltenham: Edward Elgar.

Lipset, Seymour Martin. 1959. *Political Man*. New York: Doubleday.

Margalit, Yotam. 2013. "Explaining Social Policy Preferences: Evidence from the Great Recession." *American Political Science Review 107*(1): 80–103.

McLaren, Lauren. 2003. "Anti-Immigrant Prejudice in Europe: Contact, Threat Perception, and Preferences for the Exclusion of Migrants." *Social Forces 81*(3): 909–936.

Owens, Lindsay A., and David S. Pedulla. 2013. "Material Welfare, Ideology, and Changing Political Preferences: The Case of Support for Redistributive Social Policies." Unpublished paper, Stanford University and Princeton University.

Powell, G. Bingham, and Guy D. Whitten. 1993. "A Cross-National Analysis of Economic Voting: Taking Account of the Political Context." *American Journal of Political Science 37*: 391–414.

Przeworski, Adam, and Fernando Limongi. 1993. "Political Regimes and Economic Growth." *Journal of Economic Perspectives 7*(3): 51–69.

Rehm, Philipp. 2011. "Social Policy by Popular Demand." *World Politics 63*(2): 271–299.

Rehn, Olli. 2013. "Press Speaking Points at the European Semester Press Conference." May 29, http://europa.eu/rapid/press-release_SPEECH-13-481_en.htm.

Reinhart, Carmen M., and Kenneth S. Rogoff. 2009. *This Time Is Different: Eight Centuries of Financial Folly*. Princeton, NJ: Princeton University Press.

Reuters UK. 2013. "Greece's Ruling Conservatives Extend Lead." May 28, 10:37 A.M. BST.

Richards, David, and Ronald D. Gelleny. 2006. "Banking Crises, Collective Protest and Rebellion." *Canadian Journal of Political Science 39*(4): 777–801.

Romer, Christina. 1993. "The Nation in Depression." *Journal of Economic Perspectives 7*(2): 1939.

Schlozman, Kay Lehman, and Sidney Verba. 1979. *Injury to Insult: Unemployment, Class, and Political Response*. Cambridge, MA: Harvard University Press.

Stimson, James A. 1998. *Public Opinion in America: Moods, Cycles, and Swings*, 2nd ed. Boulder, CO: Westview Press.

Tarrow, Sidney. 1994. *Power in Movement: Social Movements, Collective Action and Politics*. New York: Cambridge University Press.

Tarrow, Sidney. 2012. "Class Contentious Language and the Rise of Classless Protest." Unpublished paper presented at Oxford University, November 9.

Taylor-Gooby, Peter. 2013. "Riots, Demonstrations, Strikes and the Coalition Program." *Journal of Social Policy and Society 12*(1): 1–15.

Treas, Judith. 2010. "The Great American Recession: Sociological Insights on Blame and Pain." *Sociological Perspectives 53*(1): 3–17. Presidential address to the Pacific Sociological Association.

Van der Brug, Wouter, Cees van der Eijk, and Mark Franklin. 2007. *The Economy and the Vote: Economic Conditions and Elections in Fifteen Countries*. Cambridge: Cambridge University Press.

2

Crisis of Confidence?

THE DYNAMICS OF ECONOMIC OPINIONS DURING THE GREAT RECESSION

Christopher J. Anderson and Jason D. Hecht

IN GOOD TIMES and bad, public opinion is an essential component of the demand side of politics. Few concerns are dearer to the hearts of democratic governments than what the public thinks about the state of the country's economy, as economic opinion is commonly seen to be crucial to incumbents' own survival in office. What is more, this has been particularly true in recent years, as Western democracies and the governments that lead them have grappled with the fallout of the global economic crisis that erupted in full force during 2008.

Despite the real-world importance of the opinions citizens hold about the state of the country or their own personal economic well-being, we know relatively little about the forces that shape economic opinions during times of intense crisis. It is commonly assumed that people's opinions about the economy usually mirror economic reality, but this assumption is not always supported by evidence. Even in the best of times, the subjective and the objective economy may not line up very neatly; and during a major economic crisis there is even more reason to suspect that the link between real economic conditions and economic opinions may be bent or even broken.

Note: A first draft of this chapter was presented at the conference "Popular Reactions to the Economic Crisis," Nuffield College, Oxford University. We thank the participants in the conference, and in particular Nancy Bermeo and Larry Bartels, for their constructive comments. We are also grateful to Peter Enns for advice on the data analysis.

In this chapter, we use monthly opinion data from eleven European countries to develop a novel measure of "economic mood"—an indicator that gauges the overall sense of economic well-being in each country on a monthly basis. We use this measure to examine the dynamics of aggregate economic opinion before and after the onset of the Great Recession, and we investigate whether the content and trajectory of economic opinion varied significantly across countries. In addition, we investigate how economic mood was systematically shaped by specific aspects of countries' economic performance, and whether the structure of economic opinion changed as countries moved from the normal (pre-crisis) business cycle to a period of acute economic stress.

We first discuss the connection between the objective and subjective economies in scholarship on economic voting and public opinion in order to develop a set of expectations about the forces that shape them. We then describe the dynamics of economic opinions before, during, and after the depths of the economic crisis. We examine whether common underlying economic factors shape these economic opinions, and whether these factors vary before and after the onset of the economic crisis. Finally, we explore whether and how the dynamics and determinants of a country's economic mood are shaped by its macrostructural characteristics, including the size of welfare states and the partisan color of incumbent governments.

We find that the economic crisis produced a steep, but cross-nationally variable, decline in Europe's economic mood. Economic optimism recovered somewhat following the worst of the crisis, but at an unequal pace across countries. The dynamics of economic mood in each country over the course of the Great Recession were consistently shaped by actual macro-level economic conditions—the "real" economy. Indeed, economic opinions were probably considerably more sensitive to changes in economic conditions after the onset of the crisis than they had been earlier. This was especially true in countries with a low level of social spending—perhaps because their publics were less effectively shielded from the human costs of the economic downturn. Economic opinions were also especially sensitive to changing economic conditions in countries where left parties were especially influential—a difference we attribute to voters' tendency to view left parties and their policies as "luxury goods" unaffordable during economic hard times. Thus, our analysis suggests that the very nature of the relationship between objective economic conditions and subjective economic opinions may be strongly shaped by key aspects of a country's political context.

Economic Reality and Economic Opinions

The economy has long featured as a prominent element in models of democratic politics. It is, for example, commonly believed that hard economic times accelerated the disintegration of the Weimar Republic, and that a bad economy can contribute to the collapse of democratic regimes generally. Moreover, a long line of scholars has contended that economic grievances can lead to rebellion and revolution, or that material well-being shapes citizens' political values and preferences. But perhaps the most voluminous literature relating the state of the economy to political behavior has evolved in the area of voter behavior. At its most basic, this research purports to show that governments lose support during hard economic times (Anderson 1995).[1]

This research is commonly based on the assumption that the real economy—unemployment, growth, inflation, and the like—matters because it is systematically reflected in the subjective economy—what people think about the economy. The conventional model connecting the economy and voter behavior has long assumed a chain of causality that runs from the objective economy to political behavior via voters' economic opinions (Anderson 2007).[2] The plausibility of this assumption rests, in good part, on its consistency with existing evidence on economic voting (especially in the aggregate), and with research on aggregate public opinion, which has reported significant congruence between objective economic conditions and subjective economic opinion (see, for example, Hibbs 1987; MacKuen, Erikson, and Stimson 1992; Haller and Norpoth 1994).

In perhaps the best known example of this sort of work, Benjamin Page and Robert Shapiro's *The Rational Public*, American public opinion is described as moving in response to "real world conditions," particularly unemployment and inflation (Page and Shapiro 1992: 121–22). The authors concluded, "Opinions about employment, inflation, taxes, and energy, for example, related in systematic and consistent ways to objective trends in prices and unemployment rates" (169). Similarly, Brandon Haller and Helmut Norpoth's analysis of U.S. public opinion came to the conclusion that economic opinion "has a firm footing in the real world" (Haller and Norpoth 1997: 26).

However, these findings of a link between macroeconomic outcomes and economic opinions have run up against a growing body of research into the connection between objective economic facts (the "real" economy) and people's opinions of them. Much of this work has emphasized (1) informational and cognitive limits to perceptual accuracy, and (2) the impact of values and predispositions on the formation of economic perceptions. Thus, even though the assumption that economic facts and economic opinions are predictably connected is certainly plausible, there also are good reasons to question it.

The translation of "objective" economic conditions into accurate perceptions involves several necessary steps. First of all, it assumes there is such a thing as the "objective" economy that can be perceived by voters, and it requires that this objective economy actually be perceived by voters at least somewhat accurately. These perceptions, then, are presumed to translate into negative, positive, or neutral evaluations of the economy (e.g., is it good or bad, or better, worse, or no different from before?).

In recent years, scholars have investigated how each link of this chain can be broken. Accurate "objective" information about the economy is frequently difficult for the average citizen to come by, and the interpretation of "objective" facts about the state of the economy is often politically contested (Keech 1995). Most people learn about the national economy indirectly from mass media, which tend to overreport negative economic conditions (Goidel and Langley 1995). Via mass media, people also learn of the economic forecasts of elites (MacKuen, Erikson, and Stimson 1992). However, these forecasts do not always faithfully convey economic information (Nadeau et al. 1999). These negative and perhaps biased reports heavily condition voters' economic perceptions (Hetherington 1996), and economic evaluations potentially derive to a greater extent from how the media present economic developments than they do from objective changes in the real economy (Sanders and Gavin 2004; see also Nadeau et al. 1999).

All this can limit the accuracy of voters' perceptions of macroeconomic conditions. In addition, citizens' cognitive limits reduce the extent to which they are likely to code objective information accurately (Krause 1997; Krause and Granato 1998; however, also see Sanders 2000). Moreover, people do not learn about different aspects of the economy in the same way or at the same pace (Nannestad, Paldam, and Rosholm 2003; Weatherford 1983).[3] What is more, citizens' own political biases and values work against a close relationship between perceptions of economic conditions and economic evaluations at the individual level. For example, partisans' evaluations of the state of the economy tend to be consistent with their political predispositions (Wlezien, Franklin, and Twiggs 1997; Anderson, Mendes, and Tverdova 2004; Evans and Andersen 2006).

Researchers long thought that all these individual differences mattered little for understanding the efficacy of the electorate's collective choice or judgment; this thinking was based on the assumption that a significant portion of individual-level differences was simply the result of "noise" or random variation associated with survey data (e.g., Page and Shapiro 1992; Sanders 2000). As a result, aggregation of individual responses was expected to "cancel out" the random variation, thereby leaving only the underlying meaningful (or rational) component of public opinion (Kramer 1983; Wittman 1989).

This argument presumes, however, that individual errors in measures of public opinion are truly random. As Bartels (1996) notes, however, if these individual errors are systematic, aggregation will not produce unbiased aggregate measures of public sentiment. Rather, these aggregate measures will vary systematically with factors unrelated to objective economic performance, such as partisanship or personal experiences. As it turns out, the various sources of individual error terms in national economic evaluations are not necessarily random (Duch, Palmer, and Anderson 2000). As a consequence, aggregate deviations of individual-level economic evaluations from objective economic conditions are not idiosyncratic but rather reflect the systematic effects of respondent characteristics.

Taken together, this means that economic evaluations are predictably biased and inaccurate at the individual level, but also that some of this individual-level heterogeneity will not cancel out in the aggregate (Duch, Palmer, and Anderson 2000). This could explain why aggregate assessments of specific economic indicators (interest rates, inflation rates, etc.) on occasion are quite inaccurate (Haller and Norpoth 1994), and why some of the aggregate variation in economic perceptions is driven by factors other than simply macroeconomic fluctuations (Bechtel 2003). Analyses of aggregate data have also pointed to the critical role played by political events, such as wars and crises, in people's economic perceptions (Clarke et al. 1992; DeBoef and Kellstedt 2004).[4]

Taken together, this literature suggests several things: first, that there is significant and systematic variation in economic opinions; second, that aggregate indicators of the perceived economy therefore can be systematically biased at certain times and under certain conditions; and third, that political events and attitudes can shape these opinions to a considerable degree. Put simply, this revisionist literature challenges the assumption of an unfailingly truthful translation of the real economy into people's economic attitudes as well as the assumption that economic opinions are exogenous to politics and political behavior.

How these literatures relate to public opinion in crisis situations is far from clear. For example, it is difficult to posit a priori whether we should expect to see the same kinds of patterns in times of crisis that we see in more "ordinary" times. On one hand, all the reasons for expecting discrepancies between the objective and subjective economy may be exacerbated in times of economic crisis—perhaps most directly for reasons related to information (or a lack thereof) and the stress in processing whatever information is indeed available.

Consider, for example, the difficulty of separating economic fact from fiction in the middle of an economic crisis, or how mass media are likely to report, interpret, and possibly skew the content and tone of information about the economy. As well, the stress brought on by the threat inherent in an acute crisis is likely to impede and stretch citizens' ability to collect, decode, and interpret complex information. Finally, voters' motivations to see what they want to see—for political or personal reasons—when things are not going well are likely to be fully engaged when few people have all the facts and governments are actively working to mitigate the worst economic and political effects of the crisis.

Conversely, an alternative perspective would see the crisis as the kind of environment where information is plentiful—in fact, more plentiful than at any other time, save perhaps election campaigns. In particular, economic information of all kinds and from a variety of sources is likely to be abundant, much of which may be highly relevant to people's opinion-formation process. As well, the stress of an unusual situation like a sudden economic crisis may make people more vigilant, and there is evidence in psychology that moderate amounts of stress actually improve cognitive performance (though excessive amounts degrade it). If this is the case, then unusually bad economic times may in fact enhance the link between economic fact and perception, and at least one published study has found that assessments of economic performance are more closely linked to objective indicators when the economy is in decline (Duch, Palmer, and Anderson 2000).

By answering the questions we investigate here—whether macroeconomic performance explains economic opinions, and whether it does so differently during times of economic crisis—we seek to build on these sometimes contradictory strands of scholarship. We are agnostic but curious as to the effect of the Great Recession on the connection between economic facts and opinions. Thus, we put these varying expectations to the test by estimating a set of regression models relating economic opinions to macroeconomic conditions and examining whether the results differ before and after the start of the economic crisis. But before we can do that, we must turn to the issue of measuring public opinion about the economy: What, exactly, were European publics saying about the economy before and during the Great Recession?

Measuring Economic Opinions in Europe

Knowing how to interpret what the public is saying about the economy requires a way of measuring aggregate public opinion. We rely on a series of monthly surveys conducted by the European Commission since 1985 with representative samples of national populations.[5] These surveys, originally designed to gauge consumer confidence in each member state, contain a series of questions about the economy, including standard evaluations of personal and national economic conditions (including the overall economy as well as specific questions about unemployment and prices), both retrospective and prospective. (The full list of questions and question wording appear in Appendix A of this chapter.)

The multiple items used in the surveys are well suited for gauging European electorates' overall sense of how the economy is doing—a kind of "economic mood"—as the items tend to be highly correlated over time but capture different dimensions of subjective economic well-being in a country. Because these opinions cover a variety of economic opinions, among them people's opinions of their own and the country's economy, as well as forward- and backward-looking evaluations, jointly, they measure people's overall sense of how the economy is doing.

But instead of relying on the index of consumer sentiment supplied by the European Commission, we constructed our own country-level summary indicator of Europeans' economic opinions, based on the statistical properties of the items with the help of Stimson's dyad ratios algorithm (Stimson 1999).[6] The algorithm, which has been widely used by students of public opinion in a variety of domains,[7] is designed to identify and extract the common dynamic elements of public opinion aggregates from multiple indicators across surveys by focusing on the relative changes within an item rather than their absolute values (we describe the technical details in Appendix B).[8] Having developed the measure of economic mood, our next question is this: What did economic opinion look like during the Great Recession of 2008? This is the question we turn to next.

Economic Opinions in the Great Recession

To get a handle on the dynamics of public opinion over the course of the crisis, we start by describing Europeans' economic moods from the onset of the crisis, starting immediately before the crisis erupted in mid-2007 and continuing through early 2011 (our data end in February 2011). Figure 2.1, which shows the economic opinion series for each of the countries included here from 2007 onward, reveals several important dynamics. First, we see significant cross-national differences in countries' overall level of economic mood; for example, economic opinion is significantly more positive in Denmark

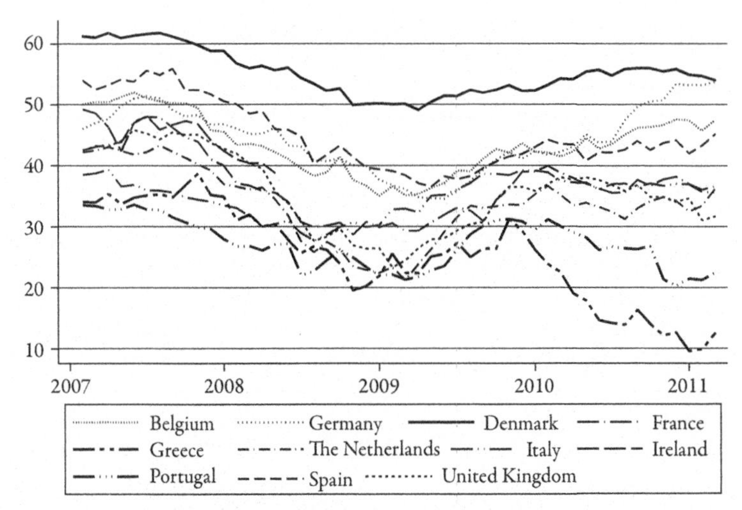

FIGURE 2.1 Economic Opinion in Europe, 2007–2011.

than in Portugal. Although Denmark and Portugal (along with Greece) are the countries with the best and worst economic moods, more generally there is significant variation across countries.

Second, and perhaps more importantly, economic opinion in Europe appears to have moved in three distinct phases. In phase 1, all countries experienced a notable and almost simultaneous dip starting in the middle of 2007. Thus, by the time the U.S. government marked the Great Recession as having started in December 2007, consistent with the official definition of a recession as negative growth for two consecutive quarters, public opinion had already been expressing it. This decline in "economic mood" was markedly parallel across countries, amounting to a decrease of about ten points in each case. This dip bottomed out in a very parallel fashion as well, in early 2009 (we would put it at February 2009).

Though virtually all European states' economic moods bottomed out in early 2009, the next period (phase 2) comprised a parallel uptick in economic opinion through the end of 2009. Thus, during much of 2009, economic opinion recovered about half of what it had lost during the early months of the crisis. Finally, phase 3 saw economic opinions diverge quite sharply. The economic mood in countries such as Germany and Belgium became significantly more positive and opinion in Denmark and the Netherlands modestly so throughout 2009 and into 2010 to pre-crisis or even above pre-crisis levels, but it soured again in 2010 in several other states, most notably Portugal and Greece, and also the United Kingdom. In contrast, the economic moods of Italy, France, and Spain, economic opinion stagnated after early 2010.

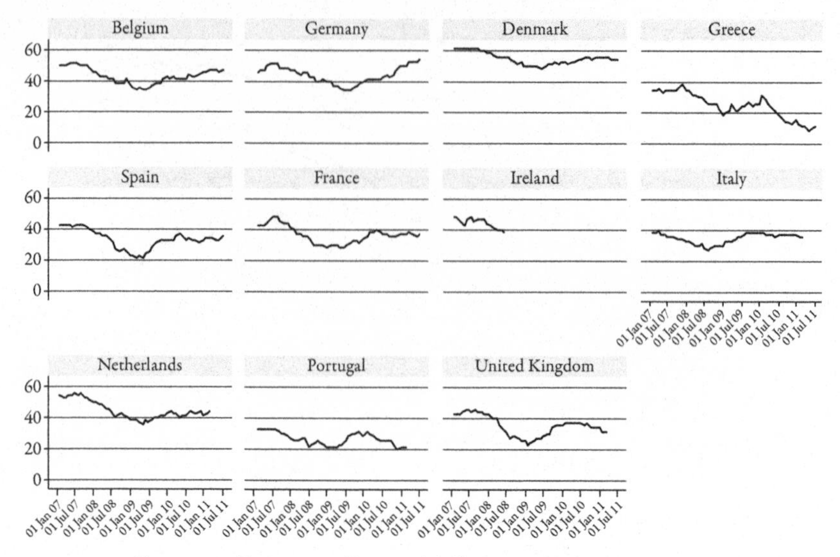

FIGURE 2.2 Economic Opinion in Europe, by Country, 2007–2010.

Taken together, the three phases of economic opinion during the crisis reveal a uniform drop across countries and a brief if somewhat shallow recovery followed by a divergence in assessments of economic conditions across the European states investigated here. These patterns can also be seen very clearly country by country in Figure 2.2, which depicts each country's unique trajectory in economic opinions.

So, what drives these opinions? And do their determinants vary across countries or change over time? Having briefly described the most notable trends in European economic opinions over the course of the crisis, we turn to answering these questions by examining more systematically the bases of those opinions.

The Impact of Economic Performance on Economic Opinions

To establish the presence or absence of a link between economic performance and economic opinion in Europe during the Great Recession, we are primarily interested in whether commonly used indicators of macroeconomic performance—here, unemployment, growth, and inflation rates—predict economic opinions. Following the existing literature, we hypothesize that macroeconomic indicators would be significant determinants of economic opinions; but we also expected that these relationships would vary during times of crisis. Presumably, they would vary as a function of the contextual conditions of heightened crisis and as a function of people's relative ease or difficulty in deciphering their country's actual economic conditions.

To investigate these relationships, we collected monthly economic performance indicators to match the public opinion data for each country. (Details appear in Appendix C.) Modeling the relationships among these variables using aggregate time-series data first requires identification of the underlying dynamic properties of the public opinion series. Specifically, we conducted a set of formal diagnostic tests to investigate whether the series are stationary or have a unit root. Unit root (Dickey Fuller) and stationarity (KPSS) tests revealed every country's series to have a unit root. Therefore, the appropriate multivariate modeling strategy involves differencing the dependent variable to make it stationary.

As a next step, we estimated a series of multivariate regressions with changes in public opinion as the dependent variable and the main economic aggregates as the independent variables. Because diagnostic tests showed the times series to be cointegrated, we estimated a single equation error correction model, which estimates both contemporaneous and long-term relationships between the independent and dependent variables with the help of differenced and lagged independent variables (DeBoef and Granato 1997; DeBoef and Keele 2008). In an error correction model, we can interpret the coefficients on the differenced independent variables as estimates of the contemporaneous relationship with the dependent variable. For example, a negative and significant coefficient on the differenced unemployment rate indicates that an increase in joblessness results in an immediate decrease in economic mood. In contrast, the coefficients for the lagged independent variables estimate the long-term effect of a variable, where a significant long-term effect implies that the independent and dependent variables move in equilibrium. Thus, a negative and significant coefficient on the lagged unemployment rate would suggest that, when the unemployment rate changes, the long run equilibrium will, over several time periods, reflect a change in the economic mood (see Enns 2010 for an application).

We begin by reporting the results for a baseline model against which subsequent results can be compared. In this baseline model (Model 1 in Table 2.1), we estimated the effect of economic variables on economic opinions for all countries over the entire period for which we have data, from 1985 to 2011. In addition to the economic variables, this model included a dummy variable for the crisis (scored 1 from July 2007 onward). In addition, we estimated an identical pooled model of economic opinions for a shorter time frame, from

Table 2.1 Macroeconomic Determinants of Economic Opinions in Eleven European Democracies: Pooled Models.

Independent Variables	Δ Economic Opinion	
	1985–2011 (Model 1)	2004–2011 (Model 2)
Economic opinion (t–1)	–.0299***	–.0791***
	(.005)	(.0140)
Δ Unemployment	–.4395*	–.5331
	(.213)	(.3482)
Unemployment (t–1)	.0016	–.0538
	(.0111)	(.0327)
Δ Growth	.2885***	.1977***
	(.0321)	(.0523)
Growth (t–1)	.0560***	.0471***
	(.0064)	(.0113)
Δ Inflation	–.2698***	–.3496*
	(.0753)	(.1481)
Inflation (t–1)	–.0246***	–.2677***
	(.0131)	(.0575)
Crisis	–.1539*	–.4861***
	(.0754)	(.0998)
Country dummies	Yes	Yes
Constant	1.3225***	4.3449***
	(.2706)	(.7776)
N	3,030	893
R^2	.08	.16

Ordinary least squares regression parameter estimates (with robust standard errors in parentheses).

Note: †p < .10, *p < .05, **p < .01, ***p < .001.

2004 onward (Model 2 in Table 2.1), to see if these results were dependent on the particular time period during which the data were collected.[9]

The results for the first model in Table 2.1, covering the entire time period since 1985, reveal that unemployment has a negative contemporaneous effect on countries' economic moods. However, even though an increase in joblessness resulted in an immediate decrease in economic mood, the insignificant coefficient for the lagged unemployment variable indicates there is no perceptible long-run equilibrium relationship between unemployment and the economic mood of European publics. This is not altogether surprising, given the persistently high unemployment rates across a number of European states over the past thirty years (Bermeo 2002).

The results from Model 1 also show that growth and inflation had the expected contemporaneous effects on economic opinion. Growing economies improved the economic outlook of European publics, while rising prices led to a worsening in Europeans' economic moods. As well, the long-term effects of growth and inflation are readily apparent, as the coefficients on their lagged levels achieved a high level of statistical significance. Thus, both high and rising inflation rates darkened Europeans' economic mood, while both high and rising growth rates cheered them up. Finally, the coefficient on the crisis variable indicates that, indeed, economic mood dipped significantly during the course of the Great Recession—even beyond what would have been expected on the basis of observed changes in unemployment, growth, and inflation, and even when considered in the context of a twenty-five-year time series.

This model of economic opinion change is very basic, including only a few key macroeconomic indicators and a period dummy for the crisis (along with cross-national intercept differences), but taken together, the content of economic opinions in Europe over the twenty-five years covered by our data is unmistakably macroeconomic in nature. Economic opinion moves predictably in tandem with economic performance, and the post-2007 period on average revealed a significant drop in Europeans' economic mood.

Model 2 in Table 2.1 is a replication of Model 1 but covers a shorter time period, from 2004 to early 2011, in order to see if the content of economic opinions changed as a function of which historical period we investigate. The results indicate a fair amount of similarity in the estimates, despite the shorter time frame and the fact that European economies in the 2000s were very different structurally from the 1980s or 1990s.

Again, we see that the main economic aggregates correlate with economic opinion change in a manner suggested by traditional economic voting theories, though there are some differences. One notable difference from the results for the longer period is the much bigger coefficient on inflation level. Short-term changes in inflation also seem to have mattered somewhat more in recent years, as have short-term changes in unemployment, while European publics seem to have become somewhat *less* sensitive to short-term changes in growth. As well, the impact of the crisis variable is much more pronounced for the shorter time series. However, tests show that the only statistically significant differences between the two sets of coefficients are for the level of inflation and lagged economic mood, indicating that the relationship between inflation level and economic opinion has changed over the period investigated here.

Did the Crisis Alter the Bases of Economic Opinions?

The results presented so far lead us to conclude that macroeconomic aggregates—both in the long run and the short run—are consistent determinants of changes in economic opinion in this set of European states. The next question, of course, is whether the determinants of economic opinions changed before and after the onset of the Great Recession. To test for this possibility, we divided the period since into pre- and postcrisis periods of equal length and estimated a model for the period before (Model 3) and one for the period after the onset of the crisis (Model 4).

These results are shown in Table 2.2. They demonstrate a good deal of stability in the estimates. In particular, we did not uncover any changes in direction of the coefficients, or any kind of fundamental reorientation of public opinion about the economy during the Great Recession. However, the results do appear to show that European publics generally became more responsive to macroeconomic conditions after the onset of the crisis than they had been earlier.

For example, the contemporaneous effects of unemployment and inflation were substantially larger in magnitude in the crisis period compared to the pre-crisis period (though the coefficients were statistically significant only at the 0.1 and 0.05 levels, respectively). Moreover, the coefficient on changes in growth rate was statistically highly significant during the crisis months, but not before. Another piece of evidence for the increased responsiveness of European economic opinion to short-term changes in the economy can be found in the model's R-squared value; whereas the model explained 8 percent of the variance in the pre-crisis period from 2004 to mid-2007, it explained about three times as much (22 percent) in the mid-2007 to 2011 period. However, despite this apparent increase in sensitivity to the real economy, *t*-tests of differences in specific coefficients across the two models revealed that these differences were not large enough to indicate statistically significant differences in the effects of the real economy on economic mood in the pre- and postcrisis periods.

Welfare States as Buffers

As our next step, we estimated similar models of economic opinion separately for two sets of countries included in this study, in order to investigate whether the content of economic opinion varied between countries with more and less extensive systems of social protection. Specifically, we hypothesized that the impact of macroeconomic performance on economic opinion should be

Table 2.2 Macroeconomic Determinants of Economic Opinions in Eleven European Democracies Before and After the Great Recession: Pooled Models.

Independent Variables	Δ Economic Opinion	
	2004–Crisis (Model 3)	Crisis–2011 (Model 4)
Economic opinion (t−1)	−.0899**	−.1027***
	(.0286)	(.0191)
Δ Unemployment	−.2523	−.9236†
	(.5562)	(.4720)
Unemployment (t−1)	−.1661†	−.0415
	(.0968)	(.0423)
Δ Growth	.1942	.1765**
	(.1486)	(.0626)
Growth (t−1)	.0768*	.0539***
	(.0396)	(.0138)
Δ Inflation	−.0470	−.4776*
	(.1916)	(.2065)
Inflation (t−1)	−.2287†	−.2882***
	(.1185)	(.0773)
Country dummies	Yes	Yes
Constant	5.4130***	4.5776***
	(1.4908)	(.9841)
N	451	442
R^2	.08	.22

Ordinary least squares regression parameter estimates (with robust standard errors in parentheses).

Note: †p <.10, *p <.05, **p <.01, ***p <.001.

less pronounced in countries with highly developed welfare states. After all, these systems are designed to insure against social risks, such as unemployment, poverty, and income loss, and thus should serve to cushion the harshest impact of the recession.

To investigate this hypothesis, we split our sample of countries in two, using the median level of overall social welfare spending (from OECD sources) as the cutoff, and estimating identical models to those presented in Table 2.2 separately for the two sets of countries. Incidentally, this classification also groups

Table 2.3 Macroeconomic Determinants of Economic Opinions in Eleven European Democracies During the Great Recession, by Level of Social Spending.

Independent Variables	Δ Economic Opinion	
	Low Social Spending[a]	High Social Spending[b]
Economic opinion (t−1)	−.111***	−.092***
	(.0311)	(.026)
Δ Unemployment	−1.238*	−.024
	(.605)	(.597)
Unemployment (t−1)	−.056	−.024
	(.055)	(.087)
Δ Growth	.325**	.074
	(.102)	(.079)
Growth (t−1)	.048†	.059**
	(.027)	(.017)
Δ Inflation	−.476	−.356
	(.313)	(.250)
Inflation (t−1)	−.278*	−.266*
	(.116)	(.110)
Country dummies	Yes	Yes
Constant	5.011**	3.545*
	(1.553)	(1.451)
N	225	217
R^2	.24	.22

Ordinary least squares regression parameter estimates (with robust standard errors in parentheses).

[a] Greece, Ireland, Italy, Portugal, Spain, United Kingdom.
[b] Belgium, Denmark, France, Germany, Netherlands.

Notes: †p < .10, *p < .05, **p < .01, ***p < .001.

most countries from the so-called PIIGS group[10] (Kriesi 2011; see also discussion of GIIPS, and the maliciously intended acronym PIIGS, in Chapter 5 of this volume) together, since the set of countries with less extensive levels of social protection includes Greece, Ireland, Italy, Portugal, and Spain (along with the United Kingdom); the group with more extensive welfare states includes Belgium, Denmark, France, Germany, and the Netherlands.

The results are reported in Table 2.3. They show, first of all, that the long-term dynamics of opinion were generally similar in the two sets of countries, as evidenced by the similarly sized coefficient for the lagged dependent variable and for the lagged levels of unemployment, growth, and inflation. (Interestingly, longer-term levels of unemployment failed to affect economic moods in both sets of countries.) However, the results reveal a distinct divergence in the contemporaneous effect of macroeconomic aggregates on Europeans' economic mood. Specifically, we find that the short-term impact of changes in economic conditions was much more pronounced in countries with less extensive systems of social protection.

This distinction is particularly notable with regard to unemployment and growth. The contemporaneous effect of changes in the unemployment rate is sizable and statistically significant in countries with a lower level of social protection, indicating that a rising unemployment level brought on by the crisis was immediately reflected in the economic moods of those countries. However, this effect is completely absent in countries with more extensively developed welfare states, which typically include sizable spending on unemployment benefits and labor market policies.

Similarly, the results show clear evidence that short-term changes in countries' economic fortunes—as measured by changes in economic growth—had very strong contemporaneous effects on economic opinions in countries with a lower level of social spending. In stark contrast, the estimates show no evidence of a parallel effect in countries with a higher level of social spending. (A *t*-test showed that this difference in coefficients between the two models was statistically significant.) As in the case of unemployment, *changes* in economic activity thus had a differential short-term impact across the two groups of countries, while the long-term effect of *level* of economic activity on economic opinions was similar across the two groups of countries.

Finally, the results for inflation are suggestive and consistent with the results we see for unemployment and growth, as the coefficient on changes in inflation rate is negative and larger in countries that spend less on social welfare than in the countries that spend more. However, the coefficient is significant only at the $p = .13$ level. Similarly, the coefficients for the lagged inflation variable are almost identical across the sets of countries; thus the results for inflation do not contradict the results we see for the other macroeconomic indicators.

To further understand how welfare states can function as buffers during times of economic recession, we produced simulations demonstrating how economic opinion would shift if a country with a low level of social spending switched to having a high level of social spending and vice versa. Figures 2.3 and 2.4 simulate these counterfactual scenarios for Spain and Denmark, respectively. To construct our counterfactual series for Spain and Denmark,

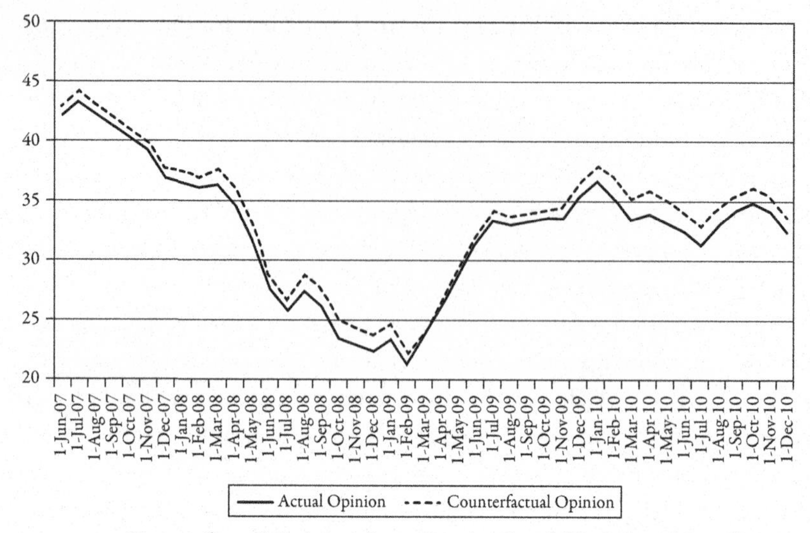

FIGURE 2.3 Counterfactual Opinion: Spain Simulated with High Social Spending June 2007– December 2010.

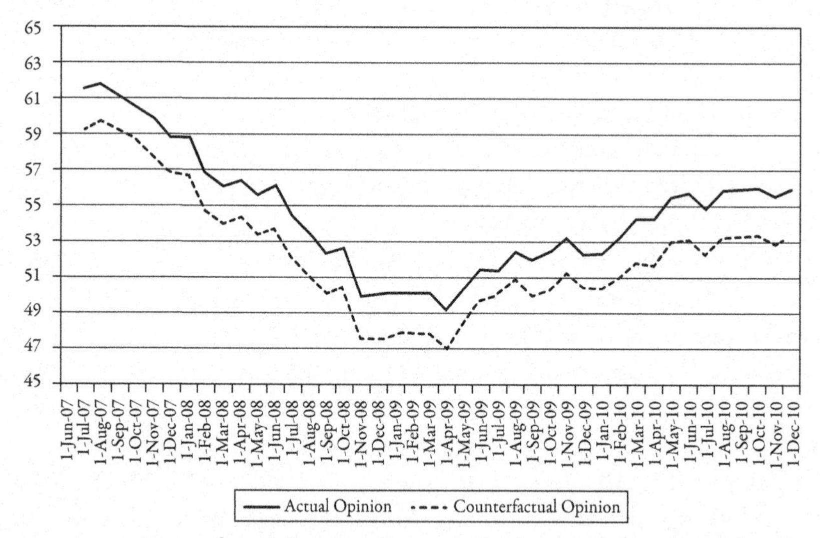

FIGURE 2.4 Counterfactual Opinion: Denmark Simulated with Low Social Spending June 2007–December 2010.

we calculated what opinion would have looked like given our coefficient estimates for both high- and low-social-spending countries, as well as the observed levels of the economic variables in both countries. Specifically, for Spain, we added the effect of being a high-social-spending country and subtracted the effect of being a low-social-spending country. We followed the reverse process for Denmark. (In both cases, we assumed that each country's observed levels of the economic variables would have remained the same in the other social spending regime.)

Figure 2.3 presents the results for Spain. The simulation reveals that a higher level of social protection would have done relatively little to change the country's economic mood during the crisis. Specifically, Spain's economic mood would have been, on average, about one point per period higher if it possessed a generous welfare state similar to that of Belgium, Denmark, France, Germany, or the Netherlands. The results for Denmark are more dramatic, however, as shown in Figure 2.4. For Denmark, we simulated what economic mood would have looked like if Denmark had a welfare state similar to that of Greece, Ireland, Italy, Portugal, Spain, or the United Kingdom. As can be seen in the figure, economic mood would have been, on average, about two and half points per period lower if Denmark possessed a less-generous welfare state.

These results provide further support for the notion that generous welfare states have the capacity to act as a kind of buffer during periods of economic downturn. As institutions designed to insure individuals against social risks, it appears that the safety net provided by welfare states also shapes how citizens respond to shifts in their country's macroeconomic performance. At the same time, these are hardly radically different worlds of economic opinion.

Someone Has to Be Responsible: Left Parties and the Great Recession

As a final step, we wanted to evaluate how a country's political context might shape economic opinions on the recession. In particular, we were curious whether left party control of government changed individuals' sensitivity to changes in the macroeconomy. Prior research suggests that citizens are especially unforgiving of left parties and politicians when the economy takes a turn for the worse. The logic underlying this "luxury model" is that voters turn away from left parties during periods of recession because they are less willing to tolerate a high level of public spending as economic conditions deteriorate (Durr 1993; Stevenson 2001). However, when the economy improves, voters' inclination to support left parties and greater public spending increases. Hence, support for left parties can be seen as a kind of "luxury" good for voters.

We bracket for this analysis the extent to which there actually were clear and detectable differences in policy content between left and right parties during this period. Although some scholars have made note of economic policy convergence during this period (e.g., Evans and Tilley 2012), the luxury model merely requires that left parties be symbolically distinct from right parties in the minds of voters, a condition other scholars have found empirical support for in recent years (Ellis and Stimson 2012; Popp and Rudolph 2011). For our purposes, the luxury model suggests that public skepticism of left party control during periods of economic downturn should heighten the sensitivity of citizens to changes in the macroeconomy in countries with a high level of left party control.[11] To see if this was indeed the case during the Great Recession, we coded the percentage of a government's cabinet controlled by

Table 2.4 Macroeconomic Determinants of Economic Opinions in Eleven European Democracies During the Great Recession, by Left Party Control.

Independent Variables	Δ Economic Opinion	
	Low Left Control[a]	High Left Control[b]
Economic opinion (t−1)	−.1156**	−.1184***
	(.0411)	(.0234)
Δ Unemployment	.1306	−1.562**
	(1.004)	(.5340)
Unemployment (t−1)	−.0799	−.0511
	(.2609)	(.0487)
Δ Growth	.2521	.1734*
	(.2323)	(.0741)
Growth (t−1)	.0245	.0612***
	(.0410)	(.1049)
Δ Inflation	.4410	−1.005***
	(.3322)	(.02576)
Inflation (t−1)	−.1906	−.2958**
	(.1414)	(.1088)
Country dummies	Yes	Yes
Constant	6.368**	5.314***
	(2.745)	(1.624)
N	159	283
R^2	.22	.30

Ordinary least squares regression parameter estimates (with robust standard errors in parentheses).

a: Left parties control less than 37.5% of cabinet seats.

b: Left parties control more than 37.5% of cabinet seats.

Notes: †p < .10, *p < .05, **p < .01, ***p < .001.

left parties with the help of the Comparative Political Data Set constructed by Klaus Armingeon and his colleagues (2011).[12] We then split our sample to investigate the responsiveness of citizens' economic mood under high and low levels of left party control of government. The results of this analysis are shown in Table 2.4.

The table reveals that individuals living under governments controlled by left parties were indeed more responsive to changes in the macroeconomy than individuals whose governments were controlled by nonleft parties. With the exception of long-term unemployment, the coefficients for all other macroeconomic variables indicate that governments controlled by left parties induced heightened sensitivity among the public to macroeconomic shifts. The results for both contemporaneous and long-term inflation are of particular note, as they suggest that the public's economic mood tends to sour to a much greater degree when inflation rises under left governments than under right governments. (A *t*-test revealed that the differences in the effect of contemporaneous inflation were highly significant.) These results provide some evidence that individuals may be quicker to find fault with left parties and politicians than with those on the right when the economy takes a turn for the worse.

Conclusions: Economic Opinions in the Great Recession

The Great Recession of 2008 seemed to come as a surprise to political elites and economists, and for average citizens it meant the sudden imposition of economic uncertainty—including income and job insecurity—as well as actual economic hardship. Although it emanated from the United States outward, the European economies were hardly spared from the financial and banking crisis and experienced the most pronounced economic downturn since the 1970s. Ironically, although elites may have been blindsided by the crisis, our analysis of public opinion data collected in eleven European states showed that publics across Europe felt and expressed the recession—in fact, even before it was officially designated as such. Thereafter, economic opinion recovered somewhat, only to diverge significantly across countries over the course of 2010.

We investigated the sources of economic opinions to see whether they are, as many would expect, a reflection of economic outcomes. We found that indeed they are, and in ways that were in fact sensible, especially over the long run. However, our analyses also revealed that there are important discontinuities in the short run. Specifically, we found that European publics became more sensitive to macroeconomic outcomes during the crisis than they had been prior to its onset. Our examination of cross-national differences also showed that the connection between real and perceived economy appears to have been stronger in countries with less extensively developed systems of social protection. Thus, extensive welfare states and their associated programs insuring labor market and income risks appear to have cushioned the blow dealt by the economic crisis.

Whether this latter finding—that the connection between economic reality and mass opinion can be weakened by public policy—is desirable in a democracy is a normative question we bracket for the moment. But we also believe that it is important to consider what the results do not show. They reveal that aggregate electorates did not panic in their reaction to the crisis. This is particularly impressive given the onslaught of negative attention that European economies received during this period, from politicians and pundits alike, concerning the need for these economies to better accommodate the demands of capital markets.[13] European publics resisted any urge to overreact and instead responded in a generally sensible manner to shifts in the macroeconomy. In those countries that weathered the crisis well, publics soon went back to business as usual. By zooming in on one country's example, we can clearly see this pattern. In Figure 2.5, we chart the most important issues on voters' minds in 2008 and 2009 from data collected by

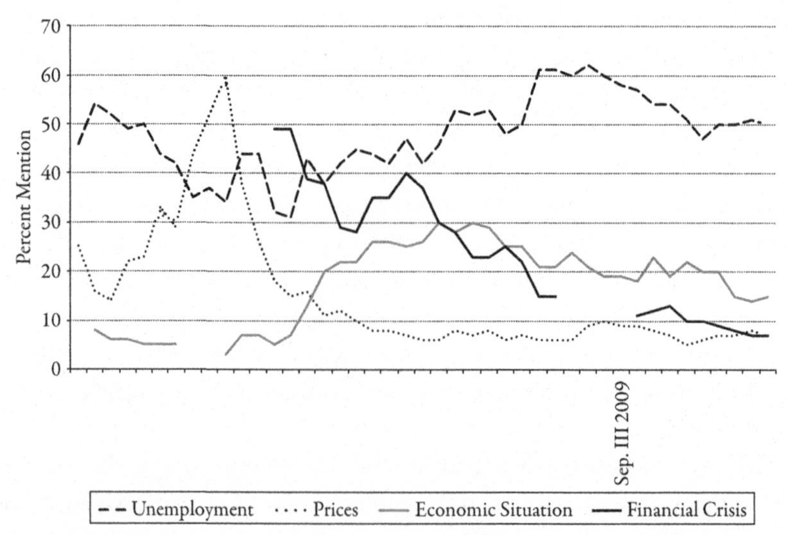

FIGURE 2.5 Mention of Economic Issues as Most Important Problem Facing Country, 2008–09.

the Forschungsgruppe Wahlen. The graph shows that economic issues clearly topped the list of important issues, but not all of them were created equal in voters' minds. The 2008–09 period saw significant changes in the economic priorities voters expressed in public opinion polls.

Among the most notable patterns in the data is the consistent mention of unemployment as one of the most important problems. Clearly, German voters were concerned about unemployment, while other issues (such as prices and wages) or generic mention of the economy tended to be less common. But perhaps the most notable pattern to emerge from the graph is the significant change in *relative* priorities over the course of the year preceding the election. Specifically, 2008 was a year that jumbled Germans' economic priorities, which were focused on unemployment (by far) as well as prices and wages and the general economy at the beginning of the year. By the end of the year, however, unemployment as an issue had been eclipsed by mention of the banking and financial crisis, which dominated opinion in the last quarter of the year, while mention of unemployment and other issues declined.

As the year progressed, however, two things happened: the importance of the banking and financial crises gradually but continuously receded in the public mind, and all the while, unemployment regained its importance as a political problem. By August, more than 60 percent of Germans thought of unemployment as the most important problem, while only about 15 percent mentioned the banking crisis as the most important problem. And by early 2010, problems associated with the economy such as unemployment (44 percent) and prices and wages (26 percent) were on the public mind, while the banking crisis was not even important enough to be mentioned by more than 5 percent. This indicates a striking reversal compared to a year earlier (October 2008), when 49 percent mentioned the banking crisis, 32 percent unemployment, and a mere 10 percent prices and wages.

Thus, on the whole, the exogenous shock of the global financial crisis and its impact on Germany's economy was in fact noticed by German voters and seen as a primary challenge to policy makers during the most difficult time of the crisis in 2008 (incidentally also the time of the presidential election in the United States). However, during the run-up to the German federal election in September 2009, the public's priorities shifted back to "business as usual" when it came to the economy, with unemployment reemerging as a primary concern. Unemployment was seen as even more pressing right before the 2005 election (with 85 percent mentioning it as the most important problem then and 56 percent mentioning it in 2009), but the relative economic and

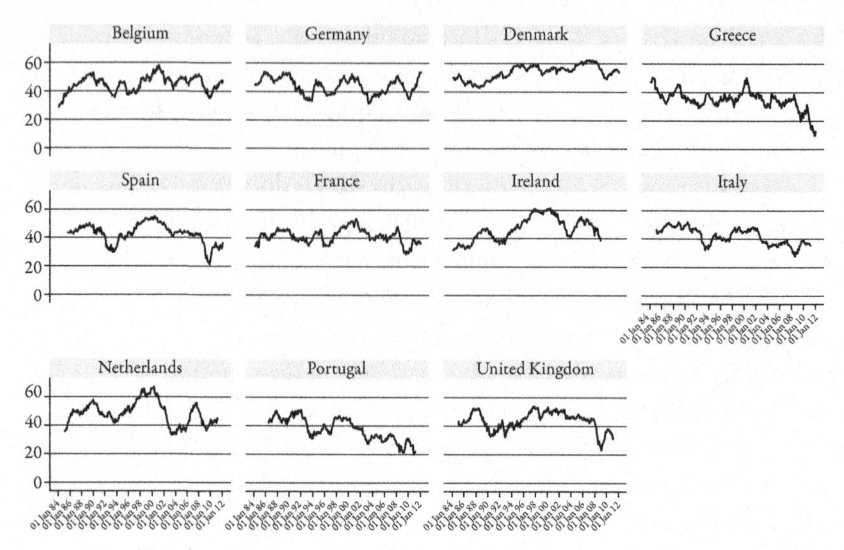

FIGURE 2.6 Trends in Economic Opinion in Eleven European Countries, 1985–2010.

political priorities in 2009 were largely similar to 2005 (with the exception of 14 percent mentioning the financial crisis).

When we zoom out from a single country and the very short run and instead consider the 2008 crisis in the context of economic opinion dynamics over the past twenty-five years more generally, a slightly different picture of the crisis emerges. Figure 2.6 shows the evolution of economic opinion in all of the countries investigated here since 1985. Here, we see that there surely was a downturn in Europeans' economic moods after 2007. At the same time, this downturn was not historic in proportions across countries, as the graph makes clear. In fact, when put in a broader historical context, the 2008 downturn was not historic in size, at least perceptually, in six of the eleven countries investigated here (Belgium, Germany, Denmark, France, Spain, Ireland), and even in countries where 2008 revealed a nadir in economic mood, it was not off the chart, so to speak. Why some countries experienced a historic trough and others did not is difficult to say. It may in part be a function of a kind of cushioning effect produced by the welfare state (Belgium, Germany, Denmark, and France) we mentioned above; but this cannot be the whole story, given Spain's or Ireland's relatively low spending.

Instead, and especially in the Southern European states—especially Greece, Italy, and Portugal, but also Spain—the numbers show a distinct long-term downward trend in economic opinions that started well before the crisis and in fact extends over the past two and a half decades. Given the historic problems faced by these countries in recent years, it almost appears as if public opinion was the canary in the coalmine presaging the structural, and heretofore unsolved, economic challenges these countries have faced, and now face with a vengeance in the context of fiscal austerity and the constraints of a common currency.

Certainly, paying attention to long-term trends in people's economic mood would have provided reason for caution in the southern European countries. Elsewhere in Europe, economic mood appears to follow a mean-reverting process, which our analysis suggests sensibly follows shifts in the macroeconomy. Absent the kind of historic economic problems faced by Southern European countries, the economic mood appears to cycle up and down alongside developments in the real economy. Taken together, these results indicate that economic mood is able to pick up on both shorter- and longer-term economic trends, responding reasonably to both.

These results also dovetail nicely with the findings of other research presented in this volume. Bartels (Chapter 7) finds that economic retrospective evaluations did matter for election outcomes during the crisis. Electorates consistently punished governments in power during periods of economic slowdown, while also rewarding those who shepherded economies during periods of growth. Kriesi (Chapter 10) also finds that political incumbents were punished for subpar economic performance, with incumbents in majoritarian settings being punished most severely due to the clarity of responsibility in such contexts. Combined, our chapters suggest that mass publics were able to translate information about the state of their respective economies into reasonable opinions and behaviors, which held elites accountable for economic outcomes without generating systemic panic.

Our results do leave a number of interesting questions unanswered. For example, they do not take into account political variables or cross-national differences beyond social protection and partisan control of the government. Nor were our analyses designed to pinpoint heterogeneous reactions among subgroups of the population—stratified by income, skill, or exposure to the world economy, for instance. The chapters in this volume by Duch and Sagarzazu and by Soroka and Wlezien compare trends in the economic opinions of different income groups in two of our countries, Germany and Britain. Differences of this sort in the dynamics of economic opinions will, we suspect, help to shape the lessons that citizens and policy makers draw from this particular crisis.

Finally, we have not explored the political consequences of changes in economic mood—for instance, with regard to political mobilization and contention. The chapters in this volume by Bartels and Kriesi shed light on these processes, confirming our suspicion that economic downturns resulting from the crisis had significant political consequences. Indeed, in most of the countries included in our analysis, the largest party in government before the onset of the crisis in June 2007 lost power soon thereafter. Maintaining political power during a period of significant economic turmoil has proven to be quite a tall order.

Appendix A: Question Wording of the Joint Harmonized EU Consumer Survey

Financial Situation Household (Retrospective): How has the financial situation of your household changed over the last 12 months? It has...got a lot better; got a little better; stayed the same; got a little worse; got a lot worse; Don't know.

Financial Situation Household (Prospective): How do you expect the financial position of your household to change over the next 12 months? It will...get a lot better; get a little better; stay the same; get a little worse; get a lot worse; Don't know.

National Economic Situation (Retrospective): How do you think the general economic situation in the country has changed over the past 12 months? It has...got a lot better; got a little better; stayed the same; got a little worse; got a lot worse; Don't know.

National Economic Situation (Prospective): How do you expect the general economic situation in this country to develop over the next 12 months? It will...get a lot better; get a little better; stay the same; get a little worse; get a lot worse; Don't know.

Unemployment Expectations: How do you expect the number of people unemployed in this country to change over the next 12 months? The number will...increase sharply; increase slightly; remain the same; fall slightly; fall sharply; Don't know.

Major Purchases Right or Wrong: In view of the general economic situation, do you think that now it is the right moment for people to make major purchases such as furniture, electrical/electronic devices, etc.? Yes, it is the right moment now; It is neither the right moment nor the wrong moment; No, it is not the right moment now; Don't know.

Personal Major Purchases (Prospective): Compared to the past 12 months, do you expect to spend more or less money on major purchases (furniture, electrical/electronic devices, etc.) over the next 12 months? I will spend...much more; a little more; about the same; a little less; much less; Don't know.

Good or Bad Time for Savings: In view of the general economic situation, do you think that now is...? A very good moment to save; a fairly good moment to save; not a good moment to save; a very bad moment to save; Don't know.

Personal Savings (Prospective): Over the next 12 months, how likely is it that you save any money? Very likely; fairly likely; not likely; not at all likely; Don't know.

Appendix B: Measuring Economic Mood

Stimson's algorithm is analogous to conducting a factor analysis on aggregate time series data. Starting with changes over time in the marginal distributions for each survey question and calculating relative change scores for each individual survey question series, the algorithm then extracts the latent dimensions underlying the shared patterns of variance across these changes and produces the relevant number of summary series of public opinion. The algorithm is also equipped with an optional smoothing function, which we choose to employ in order to minimize the "noise" inherent in this kind of survey data. The algorithm uses exponential smoothing to account for sampling error because "one wishes to observe common movements in the evolution of issue series and not tailor a fit to particular zigs and zags that may be random variation around a deterministic process" (Stimson 1999, 135). As with any data reduction technique, the number of latent variables produced by the procedure is a function of the number of dimensions the data provide.

To examine consumer confidence in Europe both across countries and over time, we proceeded in several steps. We started by estimating the extent to which attitudes about a country's economy expressed in responses to a variety of survey questions share an underlying, latent construct over time. Specifically, we first examined the dimensionality and scores of the variables measuring economic opinions over time and across countries. To examine whether economic mood has one dimension or two (or more), we examined eigenvalues using all survey items available since 1985. As a first step, we assumed two dimensions of support to see if the items separate into more than one factor. The results revealed that eigenvalues were always greater than 1.0 on the first dimension—in some cases considerably so—and never close to 1.0 on the second dimension. However, as may be expected when there is only one real dimension, the loadings of the item did not line up very neatly along preconceived lines (e.g., personal and national or prospective and retrospective items); nor did all items load strongly on this dimension. Most items loaded very strongly across countries. Items that did not load consistently highly related to assessments of prices (retrospective and prospective) as well as whether the household was currently saving money. We chose to exclude this latter item in particular because it loaded very highly in a couple of countries but not at all highly in the others.

Moreover, the results showed that this first factor explained the vast majority of the variance in the opinion series and that the second factor contributed very little. Taken together, the patterns of eigenvalues led us to conclude that, when considered over the long run of about twenty-five years for which we have survey data, aggregate public opinion about the economy is one-dimensional. (The full results are shown in Table 2.A1.) On the basis of these analyses, we generated a measure of economic mood over the long run of twenty-five years for all eleven countries investigated here. This measure represents the dynamics of the latent construct over time.

Table 2.A1 Factor Loadings for Variables Constituting Cross-National Consumer Evaluation Series, by Country.

Variable	BE	DE	DK	EL	ES	FR	IE	IT	NL	PT	UK	AVG
HH financial (retrospective)	0.910	0.908	0.928	0.948	0.956	0.892	0.955	0.957	0.885	0.939	0.790	0.919
HH financial (prospective)	0.933	0.881	0.825	0.968	0.937	0.907	0.968	0.802	0.932	0.959	0.681	0.893
Nat. economic (retrospective)	0.846	0.930	0.810	0.937	0.945	0.971	0.965	0.927	0.853	0.968	0.955	0.921
Nat. economic (prospective)	0.758	0.873	0.569	0.931	0.904	0.894	0.810	0.632	0.518	0.948	0.626	0.776
Unemployment expectations	0.700	0.754	0.771	0.824	0.849	0.747	0.914	0.075	0.746	0.881	0.808	0.723
Good time to make major purchases	0.659	0.664	0.526	0.717	0.854	0.844	0.911	0.795	0.947	0.934	0.793	0.793
Expect to spend on major purchases	0.692	0.803	0.862	0.440	0.919	0.437	0.718	-0.06	0.721	0.823	0.870	0.673
Likely to save over next year	0.663	0.727	0.851	0.707	0.643	0.209	0.661	0.879	0.530	0.669	0.260	0.626
Eigen estimate (out of 9)	4.83	5.41	4.86	5.47	6.21	4.87	6.05	4.23	4.90	6.41	4.54	5.293
% variance explained	60.4	67.6	60.8	68.4	77.6	60.8	71.3	49.0	61.3	80.2	50.4	65.6

Note: Number of observations per country, per month are as follows: BE = 1,600; DE = 2,000; DK = 1,500; EL = 1,500; ES = 2,000; FR = 3,300; IE = 1,300; IT = 2,000; NL = 1,500; PT = 2,100; UK = 2,000.

Source: Joint Harmonized EU Program of Business and Consumer Surveys.

Appendix C: Macroeconomic Varaiable Descriptions

Inflation: Coded as the percentage change in the Consumer Price Index between the month in question and the same month in the previous year. This calculation relies on CPI data taken from the OECD's Main Economic Indicators. Accessed from http://stats.oecd.org/Index.aspx.

Unemployment: Coded as the harmonized monthly unemployment rate. Taken from the OECD's Main Economic Indicators. Accessed from http://stats.oecd.org/Index.aspx.

Year-on-Year Growth Rate: Calculated by the OECD by dividing the figure for a given period t (a month or a quarter in relation to the frequency of the data) by the value of the corresponding period in the previous year (see OECD Glossary for Composite Leading Indicators). Taken from the OECD's Main Economic Indicators. Accessed from http://stats.oecd.org/Index.aspx.

Notes

1. All of these claims have been qualified in some way, whether pertaining to countries, periods, or specific variables studied.
2. Another important and often untested assumption is that "real" economy is exogenous to the subjective (or "perceived") economy (Anderson and Rueda 2004).
3. For example, differently situated voters are exposed to systematically different economic experiences that help determine how they perceive the state of the economy (Weatherford 1983; Welch and Hibbing 1992; Holbrook and Garand 1996; Duch, Palmer, and Anderson 2000). As well, lag times in citizens' learning of economic trends differ for inflation and unemployment, for example (Conover, Feldman, and Knight 1986), and significant proportions of voters are predominantly static and myopic in their evaluations of economic conditions (Paldam and Nannestad 2000).
4. In a study of aggregate consumer confidence data in the United States, for example, DeBoef and Kellstedt (2004) found that political attitudes, such as evaluations of the president's management of the economy and the party of the president, had a direct effect on consumer sentiment, even after controlling for economic conditions.
5. For more information, see http://ec.europa.eu/economy_finance/db_indicators/surveys/index_en.htm.
6. An alternative would be to make use of the commission's official consumer confidence index derived from these items. We chose to follow the strategy described here in large part because it is not clear what the psychometric properties of the consumer confidence index are, nor exactly why the items have been combined in the particular constellation used by the commission.

7. The dyad ratios algorithm is implemented through the "Wcalc" program, which is made available on James Stimson's website (www.unc.edu/~jstimson). Wcalc users are responsible for providing the program with survey responses, the dates of those responses, and the number of responses collected. Wcalc is then able to sort the responses into the appropriate specified periods (daily, monthly, quarterly, annual, or multiple years as designated by the user), and it performs a weighted averaging procedure when more than one survey response is available per period (Stimson 2008). For a detailed description of the algorithm see, in particular, the appendix to Stimson (1999), esp. pp. 133–137.
8. Stimson's algorithm takes advantage of the fact that, although the absolute values of survey marginals are not directly comparable across indicators with different response categories, the ratios of change between any two points in time within an indicator are. Moreover, the algorithm helps to overcome the problem of missing data during periods when some of the questions were not asked by making use of the various pieces of information we do have, from each survey question that has been measured more than once, concerning the relative values that those particular questions take when they are measured. As Stimson points out, "it is useful to switch focus from what we don't know, the missing values, to what we do know" (Stimson 1999, 133).
9. Using data from 2004 onward conveniently splits our sample roughly in half.
10. Kriesi's list of PIIGS countries includes Portugal, Iceland, Ireland, Greece, and Spain.
11. To be clear, this does not imply that left parties were punished to a greater extent during the crisis than right parties. As Bartels (Chapter 7) and Kriesi (Chapter 10) demonstrate in their contributions to this volume, parties of all ideological stripes came under fire as economic circumstances in their countries deteriorated. Rather, the luxury model simply posits that citizens living under left party control will react more strongly to changing economic conditions than citizens living under right party control. This is due to citizens' support for more generous (i.e., costly) social programs being contingent on a strong economy characterized by high incomes and a lower level of economic insecurity (e.g., Durr 1993; Kayser 2009).
12. Armingeon et al.'s full dataset can be accessed at http://www.nsd.uib.no/macrodataguide/set.html?id=6&sub=1.
13. See for example http://www.nytimes.com/2009/12/14/business/global/14deficits.html?ref=europeansovereigndebtcrisis. The article highlights bond traders' capacity to place demands on indebted nations, with James Carville remarking that he would like to be reincarnated as a bond trader because "you can intimidate everybody."

References

Anderson, Christopher J. 1995. *Blaming the Government: Citizens and the Economy in Five European Democracies*. Armonk, NY: Sharpe.

Anderson, Christopher J. 2007. "The End of Economic Voting? Contingency Dilemmas and the Limits of Democratic Accountability." *Annual Review of Political Science 10*: 271–296.

Anderson, Christopher J., and David Rueda. 2004. "The Endogenous Economy: The Relationship Between Subjective and Objective Economy in Comparative Perspective." Paper prepared for presentation at the Workshop on Perceptions Preferences and Rationalization: Overcoming the Problem of Causal Inference in the Study of Political Behaviour, Nuffield College, University of Oxford, May 7–8, 2004.

Anderson, Christopher J., Silvia Mendes, and Yuliya V. Tverdova. 2004. "Endogenous Economic Voting: Evidence from the 1997 British Election." *Electoral Studies 23*: 683–708.

Armingeon, Klaus, David Weisstanner, Sarah Engler, Panajotis Potolidis, Marlène Gerber, and Philipp Leimgruber. 2011. "Comparative Political Data Set 1960–2009." Institute of Political Science, University of Berne.

Bartels, Larry M. 1996. "Uninformed Votes: Information Effects in Presidential Elections." *American Journal of Political Science 40*: 194–230.

Bechtel, Gordon G. 2003. "One Voice for Consumer Confidence: Case 9/11." *International Journal of Public Opinion Research 15*: 325–334.

Bermeo, Nancy (ed.). 2002. *Unemployment in the New Europe*. New York: Cambridge University Press.

Clarke, Harold, Euel Elliott, William Mishler, Marianne Stewart, Paul Whiteley, and Gary Zuk. 1992. *Controversies in Political Economy: Canada, Great Britain, the United States*. Boulder, CO: Westview Press.

Conover, Pamela Johnston, Stanley Feldman, and Kathleen Knight. 1986. "Judging Inflation and Unemployment: The Origins of Retrospective Evaluations." *Journal of Politics 48*: 565–588.

DeBoef, Suzanna, and Jim Granato. 1997. "Near-integrated Data and the Analysis of Political Relationships." *American Journal of Political Science 41*: 619–640.

DeBoef, Suzanna, and Luke Keele. 2008. "Taking Time Seriously." *American Journal of Political Science 52*: 184–200.

DeBoef, Suzanna, and Paul M. Kellstedt. 2004. "The Political (and Economic) Origins of Consumer Confidence." *American Journal of Political Science 48*: 633–649.

Duch, Raymond M., Harvey D. Palmer, and Christopher J. Anderson. 2000. "Heterogeneity in Perceptions of National Economic Conditions." *American Journal of Political Science 44*: 635–652.

Durr, Robert H. 1993. "What Moves Policy Sentiment?" *American Political Science Review 87*: 158–172.

Ellis, Christopher, and James A. Stimson. 2011. "Pathways to Conservative Identification: The Politics of Ideological Contradiction in the United States." In *Facing the Challenge of Democracy*, Paul M. Sniderman and Benjamin Highton, eds. Princeton, NJ: Princeton University Press.

Enns, Peter K. 2010. "The Public's Increasing Punitiveness and Its Influence on Mass Incarceration in the United States." Paper presented at the annual meeting of the American Political Science Association, September, Washington DC.

Evans, Geoffrey, and Robert Andersen. 2006. "The Political Conditioning of Economic Perceptions." *Journal of Politics 68*: 194–207.

Evans, Geoffrey, and James Tilley. 2012. "The Depoliticization of Inequality and Redistribution: Explaining the Decline of Class Voting." *Journal of Politics 74*: 963–976.

Forschungsgruppe Wahlen e.V. 2008, 2009. "Politbarometer Flash." Various months.

Goidel, Robert K., and Ronald E. Langley. 1995. "Media Coverage of the Economy and Aggregate Economic Evaluations: Uncovering Evidence of Indirect Media Effects." *Political Research Quarterly 48*: 313–328.

Haller, H. Brandon, and Helmut Norpoth. 1994. "Let the Good Times Roll: The Economic Expectations of U.S. Voters." *American Journal of Political Science 38*: 625–650.

Haller, H. Brandon, and Helmut Norpoth. 1997. "Reality Bites: News Exposure and Economic Opinion." *Public Opinion Quarterly 61*: 555–575.

Hetherington, Marc J. 1996. "The Media's Role in Forming Voters' National Economic Evaluations in 1992." *American Journal of Political Science 40*: 372–395.

Hibbs, Douglas. 1987. *The Political Economy of Industrial Democracies*. Cambridge, MA: Harvard University Press.

Kayser, Mark Andreas. 2009. "Partisan Waves: International Business Cycles and Electoral Choice. *American Journal of Political Science 53:* 950–970.

Keech, William R. 1995. *Economic Politics: The Costs of Democracy*. New York: Cambridge University Press.

Kramer, Gerald. H. 1983. "The Ecological Fallacy Revisited: Aggregate- Versus Individual-Level Findings on Economics and Elections and Sociotropic Voting." *American Political Science Review 77*: 92–111.

Krause, George A. 1997. "Voters, Information Heterogeneity and the Dynamics of Aggregate Economic Expectations." *American Journal of Political Science 41*: 1170–1200.

Krause, George, and James Granato. 1998. "Fooling Some of the Public Some of the Time? A Test for Weak Rationality with Heterogeneous Information Levels." *Public Opinion Quarterly 62*: 135–151.

Kriesi, Hanspeter. 2011. "About Cows and PIIGS: Contention and Convention in the Popular Reactions to the Financial and Economic Crisis in Western Europe." Paper presented at the conference on Politics, Power, and Movements in Honor of Sidney Tarrow. Ithaca, NY, Cornell University, June 3–4.

MacKuen, Michael, Robert Erikson, and James Stimson. 1992. "Peasants or Bankers: The American Electorate and the U.S. Economy." *American Political Science Review 86*: 597–611.

Nadeau, Richard, Richard G. Niemi, David P. Fan, and Timothy Amato. 1999. "Elite Economic Forecasts, Economic News, Mass Economic Judgments, and Presidential Approval." *Journal of Politics 61*: 109–135.

Nannestad, Peter, Martin Paldam, and Michael Rosholm. 2003. "System Change and Economic Evaluations: A Study of Immigrants and Natives in Israel." *Electoral Studies 22*: 485–501.

Page, Benjamin, and Robert Shapiro. 1992. *The Rational Public: Fifty Years of Trends in Americans' Policy Preferences.* Chicago: University of Chicago Press.

Paldam, Martin, and Peter Nannestad. 2000. "What Do Voters Know About the Economy? A Study of Danish Data, 1990–1993." *Electoral Studies 19*: 363–392.

Popp, Elizabeth, and Thomas J. Rudolph. 2011. "A Tale of Two Ideologies: Explaining Public Support for Economic Interventions." *Journal of Politics 73:* 808–820.

Sanders, David. 2000. "The Real Economy and the Perceived Economy in Popularity Functions: How Much Do Voters Need to Know? A Study of British Data, 1974–1997." *Electoral Studies 19*: 275–294.

Sanders, David, and Neil Gavin. 2004. "Television News, Economic Perceptions and Political Preferences in Britain, 1997–2001." *Journal of Politics 66*: 1245–1266.

Stevenson, Randolph T. 2001. "The Economy and Policy Mood: A Fundamental Dynamic of Democratic Politics?" *American Journal of Political Science 45*: 620–633.

Stimson, James A. 1999. *Public Opinion in America: Moods, Cycles, and Swings*, 2nd ed. Boulder, CO: Westview Press.

Stimson, James A. 2008. "Using WCalc and the Dyad Ratios Algorithm." Unpublished instructional guide available at http://www.unc.edu/~jstimson/Software.html.

Weatherford, M. Stephen. 1983. "Economic Voting and the 'Symbolic Politics' Argument: A Reinterpretation and Synthesis." *American Political Science Review 77*: 158–174.

Welch, Susan, and John Hibbing. 1992. "Financial Conditions, Gender and Voting in American National Elections" *Journal of Politics 54*: 197–213.

Wilcox, Nathaniel T., and Christopher Wlezien, 1996. "The Contamination of Responses to Survey Items: Economic Perceptions and Political Judgments." *Political Analysis 5*: 181–213.

Wittman, Donald. 1989. "Why Democracies Are Efficient." *Journal of Political Economy 97*: 1395–1424.

Wlezien, Christopher, Mark N. Franklin, and Daniel Twiggs. 1997. "Economic Perceptions and Vote Choice: Disentangling the Endogeneity." *Political Behavior 19*: 7–17.

3

Political Understanding of Economic Crises:

THE SHAPE OF RESENTMENT TOWARD PUBLIC EMPLOYEES

Katherine J. Cramer

THE STATE OF Wisconsin made headlines around the world in February 2011, when newly inaugurated Republican Governor Scott Walker introduced some of the most controversial budget measures in the state's history. Walker had campaigned on a Tea Party platform, vowing in the midst of a deep recession to balance the state's budget without raising taxes. He won with 52 percent of the vote. Six weeks after taking office, Walker introduced a "budget repair" bill that called for an end to collective bargaining rights, except with respect to wages, for all public employees (police and fire employees excluded). It also required all public employees to increase their payroll contributions for health and pension benefits.

Over the following weekend, union leaders organized protests at the State Capitol in Madison. Within days, thousands of protesters occupied the Capitol building, while ten thousand more gathered on the Capitol

Note: I am sincerely grateful to the people who allowed me to take part in their conversations for this study. I also thank Tim Bagshaw, Emily Erwin-Frank, Valerie Hennings, Ryan Miller, Tricia Olsen, Kerry Ratigan, and especially Sarah Niebler for transcription, translation, and research assistance. I am grateful to the Ira and Ineva Reilly Baldwin Wisconsin Idea Endowment Grant and the University of Wisconsin-Madison Department of Political Science for funding that made this research possible. I sincerely thank Kent Tedin, Alexander Shashko, Nancy Bermeo, Larry Bartels, participants in the Oxford conference on "Popular Reactions to the Economic Crisis," and seminar participants at the Center for the Study of Democratic Institutions, Vanderbilt University, for comments on earlier versions.

Square outside. In an effort to block passage of the governor's bill, the fourteen Democrats in the state senate fled to the neighboring state of Illinois. Although they succeeded in postponing action for a few weeks, the governor's allies achieved a quorum by stripping the fiscal components from the bill, allowing them to pass the collective bargaining provisions despite the Democrats' absence. Public protests intensified, with approximately one hundred thousand protesters packing the Capitol Square. By mid-March, efforts to recall state senators (of both parties) and the governor were under way.

The events in Madison in early 2011 constituted the most intense political uproar the state of Wisconsin had seen in decades, perhaps in its history; and they involved the most extensive popular mobilization anywhere in the United States in the wake of the economic crisis. Walker's campaign was a reaction to the economic crisis, and as governor he used the context of the recession to argue for the necessity of his controversial budget measures. What can the people of Wisconsin teach us about how people make sense of economic crises?

This chapter explores how people in Wisconsin made sense of the economic crisis by examining how they talked about it with people in their everyday social networks. That is, it examines the process of making sense of public affairs. More specifically, it examines how people made attributions of blame and how they used perceptions of in-groups and out-groups to interpret their economic circumstances. If they see an economic crisis as an act of will, rather than an act of nature, what causal story do they use? When people attribute the cause to a political actor, organization, or social group the conditions are ripe for political mobilization (Stone 1989; see also Iyengar 1994). Thus understanding the nature of causal stories for economic crises helps us understand the policies and the arguments that become possible and effective in their wake.

My account of how people achieve these understandings is based on participant observation of more than eighty conversations, involving thirty-seven groups of people in twenty-seven communities sampled from across the state of Wisconsin. I met these people in settings in which they regularly gather of their own accord—often in daily morning "coffee klatches" in local diners. The size of the groups varied from about four to ten members. (More detailed information regarding sampling and fieldwork appears in the Appendix.) I visited most of these groups at least twice during the course of my fieldwork, which was conducted between May 2007 and June 2011. Thus I am able to trace how people's economic thinking evolved from before the onset of the Great Recession through the political fracas touched off by Governor Walker's budget bills.

The aim of my study is not to generalize to the broader population of the United States, or even to the population of Wisconsin. Rather, it is to provide a qualitative exploration of *how* people use their conceptions of "us" and "them" to make sense of economic crises.

The people I studied were much more apt to attribute blame for the economic crisis—and for economic problems more generally—to government and public employees than to Wall Street, banks, or corporations. This was true long before Governor Walker and his allies in the legislature tapped into this resentment. By examining the logic of the perspective through which public employees were blamed for the recession, my analysis reveals the social and political roots of the profound split between public employees and private employees that erupted in protests in Madison and across the state of Wisconsin in 2011.

Understanding the Economy: Self Interest as Group Interest

How do people make sense of economic conditions? What tools do they rely on, and how do they do so? In the United States, indicators such as the unemployment rate and the Dow Jones Industrial Average serve as points of reference, but people presented with the same facts often interpret the economy differently (Herrera 2010).

In many realms of politics, there is only a weak link between objectively defined self-interest (e.g., income, education, and occupation) and policy preferences (Citrin and Green 1990; Stoker 1994; Bartels 2008, chap. 6). Thus interests are in the eye of the beholder (Stoker 1994). Often, how people interpret their interests depends on their attitudes toward social groups related to the issues under consideration. One prominent example is the influence of attitudes toward African Americans on whites' attitudes toward school desegregation busing (Sears, Hensler, and Speer 1979; Tedin 1994).

To put it differently, people often understand their self-interests as group interests. We commonly interpret "How does this affect me?" as "How does this affect people like me?" (Walsh 2004). Similarly, we often answer "What do I think about this policy?" by considering "What do I think about the social groups affected by this policy?" (Nelson and Kinder 1996; see also Schneider and Ingram 1993).

In general, social groups serve as a powerful tool for political thinking (Campbell et al. 1960, chaps. 12, 13; Conover 1984, 1988; Sears and Kinder 1985; Huddy 2003), since they act as reference points for social comparison and boundaries of allegiance, help guide notions of appropriate behavior and attitudes, and influence which messages people pay attention to and incorporate into prior beliefs. Part of this is the work of categorizing the world into social groups and developing psychological attachments to some of them (e.g., Tajfel et al. 1971; Tajfel and Turner 1986). The act of viewing politics through the lens of us versus them is ubiquitous and powerful for policy preferences (Kinder and Kam 2009).

When we turn specifically to understanding how people interpret political issues such as economic crises, we should also expect social groups to be powerful tools. Understanding in general (not just about politics) is fundamentally about categorization (Hinsley, Hayes, and Simon 1978; Chi, Feltovich, and Glaser 1981; Medin and Cooley 1998). Typing events, people, and things as an instance of *X* simplifies the information environment, and it also provides clues about how one ought to respond to the stimuli.

Work on group consciousness stresses the mobilizing effects of perspectives that link group identities and blame. This work argues that with respect to political participation, group identity is particularly likely to mobilize individuals when it is connected to a preference for one's in-group, a sense that one's in-group is disadvantaged, and a perception that one's position in society is the fault of the political system rather than individual behavior (Miller et al. 1981).

The extensive literature on attribution bias also suggests that people are likely to lean on us-them categorizations when attempting to understand broad economic events. This literature focuses on the causal stories people generate for intergroup interactions—not economic events—but it reveals that people have a tendency to perceive causes so as to favor in-groups and denigrate out-groups (e.g., Islam and Hewstone 1993).

Since us-them distinctions are powerful tools for understanding, and for understanding politics in particular, they are likely to play a central role in people's attempts to make sense of a major event such as an economic crisis. Knowing how people are carving up the world into us-them enables us to understand the politics that arise in the wake of economic crises. The sentiments that exist among members of the public form the pool of understandings from which politicians can pick divisions to exploit. Much of the shape of mass opinion is undoubtedly elite-driven, but predispositions are powerful (Zaller 1992). That is, mobilization is best achieved by sending messages that resonate with individuals' preexisting perspectives and preferences.

Understanding the public sentiments that elites can capitalize on requires listening to how normally occurring groups of people make sense of public affairs together in casual conversation. This is admittedly an unusual conception of public opinion. It assumes that public opinion is not just the aggregation of opinions expressed by individuals via mass sample scientific surveys. Instead, it harkens back to a somewhat forgotten conception in which public opinion is the product of groups of people competing with one another (Blumer 1948) or the product of people reacting to each other's communications (Bryce 1913). That is, I am intentionally not attempting to describe opinions of the sort that would be offered to pollsters by solitary individuals. Rather, I am focusing on the understandings that groups of people generate and articulate when talking together.

Tracking the Crisis

The fieldwork on which this study is based began as an investigation of the role of social class identity on political understanding. I first visited twenty-three of my thirty-seven groups in May and June 2007, before the economic crisis had begun. At that time, the Dow Jones was still rising (it hit a peak in October 2007). By most accounts, the recession did not begin until August 2007, when news of the subprime mortgage-backed securities first came to light and the credit markets froze.

Attention to the crisis intensified over the course of my fieldwork, but many of the groups—especially those meeting in rural communities—had serious concerns about the economy even before the recession. During my first visits in the spring of 2007, no group talked about the "recession." However, when I asked, "What are the big concerns in your community?" the top three responses were the cost of health care, lack of jobs, and high taxes. This was consistent across group location and apparent class type. Many people also mentioned gas prices, which soared to more than three dollars per gallon in the Midwest in May 2007. People outside the major metropolitan areas described their communities as enduring a long-term economic decline. They said their communities were dying, and they lamented the ongoing drain of jobs that provided decent wages and benefits.

I conducted my second round of fieldwork in January and February 2008. By that time, several major events in the recession had occurred. Gas prices continued to rise, but more significantly, the U.S. Federal Reserve had injected more than $80 billion for banks to borrow at a low rate in November and December, and it lowered the interest rate several times, to 3.50 by January 11, 2008. In the first months of 2008, the main concerns across all groups continued to be health care and jobs. Occasionally, someone would mention "recession," but others would also argue a recession was not occurring.

Then in March 2008, Bear Stearns collapsed. When I returned to many of the communities in April and May 2008, the reality of the economic crisis was setting in. In one logging community in northwestern Wisconsin, one person in a group of men on their way to work (G6)[1] explained, "Well, the company my brother works for, last summer they had 86 guys working. This winter they had 43 or something. Now they're down to 12, and they're having a hard enough time finding part-time work for 12 guys." When I returned in April 2009:

KJC: So my big question is what are the big concerns in [this town] or in the area these days?

JIM: Probably more jobs to lose. [The mill in town was about to lay off eighty people.]

[...][2]

FRED: The only good thing is we don't have enough money to leave town.

By May 2009, all of the groups recognized the difficult economic times, although some avoided the term *recession*. One visible impact was the size of a morning coffee klatch of professionals in a central Wisconsin city (G16). In June 2007, it was difficult to find a space among the ten or so regulars. By May 2009, the group had dwindled to three. The rest had been fired or laid off and thus were no longer making their usual morning stops. By June 2010, five months before Governor Walker's election, 85 percent of Wisconsinites perceived that the state was in "bad times" economically (up from 40 percent in June 2007), and 95 percent felt this way about the United States as a whole.[3]

In the analyses below, I divide my fieldwork into three periods: a pre-recession period (prior to January 2008), reactions to the crisis (2008–2010), and the period following Governor Walker's budget proposals (2011).

Who Is to Blame?

Given the milestone events of the financial crisis, one might expect that people generally blamed Wall Street and financial institutions. Instead, I heard very little discussion of banks or financiers, before or after the crisis, by any type of group. Several groups did mention blame of corporations and wealthy CEOs—but I heard such mentions only three times in eighty visits to twenty-seven groups. Also, only five groups mentioned economic inequality as the culprit of economic woes. For example, even after the crisis began, members of a Democratic-leaning group in a logging town in central Wisconsin (in April 2008) nodded in agreement as one member said, "Well, on the other hand, you can't blame the corporations, they're responsible to their stock holders" (G11b). In other words, in many of these groups, corporations were not treated as an appropriate target.

Instead, the majority of blame was placed on government largesse and spoiled public employees. The attribution of blame toward the public sector and public sector employees was evident across groups of various partisan leanings, geographic location, and socioeconomic status.

Liberals and conservatives alike blamed the government for economic problems *even before the crisis began.* In liberal-leaning groups, people would complain that economic policy was flawed because the government conspired with the rich to leech off ordinary taxpayers. Also, they would complain that the influence of money on elections meant the playing field was tilted toward the rich. Conservative groups would complain that the government was too large and not run enough like a business. Groups displaying a mix of ideological leanings would often complain about the private sector, but in the same conversation criticize the government.

Criticism of the government was more common in these conversations after the crisis began. For example, an ideologically mixed group of loggers, meeting in a Democratic-leaning northwestern community, complained that the 2008 presidential race was all about money (G6, April 2009):

SAM: Well those outfits donate all that money and the congressmen vote to let them steal out of our 401k's for all kinds of fees and, and just the people with all the money control everything. (Pause.) Whoever makes the big donations gets their way.

FRED: It's kinda hard to trust politicians to put it that way, no matter what side you're on. You know.

KJC: Yeah. You think it's different today than it used to be?

FRED: No, it's just on a bigger scale.

SAM: More money involved.

[...]

RANDALL: Well yeah then you get this economist: "When them oil prices start going more than 4 dollars, boy that isn't gonna bother the economy." Well how can it not bother the economy?! Jeez, how much b.s. do you think we can swallow?

A similar claim that the government and the private sector were conspiring came from the group meeting on their way to work in a diner in the north central tourist town (G9). They lumped Wall Street and the secretary of the treasury together as enemies of the public.

COREY: My whole point of that thing is that they're just throwing this money to Wall Street and the banks right away, no questions asked. AIG goes and has a hunting party in England, they go to a party down there and Henry Paulson [then secretary of the treasury] is gonna take care of the whole thing. But you haven't even seen that guy, they gave him control of $300 billion but you haven't seen nothing.

[...]

DAVE: Well the secretary of the treasury. Just think, wow that guy didn't pay his taxes.... Well you're putting a guy in there that cheated the government, that's stealing. How can he be the treasury secretary? Just ridiculous.

Conservative groups complained about the size of government and suggested its very structure meant it was unable to trim excess. One man in a group of people on their way to work in a south central hamlet, said (G8, January 2008), "It's like, have you ever seen a politician ever cut out a program? No, because the more programs you have the more politicians and government employees it takes to run them. So they want as many programs as possible, whether they're any good or not."

One conservative group of professionals meeting in the central Wisconsin city treated government, not financial institutions, as "the big money," and complained that the government spent its money against the interests of taxpayers (G16, April 2008). Like other Republican-leaning groups, as the mortgage crisis gained prominence in the 2008 presidential campaign, they blamed it on former President Clinton and the Democrats, not banks or lending institutions. One man said, "The Clinton administration they forced them [speculators] to make money so easy that people did this."

Even groups whose ideological and partisan leanings were more ambiguous also blamed the government and its inability to run more like a business (see Gangl 2007). For example, one small business owner in the group of loggers in a northwestern town noted his own need to balance a budget and lamented the lack of accountability in government spending (G6, April 2008). Other mixed-ideology groups blamed the government's lack of performance on the fact that government officials were wealthy people with little experience in the real world. For example, in April 2008, in the logging community in central Wisconsin, the regulars meeting in the back room of a diner blamed the mortgage crisis on government deregulation (G11b):

MARK: Nobody has any idea what real life is like. None of them work for a living. They're legislators. They don't have outside jobs. And they, they lose touch, they don't have to deal with it.

HENRY: I mean I laugh now, you listen to all this thing now over the mortgage crisis. You could see this train wreck coming years ago.

In sum, people of a wide range of political leanings viewed the government in general as the source of blame for the economic crisis.

Resentment Toward Public Employees

Complaints about the government were often accompanied by complaints about public employees. The resentment toward public employees was ubiquitous—arising in groups of a range of political leanings, and in a range of places—and well developed. That is, there were multiple aspects of the resentment, and people talked freely about how these various elements fit together. Not all Wisconsinites are resentful of public employees, at least according to the best available public opinion poll measures. In a June–July 2011 Badger Poll just 27 percent said that public employees had "too much influence." Although perceptions of influence are not necessarily the same as sentiments of resentment, this level of negative attitudes toward public employees is arguably sizeable enough to influence the political arguments that gain traction. It is larger than the level of support for the Tea Party expressed in the same poll—18 percent—in a state in which a Tea Party–backed candidate for U.S. Senate had defeated a popular longtime incumbent in 2010.[4]

Looking across the conversations from all of the thirty-seven groups, one sees the resentment toward public employees having five central elements. Public employees were perceived as (1) lazy, (2) inefficient bureaucrats who get (3) exorbitant benefits paid by hard-earned taxpayer money, (4) are guilty by association with the government (which they perceived ignored their concerns), and (5) are often represented by greedy unions. For many people in rural areas, the resentment of public workers often had an additional layer: public employees were perceived as members of another out-group, urbanites. The next section will briefly explain each of these elements, and then, by referencing the conversations of three groups with Democratic sympathies, will illustrate how people wove them together.

First, people viewed public employees as people who do not work hard and are thus undeserving. For example, manual laborers especially argued that public workers do not work with their hands. They argued that teachers and university professors "only work nine months out of the year!" A group of loggers in northwestern Wisconsin (G6, April 2009) remarked that public employees can retire early, which they said was ironic since their work does not wear their bodies out.

Second, people also conceptualized public employees as an out-group and the target of blame by claiming that they routinely wasted taxpayer money. People claimed that public employees were out of touch with the lives of real people and were focused on their own salaries, benefits, and continuation of their jobs more than on the public good.

Third, people perceived that public employees had benefits that were way out of step with the benefits of private-sector workers. Across groups of varying occupational type, people argued it was unjust that they worked hard and struggled to make ends meet to pay high taxes that went to pay for extravagant benefits for lazy state workers.

The fourth main element of resentment toward public employees was that people occasionally recognized that such employees are part of the government, and the widespread resentment toward government and resentment toward public employees fed each other. People in many communities felt that government ignored and failed to understand their concerns. In addition, especially in rural areas and with respect to health care, people perceived that public officials were out of touch with their concerns because they were economically in a higher-income class.

Fifth, resentment toward public employees was intertwined with resentment toward unions. Particularly in groups that did not contain current or retired union members, people claimed that unions were the reason public employees did not have to work hard and had exorbitant benefits and salaries that were busting the public budget. In addition, unions prevented school districts, universities, or other parts of the government from firing inefficient or ineffective workers.

Finally, in rural areas, geography provided an additional layer to the resentment toward public employees. There are two main urban areas in Wisconsin: (1) the largest and most industrial city, Milwaukee, and its surrounding suburbs; and (2) the state capital, Madison, and surrounding communities. The rest of the state is predominantly rural.

For many people in rural Wisconsin, this urban versus rural distinction represented the distribution of political power, the location of people who worked hard, and the distribution of wealth and resources. That is, many rural residents perceived that:

- All of the political decisions were made in the cities and communicated out to rural areas without taking into account rural concerns.
- People in the cities were generally lazy bureaucrats who did not know how to work with their hands.
- All of the good jobs, wealth, and taxpayer money were located or diverted to the cities (Walsh 2012).

When discussions of public workers arose in rural areas, these conversations generally entailed talking about public employees from Madison or Milwaukee who displayed a lack of common sense when descending upon the residents' community, or local public workers such as public school teachers who displayed laziness and inappropriate expenditures of tax dollars enabled by decision makers in the urban areas. That is, people did not claim all public employees were themselves urbanites, but they conveyed that the values and priorities public employees pursued were the products of urban areas.[5]

The prominence of public employees in the groups' comments may have been partly generated by my presence as a faculty member of a public university. However, the resentment toward public employees was ubiquitous, many-layered, and intense. Although my presence may have brought the public employee versus other workers divide to the fore, it did not manufacture it.

To illustrate how people wove these various elements of resentment toward public employees together when talking about the economy, I turn to conversations among the members of three example groups. The first is a group of people who meet on their way to work in a rural tourist community in north central Wisconsin (G9). The second is a group of loggers who meet in the grocery store/gas station/tackle shop/hardware store/liquor store in a rural northwestern town (G6), and the third is a group of retirees who meet in a coffee shop in Madison (G22b). All the groups contained members who expressed support for the Democratic Party but nevertheless exhibited resentment toward public employees.[6] All of these groups contained a mix of people who called themselves "working" or "middle" class, with many of them working in or retired from jobs involving manual labor.

Before the Crisis

Notably, the outlines of the resentment toward public employees did not change as the economic crisis took hold, or as Scott Walker came into office and proposed his budget measures. Even before the crisis, the three groups expressed resentment toward public employees. The first group met in a diner in a rural tourist community (G9), but contrary to the typical association in the United States of rural areas with Republican leanings, the most vocal members of this group supported Democratic candidates. One of them had held local public office as a Democrat. They portrayed their community as poor and complained that state government swallowed their money in order to feed itself. On my very first visit, in June 2007, one man complained that "all of our money goes to Madison, gets distributed back down to us... the bureaucracy gets bigger and bigger. Their secretaries have to have secretaries!"

The second, the group of loggers meeting before work around the coffee urns in the multipurpose store in northwestern Wisconsin (G6), also met in a rural town and included many members who were outspoken Democrats. They often laughed about the fact that as loggers they were "voting with the tree huggers." This part of the state has leaned Democratic for decades. But even in this group, with its potential for support for the public sector, the seeds of resentment toward public employees were still evident.

During my first visit, in June 2007, I asked the group whether they thought they paid their fair share in taxes, and their resentment toward public workers came through:

JIM: Who doesn't think they pay their fair share? We're all paying too much, the way they waste money. They should have to run the state like you do your own business. If they had to, they'd all go broke. Every government agency.

KJC: What do you see them wasting money on?

FRED: Well we get road jobs out here and they come up two years ahead of time, to survey the sucker, and they are getting 50 dollars an hour and extra to resurvey it again, and the next year to resurvey—to me it is a waste of money.

JIM: Too many studies.

FRED: Not enough work.

JIM: Too much bureaucracy in the system.

FRED: They do waste a lot of money on surveying roads.

SAM: All those state employees, we look at 'em and we don't think they do much.

Later in the conversation, I asked the group about hard work:

KJC: Sometimes people say—survey researchers ask about different occupations and they ask people which one they think works the hardest. Tell me what you think—if you compare a professor, a public school teacher, a waitress, a farmer, and a construction worker, which ones do you think work the hardest?

SAM: The last three—and for no benefits.

STEVE: Yeah.

KJC: Yeah? How about those first two—like—

SAM: I think a school teacher—I know it can be hard. But they got great benefits. Tremendous benefits. And if you've been there for fifteen, twenty years, you're making fifty grand a year. There's nobody in town other than them making fifty grand a year. The guys in the [local] mill make twenty thousand.

The resentment toward public employees in this group was not extreme. However, in their comments, one can notice the connection between government inefficiency and laziness, and the construction of public employees as an "other." Their comments convey the following reasoning: government workers do not work hard; thus they do not deserve our hard-earned money (via taxes).

These comments before the crisis also were illustrative of how rural residents intertwined resentment toward public employees with resentment toward the metro areas. When they talked about the current difficult economic times in their community, they explained that unlike the urban areas, they were not in a temporary downturn or recession; they were in a fatal long-term decline. During that same visit in June 2007, they described their town this way:

LOUIS: [It's a great place to live] if you like poverty.

FRANK: Yeah, it *is* poverty [describing their town]. [Chuckles.] There ain't no businesses going in up here.

KJC: Yeah, a lot of folks leaving?

LOUIS: No, most of us can't afford to leave.

FRANK: Yeah.
CHARLIE: Well I stayed here all my life, I never made enough money to leave.
KJC: Gosh.
FRANK: No industry *up here* [emphasis added].
JIM: Only thing we have up here is lumbering, trees or logs or what have you. Every one of us here—
FRED: We're all a bunch of sawdust heads.

Members of the third group, retirees who met every morning in a coffee shop in Madison (G22b), were generally union supporters. Most of them had been members of nonpublic unions during their working life, as electricians and other tradesmen, and several of them proudly displayed their union emblems on insulated coffee mugs or jackets. Like the other two groups above, their animosity toward public employees was clear even during my first visit. After I had explained that I was a UW-Madison faculty member (and thus a state employee) and given each a business card displaying this, they talked about the university people "on the hill," removed from ordinary people like themselves. One man, Harold, complained about the elitism among the state employees in his neighborhood: "You take some guy if he hasn't got a couple of college degrees and a master's or whatever and all that, he's a nothing. And I live on Lake Mendota, and I've lived on it for like I don't know how many years, I've got guys who come in now who don't even talk to me because I get my hands dirty, see?"

Reactions to the Crisis

The resentment toward public employees persisted as the recession took hold. By April 2008, the group meeting in the northern tourist town (G9) was worrying about their level of debt, and the high cost of health care. They talked about how even a middle-class salary was not enough to cover basic expenses. "How in the heck can you afford to do anything? Can't even afford to live," one man said. But these sentiments were not unlike those expressed before the crisis began. The group of loggers (G6) similarly spoke as though conditions under the recession were not that unusual for them. In April 2008, they said the outcome of the presidential race did not matter to people so far removed from the urban centers. As Steve put it, "I can't see the difference it's gonna make up here anyway. We've been in a recession up here for thirty years, forty years. We don't know any different. People talk about recession, you oughta come up here."

In the tourist town (G9), the group mentioned different reasons for the crisis, including the lack of manufacturing in the United States, and then government inefficiency, and government corruption, until finally landing on public employees, as one man piped in (with a laugh), "I think those people that work for the UW should take a pay cut" and at least one other nodded in agreement, adding, "professors—professors have student teachers" (implying professors are lazy).

Later on in the recession, in February 2009, I asked the group what they thought the government ought to do to jump-start the economy. They responded by criticizing the United Auto Workers (UAW) for not making concessions, and then government corruption, and then their conversation turned back to public employees and the state bureaucracy in (urban) Madison:

PAT: Well you gotta think how many people that you got down in Madison—secretaries, with secretaries, with secretaries.

COREY: It's Madison's schools, it's everything, it's just getting pathetic you know. No, I can know one thing, there was a chart this morning on there, you know showing the Republican stimulus package and what they wanted... and Republicans had nothing for schools.... I don't know what the hell the answer is. I've never blamed any president, you know, because it's the same thing about the war: the Democrats have been bitching about the war but when Bush always asked for another $400 million, if the Democrats hadn't voted otherwise they wouldn't never have had it, you know?

In this, as in many of the conversations, resentment toward public employees was not a given for many people. That is, they struggled to make sense of who was to blame for the poor economy. In the conversation above, Corey tried to balance his concern that Republicans wanted to allocate too little for schools with his perception that Democrats were willing to allocate too much for war. Nevertheless, even in conversations in which some people wavered in their portrayals of public employees as a target of blame, others (like Pat, above) stepped in to reinforce antipublic employee sentiment.

The group meeting in Madison (G22b) similarly touched upon different targets of blame for the crisis, both before and after the crisis. They talked about the lack of manufacturing in the United States, and they worried openly about the cost of health care. They placed some blame on drug companies and malpractice insurance but resisted supporting government-based solutions to the health care crisis because they believed it was corrupt and bloated.

In February 2008, one man brought up wages during a meandering conversation about health care and a statewide smoking ban. This quickly turned to a criticism of public employees, especially university employees.

BILL: How about wages for people? Ya educated people get all the money. (Laughs.) I worked, we worked in the trades, we don't get anywhere that kind of money that they get, and all the benefits they get.

KJC: And it used to be different, right? I mean, correct me if I'm wrong, but it used to be the case that if you got out of high school and did a trade, you made a pretty decent living. Right? And that's just not the case anymore.

LUTHER: Now you got the firemen, the policemen, school teachers—ridiculous.

HAROLD: [Looking at KJC.] That includes you, too. They bleed the rest of us to death.

KJC: You think?

BILL: The schoolteachers, what they used to make a hundred years ago. And now my daughter makes sixty-four thousand dollars a year plus all the benefits.

KJC: That's a good deal.

BILL: That's education.

HAROLD: The university. And they're telling us we got to pay more money for them smart guys to come here and stay here [referring to pleas from the university for more money to retain faculty]. Well I'll tell ya what, if they let that smart guy go, there's another smart guy looking for the job and he'll be here tomorrow. . . .

After a few additional comments, the conversation turns toward blaming immigrants.

HAROLD: I think that they can get, let's put it this way, we don't have a corner on the market on smart people at the University of Wisconsin. [Chuckling in the background.] We probably got—but overall, I still say, it's just like the Mexicans, they can tell me with all these Mexicans coming in here. And this is the biggest problem we got, really. See? Oh sure! . . . But anyway, the long and short of it is they're working for a little less money, now. But we're paying for the education, the hospitalization, the food stamps, the whole ten yards. Not nine yards. Ten yards.

LUTHER: But you know why we have all the Mexicans here?
STU: Because nobody wants to work!

From there, the group launched into an argument about whether immigrants are taking jobs that Americans do not want, and claims that immigrants in the past had to work harder, even at learning English, to survive. Harold was the most outspoken critic of Mexican immigrants, but others' comments resonated with his resentment of people whom he perceived get something for free, as well as his perception that people do not work as hard for a living as they used to.

These comments underscore that when people make sense of government benefits, they often consider deservingness, and deservingness centers on the value of hard work (Soss and Schram 2006). This group, as with many others in this study, conveyed that only those workers who truly work hard are deserving of good pay and benefits.[7]

The comments also exemplify how perceptions of deservingness are often intertwined with racial and ethnic prejudice. Wisconsin is a very racially segregated state, with the majority of people of color residing in specific neighborhoods in Madison and Milwaukee. Comments about "those people" in Milwaukee were often references to African Americans in particular. Thus rural residents' resentment toward urbanites, suburbanites' resentment of people in the core city, and residents' animosity toward Mexican immigrants were undoubtedly racially coded. Racial resentment continues to drive public opinion in the U.S. context on many issues (Kinder and Kam 2009). However, the resentment toward public employees voiced in these conversations cannot be explained away simply as racism, since most of the people they referred to—public school teachers, university employees—are predominantly white. Nevertheless, the manner in which conversations would touch on immigrants, welfare recipients (widely, though erroneously, perceived to be predominantly African Americans; Gilens 1999), and public employees in a short span of time underscores the centrality of notions of laziness or hard work in constructions of targets of blame.

Reactions to Governor Walker's Budget Initiatives

Although the three groups I have focused on here contained members who reported voting for Democrats, their antipublic employee comments well before the 2010 election suggested the groups would be supportive of Walker's budget initiatives. When I returned to these groups in the spring of 2011, that was indeed the case.

When I visited the group of loggers (G6) in May 2011, there were just three people at the table when I first sat down, and all were strongly supportive of Walker. I told them that the group had previously described themselves as Democrats. One man said the group was about fifty-fifty Democrats and Republicans, and many of them were small-business owners "and we know what it is to make a dollar . . . and the government doesn't run that way. It's just a big free-for-all. Throw it in the pot and see who can spend the most. Isn't that the truth?" As in earlier conversations, the group stressed the notion of hard work. Walker's proposal to make state employees pay more for their benefits was fair and necessary, since public employees had been reaping the rewards of hard work put in by nonpublic employees like themselves, they argued. "You've got 50 percent of the people workin' for the government, you got 12 percent unemployment, so what have you got left to pay the bills? Thirty-five percent of the working people that are payin' the bills."

Across the state, in the tourist town (G9), the people at the diner were also strongly supportive of Walker's proposals. "Enough is enough," the former Democratic county board member said. "Public employees gotta pay their share." He also favored reducing the collective bargaining rights of public unions, arguing that public school teacher unions in particular enable poor performance. He perceived that the thousands of protestors at the State Capitol were not representative of people in the state, especially rural Wisconsin, and that "those folks downstate have little understanding of what life is like up here."

I also visited the retired union members meeting in Madison (G22b) during the protests, in February 2011. There were six men present, four of whom were current or former union members. One other owned a used-car dealership, and the final member, Harold, had been a member of the UAW and also a union steward, for a few years before quitting because he believed the union was corrupt. All of the members except Harold were highly critical of Walker's attempts to eliminate most collective bargaining rights for most public employees—a pattern consistent with the tendency of people in union households in the state to disapprove of Walker's performance.[8] They asserted that collective bargaining is a democratic right, and that the governor had gone too far by trying to take it away. But Harold strongly dissented, invoking an argument steeped in the concept of hard work: "The teachers' union—they been in there—they were in there like the cat at the bowl of milk. Then they turned it to cream. And then they turned it to *ice* cream. And finally it's *gonna melt*!"

And then one of the pro-union members of the group said:

STU: Oh no it's not only the teachers' union, it's all the unions—state employees.

HAROLD: You name me one thing that they've given up in the past 45 years. It's nothing, nothing, nothing.

STU: It's not a matter of what they are giving up. It's taking away collective bargaining.

HAROLD: I'm sick of collective bargaining. And I'm a taxpayer. And you are too! And you sit here bellyaching about paying taxes and you don't want to....

STU: No no no no!

["TIME OUTS!" FROM SOME MEMBERS. *KJC*: "I don't mean to start a fight here."]

HAROLD: Let me tell you something. There is nobody that had a rougher childhood and place to stay than I did.

STU: I'm not—

HAROLD: Now wait a second (wagging his finger). I used to work and swing a sixteen-pound maul. I built the first pier in front of the Edgewater (a lakeside hotel in town), see, and I was about twelve, thirteen years old and swinging a sixteen-pound sledge from the minute I got out of school until the sun went down.... I used to have to catch a hundred fish before breakfast if the whole family was going to eat that day. Clean 'em and skin 'em and sell them for a quarter a dozen or two cents a piece. *So I know what it is to be on the bottom.* And I would do it all over again. But the people at the top, they are just milking us dry on taxes. That's what it is. And 90 percent of 'em, up in that state office building or wherever the hell they are working, if they lost the job they got, they would lay down in the gutter outside here and die, since they don't know how to do anything else. There ain't very many of 'em that sweat.... I still know how to work. I'm eighty-two years old and I'm driving a semi [truck]!

KJC: So let me ask you this. You mentioned the people at the top milking the rest of us dry.

HAROLD: Yeah!

KJC: Is it the people at the top versus the rest of us, or is it the public employees versus the workers who aren't public employees? (pause) You know what I mean?

HAROLD: Hey—Can you tell me why Lizard Doyle [Jim Doyle, the former governor] gave the guy the two hundred and fifty thousand dollar a year job and he just walked in the door and got it? Can anybody back that up and apologize for it with one word even if it means anything? Hell no! See it's just—on and on and on.

My last question above was an attempt to clarify whether Harold perceived the greatest division was between the haves and the have-nots, or between public and private employees. His answer suggested that in his mind, public employees *are* among the haves. His comments convey the following understanding of the world:

People like me = hard-working people = nonpublic employees
vs.
People who don't work hard = public employees = corrupt government

Although his pro-union friends disagreed that public employees do not deserve collective bargaining rights, there was little disagreement in this visit, as in other visits, about public employees' lack of work ethic and exorbitant benefits.

Summary and Discussion

This study was designed to examine in depth the causal stories people used to understand the economic crisis, focusing especially on the assignment of blame and designations of in-groups and out-groups. It used participant observation of conversations of thirty-seven small groups meeting regularly in twenty-seven municipalities across the state of Wisconsin from May 2007 to June 2011. The resulting data are best suited to understanding *how* people made sense of the crisis, rather than *what* a broad cross-section of the public thought about the crisis.

Few people in the conversations I observed blamed actors in the private sector, such as corporations or financial institutions, for the economic crisis. More often, people blamed government, unions, and public workers. Underlying these attributions was a multilayered resentment toward public employees that consists of five main elements: a perception that public employees are (1) lazy, (2) inefficient bureaucrats who get (3) exorbitant benefits paid by hard-earned taxpayer money, (4) are guilty by association because they are part of government, which ignores their concerns, and (5) are often represented by greedy unions. In rural areas, many people expressed yet another layer to this us versus them categorization: public employees were also guilty by association because they were perceived as largely urbanites or enabled by urban decision makers.[9]

This last result underlines the importance of geography as an element of public opinion. For many rural residents, the rural versus urban divide was an important part of the animosity toward public workers. Predispositions such as partisanship and attitudes toward limited government clearly mattered for how people talked about the economic crisis, but the framework of place mattered as well. This geographic element of the attribution of blame means that politicians could mobilize rural voters against public employees if they could convincingly portray the target as urban.

Rural groups in this study, even when they expressed support for public employee unions (such as groups of retired teachers), showed a willingness to demonize urban entities such as the decision makers in Madison and Milwaukee who designed school funding formulas, administrators of corporate farms, and Wal-Marts. Thus, Governor Walker may have been able to win the support of people otherwise inclined to side with public employees by portraying public workers as urbanites who were out of touch with hard-working small-town Americans. His success in rural areas of the state in the 2010 election[10] suggests he was able to tap into anti-Madison sentiment (see Fanlund 2010) as well as anti-Milwaukee sentiment (Fanlund 2011).

In the spring of 2011, after the protests in Madison, I revisited seven of my thirty-seven conversation groups. In many of these groups, men who were themselves in favor of Walker's budget proposals told me that female family members (wives or sisters) were strongly opposed to these proposals. (Some of these women were reportedly public school teachers.) Public opinion survey data suggest that the strong relationship between gender and attitudes toward the governor's proposals was not limited to my conversation groups. For example, in the summer of 2011, 40 percent of men in Wisconsin said public employees have too much influence, while just 27 percent of women gave that response.[11] Thus, if I had studied primarily women rather than older, white men, it is likely that I would have heard less resentment toward public workers, or that this resentment would have taken a different form.[12]

These variations do not erase the broader point of this study, however: that when people make sense of economic crises, their causal stories are less a product of facts than of social categorizations and social identities. These causal stories involve more than simply claims that "it's their fault." They build on perceptions of who does and does not share their values, who is listening to (or ignoring) their concerns, and who is deserving of the assistance of people like themselves.

The resentment voiced in these groups toward public employees in the three and a half years prior to the state's 2011 budget crisis is also a lesson in how issues bubble up when elite-driven and bottom-up forces collide. Some critics of Governor Walker have argued that it was his proposed budget legislation that created a divide in Wisconsin between public workers and the rest of the public (Lueders 2011). However, the discussions in this study clearly show that the seeds of this divide predated the 2011 legislation, and even the 2010 election that brought Walker to power.

To some degree, these battle lines are learned from elite communication via mass media. The current animosity toward public unions is arguably part of a decadeslong battle against unions among conservative and Republican elites (Zernike 2011). Unions in general are often portrayed in policy and by policy makers as undeserving (Schneider and Ingram 1993). But it is the bottom-up process of people teaching in-group, out-group categorizations to each other—including the many layers and associations that those distinctions contain—that clarifies, reinforces, and keeps alive these divisions that politicians can then exploit. As people made sense of the economic crises, they tried out various scapegoats. However, Walker's budget bills (like the budget bills offered by Republican governors in Ohio, Indiana, New Jersey, Florida, and other states in 2011) put two particular targets of blame front and center: public employees and the unions through which they organize.

In other words, this study suggests that public opinion and the political process are not driven by elites *or* driven from the bottom up: politics occurs at the confluence of these forces. In order to fully understand the origins of the shape of mass opinion at a given point in time, we need to acknowledge processes taking place among members of the mass public as well as among political elites.

The events of early 2011, and the results conveyed in this chapter, suggest *both* that there are limits on how much power elites have to pit citizen against citizen *and* that their power to do so is quite extensive. First, with respect to the limits of this power, it is helpful to revisit the concept of stereotypes. The best scapegoats are those that are easy to dislike and are readily understood via negative stereotypes. But stereotypes, we know, are best disabled by conditions that encourage people to view members of out-groups as something other than "them": as unique individuals (Miller 2002), or people like themselves (Gaertner and Dovidio 2000). The intensive attention placed on the protestors in Madison may have complicated the ease with which some members of the public viewed public employees as an out-group. News coverage often portrayed the protestors as ordinary people—teachers, nurses, police officers, firefighters—not just radical UW-Madison students with nothing better to do. The arguments that Walker overreached may have drawn attention away from the division of public employee versus the rest of us and onto a new one: Governor Walker versus the rest of us.[13]

However, the events of early 2011 and the fieldwork I conducted in the wake of the state budget crisis also suggest that elites nevertheless have a great deal of power to foment divides. Every group I revisited after the protests reported a divide in their opinions on Walker's handling of the budget with respect to public employees. Indeed, most said they had decided, as a group, not to talk about the issue in order to avoid damaging their friendships. The desire to prioritize friendship over political debate illustrates, once again, how profoundly group attachments and identity shape political experience.

Appendix: Case Selection and Fieldwork

The purpose of this study is not to generalize to a population in the statistical sense. Therefore, my primary concern in case selection was not whether Wisconsin is more or less typical of all U.S. states. Rather, I chose a state that has a good deal of economic heterogeneity across communities and therefore was likely to provide variety in how people conceptualized their own economic situations.

I chose the sites to study within the state by sampling particular communities using a stratified purposeful approach (Miles and Huberman 1994, 28). I categorized the counties into eight distinct regions, based on partisan leaning, median household income, population density, size of community, racial and ethnic heterogeneity, local industry, and agricultural background. I then purposively chose the largest city or population center in each region, and I also randomly chose a smaller municipality. I included several additional municipalities to provide more variation, resulting in a sample of twenty-seven communities.

To identify groups to study in each of these communities, I asked university county extension offices and local newspaper editors to suggest places where I might find a group of people who met regularly and casually of their own accord, to which I could gain access. They typically suggested informal groups that met in local restaurants, cafes, or gas stations early on weekday mornings. (See Table 3.A1 for descriptions of these groups and communities.) When possible, I spent time with multiple groups in a given municipality to provide greater socioeconomic and gender variation. I visited each group one to five times between May 2007 and June 2011. To protect the confidentiality of the people I studied, I use pseudonyms and do not identify the communities by name except for Milwaukee and Madison.

When I first spent time with a group, I arrived at the time and place an informant suggested. I greeted the members and asked for permission to sit with them. I explained that I was a public opinion researcher from the University of Wisconsin-Madison (the

Table 3.A1 Descriptions of Groups Observed and Municipalities in Which They Met.

Group No.	Municipality Description	Group Type	Municipality Population (2000)	Median Household Income (1999)	2010 Republican Gubernatorial Vote	Dates of Site Visits
1	Central hamlet	Daily morning coffee klatch, local gas station (employed, unemployed, and retired men)	500	$38,000	55%	May '08, April '11
2	Northwestern village	Weekly morning breakfast group, restaurant (women, primarily retired)	500	$32,000	25%	June '07, Jan '08, April '08, April '09, May '11
3	Northwestern hamlet	Weekly morning coffee klatch, church (mixed gender, primarily retirees)	500	$35,000	50%	June '07, Jan '08
4a	North central village	Group of library volunteers at library (mixed gender, retirees)	500	$34,000	70%	June '07
4b	North central village	Daily coffee klatch of male local leaders meeting in the municipal building	500	$34,000	70%	Jan '08, June '08
5	Northeastern resort village	Group of congregants after a Saturday evening service at a Lutheran church (mixed gender)	1,000	$41,000	45%	June '07

(*Continued*)

Table 3.A1 (Continued)

Group No.	Municipality Description	Group Type	Municipality Population (2000)	Median Household Income (1999)	2010 Republican Gubernatorial Vote	Dates of Site Visits
6	Northwestern village	Daily morning coffee klatch, gas station (employed, unemployed, and retired men)	1,000	$32,000	35%	June '07, Jan '08, April '08, April '09, May '11
7	Northern American Indian reservation	Group of family members, during a Friday fish fry at a gas station/restaurant (employed and retired, mixed gender)	1,000	$35,000	50%	June '07
8	South central village	Daily morning coffee klatch, gas station (mixed gender, employed and retired)	1,500	$31,000	50%	June '07, Jan '08, April '08, April '11
9	North central village	Daily morning breakfast group, diner (employed and retired, mixed gender)	2,000	$38,000	65%	June '07, Jan '08, April '08, Feb '09, June '11
10a	South central village	Women's weekly morning coffee klatch at diner	3,000	$43,000	40%	June '07
10b	South central village	Daily morning coffee klatch of male professionals, construction workers, retirees	3,000	$43,000	40%	Feb '08, July '08
11a	Central west village	Daily morning coffee klatch of men at gas station (employed and retired)	3,000	$43,000	60%	May '07, Jan '08, April '08

11b	Central west village	Daily morning coffee klatch of men at diner (employed and retired)	3,000	$50,000	60%	May '07, Jan '08, April '08, April '11
12a	Central east village	Kiwanis meeting (mixed gender, primarily retirees)	3,000	$45,000	55%	June '07
12b	Central east village	Daily morning coffee klatch of male retirees at fast food restaurant	3,000	$45,000	55%	May '08
13	Suburb of Minneapolis/ St. Paul, Minnesota	Daily morning coffee klatch of male local business owners, lawyers, retirees at diner	9,000	$51,000	55%	June '07, Jan '08, April '08
14	Milwaukee northern suburb	Dailey morning coffee klatch of male retirees and construction workers	10,000	$54,000	70%	June '07, Jan '08, May '08
15	South central city	Middle-aged man and woman taking a midmorning break at café	10,000	$36,000	50%	June '07
16	Central city	Daily morning coffee klatch of middle-aged professionals and a few retirees, mixed gender, at café	38,000	$37,000	50%	June '07, Jan '08, April '08, Feb '09, May '09
17	East central city	Daily morning coffee klatch, gas station (retired men)	42,000	$41,000	60%	June '07, Jan '08, April '08, Jan '09

(*Continued*)

Table 3.A1 (Continued)

Group No.	Municipality Description	Group Type	Municipality Population (2000)	Median Household Income (1999)	2010 Republican Gubernatorial Vote	Dates of Site Visits
18a	Milwaukee suburb (western edge)	Group of teachers and administrators at high school (mixed gender)	47,000	$55,000	50%	June '07
18b	Milwaukee suburb (western edge)	Daily lunch group of employed and unemployed middle-aged men	47,000	$55,000	50%	April '08, Jan '09 (twice), Feb '09
18c	Milwaukee suburb (western edge)	Daily morning breakfast group of male and female small-business owners and retirees	47,000	$55,000	50%	Jan'09, Feb'09 (twice)
19	Western city	Daily morning coffee klatch, café (middle-aged professionals and retirees, mixed gender)	52,000	$31,000	40%	June '07, Jan '08, April '08
20	Southeastern city	Weekly morning breakfast group, diner (mixed gender, retirees and employed)	82,000	$37,000	40%	July '08
21a	Northeastern city	Daily morning breakfast group, diner (employed and retired men)	100,000	$39,000	50%	June '07
21b	Northeastern city	Daily morning breakfast group, diner counter (employed and unemployed, mixed gender)	100,000	$39,000	50%	May '08
22a	Madison	Middle-aged, female professionals' book club	200,000	$42,000	20%	July '07

22b	Madison	Daily morning coffee klatch of male and female retirees at bakery	200,000	$42,000	20%	Feb '07, March '07, Feb '08, July '08, Feb '11
22c	Madison	Female resident volunteers in food pantry in low-income neighborhood (employed and unemployed)	200,000	$42,000	20%	Multiple visits, Fall '06
23a	Milwaukee, northern neighborhood	Activist group meeting after services in a Baptist church (mixed age and gender, employed)	600,000	$32,000	25%	July '07
23b	Milwaukee, southern neighborhood	Mexican immigrants waiting at a pro bono health clinic (mixed age and gender, employed and unemployed)	600,000	$32,000	25%	June '07
24	Southwestern village	4H group (mixed gender)	4,000	$42,000	45%	Feb '10
25	Central village	4H group (mixed gender)	10,000	$33,000	50%	March '10
26	South eastern city	4H group (mixed gender)	28,000	$48,000	70%	April '10
27	Central east village	4H group (mixed gender)	4,000	$38,000	60%	April '10

Note: Population and income figures have been rounded to preserve confidentiality of groups observed. Vote figures are rounded to nearest 5%.

state's flagship public university), studying the concerns of Wisconsinites. I asked for their permission to record our conversation and passed out "small tokens of my appreciation" for their time, such as football schedules, donated from the university alumni association. I then asked, "What are the big concerns for people in this community?" and continued with other questions on my protocol, adjusting the order and number of questions asked when necessary. All of the conversations were recorded and transcribed, except for two groups that permitted me to take handwritten notes instead.

My strategy for finding groups meant the people I spent time with were predominantly male, non-Hispanic white, and of retirement age. Of the thirty-seven groups I studied, twelve were composed of only men, four were exclusively female, and the rest were of mixed gender, but predominantly male. Twenty groups were composed of a mix of retirees and currently employed people, though retirees were in the majority in these groups. Of the other groups, five were composed of solely of retirees, eight of people currently employed or unemployed, and four of high school students (4H groups). Each of the thirty-seven groups was composed of people of a similar occupational and educational background, though almost every group contained some variety in that respect (e.g., one group of loggers included a real estate agent). My strategy resulted in a good deal of socioeconomic variation across groups, from people who were "one step from homelessness" to wealthy business owners. I label the groups lower-income and upper-income on the basis of members' stated occupations. (Asking directly about income in a pilot study was unproductive.)

The people in this study were opinion leaders in their community, often local leaders in politics or in their occupational community (Lazarsfeld, Berelson, and Gaudet 1944; Katz and Lazarsfeld 1955). Their perceptions and preferences may not be representative, but they are likely consequential for the way others in their community think about many public issues. Since the communities varied economically, the occupation of these leaders varied across place. Sometimes they were farmers. In other places they were retired executives of multinational corporations.

Of course, my presence altered these conversations. I intentionally steered the conversations, and the participants likely altered what they said somewhat because of my presence. My presence as an outsider, urbanite, and university faculty member likely raised the salience of the divides of public employees versus other employees and rural versus urban. Because the purpose of this study is primarily to investigate *how*—not *whether*—people use perceptions of in-groups and out-groups, drawing attention to these divides facilitated the investigation.

I designed my interview protocol to generate talk about topics that pilot studies suggested were likely to evoke economic considerations and references to social class: tax policy, immigration, higher education, and health care. To analyze my data, I used data displays to study patterns in the conversations across groups with respect to the kinds of blame attribution people made when talking about the economy, and the considerations people used when talking about public employees, after it became evident that public employees were a prominent element in interpretations of the economic crisis (Miles and Huberman 1994).

As I proceeded, I wrote memos detailing the patterns I perceived (Feldman 1995). I analyzed what additional evidence I would need to observe in order to validate my conclusions, and used the visual displays to test whether the patterns were as pervasive as I had first concluded and whether they varied across type of group (Miles and Huberman 1994, chap. 10). To further verify my conclusions, I considered how the conversations might have been affected by my presence, reexamined conversations that were not consistent with the patterns I identified, considered spurious relations, added additional groups to the study to investigate whether conversations among people of different demographic backgrounds exhibited patterns similar to the groups already in my study, and sent reports of my results to the groups I had visited, giving them brief verbal reports on subsequent visits so that they could comment on the conclusions I was reaching (Miles and Huberman 1994, pp. 262–277).

Notes

1. This notation refers to Table 3.A1 in the Appendix, which lists the groups by number (G#) and describes their characteristics.
2. This denotes several comments have been omitted for brevity.
3. University of Wisconsin-Madison Survey Center Badger Polls #30 (N = 500) and #24 (N = 502).
4. Badger Poll #32, June 17–July 10, 2011. N = 556. "Some people think that certain groups have too much influence in Wisconsin life and politics, while other people feel that certain groups don't have as much influence as they deserve. For each of the groups that I read to you, tell me whether you think this group has too much influence, just about the right amount of influence, or too little influence.... Do public employees have too much influence, just about the right amount of influence, or too little influence?" "Do you consider yourself to be a supporter of the Tea Party movement or not?"
5. It is not necessarily the case that resentment of public employees was stronger in rural areas. Using the question detailed in note 4 the percentage of self-reported rural respondents saying public employees had "too much influence" was statistically indistinguishable from self-reported suburban and urban residents.
6. The influence question (see note 4) suggests a strong partisan dimension in resentment toward public employees in 2011. Fifty-four percent of Republicans said "too much" while just 15 percent of Democrats gave that response (29 percent of independents did so as well).
7. This resonates with Williamson, Skocpol, and Coggins's finding (2011) that Tea Party activists are not opposed to government handouts per se, just opposed to handouts to groups they perceive as not working hard.
8. In a Badger Poll conducted between June 17 and July 10, 2011, 77 percent of people in union households said they disapproved of "the way Scott Walker is handling his job as Governor of Wisconsin" (N = 556).

9. This perception is challenged by empirical evidence that more than three-quarters of Wisconsin's 283,000 public workers are employees of (mostly nonurban) local governments and school districts (Wisconsin Taxpayer Alliance report, March 2010, www.wistax.org/news_releases/2010/1002.html). However, the mismatch between those perceptions and the employment data underscores that people base their evaluations on perceptions, not hard facts.
10. In the 2006 gubernatorial election, the Democratic incumbent Jim Doyle won forty of the sixty-four counties outside the Milwaukee Combined Statistical Area and the Madison Metropolitan Statistical Area. In 2010 the Democratic candidate for governor lost all but eight of the nonmetro counties to Walker.
11. Badger Poll #32, June 17–July 10, 2011. N = 556. Chi-square = 12.046, p = .002.
12. See Vargas-Cooper (2011) for an intriguing commentary on the gender component of contemporary opinion toward unions, including the controversies in Wisconsin. The one all-female group that I visited, in northwest Wisconsin, was almost unanimously opposed to Walker's budget.
13. Identical survey questions fielded by the Wisconsin Policy Research Institute, a conservative think tank, in November 2010 and then in late February–early March 2011 suggested that after several weeks of the protests, support for teachers' unions increased, while support for Walker dropped http://www.wpri.org/polls/March2011/poll0311.html.

References

Bartels, Larry. 2008. *Unequal Democracy: The Political Economy of the New Gilded Age.* Princeton, NJ: Princeton University Press and Russell Sage Foundation.

Blumer, Herbert. 1948. "Public Opinion and Public Opinion Polling." *American Sociological Review* 13(5): 542–549.

Bryce, James. 1913. "The Nature of Public Opinion." In *The American Commonwealth,* Vol. II, 251–376. New York: Macmillan.

Campbell, Angus, Philip E. Converse, Warren E. Miller, and Donald E. Stokes. 1960. *The American Voter.* Chicago: University of Chicago Press.

Chi, Michelene T. H., Paul J. Feltovich, and Robert Glaser. 1981. "Categorization and Representation of Physics Problems by Experts and Novices." *Cognitive Science* 5: 121–152.

Citrin, Jack, and Donald Phillip Green. 1990. "The Self-Interest Motive in American Public Opinion." *Research in Micropolitics* 3:1–28.

Conover, Pamela Johnston. 1984. "The Influence of Group Identifications on Political Perception and Evaluation." *Journal of Politics* 46: 760–785.

Conover, Pamela Johnston. 1988. "The Role of Social Groups in Political Thinking." *British Journal of Political Science* 18: 51–76.

Fanlund, Paul. 2011. "Barrett Steps Up, But for Another Shot at Walker?" *Capital Times,* May 18, 5.

Fanlund, Paul. 2010. "Madison 360: Mayor Dave Ponders Response to Attacks on Madison." *Capital Times*, December 15.

Feldman, Martha S. 1995. *Strategies for Interpreting Qualitative Data*. Thousand Oaks, CA: Sage.

Gaertner, Samuel L., and John F. Dovidio. 2000. *Reducing Intergroup Bias: The Common Ingroup Identity Model*. Ann Arbor: Taylor and Francis.

Gangl, Amy. 2007. "Examining Citizens' Beliefs That Government Should Run Like Business." *Public Opinion Quarterly* 71(4): 661–670.

Gilens, Martin. 1999. *Why Americans Hate Welfare: Race, Media, and the Politics of Antipoverty Policy*. Chicago: University of Chicago Press.

Herrera, Yoi. 2010. "Imagined Economies: Constructivist Political Economy, Nationalism and Economic-based Sovereignty Movements in Russia." In Rawi Abdelal, Mark Blyth, and Craig Parsons, eds., *Constructing the International Economy*, 114–134. Ithaca, NY: Cornell University Press.

Hinsley, Dan A., John R. Hayes, and Herbert A. Simon. 1978. "From Words to Equations: Meaning and Representation in Algebra Word Problems." In P. A. Carpenter and Marion A. Just, eds., *Cognitive Processes in Comprehension*, 89–106. Hillsdale, NJ: Erlbaum.

Huddy, Leonie. 2003. "Group Identity and Political Cohesion." In David O. Sears, Leonie Huddy, and Robert Jervis, eds., *Oxford Handbook of Political Psychology*, 511–558. New York: Oxford University Press.

Islam, Mir. R., and Miles Hewstone. 1993. "Intergroup Attributions and Affective Consequences in Majority and Minority Groups." *Journal of Personality and Social Psychology* 64(6): 936–951.

Iyengar, Shanto. 1994. *Is Anyone Responsible? How Television Frames Political Issues*. Chicago: University of Chicago Press.

Katz, Elihu, and Paul F. Lazarsfeld. 1955. *Personal Influence: The Part Played by People in the Flow of Mass Communications*. New York: Free Press.

Kinder, Donald, and Cindy Kam. 2009. *Us Against Them: Ethnocentric Foundations of American Opinion*. Chicago: University of Chicago Press.

Lazarsfeld, Paul F., Bernard Berelson, and Hazel Gaudet. 1944. *The People's Choice: How the Voter Makes Up His Mind in a Presidential Campaign*, 2nd ed. New York: Columbia University Press.

Lueders, Bill. "Scott Walker's War." 2011. *The Isthmus*, February 24, http://www.thedailypage.com/isthmus/article.php?article=32445.

Medin, Douglas L., and John D. Coley. 1998. "Concepts and Categorization." In *Perception and Cognition at Century's End*, ed. Julian Hochberg, 403–440. San Diego: Academic Press.

Miles, Matthew B., and A. Michael Huberman. 1994. *Qualitative Data Analysis: An Expanded Sourcebook*, 2nd ed. Thousand Oaks, CA: Sage.

Miller, Arthur H., Patricia Gurin, Gerald Gurin, and Oksana Malanchuk. 1981. "Group Consciousness and Political Participation." *American Journal of Political Science* 25: 494–511.

Miller, Norman. 2002. "Personalization and the Promise of Contact Theory." *Journal of Social Issues* 58(2): 387–410.

Nelson, Thomas E., and Donald R. Kinder. 1996. "Issue Frames and Group-Centrism in American Public Opinion." *Journal of Politics* 58: 1055–1078.

Schneider, Anne, and Helen Ingram. 1993. "Social Construction of Target Populations: Implications for Politics and Policy." *American Political Science Review* 87 (2): 334–347.

Sears, David O., Carl P. Hensler, and Leslie K. Speer. 1979. "Whites' Opposition to Busing: Self-Interest or Symbolic Politics?" *American Political Science Review* 73: 369–384.

Sears, David O., and Donald R. Kinder. 1985. "Whites' Opposition to Busing: On Conceptualizing and Operationalizing Group Conflict." *Journal of Personality and Social Psychology* 48: 1141–1147.

Soss, Joe, and Sanford F. Schram. 2006. "A Public Transformed? Welfare Reform as Policy Feedback." *American Political Science Review* 101 (1): 111–127.

Stone, Deborah A. 1989. "Causal Stories and the Formation of Policy Agendas." *Political Science Quarterly* 104(2): 281–300.

Stoker, Laura. 1994. "A Reconsideration of Self-Interest in American Public Opinion," ANES Pilot Study Report, No. nes010876.

Tajfel, Henri, M. G. Billig, R. P. Bundy, and Claude Flament, 1971. "Social Categorization and Intergroup Behavior." *European Journal of Social Psychology* 1: 149–178.

Tajfel, Henri, and John Turner. 1986. "The Social Identity Theory of Intergroup Behavior." In Stephen Worchel and William G. Austin, eds., *Psychology of Intergroup Relations*, 7–24. Chicago: Nelson-Hall.

Tedin, Kent L. 1994. "Self-Interest, Symbolic Values, and the Financial Equalization of the Public Schools." *Journal of Politics* 56 (3): 628–649.

Vargas-Cooper, Natasha. 2011. "We Work Hard, But Who's Complaining?" *New York Times*, April 2.

Walsh, Katherine Cramer. 2004. *Talking About Politics: Informal Groups and Social Identity in American Life*. Chicago: University of Chicago Press.

Walsh, Katherine Cramer. 2012. "Putting Inequality in Its Place: Rural Consciousness and the Power of Perspective." *American Political Science Review* 106 (3): 517–532.

Williamson, Vanessa, Theda Skocpol, and John Coggin. 2011. "The Tea Party and the Remaking of Republican Conservatism." *Perspectives on Politics* 9:25–43.

Zaller, John R. 1992. *The Nature and Origins of Mass Opinion*. New York: Cambridge University Press.

Zernike, Kate. 2011. "Wisconsin's Legacy of Labor Battles." *New York Times*, March 5. http://www.nytimes.com/2011/03/06/weekinreview/06midwest.html?_r=2&ref=weekinreview.

4

Economic Crisis and Support for Redistribution in the United Kingdom

Stuart Soroka and Christopher Wlezien

THERE IS LITTLE doubt that public reactions to economic trends have important political consequences. We also know that public preferences on a wide range of policies, particularly redistributive policies, vary with shifts in the economic climate (e.g., Durr 1993; Stevenson 2001; Erikson, MacKuen, and Stimson 2002; Soroka and Wlezien 2005). In particular, publics seem to be more supportive of redistributive policies in times of economic security (see especially Durr 1993; Stevenson 2001). Thus, paradoxically—and perhaps unfortunately—redistributive policies may be least likely to garner public support at times when they are most needed.

We also know that there is a connection between what publics support and what governments do. In the United States, across a broad range of government policies, there is a connection between "public mood" and policy liberalism (Erikson et al. 2002). And looking at specific policy domains, there appears to be a strong connection between public preferences and spending in major social welfare domains, including welfare, education, and health, in

Note: An earlier version of this chapter was presented at the June 2011 conference "Popular Reactions to the Economic Crisis" at Nuffield College, Oxford. We are grateful to participants, and especially to Larry Bartels, Nancy Bermeo, and Stephen Fisher, for helpful comments. We are also grateful to Quinn Albaugh for his ongoing work on this project, and to Roger Mortimer, director of political analysis at Ipsos MORI, who was, as always, very helpful in our search for data. Our work was funded in part by the Quebec Fonds de recherche sur la société et la culture (FQRSC) through the Soutiens aux equipes de recherche program.

the United States, the United Kingdom, and Canada (Soroka and Wlezien 2010). As a consequence, public preferences for redistributive policy can be of fundamental importance not only in determining who governs but also in determining how they govern.

The Great Recession provides a unique opportunity—and perhaps a heightened need—to look more closely at the potentially problematic relationship between the economy, public opinion, and public policy. How did public opinion on economic matters evolve over the course of the Great Recession? Did the economic crisis lead to a somewhat different relationship between the state of the national economy and public opinion? Did public opinion about taxation or redistribution shift fundamentally during this especially hard economic time? Did some income groups react differently to economic crisis than others?

These are the questions motivating this chapter. Our aim is to provide a preliminary look at the distribution of opinion during the Great Recession, and to explore the possibility that public opinion shifted or reacted to the economy uniquely during this period of economic crisis. Doing so requires that we look at data not just from the very recent past but over an extended period of time. The chapter accordingly focuses on British public opinion over the past thirty years, drawing mainly on data from British Social Attitudes (BSA) surveys. Our primary variables of interest relate to redistributive policy; and we are particularly interested in differences in opinion across low-, middle-, and high-income respondents.

As it turns out, our story is much more about long-term trends in opinion than about short-term changes in the current period of economic crisis. As of 2011, at least, the Great Recession has not led to major shifts in British opinion on issues of redistribution. But changes over the past thirty years are important. Multiple variables across large bodies of survey data suggest a similar dynamic: a gradual rightward shift in British public preferences for redistribution, even (in fact, particularly) amongst low- and middle-income respondents. On some dimensions it thus appears as though differences in preferences for redistribution across income groups are narrowing; one consequence is that on some issues the median British voter has been moving toward the right. This is true even as the British public recognizes income inequality as a problem, and even in the recent period of crisis. This long-term, three-decade trend has, to our knowledge, not been previously noticed or discussed in the scholarly literature on British public opinion; though the more recent rightward shift in preferences is found in a number of countries investigated in this volume (e.g., by Cramer in Chapter 3, Dancygier and Donnelly in Chapter 6, and Mayer in

Chapter 9). Nevertheless, it may have important consequences where British governments' reactions to economic crisis are concerned.

The Great Recession in the United Kingdom

We begin with a review of the British economic climate in the years leading up to the Great Recession. Figure 4.1 puts the current economic situation in the United Kingdom in historical context. The black, solid line in the figure is a (lowess-smoothed) measure of prospective economic perceptions over the past three decades. It is based on a question asked by MORI and used as their Economic Optimism Index (EOI): "Do you think that the general economic condition of the country will improve, stay the same, or get worse over the next twelve months?" Here, we subtract the proportion of respondents in the negative categories from the proportion of respondents in the positive categories to produce a single measure that captures both the direction and the magnitude of the difference between positive and negative assessments at a given time. The gray dashed line in the same figure shows the OECD's Composite Leading Indicator (CLI) for the United Kingdom. The leading indicator series includes a range of measures, among them GDP, output variables, money aggregate, consumer and producer prices, a trade measure, labor indicators, and so on, and, importantly, *not* public opinion. (This is in

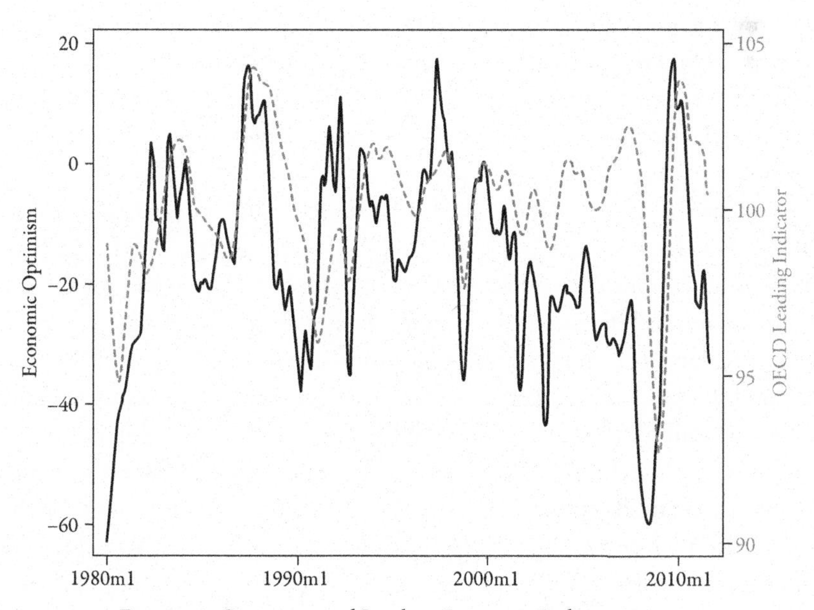

FIGURE 4.1 Economic Optimism and Leading Economic Indicators.

contrast with the Conference Board's Index of Leading Economic Indicators for the United States.) We use leading economic indicators because they presumably best correspond with our public opinion measure, which taps prospective perceptions.

The two series are correlated, though perhaps not as closely as one might expect; the Pearson's r is .44 ($p < .01$). Both indicators make clear, however, that the Great Recession in the UK was markedly worse economically than any other period in the last thirty years. This is readily evident from the sharp drop in both series toward the end of our timeline, which comes as no surprise, of course; what may be most surprising is how sharply things bounced back, at least temporarily. The low point for economic optimism, −64.0, was in July 2008 (the CLI index was already very low at that stage but did not bottom out until January 2009, at 92.7). But optimism shot up to +23 by November 2009 (again, the CLI index lagged somewhat, peaking in February 2010 at 103.9). Clearly, economic indicators and public sentiment pointed to a quick recovery. That was not to be, however, and both optimism and the composite index have declined since that time, at least through 2010, when our series ends.

Of course, subgroups may react to macroeconomic trends in their own particular ways. Income subgroups seem especially likely to be relevant, since people with higher incomes may be affected differently by changing economic conditions from those with lower incomes.[1] In the United States, there is a growing body of scholarship examining inequalities across income groups in both public responsiveness to the economy and political representation. Differential reactions to economic circumstances may matter in British politics as well; but there has thus far been relatively little work considering that possibility.[2]

Income is not available in MORI survey data, but social class is. MORI divides respondents using the NRS social grades, on the basis of head-of-household occupation.[3] Figure 4.2 shows (lowess-smoothed) data for 2003 onward, the time period for which data on social class are available, breaking the sample into two groups: (1) middle-upper class and (2) middle-lower class.[4] Results for the two groups are not fundamentally different; indeed, they are relatively similar both in levels, and in the direction of monthly changes.[5] To the extent that there are differences, it may be that the middle-upper cohort is slightly more optimistic most of the time. Alternatively, given that the middle-upper cohort drops below the middle-lower cohort at the low point of the Great Recession, they may simply show somewhat more variance over time, perhaps a product of greater

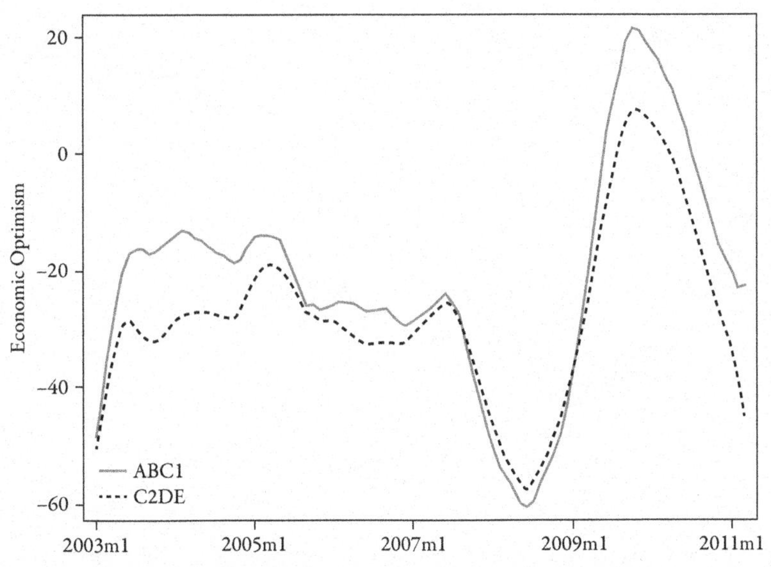

FIGURE 4.2 Economic Optimism Across Social Classes, MORI Surveys.
Source: MORI surveys.

education or sophistication. From these aggregate-level data, we cannot easily distinguish the two possibilities.

In any case, there is not much evidence here that people with lower incomes react fundamentally differently to economic information than those with higher incomes. There also is little evidence that the recent crisis produced a differential pattern of change in economic optimism across social classes.

The modest differences in economic optimism evident in Figure 4.2 may be surprising in light of the high (and rising) level of income inequality in the contemporary UK. Figure 4.3 charts changes in income inequality over the past half-century, as measured by the Gini coefficient.[6] Although there were periods in the mid-1990s and mid-2000s when inequality held steady, the overall trend since 1980 has been sharply and fairly consistently upward, with the Gini coefficient at the outset of the Great Recession roughly 60 percent higher than it was in the late 1970s. Thus, the UK in 2008–09 was experiencing its worst economic slump since 1980 in a context of historically high economic inequality.

It is worth noting, as well, that there appears to have been a partisan tinge to the rise in economic inequality over the past fifty years. The major rise in inequality charted in Figure 4.3 occurred under Conservative rule. Indeed,

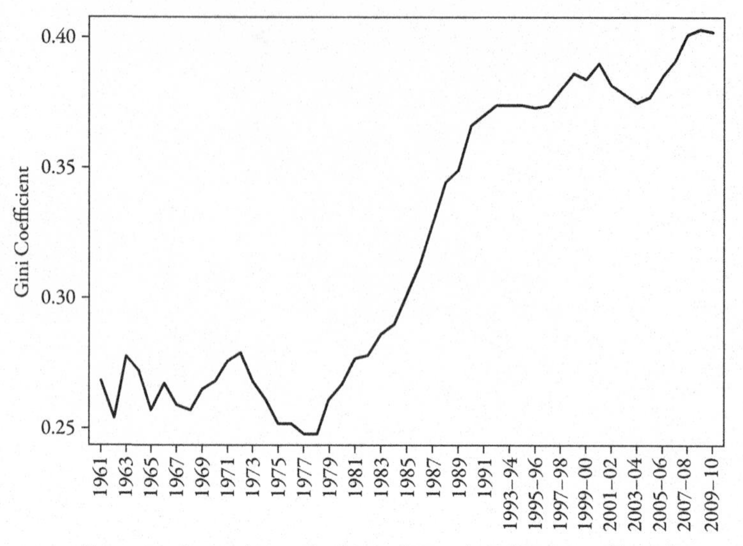

FIGURE 4.3 Economic Inequality in the United Kingdom (Gini Coefficient).

over this fifty-year period the mean annual increase in the Gini coefficient under Conservative governments was .005, while the mean for Labour governments was .00004.[7] This finding is in line with recent work by Brewer et al. (2009), which points to rising inequality in the UK through a combination of increasing incomes for the wealthy and decreasing incomes for the poor; and differences in the distribution of income across Conservative and Labour governments, where the latter produce income gains across the spectrum and the former produce gains mainly for the wealthy. In short, Brewer et al. argue that inequality is worsening, particularly during Conservative rather than Labour governance.

The partisan difference is less important for our current purposes than is the general economic climate: a faltering economy, coupled with growing inequality. But the three trends together are notable for their similarity with what Bartels (2008) has recently observed in the United States.[8]

Public Opinion About Redistribution

Has the Great Recession had an impact on attitudes about redistributive policies? As we have already noted, a growing body of scholarly work shows that public attitudes toward redistribution react to economic trends—and that those attitudes affect government policies. The state of Britons' attitudes toward redistribution may thus be critical to their government's reactions to the current economic crisis. What do those attitudes look like, leading up to and following the Great Recession?

We turn to these analysis with two bodies of work in mind: (1) work that has emphasized parallelism in policy preferences over time, particularly (but not exclusively) in the United States (Page and Shapiro 1992; Soroka and Wlezien 2008, 2010); and (2) literature focused on differences in representation of the preferences of the wealthy versus the poor (e.g., Bartels 2005, 2008; Gilens 2005; Jacobs and Page 2005; Enns and Wlezien 2011). Do British policy preferences differ across income groups? What is the nature of those differences—is it simply in levels, or also in trends over time? How policy preferences vary from one income group to the next (if they do) matter to the potential for differential representation, of course. But just as importantly, over-time changes in policy preferences also shed light on how various income groups react to economic crisis.

The parallelism in economic optimism across income cohorts evident in Figure 4.2 is echoed, at least in part, in preferences on redistribution from the British Social Attitudes surveys. The BSA has surveyed a range of political opinion annually since 1983. Two regular questions are of particular interest here:

> *Opinion about the Income Gap*: Thinking of income levels generally in Britain today would you say that the gap between those with high incomes and those with low incomes is... [too large, about right, too small]?
>
> *Support for Redistribution*: How much do you agree or disagree that government should redistribute income from the better-off to those who are less well off? [agree strongly, agree, neither agree nor disagree, disagree, disagree strongly][9]

We look at trends over time in responses to both questions. For the income gap measure, the variable is recoded so that +100 is "too large," 0 is "about right," and −100 is "too small." For redistribution, a net support measure is produced that is based on the annual average of responses, where "agree strongly" is coded as +100, "agree" as +50, "neither agree nor disagree" as 0, "disagree" as −50, and "disagree strongly" as −100. The resulting measure takes on a value of +100 when all respondents agree strongly and −100 when all respondents disagree strongly. Of course, average values tend to be somewhere in between.

Figure 4.4 shows opinion about the income gap by income level, where incomes are divided into terciles.[10] Here we see a consensus about the income

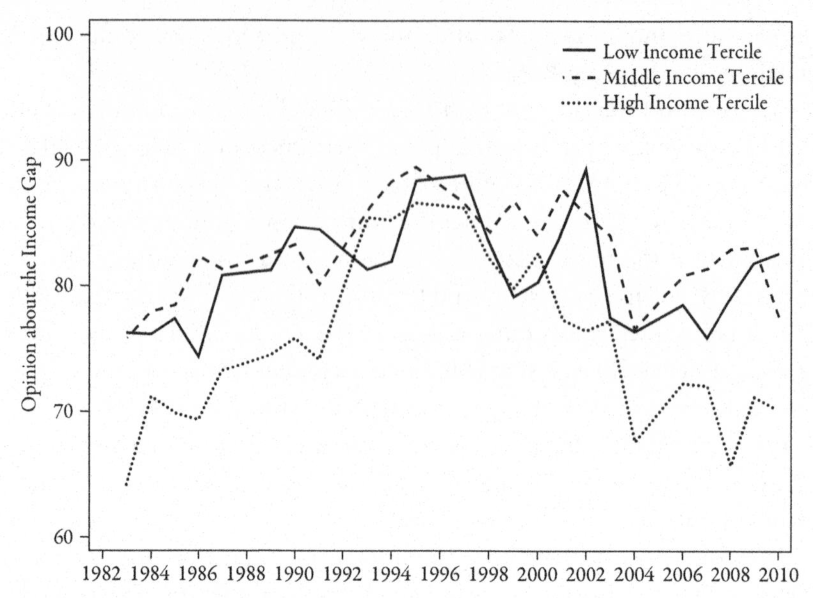

FIGURE 4.4 Public Opinion About the Income Gap, by Income Group.
Source: BSA surveys.

gap. Indeed, supermajorities at all three income levels think that the gap is "too large." Trends across the three income groups are also strongly parallel—the average bivariate correlation is .68. Even so, there are slight differences in opinion across income levels. The low- and middle-income groups both are more inclined to think that the gap is "too high," and with virtually identical numbers. High-income earners are less likely to believe the income gap is "too large." This is perhaps as we should expect; both the low- and middle-income groups presumably have an interest in a more equal allocation of income. Note also that differences between income groups vary over time. Even though opinions flow together, they do not move in perfect sync—there was near-convergence across groups through much of the 1990s that has disappeared in the new millennium.[11] Upper-income respondents now are less inclined than ever to see the income gap as a problem; middle- and low-income respondents continue to have very similar opinions.

Interestingly, this divergence emerged after Labour took control of government in the late-1990s. Trends in inequality cannot easily explain this timing. It is clear from Figure 4.3 that the sharp rise in inequality occurred decades before—and that by 2004 the Gini coefficient had been fairly stable for more than a decade. The divergence in attitudes occurred during a period of relative economic success, when economic

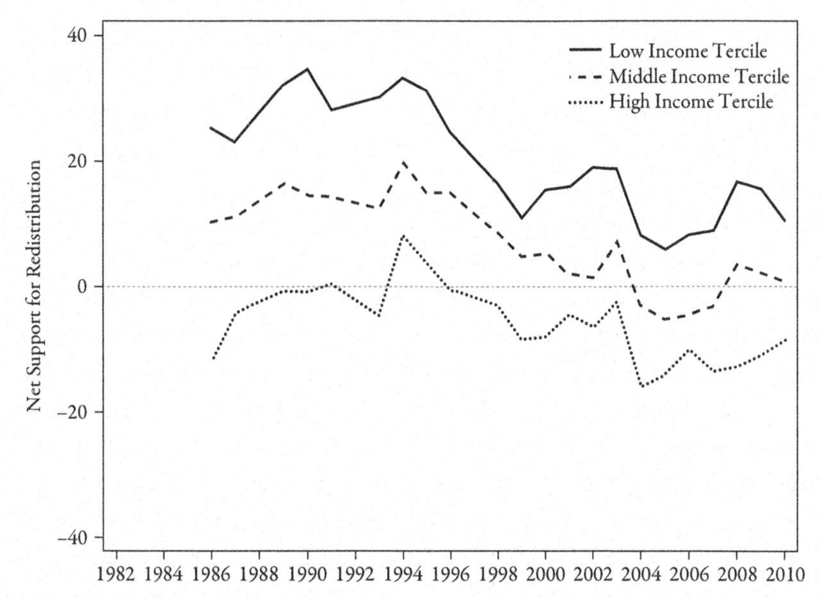

FIGURE 4.5 Net Support for Redistribution, by Income Group.
Source: BSA surveys.

optimism was comparatively high, particularly for high-income respondents (Figure 4.2); however, the recent shift in the economic climate has done little to narrow the gap.

Differences across income groups are somewhat clearer when the question focuses on preferences for redistribution, shown in Figure 4.5. Low-income citizens tend to favor redistributing income and high-income citizens oppose it, with middle-income citizens clearly in between. Note, then, that even though clear majorities across all income groups identify the income gap as a problem (Figure 4.4), citizens are divided when it comes to actually doing anything about it. This is especially true for low- and middle-income citizens, who share almost identical perceptions of the income gap but quite different opinions about redistribution. As we move away from general opinion about income inequality toward questions of redistribution, people in the middle are just not as willing to try to address the problem in government policy.

Such differences between low- and middle-income respondents and/or middle- and high-income respondents are likely of real consequence (see Soroka and Wlezien 2008, 2010; Wlezien and Soroka 2011). There are strong theoretical reasons to expect policy makers to follow the median voter or high-income voters; there are fewer reasons to expect them to follow low-income voters. So, to the extent that the level of policy matches levels of policy support,[12] the representation of the poorest voters' preferences in policy is likely to be greatest when their preferences are closer to the median voter.[13] This representation of low-income preferences is less likely when they are further from the median voter, especially when middle- and high-income preferences are close.

Differences in levels do not preclude a very high degree of parallelism, of course, and the average correlation between the three series in Figure 4.5 is .86.[14] This parallelism should not mask an important over-time difference, however; in 2010, net support for redistribution for the wealthiest group is at roughly the same level as in 1986, while net support for the other two cohorts is markedly lower than their 1986 levels. Overall, then, the difference across income cohorts is narrowing—not through upward shifts in the high-income group, but through downward shifts in the middle- and low-income groups. The result is that the median British voter has, over the past twenty years, been moving to the right (at least where preferences for redistribution are concerned). Low-income voters in the UK were as a consequence less supportive of redistribution before the Great Recession, and though support increased in 2008, 2009, and 2010, preferences for redistribution were lower even in the thick of the recent recession than they had been during the recession in the early 1990s. In short, although most people now consider the income gap at least as big as it was twenty-five years ago (recall data in Figure 4.4), they are less inclined to actually support redistribution.

Are there no significant changes in support for redistribution surrounding the Great Recession? Table 4.1 brings this period into closer focus. It presents basic descriptive data for each question for the three years before, and the three years during and after, the recession. Results for Opinion About the Income Gap make clear that there is no significant shift over this period; roughly 20 percent are not in the "too large" category, and they are unaffected by the recession. Results for Support for Redistribution do show an upward shift from one period to the next. The overall shift is statistically significant but very small in magnitude, a shift of roughly four points from the "disagree" categories to the "agree" categories.[15] To the extent that the Great Recession has affected attitudes on redistribution—as of 2010, at least—the effect has been marginal.

These results seem to raise questions about the relationship between perceptions of inequality and support for redistribution: 80 percent of respondents believe the gap between the rich and poor is too large, but fewer than 40 percent believe the government should redistribute income. We can explore these relationships more directly, of course, by examining preferences

Table 4.1 Views About Inequality and Support for Redistribution, Before and After the Great Recession.

	2005–2007	2008–2010
Opinion About the Income Gap		
...would you say that the gap between those with high incomes and those with low incomes is...		
Too small	2.2%	2.0%
About right	18.2%	17.8%
Too large	79.5%	80.1%
N	4,100	5,392
Chi square	0.703, p = 0.70	
Support for Redistribution		
...government should redistribute income from the better-off to those who are less well-off...		
Disagree strongly	7.2%	6.3%
Disagree	32.1%	29.0%
Neither agree nor disagree	27.5%	26.8%
Agree	26.1%	29.5%
Agree strongly	7.0%	8.5%
N	10,672	9,511
Chi square	58.431, p = 0.00	

Note: Cell entries are column percentages.

Source: BSA surveys.

for redistribution separately among those who believe the income gap is too large and those who do not. (Since very few respondents—fewer than 5 percent—say the income gap is too small, we combine the "too small" and "about right" categories.) The separate time trends are shown in Figure 4.6.

Clearly, there is a strong relationship between opinion about the income gap and redistributive preferences: those who believe that the income gap is too large are most supportive of redistribution. That said, the gap in redistributive preferences across the two groups has narrowed over time. This is not a consequence of shifting redistributive priorities among the groups that believe the income gap is too small or about right; it is a consequence of declining support for redistribution among those who feel the income gap is too high. Figure 4.6 lends further support, then, to the finding implicit in Figures 4.4 and 4.5: a

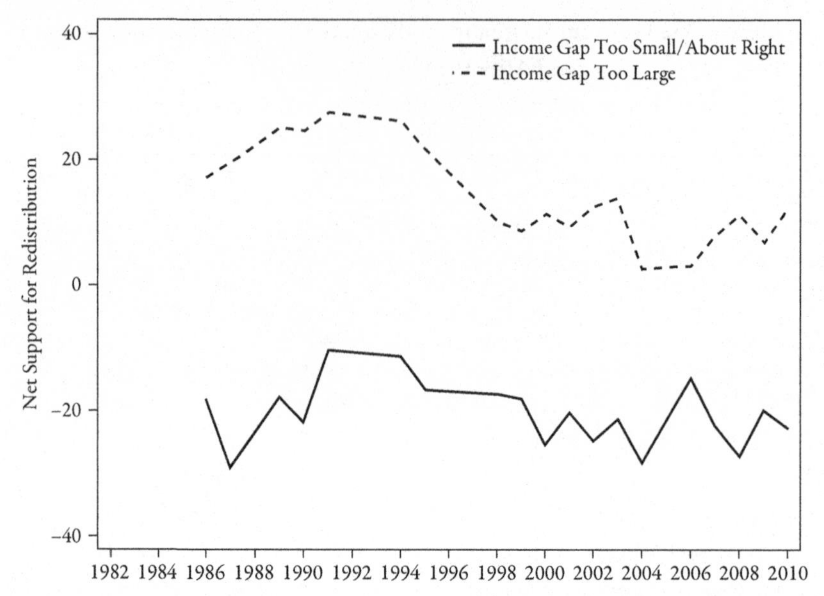

FIGURE 4.6 Net Support for Redistribution, by Opinion About the Income Gap.
Source: BSA surveys.

growing proportion of the (largely middle income) BSA respondents believe the income gap is too large, but they do not support greater levels of redistribution. The Great Recession has done little to change this long-term trend.

Preferences for Taxes and Spending

Thus far we have focused on general support for "redistribution." To what extent do the patterns we have observed apply to the two policy instruments themselves: taxing and spending? We rely here on three measures, again from BSA surveys:

> *Support for Taxes and Spending*: Suppose the government had to choose between the three options on this card. Which do you think it should choose? [Reduce taxes and spend less on health, education, and social benefits; keep taxes and spending on these services at the same level as now; increase taxes and spend more on health, education, and social benefits.][16]
>
> *Support for Welfare*: The government should spend more money on welfare benefits for the poor, even if it leads to higher taxes. [agree strongly, agree, neither agree nor disagree, disagree, disagree strongly]

> *Support for Taxes by Income Group*: How would you describe taxes in Britain today...for those with high incomes? / For those with middle incomes, are taxes... / For those with low incomes, are taxes... [much too high, too high, about right, too low, much too low]?[17]

Note that the first deals with taxes and spending combined, while the others deal with spending and then taxes independently. We code responses as with the previous questions: for support for taxes and spending, "reduce" is coded as −100, "same" as 0, and "increase" as +100; for support for welfare, a net support measure is produced that is based on the annual average of responses where "agree strongly" is coded as +100, "agree" as +50, "neither agree nor disagree" as 0, "disagree" as −50, and "disagree strongly" as −100; the tax question is coded similarly, with "much too high" as +100 and "much too low" as −100.

Figure 4.7 shows results for the taxes and spending question. Note that there is always more support for increasing taxes and spending than for decreasing them—the y-axis shows only positive values, though the variable could in principle range from +100 to −100. Preferences evolve almost parabolically, rising sharply through the 1980s and into the 1990s before dropping sharply thereafter. Support for taxing and spending in 2010 is essentially

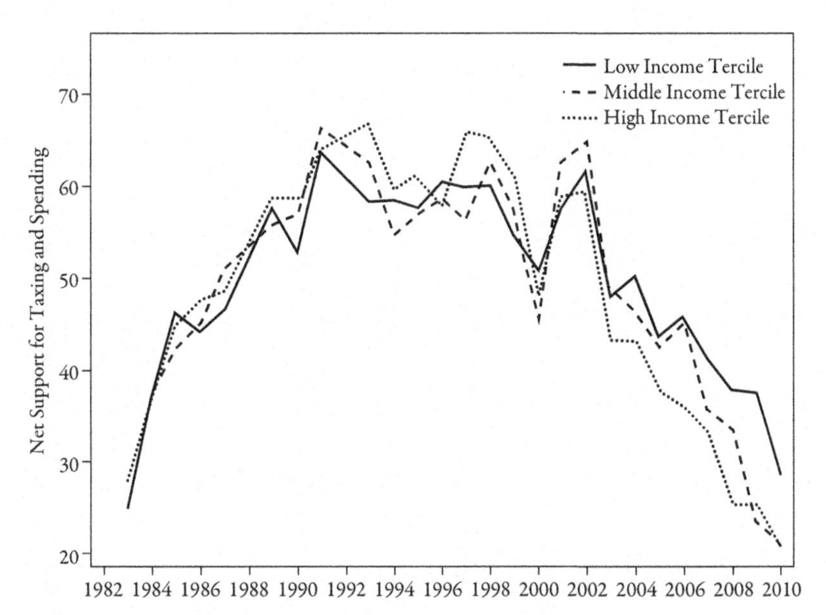

FIGURE 4.7 Public Opinion About Taxes and Spending, by Income Group.
Source: BSA surveys.

the same as it was in 1982. The figure also demonstrates a very high degree of identity across the three groups. Support is virtually indistinguishable until the very end of the series. There, middle- and high-income preferences diverge from low-income preferences, though even here the differences are not fundamental.

It is difficult to know just how much of the dynamic in Figure 4.7 is a consequence of shifting opinion about spending and/or how much of shifting opinion about taxing. The two need not move together, of course—and data that capture opinions on spending and taxing suggest, in fact, that they did not. Consider first Figure 4.8, which displays net preferences for welfare spending. The lowest income group is clearly the most supportive of welfare, though as of 2010 they are only barely so. Perhaps most importantly, the preferences of the middle-income group are nearly identical to those of the high-income group. This contrasts sharply with what we see for opinion about the income gap and also preferences for redistribution. It does comport with our own past work on preferences for welfare spending in the United States, however (Soroka and Wlezien 2008, 2010; Wlezien and Soroka 2011). Thus, even if policy makers are following the preferences of the median voter, they will tend to produce welfare policy that better matches the preferences of high-income earners than those of the poor.

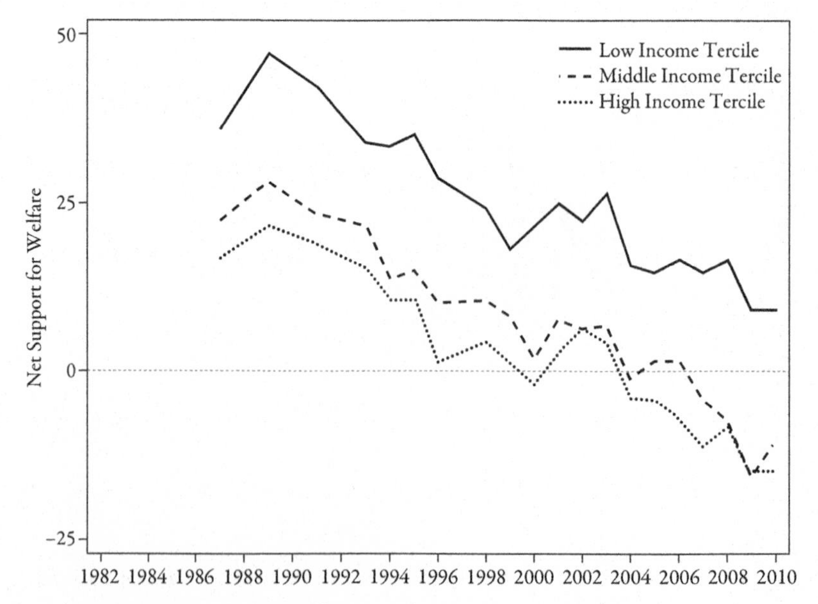

FIGURE 4.8 Net Support for Welfare Spending, by Income Group.
Source: BSA surveys.

Figure 4.8 also reveals certain similarities in welfare spending preferences across income groups. First, they move in parallel over time. Second, they all have declined markedly over time. From a consensus for more spending in the middle 1980s, public support has in a secular fashion in the wake of the Great Recession. In 2011, middle- and upper-income citizens express support for less spending on welfare and low-income citizens are approaching neutral.

The trend is rather different for preferences on taxing. Unfortunately, the BSA tax questions were not asked as regularly as the others investigated here. Even so, we have four years' worth of data, spanning three decades. Table 4.2

Table 4.2 Tax Preferences for Low-, Middle-, and High-Income Earners, by Income Group.

	Overall	by Respondents' Income Tercile		
		Low	Middle	High
		Taxes on Low Incomes		
1987	+62.0	+67.6	+62.4	+55.3
1996	+49.3	+63.3	+49.9	+37.9
2006	+44.4	+52.0	+47.2	+35.3
2009	+47.4	+54.6	+50.6	+38.3
		Taxes on Middle Incomes		
1987	+21.7	+18.4	+20.7	+26.8
1996	+13.9	+16.8	+13.2	+11.3
2006	+26.5	+26.5	+26.6	+25.4
2009	+23.8	+21.9	+24.6	+23.0
		Taxes on High Incomes		
1987	−9.3	−12.3	−17.2	+2.3
1996	−15.4	−13.5	−20.6	−16.2
2006	+2.2	−0.4	−2.0	+7.4
2009	−2.5	−6.1	−6.8	+0.6

Note: Cell entries are mean values for a variable ranging from −100 (too low) to +100 (too high).

Source: BSA surveys.

shows results for the three questions asking about tax levels for low-, middle-, and high-income earners. Results are shown by income tercile; recall that the measure ranges from −100 (much too low) to +100 (much too high).

Not surprisingly, high-income tercile respondents are more likely to say their taxes are too high, and low-income tercile respondents are more likely to say their taxes are too high. Opinions about taxes on middle-income earners hover midway between "about right" (0) and "too high" (50) over time, and in 2009 they are only slightly different from what they were in 1987. There are some interesting shifts in opinions about taxes on high- and low-income earners, however. Regarding the former, the low and middle tercile respondents seem to have shifted upward—away from "too low" and toward "about right"—over the past decade or so. That is, middle- and low-income tercile respondents seem to be more sympathetic to the tax plight of high-income earners. The opposite is true regarding opinions about taxes for low-income respondents. Here, even though preferences are still closer to "too high" than to "about right," there is clearly a downward shift (of 13 to 17 points), across all three income terciles.

The end result is that opinions about tax levels overall are roughly as they were twenty years ago, but the gap between opinions on taxes for high- and low-income earners has narrowed a little. Consider the first column in Table 4.2, which shows tax preferences for all respondents combined. The difference between preferences for low- and high-income earners in 1987 was 62.0 versus −9.3 respectively; by 2009, the difference is 47.4 versus −2.5. Put differently, opinions about taxes on high-income earners now sit firmly at "about right" (0); opinions about taxes on low-income earners sit at "too high" but are down nearly 15 points from their 1987 level.

This narrowing fits with what we have seen above: (bare) majority support for redistribution in 2010, with a marked decline in support since the early 1990s (see Figure 4.5). Declining support for taxation over the past twenty years roughly parallels the decline in support for welfare spending (see Figure 4.8). Although the downward trends are similar, we should not lose sight of one divergence between public opinion about taxes and spending: the former is very similar across income groups while the latter differs fundamentally. In short, low-income respondents are more supportive of spending on welfare but are not markedly more supportive of taxes, even when those taxes are directed at more prosperous cohorts.

Figure 4.9 draws together data reviewed in this and the previous sections. The figure shows trends in support for welfare spending for different groups according to their opinions about the income gap. This figure serves three

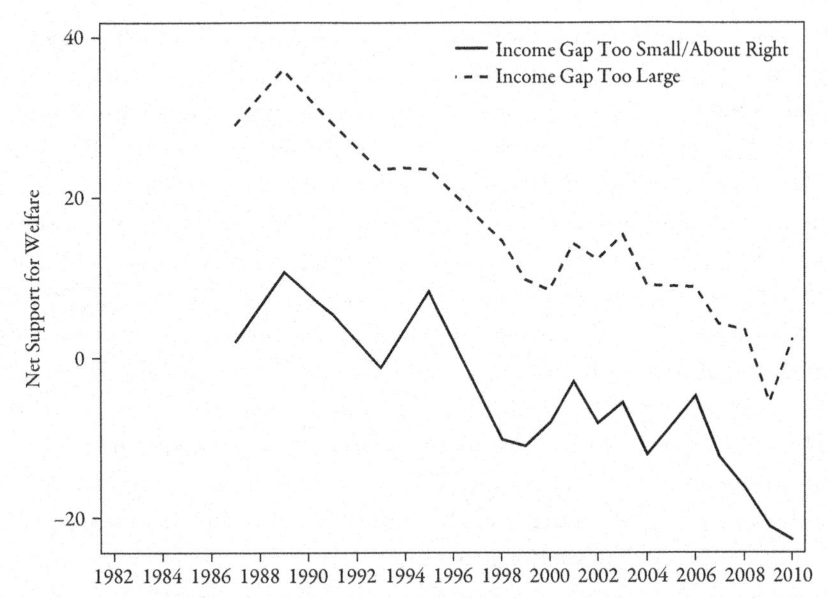

FIGURE 4.9 Net Support for Welfare Spending, by Opinion About the Income Gap.
Source: BSA surveys.

purposes. First, it illustrates (again) a weakening of support for redistribution, particularly among those who think the income gap is too large (many of whom would likely benefit directly from increased spending). Second, it confirms that the decoupling of perceptions of inequality and demand for redistribution seen in Figure 4.6 is also evident when we look at more concrete policy opinion, such as support for welfare. Third, it hints at a possibility only barely evident (if at all) in preceding figures: a potential shift in opinion on welfare since the start of the Great Recession. That is, in 2010 there is an increase of more than five points in support for welfare spending among those who believe the income gap is too large. It is of course too soon to know whether this reflects a permanent or ongoing shift, and it is important to note that it follows on an equal and opposite shift in preferences in 2009. But it is one of the very few hints in the BSA data that the Great Recession has had an impact on public opinion about redistribution in the United Kingdom.

Discussion and Conclusions

In the midst of the Great Recession, results from the BSA surveys point toward a middle-income group that is more closely allied with the poor when it comes to support for a reduction in the income gap, but—by some measures at least—more closely allied with the well-to-do when it comes to support for redistributive policy. (This is not clear in generic support for redistribution but is clear in support for welfare spending and taxing.) These findings are not unlike Bartels' in his influential 2005 article "Homer Gets a Tax Cut." Bartels argues, "The results of my analysis suggest that most Americans supported tax cuts not because they were indifferent to economic inequality, but because they largely failed to connect inequality and public policy" (16; see also McCall 2013). We see hints of a similar possibility here; at least, we see increasing inequality in Britain, alongside a disjuncture in public preferences that may well encourage policy outcomes most beneficial to the wealthy. This may mean the British public suffers from the same failure to "connect inequality and public policy" that Bartels identifies in the United States. It may, alternatively, mean that even though they correctly identify the inequality, the British public simply does not really want to do anything about it using redistributive policy.[18] (For instance, it may be, as Cramer describes in Chapter 3, that people think the government is more of a problem than it is a solution.)

Either way, it is striking that in the mid-1980s the average BSA respondent identified inequalities and was supportive of redistributive policy generally and welfare specifically; but in 2010, though the average respondent is more acutely aware of inequality, he or she is ambivalent about redistribution and welfare. (Of course, whether the British government represents the average voter is another issue; we use the average here simply to capture the overall shift in the distribution of British preferences for redistribution over time.) This change over time is one difference between what we see in the BSA data and what Bartels (2008) found in the United States: Bartels argued that public opinion about redistribution had not changed over time in the United States, but the same clearly is not true in the UK. Over the past twenty-five years or so, support for redistributive policy has declined across all income cohorts—and particularly among the low-income cohort. The end result is that the average voter in the UK during the Great Recession is clearly to the right of the average voter in either of two previous recessions.

What accounts for this shift? One notable possibility is the impact of party politics—a critical part not just of Bartels' story but of a wide body of work focused on the relationship of preferences, politics, and policies over time (e.g., Erikson et al. 2002; Soroka and Wlezien 2010).[19] The general trend in the preferences of partisans is as we might expect given the results above, however. As an illustration, Figure 4.10 shows preferences for redistribution

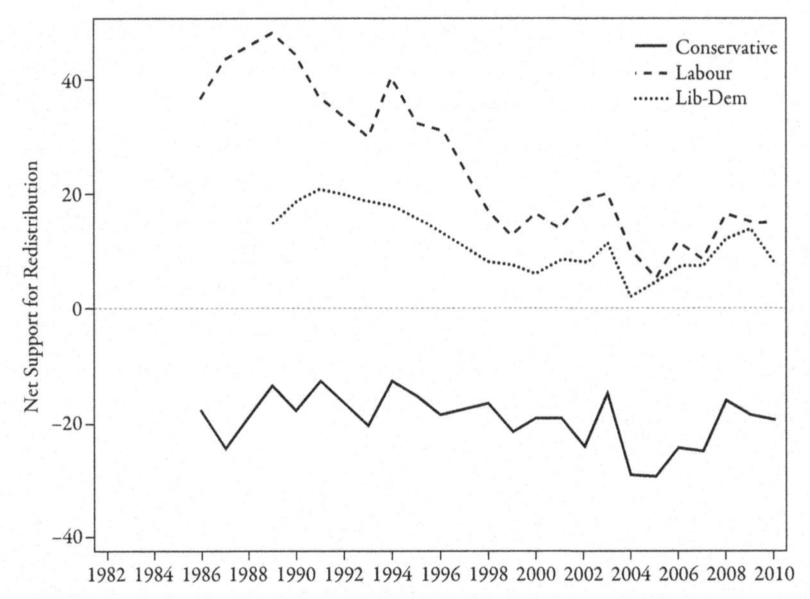

FIGURE 4.10 Net Support for Redistribution by Partisanship.

separately for Conservative, Labour, and Lib-Dem party identifiers. The story where partisanship is concerned is pretty clear: Conservative Party supporters are now roughly where they were in the early 1980s, while—despite a modest reversal over the past six years—Labour Party supporters are much farther to the right than they had been.

Results in Figure 4.10 are in line with previous analyses of BSA data by Curtice and Fisher (2003). These authors probe in more detail the composition of the Labour and Conservative parties and note a rightward shift in the opinions of Labour supporter in the mid-1990s—a shift linked, they argue, to Tony Blair's effort to move Labour to the center and thus win over previously Conservative voters. Results above suggest that the trends in Figure 4.10 are not just about shifting voting patterns, however. As Curtice and Fisher note, the apparent change in preferences among Labour voters reflects both actual changes in their preferences and shifting party identifiers. What is striking in our more recent data, then, is the fact that the trends evident in 2002 have largely continued.

Indeed, the trends have continued into, and thus far through, the Great Recession. In spite of rising inequality, and in spite of economic expectations falling to their lowest level since Thatcher's first term in government, the British public remains markedly less supportive of redistributive policy. This is true not just at the outset of the Great Recession, in 2008; it is true in 2010, two years (and one election) into the recession. The Great Recession has done little to reverse the rightward trend in preferences evident since the early 1990s.

These public preferences may have had consequences for policy reactions to the recession. In attempting to address fiscal imbalance in recent years, governments have sometimes increased taxes on the rich and sometimes cut spending on welfare. We have seen hints of majority support for both of these actions in our figures, particularly for welfare spending cuts. But party control evidently has mattered as well. After all, it presumably is no accident that the sitting Conservative-led coalition government has cut spending, while the preceding Labour government raised taxes. This is what we have come to expect, not just in the United States but in the UK as well (Erikson et al. 2002; Wlezien 2004; Soroka and Wlezien 2010).

Notes

1. Whether they are *less* or *more* affected is unclear; surely this depends on which aspects of the economy are changing.
2. On responsiveness to the economy, see especially Page and Jacobs (2009) and Duch and Sagarzazu in this volume, Chapter 8. On political representation, see citations below.
3. Full information on NRS social grades is available at http://www.nrs.co.uk.
4. The middle-upper group combines upper-middle and upper classes; it includes NRS social grades A, B, and C1. The middle-lower group combines lower-middle and lower classes; it includes NRS social grants C2, D and E. Breaking down the sample further would introduce more error due to smaller samples, but makes no real difference for the results.
5. The Pearson's r for the two (unsmoothed) series is .94.
6. Data are from the Institute for Fiscal Studies' Inequality and Poverty Spreadsheet, available at ifs.org.uk. For work using these data, see Brewer et al. (2009); for similar data, see Hills et al. (2010).
7. Party coding is based on the party in power for the majority of the year. The difference in means is statistically significant at $p < .05$.
8. There are earlier observations on the link between partisanship and changes in inequality in the United States as well (e.g., Hibbs and Dennis 1988). For a recent take, see Kelly (2009).
9. There are other related questions in the BSA. The one most regularly asked and most clearly related to the income gap and redistribution is, "How much do you agree or disagree that ordinary working people do not get their fair share of the nation's wealth [agree strongly, agree, neither agree nor disagree, disagree, disagree strongly]?" Trends in responses to this question (as well as differences across income groups) are not very different from the *Support for Redistribution* question examined here.

10. Income terciles are based on the distribution of incomes in the BSA datasets. As both the distribution of income and survey response categories shift from year to year, we estimate terciles for each year independently before merging the annual datasets.
11. Of course, preferences differ from year to year partly due to sampling error, but there also are more systematic patterns.
12. It is very hard to tell if this is the case. Matching change in policy to preference for change is relatively easy; comparing level of policy to level of preference is very difficult in all but a few policy domains. See Soroka and Wlezien (2010).
13. It also may be that representation is greatest when the preferences of poorer citizens are close to those of the richest voters, though this is unlikely in the case of redistributive policy. It is more likely (and in fact sometimes the case) in a range of other policy domains (Soroka and Wlezien 2008).
14. In a principal components factor analysis, a single factor accounts for 91 percent of the variance in the three series.
15. Results are not markedly different if we look at each year independently, rather than in three-year intervals. In fact, the greatest shift in support for redistribution occurred in 2008; subsequent years show a slight retreat from this (already minor) shift in preferences.
16. We view this as an imperfect measure of tax preferences; but although there are other questions dealing more directly with taxes (without spending) in BSA surveys, none are asked as consistently as this one. Indeed, no question dealing with taxes directly is asked more than four times over the past thirty years, and we do use these data to assess the balance and structure of preferences below.
17. Another question in the BSA surveys asks, "Do you think people with high incomes should pay a larger share of their incomes in taxes than those with low incomes, the same share or a smaller share? [much larger, larger, the same share, smaller, much smaller]." Results from this question are not very different (over time, or across income groups) from the combined results from the *Support for Taxes by Income Group* questions examined here.
18. The same may be true in the United States.
19. Another possibility is that our measures of preferences are relative rather than absolute—that is, they reflect a combination of preferences for policy alongside current levels of policy (Wlezen 1995). Policy change may in fact have more impact—in the form of thermostatic responsiveness—on preferences than the Great Recession itself.

References

Anderson, Christopher J. 1995. *Blaming the Government*. Armonk, NY: Sharpe.

Bartels, Larry M. 2005. "Homer Gets a Tax Cut: Inequality and Public Policy in the American Mind." *Perspectives on Politics* 3(1): 15–31.

Bartels, Larry M. 2008. *Unequal Democracy: The Political Economy of the New Gilded Age*. Princeton, NJ: Princeton University Press.

Bloom, Howard S., and H. Douglas Price. 1975. "Voter Response to Short-Run Economic Conditions: The Asymmetric Effect of Prosperity and Recession." *American Political Science Review 69*: 1240–1254.

Brewer, Mike, Alastair Muriel, David Phillips, and Luke Sibieta. 2009. *Poverty and Inequality in the UK: 2009*. London: Institute for Fiscal Studies.

Claggett, William. 1986. "A Reexamination of the Asymmetry Hypothesis: Economic Expansions, Contractions, and Congressional Elections." *Western Political Quarterly 39*: 623–633.

Curtice, John, and Stephen Fisher. 2003. "The Power to Persuade? A Tale of Two Prime Ministers." In Alison Park et al., eds., *British Social Attitudes: The 20th Report*, 233–254. London: Sage.

Durr, Robert H. 1993. "What Moves Policy Sentiment?" *American Political Science Review 87*(1): 158–170.

Enns, Peter, and Christopher Wlezien, eds. 2011. *Who Gets Represented?* New York: Russell Sage Foundation.

Erikson, Robert S., Michael B. MacKuen, and James A. Stimson. 2002. *The Macro Polity*. Cambridge: Cambridge University Press.

Gilens, Martin. 2005. "Inequality and Democratic Responsiveness." *Public Opinion Quarterly 69*: 778–796.

Goidel, Robert K., and Ronald E. Langley. 1995. "Media Coverage of the Economy and Aggregate Economic Evaluations: Uncovering Evidence of Indirect Media Effects." *Political Research Quarterly 48*(2): 313–328.

Haller, H. Brandon, and Helmut Norpoth. 1997. "Reality Bites: News Exposure and Economic Opinion." *Public Opinion Quarterly 61*(4): 555–575.

Hibbs, Douglas A. and Christopher Dennis. 1988. "Income Distribution in the United States." *The American Political Science Review 82*(2): 467–490.

Hills, John, et al. 2010. *An Anatomy of Economic Inequality in the UK: Report of the National Equality Panel*. London: Government Equalities Office.

Jacobs, Lawrence R., and Benjamin I. Page. 2005. "Who Influences U.S. Foreign Policy?" *American Political Science Review 99*: 107–123.

Kelly, Nathan. 2009. *The Politics of Income Inequality in the United States*. New York: Cambridge University Press.

McCall, Leslie. 2013. *The Undeserving Rich: American Beliefs About Inequality, Opportunity, and Redistribution*. New York: Cambridge University Press.

Nadeau, Richard, Richard G. Niemi, David P. Fan, and Timothy Amato. 1999. "Elite Economic Forecasts, Economic News, Mass Economic Judgments, and Presidential Approval." *Journal of Politics 61*(1): 109–135.

Page, Benjamin I., and Lawrence R. Jacobs. 2009. *Class War? What Americans Really Think About Economic Inequality*. Chicago: University of Chicago Press.

Page, Benjamin I., and Robert Y. Shapiro. 1992. *The Rational Public: Fifty Years of Trends in Americans' Policy Preferences*. Chicago: University of Chicago Press.

Soroka, Stuart and Christopher Wlezien. 2005. "Opinion-Policy Dynamics: Public Preferences and Public Expenditure in the UK," with *British Journal of Political Science 35*: 665–689.

Soroka, Stuart, and Christopher Wlezien. 2008. "On the Limits to Inequality in Representation." *PS: Political Science and Politics* 2008: 319–327.

Soroka, Stuart, and Christopher Wlezien. 2010. *Degrees of Democracy: Politics, Public Opinion and Policy*. Cambridge: Cambridge University Press.

Stevenson, Randolph T. 2001. "The Economy and Policy Mood: A Fundamental Dynamic of Democratic Politics?" *American Journal of Political Science 45*(3): 620–633.

Wlezien, Christopher. 1995. "The Public as Thermostat: Dynamics of Preferences for Spending." *American Journal of Political Science 39*: 981–1000.

Wlezien, Christopher. 2004. "Patterns of Representation: Dynamics of Public Preferences and Policy." *Journal of Politics 66*(1): 1–24.

Wlezien, Christopher, and Stuart Soroka. 2011. "Inequality in Policy Responsiveness?" In Enns and Wlezien, *Who Gets Represented?* New York: Russell Sage Foundation.

5

Economic Insecurity and Public Support for the Euro

BEFORE AND DURING THE FINANCIAL CRISIS

Sara B. Hobolt and Patrick Leblond

TEN YEARS AFTER the introduction of the European single currency, the *Economist* (2009) concluded that "the euro has proved a haven in the economic crisis—so much so that no country seriously wants to leave it and plenty want to join." However, as the financial crisis evolved into a European sovereign debt crisis, threatening the very survival of the eurozone, it is no longer clear whether Europeans consider the euro a "safe haven." This raises the central question of this chapter, namely, What determines public attitudes toward the euro? Specifically, how does economic insecurity shape support for the single currency? And how has the economic crisis in Europe, which began with the global financial crisis in 2008, affected the impact of economic insecurity on support for the euro? Public attitudes toward the euro are of critical importance, not only because the decision on whether or not to join the euro is often decided by popular referendum[1] but also because institutional reforms of the eurozone's economic governance are constrained by public opinion, as EU treaty changes need to be ratified by member states, either by national

Note: Previous versions of this paper were presented at the 2009 annual meetings of the American Political Science Association and the International Political Economy Society, at a workshop organized by HEC Montreal's Research Group in International Business (GRAI), and at the Oxford conference "Popular Reactions to the Great Recession" organized by the editors of this volume. We thank participants at these gatherings for their comments, most especially Larry Bartels, Nancy Bermeo, Benjamin Cohen, Jeffry Frieden, Stefanie Walter, and two anonymous reviewers. We are also grateful to Traci Wilson for research assistance.

parliaments or by national electorates in referendums. Ultimately, closer fiscal integration, as a solution to the single currency's original design flaws, is viable only if it is perceived to be legitimate in the eyes of citizens.

This chapter demonstrates that, perhaps surprisingly, support for the euro has remained high and stable within the eurozone throughout the crisis. By analyzing support across Europe, we show that in times of relative stability before the crisis citizens in countries with worsening economic prospects were generally less supportive of the euro than where it was seen as a promoter growth of prosperity. However, since the onset of the euro crisis, even for citizens in countries with severe austerity measures, recession, and high unemployment, support for staying inside the euro has remained high. We conclude this is because the relative economic uncertainty associated with euro exit or eurozone collapse is even greater in the eyes of most citizens than the cost of remaining in the euro. Outside the eurozone, where the public feels it has less to lose from a eurozone breakdown, support for the euro has dramatically declined.

Explaining Public Support for the Euro

In the extant literature, two alternative perspectives have been applied to explain variation in both individual-level and aggregate-level support for the EU's single currency: utilitarian rationality and symbolic concerns. From a utilitarian perspective, generic support for European integration is determined by a rational cost-benefit analysis: those who benefit economically from European integration (particularly trade liberalization) are supportive, whereas those who stand to lose are more hostile (Gabel 1998a, 1998b; Gabel and Palmer 1995; McLaren 2006). Given the direct economic implications of monetary integration, it is therefore not surprising that most scholars have analyzed support for the euro from the standpoint of economic self-interest. Monetary integration should lead to increased trade (see Rose and Stanley 2005) and, as a consequence, individuals with high involvement in international trade should favor the euro more than individuals employed in the nontradable sector (Banducci, Karp, and Loedel 2009; Gabel 2001; Gabel and Hix 2005). Studies of support for the euro have also found that sociotropic economic concerns play a role (Banducci et al. 2003, 2009; Kaltenthaler and Anderson 2001). In countries where the euro is expected to bring about greater economic stability, people are more in favor of joining the currency union. For instance, Gärtner (1997) found that, prior to the creation of the euro, citizens in EU member states with a looser fiscal policy and high deficit were more likely to support the euro (see also Gabel 2001).

An alternative explanation for the variation in support for the euro, and European integration more generally, focuses less on economic self-interest and more on the threat that European integration can pose to national identity and a country's symbols and values (see Carey 2002; Hooghe and Marks 2004; McLaren 2002, 2004, 2006). Several studies have shown that attachment to the nation, and particularly "exclusive" national identity, is a powerful predictor of negative attitudes toward European integration (Hooghe and Marks 2004; McLaren 2006). In the context of the euro, an important symbol of national identity is the national currency (Cohen 1998; Hobolt and Leblond 2009). Helleiner (2003) argues that the creation of national money has traditionally been closely associated with nation-state building, as a means of giving the inhabitants of a political entity a sense of collective identity. It is therefore not surprising that feelings of national identity and diffuse support for European integration influence individual opinion about monetary integration (Gabel and Hix 2005; Kaltenthaler and Anderson 2001). In the context of the referendums on joining the euro in Denmark and Sweden, Jupille and Leblang (2007) found that "identity concerns" played a greater role than "pocketbook calculations." Generally, citizens who thought that the EU undermined national sovereignty and democracy were more likely to vote against the euro's adoption. Similarly, Hobolt and Leblond (2009), arguing that the strength of a currency is positively related to its symbolic value, have found that exchange rates influenced support for the euro in both Denmark and Sweden prior to the referendums. In Denmark, where the krone has been fixed to the Deutschemark (before 1999) and the euro (since 1999) for years, the weakening (i.e., depreciation) of the euro vis-à-vis the U.S. dollar led to a decline in Danes' support for the European single currency. In Sweden, where there has been a flexible exchange rate, the strengthening (i.e., appreciation) of the krona against the euro saw opposition to eurozone membership increase.

Hence, existing work has clearly demonstrated that economic calculations and symbolic concerns play an important role in explaining variation in support for the euro between countries and across individuals within nations. Yet the question still remains about how the recent changes in economic conditions influence support for European monetary integration. To understand how the financial crisis has affected, and will continue to influence, support for the euro, we need to examine how changing economic conditions affect attitudes toward the single currency. The existing work on the euro has provided limited insights into the dynamics of public support for the euro, as most studies have focused on cross-sectional variation (across countries or individuals) in support rather than change over time. In addition to the study by Hobolt and Leblond (2009), which considers monthly changes in euro support, a notable exception is the work conducted by Banducci, Karp, and Loedel (2003, 2009), who examine public support for the euro before and after its introduction. Using pooled Eurobarometer survey data from fifteen "old" EU member states, they find, among other things, that the appreciation of the currency is associated with a higher level of support for the euro.

These studies make an important contribution to our understanding of support for European monetary integration as they show that changes in economic conditions lead to changes in support for the euro. Yet they also raise a fundamental question in the context of the current crisis: How are these determinants influenced by a severe economic crisis? The next section presents a theoretical explanation of support for monetary integration, focusing on the role on economic insecurity, and the subsequent sections of this chapter test these explanations in a time-series cross-sectional analysis of euro support since the birth of the eurozone in 1999.

The Crisis and Euro Support

Economic difficulties create a heightened sense of insecurity among individuals. If the economy slows down, people fear they will become unemployed or that the value of their assets (houses, investments, pensions, etc.) will decline. Naturally, following the utilitarian perspective outlined above, citizens' evaluations of the euro should be influenced by whether they feel monetary integration exacerbates this economic insecurity or protects them from the consequences of an economic slowdown.

In the context of Europe's financial (banking and fiscal) crisis, opinion on whether the Economic and Monetary Union (EMU) has offered protection varies considerably across countries and over time. Figure 5.1 displays the proportion of respondents who said they were in favor of a single currency across four distinct groups of countries. The first group comprises all eurozone member states, except for the so-called GIIPS countries (Greece, Ireland, Italy, Portugal, and Spain).[2] Support among citizens in the GIIPS countries is shown separately in the second group, because these countries stand at the heart of the EU's fiscal crisis, which has been partly blamed on their eurozone membership as they are prevented from devaluing the currency for their economies to remain internationally competitive without other market reforms. The term *GIIPS* has been used to describe the group of eurozone economies facing a particular severe sovereign debt crisis (it is the politically correct version of the malicious "PIIGS" moniker that has often

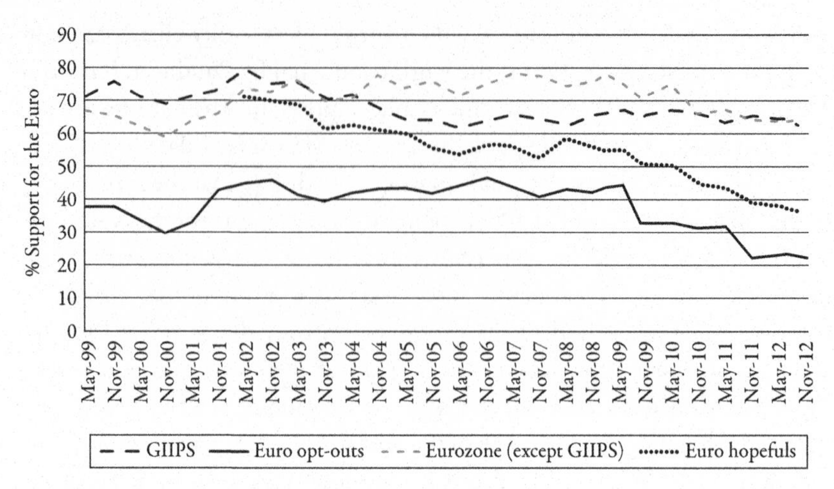

Note: Figure shows percentage of respondents in favor of "European Monetary Union with one single currency, the EURO". Eurozone: all eurozone members except GIIPS; GIIPS: Portugal, Ireland, Italy, Greece and Spain; Euro opt-outs: Denmark, Sweden, UK; Euro hopefuls: remaining non-eurozone member states.

FIGURE 5.1 Support for the Euro, 1999–2012.

Source: Eurobarometer surveys, various years.

been used to identify these countries). Individuals in the eurozone member states, without the GIIPS countries, have until recently been the most supportive of the euro (on average 71 percent of people in this group favored the euro across the period 1999–2012). Over the course of the crisis, however, their support has declined to reach the same level as that of individuals in the GIIPS countries, whose support has actually increased since 2008. Figure 5.1 illustrates that GIIPS countries were the most supportive group when the euro was introduced; but they have been relatively less so since 2004. On average across the 1999–2012 period, support in GIIPS countries was 68 percent in favor of the euro.

What is noteworthy is that support for the euro has not declined significantly inside the eurozone since the financial crisis became a sovereign debt crisis in late 2009. Two-thirds of citizens in the eurozone still favor the euro, and they did so even at the height of the eurozone crisis in 2011. Also, we find no significant differences in support between GIIPS countries and other eurozone member states. Support has remained relatively stable in both groups of countries. This may be because the distributive consequences of the crisis and euro-rescue measures are somewhat unclear within the eurozone. On the one hand, debtor states have suffered most severely from the crisis and have had to accept austerity measures imposed by the EU and the IMF. On the other hand, these countries are in the greatest need of EU intervention and have received the most tangible benefits through the bailout programs. However, what both sets of countries have in common is that a breakdown of the monetary union could have severe and very uncertain consequences for the future of their economies (Leblond 2012).

In contrast, for citizens in countries outside the eurozone, the prospect of joining the monetary union during an economic crisis may appear less than appealing. The third group, the "euro opt-outs," includes countries that have chosen to remain outside the eurozone until now, despite being able to meet the Maastricht convergence criteria: Denmark, Sweden, and the United Kingdom. In both Denmark and Sweden, the governments have been in favor of adopting the euro, but the electorate rejected the proposal in referendums in 2000 and 2003. In Britain, the current government's position is that the country should remain outside the euro. Among this group of opt-out countries, citizens have been the least supportive of the euro, averaging only 38 percent in favor. It is also within this group that we observe the largest decline in popular support for the single currency since the beginning of the euro crisis in 2010. The final group is composed of the "euro hopefuls," which are the remaining nine EU member states that have an official policy of joining the eurozone once they meet the convergence criteria. Within these countries, support for the European single currency has been in decline since 2001. This trend has only continued during the crisis period since the fall of 2008. The proportion of citizens in this group favoring the euro averages 55 percent across the period.

In sum, not unexpectedly, support for the euro is the lowest in the countries that are outside the eurozone while it is the highest among countries inside the zone. In terms of popular support during the euro crisis, it is also in the countries that have not adopted the euro that decline in support has been most significant.

We thus observe that there has been a decline in support among euro opt-outs and euro hopefuls in recent years, but that support inside the eurozone has remained stable. This raises the question of why the public inside the eurozone has continued to support the single currency in times of severe economic downturn, exacerbated by design flaws in the EMU itself (De Grauwe 2011). A plausible explanation is that the relative risks associated with abandoning the euro, for citizens in countries that have already adopted this currency, are seen as greater than the costs of staying inside (Leblond 2012). This is a narrative that has been espoused by European leaders in both creditor and debtor countries. For instance, Germany's chancellor, Angela Merkel, has repeatedly stressed the need for European unity and assistance to Southern neighbors by emphasizing the greater dangers associated with inaction. As an example, in September 2011, she stated that:

> In a currency union with 17 members, we can only have a stable euro if we prevent disorderly processes. Therefore it is our top priority to avoid an uncontrolled default, because it would hit not only Greece. The danger would be very high that it would hit many other countries ("Merkel warns" 2011).

In the same interview with the German RBB Inforadio, Merkel emphasized that Germany had benefited hugely from the euro. The warnings from national leaders of the dangers of euro exit have been even more pronounced in the GIIPS countries—which have all, with the exception of Italy, received financial assistance with strict conditions attached, mostly in the form of public finance and market reforms (the so-called austerity measures). The Greek prime minister, Antonis Samaras, warned in November 2012 that the country could be forced out of the eurozone if parliament failed to approve a new round of reform measures required by creditors: "We must save the country from catastrophe . . . if we fail to stay in the euro nothing will make sense" ("The eurocrisis live" 2012).

These warnings appear to resonate with citizens in the euro area who, despite any misgiving about the EU, generally consider that European unity will provide a more effective solution to the crisis than member states acting alone. This interpretation is supported by recent survey data on individuals' assessment of whether the EU or other institutions (such as the national government or the IMF) will handle the crisis more effectively. Since February 2009, the Eurobarometer surveys have asked this question: "Which of the following is best able to take effective actions against the effects of the financial and economic crisis?" The options include the national government, the European Union, the United States, the G20, the IMF, other, and none. This question is useful for understanding why support for the euro has remained high inside the eurozone, as it allows us to assess whether people perceive the EU to be more effective than national governments and other international institutions. Figure 5.2 shows the proportion of respondents who selected the EU as the institution best able to take effective action. It is worth noting that, on average, EU citizens perceived the EU to be the most effective at taking action against the crisis compared to all other options.

Figure 5.2 disaggregates countries into the same four groups as Figure 5.1. It shows that Europeans became more likely to name the EU as the most effective institution as the financial crisis evolved into a sovereign debt crisis in late 2009 and early 2010. This increase also coincides with high-profile EU interventions, such as the first Greek bailout and the establishment of the European Financial Stability Facility to safeguard financial stability in Europe in May 2010. In other words, as the crisis worsened in Europe and the EU started to intervene, people were more likely to think that the EU is best placed to deal effectively with the consequences of the crisis. This is especially the case in the GIIPS countries, which were arguably in the greatest need of EU intervention, closely followed by other eurozone states. Interestingly, euro hopefuls also put their faith in the actions of the EU, while the proportion is significantly lower in euro opt-out states. It is noteworthy that across the EU, except in the euro opt-out states, citizens were more likely to perceive the EU as an effective actor in taking action against the crisis than their national government. These differences are quite substantial: in GIIPS countries, 27 percent of citizens saw the EU as the "most effective institution" at handling the crisis, compared to only 17 percent who mentioned their national government. In other eurozone countries and euro-hopeful countries the difference was only slightly smaller at 8 percentage points. In contrast, in the opt-out countries, only 15 percent of citizens mentioned the EU as the most effective institution, whereas 25 percent opted for their own national government.

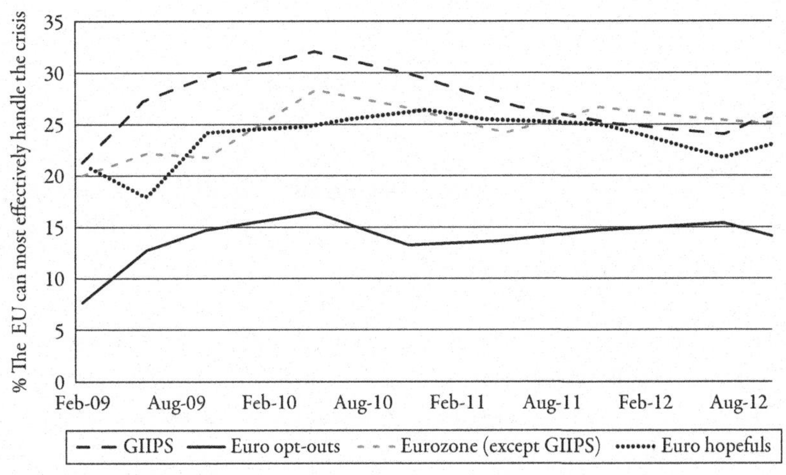

FIGURE 5.2 The EU Can Handle the Crisis Most Effectively.

Source: Eurobarometer surveys.

It is also interesting to note that this evaluation of the EU as the "most effective" institution did not decline significantly during the crisis, outside the three Euro opt-out states. This points to a plausible explanation for the otherwise puzzling finding that support for the euro remained so stable amid the crisis. In a nutshell, Europeans inside the eurozone, and in most of the countries hoping to join the euro, might have had increasing misgivings about the EU; however, they still perceived it to be more effective than their national governments in taking action against the economic crisis. This also suggests that citizens inside the eurozone were willing to support further integration to avoid the more uncertain, and potentially more sinister, consequences of a eurozone collapse.

Economic Insecurity and Euro Support

These findings concerning the impact of the crisis on support for the euro beg the more general question of how economic factors shape citizens' feelings about whether the euro protects against economic insecurity or, in fact, exacerbates it, not only in times of crisis but also in general. To begin with, we consider the effect of economic conditions on euro support. We expect citizens to view the single currency more favorably when economic conditions are good than when they are bad, since they are likely to attribute the economic climate, at least in part, to the monetary policy of the European Central Bank and the fiscal requirements of the Stability and Growth Pact.[3] Hence, when consumer confidence is higher, we expect a higher level of public support in the eurozone. Equally, we would expect that objective indicators of economic conditions such as unemployment, inflation, and economic growth influence support for the euro. For instance, higher unemployment or inflation should be associated with lower support, and the opposite should hold for economic growth. Since interest rates are directly linked to the management of the monetary union, we expect them to have an effect on support, where lower interest rates should be associated with a higher level of support. This leads us to formulate three hypotheses:

H1: Public support for the euro in eurozone countries decreases as economic conditions worsen.

H2: Public support for the euro in eurozone countries increases as consumer confidence improves.

H3: Public support for the euro in eurozone countries increases as interest rates decrease.

As discussed above, support for monetary integration may also be affected by another kind of insecurity, related to feelings of identity. In the eurozone, where the euro is the "national" currency, we would expect citizens to view the monetary union more positively when the value of the euro increases against its main "rival" currency, the U.S. dollar (Banducci et al. 2009), although in general we would expect that symbolic concerns matter more when it comes to the value of the national currency than the euro currency, since most citizens have a stronger affective attachment to their national currency (and their country) than people living in the eurozone have to the euro (and the EU). This leads to a fourth hypothesis:

H4: Public support for the euro in eurozone countries increases as the euro appreciates against the U.S. dollar.

Finally, we also expect that general levels of diffuse support for the EU will affect support for monetary integration. In countries where citizens feel the European Union poses less of a threat to national sovereignty and identity, they are more likely to favor monetary integration. This gives us a fifth hypothesis:

H5: Public support for the euro is higher when diffuse support of membership of the European Union is higher.

These hypotheses have been derived for situations that we can consider stable and "normal"; however, it seems reasonable to ask whether they also apply during a financial and economic crisis, especially one as severe as what Europe has been experiencing since 2008. The expectations concerning how the crisis affects the factors that shape support for the euro are not clear-cut. In principle, there is no apparent reason for the hypotheses mentioned above not also applying in the context of an economic crisis. After all, a crisis only represents a higher degree of economic insecurity. There are, however, two notable differences that we could expect. First, utilitarian rationality is likely to supersede symbolic concerns during a crisis. This implies that an appreciation of the euro vis-à-vis the U.S. dollar during a crisis may not have a positive effect on public support for the single currency. This is because a strong euro hurts exports to countries outside the eurozone, notably the United States, which further compounds existing economic difficulties. Second, an economic crisis that is so severe as to threaten the very existence of the euro could change how people associate economic uncertainty with the single currency. In normal times, high unemployment, high inflation, and high interest rates would all be expected to lead to a lower level of popular support for the euro, since the latter would be made responsible for the poor performance of the economy. In an exceptional situation, such as the sovereign debt crisis that began in late 2009, individuals might put the blame on other factors than the euro for their plight, such as bankers or incompetent governments. Even to the extent that citizens blame the euro and the EU more generally, they are likely to think that their economic situation would be more uncertain and worse if their country were to leave the eurozone or the euro were to disappear altogether. After all, the euro has been beneficial for eurozone members in terms of increased trade, lower inflation, and lower interest rates. This explains why Germany and other eurozone member states ended up accepting the need for financial bailouts for countries unable to finance their sovereign debt. Consequently, we can formulate three alternative hypotheses for explaining euro support during an extremely severe economic crisis, though their realization should ultimately depend on people's perception of the degree to which the euro's future is at risk:

H6: During a severe economic crisis, public support for the euro in eurozone countries increases as economic conditions worsen.
H7: During a severe economic crisis, public support for the euro in eurozone countries increases as interest rates increase.
H8: During an economic crisis, public support for the euro in eurozone countries decreases as the euro appreciates against the U.S. dollar.

In the next section, we present the data and methodology used to test the hypotheses developed above as well as the results of this test.

Data, Methods and Results

To examine public support for monetary integration in the eurozone, we rely on data from the Eurobarometer (EB), which is conducted twice a year on behalf of the European Commission, surveying citizens in all the member states with respect to their opinions on European matters. We aggregate responses to a question about whether one was for or against a "European Monetary Union with one single currency, the EURO" for each of the seventeen eurozone member states for the period from the introduction of the euro in 1999 to 2011. To differentiate between the pre-crisis and crisis period, we divide the dataset into two periods: (1) from 1999 to spring of

2008 (pre-crisis) and (2) from autumn 2008 to late 2011 (crisis). This division reflects the fact that the global financial crisis reached its apex in the fall of 2008 with the failure of Lehman Brothers, a major U.S. investment bank, and the ensuing freeze in credit markets worldwide. This dramatic situation led to the first-ever meeting of the leaders of G20 countries in Washington in November 2008 in order to coordinate an international response to the crisis. Thus it seems reasonable to assume that the general public became aware of the crisis only in the fall of 2008, even if financial market difficulties had begun more than one year earlier (see European Commission 2009).

In order to explain the changes and differences in euro support and test our hypotheses, we rely on a number of indicators. The level of diffuse EU support is operationalized as the proportion of respondents who say that "EU membership is a good thing" in each country, using EB data. We also include a number of economic indicators in our model. We include the exchange rate between the U.S. dollar and the euro. Because it reflects the central bank's ability to conduct monetary policy effectively (i.e., to keep prices relatively stable), the inflation rate is one of the economic measures included the analysis. Other economic indicators are the unemployment rate, the short-term interest rate, and the GDP growth rate. Finally, a consumer confidence index serves to measure subjective economic expectations; it gauges consumers' feelings about the current condition of the economy and their expectations about the economy's future direction. Details on data and data sources appear in Appendix 1 to this chapter.

To test the hypotheses concerning support for the euro, we pool the biannual data for the seventeen countries across the period 1999–2011, splitting the sample into pre-crisis (1999–2008) and crisis (2008–2011) periods.[4] Both the temporal and the spatial properties of this time-series cross-sectional (TSCS) dataset make ordinary least squares problematic (Beck 2001; Beck and Katz 1995; Plümper et al. 2005). In particular, models for TSCS data often allow temporally and spatially correlated errors as well as for panel heteroskedasticity. To address the serial correlation of the errors in the TSCS framework, we follow the standard practice of transforming the data (Beck and Katz 1995). We use the Prais-Winsten transformation, which assumes that there is a first-order autocorrelation process, AR(1), and that the coefficient of the autocorrelation process is common to every panel (Greene 1993: 456).[5] We also follow Beck and Katz's recommendation (1995, 1996) of using panel-corrected standard errors (PCSE) to calculate the standard errors. Although in some cases introducing a lagged dependent variable is appropriate to account for the autocorrelation process, the number of observations for each country (*t*) is sufficiently small to warrant excluding it from our models (Achen 2000). Moreover, Achen (2000) and Plümper et al. (2005) show that a lagged dependent variable can introduce biases. We also test for unit (country) heterogeneity, and the *F*-test indicates that the slopes were homogeneous across the cross-sectional units, but we detect the presence of significant heterogeneity among the units' intercepts. As a result, we estimate a fixed-effects model that assumes a separate intercept for each of the countries (Beck 2001).

To test our hypotheses, we estimate the effect of our predictors on euro support before and during the crisis in two separate models, with and without general "support of the EU" as an independent variable (Table 5.1). Unsurprisingly, general EU support is highly correlated with euro support. But we know that economic conditions also shape individuals' general support for the EU, and hence by controlling for general EU support we remove the impact of the economy on euro support that is mediated through general EU attitudes. We would thus expect much weaker effects of the economy on euro support controlling for diffuse EU support. We therefore show results both with (Model 2) and without (Model 1) EU support as a control variable.

Starting with the pre-crisis period (1999–2008), we find the results in Table 5.1 are generally in line with our hypotheses. As expected, a higher level of consumer confidence leads to a higher level of support for the euro in both models. Also, the strength of the euro vis-à-vis the dollar is positively associated with euro support. As expected, higher interest rates are strongly associated with a decrease in popular support for the euro. Equally, higher unemployment has a negative effect on support and growth as a positive effect in Model 1, as expected. When we control for EU support, the effects of growth and unemployment become insignificant, but this may be because these factors shape EU support directly, and their effect on euro support is therefore mediated through EU membership support. The only surprising result is that inflation has a positive and significant effect on euro support (in Model 1). Interestingly, Banducci et al. (2009) find no effect of the actual inflation rate on euro support within the eurozone in their aggregate-level analysis; however, in their individual-level analysis they find that a subjective belief that prices (or inflation) are high leads to low support for the euro. Survey evidence also shows considerable ambivalence among citizens about changes in price levels, which suggest that inflation rates may not have the expected impact because citizens are relatively unaware of actual inflation rates (Banducci et al. 2009). Overall, in terms of hypotheses H1 to H5, the evidence for the pre-crisis period generally points in the expected direction.

Table 5.1 Support for the Euro in the Eurozone Before and During the Crisis (1999–2011).

	Before Crisis				During Crisis			
	Model 1		Model 2		Model 1		Model 2	
	Coef.	PCSE	Coef.	PCSE	Coef.	PCSE	Coef.	PCSE
EU membership a good thing	—	—	0.36***	0.03	—	—	0.36***	0.04
$US-euro exchange rate	6.57***	1.48	7.55***	2.62	−3.01	10.07	−5.86*	2.15
Inflation	0.90**	0.40	0.71	0.47	0.19	0.70	0.20	0.49
Unemployment	−0.25**	0.12	0.07	0.18	−0.06	0.40	−0.12	0.20
Consumer confidence	0.13***	0.04	0.12**	0.04	0.23***	0.09	0.18***	0.05
Growth	0.24*	0.14	0.03	0.18	− 0.80***	0.22	−0.63**	0.27
Interest rates	−2.27***	0.38	−1.78***	0.50	0.32	1.07	0.10	0.25
Constant	69.94***	1.93	47.52***	5.07	79.02***	14.86	63.58***	4.68
N	229		229		96		96	
Countries	15		15		17		17	
R squared	0.67		0.72		0.81		0.78	
Rho	0.77		0.72		0.56		0.40	

Note: The fixed-effects models were estimated using a Prais-Winsten regression, allowing for autocorrelation in the error terms over one period (AR1), and the reported standard errors are panel-corrected (PCSE).

*** $p < 0.01$; ** $p < 0.05$; * $p < 0.1$.

When we focus on the crisis period in Table 5.1, we see that the results differ to some extent from the ones observed for the period before the crisis. First, we find that the effect of the U.S dollar–euro exchange rate is in the opposite direction, whereby public support for the euro in eurozone countries decreases as the euro appreciates against the U.S. dollar during the financial crisis. Second, a decrease in the rate of economic growth is now associated with an increase in support for the single currency. In addition, the fact that the coefficients for inflation and unemployment are no longer statistically significant in any of the models further lends credence to the argument that worsening economic conditions lead to increased support for the euro in the event of a very severe economic crisis. Third, during the crisis period higher interest rates are no longer associated with lower euro support, though they do not lead to increased support. Finally, the effect of consumer confidence on euro support during the crisis is even stronger than in the pre-crisis period. This is in line with the argument that in severe economic conditions the euro and eurozone membership offer a relatively less risky or uncertain economic environment. Overall, the results obtained for the crisis period generally support the alternative hypotheses H6, H7, and H8 that we formulated in the previous section. It is important to note, however, that these results should be interpreted with some caution, given the low number of observations available.

In sum, the time-series cross-section analyses presented in Table 5.1 lend considerable support to our hypotheses and argument about the increased economic insecurity that the threat to the euro's integrity represents for individuals inside the eurozone. As such, they suggest that economic indicators play an important role in explaining variation in public support for the euro, even when controlling for diffuse EU support. However, they also show that the economic calculations concerning the cost and benefits of the euro for citizens in the eurozone appear to have changed radically during the crisis.

Conclusion

As mentioned in the introduction, there was initially a widely held belief that the global financial crisis made the European single currency more popular. Some experts, such as Jones (2009), went so far as to suggest that without the euro, things would have been worse than if the old system of fixed exchange rate prevailed. Events that followed, namely the eurozone debt crisis, have tempered such a positive assessment of the euro as a safe haven. In fact, the euro has been blamed for being the reason behind the debt crisis in the GIIPS countries (Hobolt and Tilley forthcoming). Nevertheless, giving up on the euro would have had far worse consequences than the path chosen by eurozone leaders so far (Leblond 2012). This would explain why we find that support for the euro has remained high and relatively stable inside the eurozone during the crisis and that the EU is generally considered better placed to deal with the crisis.

To shed light on European public opinion on the euro before and during the banking and debt crises, this chapter has investigated the relationship between economic insecurity and public support for the European single currency across seventeen eurozone member states over the period 1999–2012. The conclusion is that economic insecurity negatively affects euro support, but only in "normal" times. When economic conditions are severe, economic insecurity tends instead to favor the euro. This is because the risk of a breakdown of the eurozone creates greater economic insecurity among individuals, as giving up on the euro is likely to make the economic situation worse and even more uncertain than the situation associated with keeping the eurozone intact through bailouts and economic adjustment programs.

This chapter thus expands and refines our understanding of the determinants of public support for the European single currency and considers the effect of the European banking and fiscal crises on those determinants. Although the pre-crisis results differ somewhat from the crisis ones, there is nevertheless a considerable degree of stability in the level of support for the euro inside the eurozone since the onset of the crisis. For those who are worried about the legitimacy of the euro in these difficult and uncertain economic times, the results of our analysis suggest that the choice to save the euro and maintain the eurozone's integrity through bailouts and unorthodox monetary policies has been broadly supported by citizens in the eurozone. As the risk of euro exit and eurozone breakup recedes, as a result of what is gradually proving to be a successfully (if not always efficiently) managed crisis, the economic insecurity conditions that will gradually apply to the euro's public support are likely to be those associated with the pre-crisis period (i.e., those for "normal" times). This transition from exceptional to normal times could mean a period of reduced euro support in the eurozone as fiscal and market reforms continue to be in effect for a prolonged period, which would explain why EU and IMF leaders are now increasingly turning their attention to finding ways to stimulate economic growth. This renewed focus on growth is particularly important as the EU contemplates treaty changes in order to provide a sound legal basis for creating fiscal and banking unions that would correct the EMU's original design flaws.

Appendix: Data Sources and Descriptions

Support for the Euro

Eurobarometer surveys EB51, EB52, EB53, EB54.1, EB55.1, EB56.2, EB57.1, EB59, EB59.1, EB60.1, EB61, EB62, EB63.4, EB64.2, EB65.2, EB66.1, EB67.2, EB68.1, EB69.2, EB70, EB71, EB72, EB73, EB75.3, EB76, EB77, EB78

Support for EU Membership

Eurobarometer surveys: EB51.0, EB52.0, EB53.0, EB54.1, EB55.1, EB56.2, EB57.1, EB61, EB62, EB62.2, EB63.4, EB64.2, EB65.2, EB67.2, EB68.1, EB69.2, EB70, EB71, EB72, EB73, EB75.3, EB76, EB77, EB 78

USD-Euro Exchange Rate

European Central Bank

Inflation

Eurostat: Annual rate of change in Harmonized Index of Consumer Prices (HCIP)

Unemployment

Economist Intelligence Unit, Eurostat, OECD

Consumer Confidence

Eurostat, OECD

Economic Growth

Eurostat, OECD: Quarterly GDP (expenditure approach) growth rate compared to the same quarter of previous year, seasonally adjusted

Interest Rate

Economist Intelligence Unit, Eurostat, IMF (IFS), OECD: monthly average of day-to-day money market rates

Notes

1. Both Denmark and Sweden have remained euro outsiders because of no-votes in referendums.
2. The results shown in Figure 5.1 (and Figure 5.2) do not look different if we also include Cyprus in the GIIPS category, because it received a financial bailout in the winter of 2013.
3. It should be noted, however, that the constraints imposed by the Stability and Growth Pact have been rather weak (e.g., see Heipertz and Verdun 2004, 2010; Leblond 2006), which the current debt crisis in the EU has made only too clear.
4. Data on support for the euro are not available for the entire period for the countries that joined the EU in 2004 and 2007.
5. There are no major differences to the models if we specify a panel-specific autocorrelation structure.

References

Achen, C. H. 2000. "Why lagged dependent variables can suppress the explanatory power of other independent variables." Paper presented at the 2000 Annual Meeting of the Society for Political Methodology, University of California, Los Angeles, July 20–22, 2000.

Banducci, S., J. A. Karp, and P. H. Loedel. 2003. "The euro, economic interests and multi-level governance: Examining support for the common currency." *European Journal of Political Research* 42: 685–703.

Banducci, S., J. A. Karp, and P. H. Loedel. 2009. "Economic interests and public support for the euro." *Journal of European Public Policy* 16(4): 564–581.

Beck, N. 2001. "Time-series cross-section data: What have we learned in the past few years?" *Annual Review of Political Science* 4: 271–293.

Beck, N., and J. N. Katz. 1995. "What to do (and not to do) with time series cross section data." *American Political Science Review* 89: 634–647.

Beck, N., and J. N. Katz. 1996. "Nuisance vs. substance: Specifying and estimating time-series-cross-section models." *Political Analysis* 6: 1–36.

Carey, S. 2002. "Undivided loyalties: Is national identity an obstacle to European integration?" *European Union Politics* 3(4): 387–413.

Cohen, B. J. 1998. *The Geography of Money*. Ithaca, NY: Cornell University Press.

De Grauwe, P. 2011. "Managing a fragile eurozone." *CESifo Forum* 12(2): 40–45.

"The eurocrisis live: Greece faces further delays as euro package reaches parliament." *Guardian*, November 5, 2012.

European Commission. 2009. "Economic crisis in Europe: Causes, consequences and responses." *European Economy*, No. 7, September, Brussels: Directorate-General for Economic and Financial Affairs.

Gabel, M. J. 1998a. *Interest and Integration: Market Liberalization, Public Opinion and European Union*. Ann Arbor: University of Michigan Press.

Gabel, M. J. 1998b. "Public support for European integration: An empirical test of five theories." *Journal of Politics* 60(2): 333–354.

Gabel, M. J. 2001. "Divided opinion, common currency: The political economy of public support for EMU." In B. Eichengreen and J. A. Frieden (eds.), *The political economy of European monetary unification*, 2nd ed. Boulder, CO: Westview Press.

Gabel, M. J., and S. Hix. 2005. "Understanding public support for British membership of the single currency." *Political Studies* 53(1): 65–81.

Gabel, M. J., and H. D. Palmer. 1995. "Understanding variation in public support for European integration." *European Journal of Political Research* 27: 3–19.

Gärtner, M. 1997. "Who wants the euro—and why? Economic explanations of public attitudes towards a single European Currency." *Public Choice* 93(3–4): 487–510.

Greene, William H. 1993. *Econometric Analysis*, 2nd ed. New York: Macmillan.

Heipertz, M., and A. Verdun. 2004. "The dog that would never bite? What we can learn from the origins of the Stability and Growth Pact." *Journal of European Public Policy* 11(5): 765–780.

Heipertz, M., and A. Verdun. 2010. *Ruling Europe: The Politics of the Stability and Growth Pact*. New York: Cambridge University Press.

Helleiner, E. 2003. *The Making of National Money: Territorial Currencies in Historical Perspective*. Ithaca, NY: Cornell University Press.

Hobolt, S. B., and P. Leblond. 2009. "Is my crown better than your euro? Exchange rates and public opinion on the European single currency." *European Union Politics*, 10(2): 209–232.

Hobolt, S. B., and J. Tilley. Forthcoming. *Blaming Europe? Responsibility Without Accountability in the European Union*. Oxford: Oxford University Press, forthcoming 2014.

Hooghe, L., and G. Marks. 2004. "Does identity or economic rationality drive public opinion on European integration?" *PS: Political Science and Politics* 37: 415–420.

Jones, E. 2009. "The euro and the financial crisis." *Survival* 51(2): 41–54.

Jupille, J., and D. Leblang. 2007. "Voting for change: Calculation, community, and Euro referendums." *International Organization* 61(4): 763–782.

Kaltenthaler, K. C., and C. J. Anderson. 2001. "Europeans and their money: Explaining public support for the common European currency." *European Journal of Political Research* 40(2): 139–170.

Leblond, P. 2006. "The political stability and growth pact is dead: Long live the economic stability and growth pact." *Journal of Common Market Studies* 44(5): 969–990.

Leblond, P. 2012. "One for all and all for one: The global financial crisis and the European integration project." In L. Fioramonti (ed.), *Regions and Crises: New Challenges for Contemporary Regionalisms*, 50–66. New York: Palgrave Macmillan.

McLaren, L. 2002. "Public support for the European Union: Cost/benefit analysis or perceived cultural threat?" *Journal of Politics* 64(12): 551–566.

McLaren, L. 2004. "Opposition to European integration and fear of low of national identity: Debunking a basic assumption regarding hostility to the integration project." *European Journal of Political Research* 43: 895–911.

McLaren, L. 2006. *Identity, Interests and Attitudes to European Integration*. Basingstoke: Palgrave Macmillan.

"Merkel warns against Greek default, euro exit." Reuters UK edition, September 13, 2001.

Plümper, T., V. Troeger, and P. Manow. 2005. "Panel data analysis in comparative politics: Linking method to theory." *European Journal of Political Research* 44(2): 327–354.

Rose, A. K., and T. D. Stanley. 2005. "A meta-analysis of the effect of common currencies on international trade." *Journal of Economic Surveys* 19(3): 347–365.

"Trouble at the polls." *Economist*, June 13, 2009, 15 (U.S. edition).

6

Attitudes Toward Immigration in Good Times and Bad

Rafaela Dancygier and Michael Donnelly

IMMIGRATION IS A hotly contested issue across Europe, the United States, and beyond. The large and continuing inflow of migrant newcomers has changed the face of neighborhoods, cities, and countries. In doing so, immigration has at times stirred up conflict and controversy as native citizens and politicians grapple with the implications of immigration and the ethnic diversity it produces. How has the Great Recession influenced the publics' views about immigration? Has the deteriorating economic climate generated an economic backlash against immigration? Has anger over the economic effects of immigrants spilled over into xenophobic attitudes?

A large body of research has established strong links between individuals' positions on immigration and the social and cultural threats that immigrants are perceived to represent. Culturally, ethnically, and linguistically distinct newcomers may undermine the sense of security and belonging of the native citizenry. Such identity threats may turn natives against immigrants.[1] Other research has focused on the economic factors that drive opposition against immigration. Competition in the labor market and the struggle over scarce material goods may pit migrant settlers against native publics.[2] These resource threats, rather than cultural concerns, in turn provoke a backlash among those who are most directly exposed to the potential economic costs of immigration. Lastly, some have argued that the cultural and economic threats generated by immigration are in fact closely linked. As Kriesi and colleagues (2008) argue, individuals who face economic insecurity due to the processes unleashed by globalization are especially susceptible to ethnocentrist, anti-immigrant appeals. In the wake of the financial collapse,

UNESCO predicted that xenophobia would rise, saying "All previous crises of the 1900s, including the Great Depression... affected migration in distinct ways and spurred resentment of foreigners and xenophobic actions" (Global Migration Group 2009).[3] Other analysts suggested that the Great Recession would lead to an increase in support for the anti-immigrant far right (Jones and Genugten 2009).

In this chapter, we argue that economic shocks—such as those set in motion by the worldwide financial crisis—raise the salience of the economic costs of the international flow of labor and thereby provoke hostility against immigration. It is during economically bleak times that the potential economic threats posed by immigration come to the fore. To demonstrate this relationship, we investigate Europeans' views about immigration before and during the crisis, and we do so by focusing on natives' exposure to immigrants in their industries of employment.

The economic crisis not only put the spotlight on aggregate macroeconomic indicators such as unemployment rates and GDP growth. It also led policy makers and publics to examine developments at the industry level, specifically to question the economic benefits of immigration in certain sectors during a time when job prospects for natives were drying up. Indeed, many of the sectors that experienced particularly steep declines, such as construction and manufacturing, have been important destinations for immigrant workers (OECD 2009).

Our analyses show that individuals are more likely to evaluate immigration in a negative light as the share of immigrants employed in their industry rises. However, this pattern is apparent only when public confidence in the economy is low, as it was during the Great Recession. Working in industries that hire large numbers of migrants when pessimism about the state of the economy runs high and job opportunities contract causes natives to doubt the merits of immigration. Yet when European publics are more confident about their countries' economic prospects, being surrounded by immigrant co-workers in their industries has little effect on natives' assessments of immigration. That sectoral exposure to immigrants is associated with restrictionist attitudes when confidence in the economy plummets suggests that natives are more likely to perceive economic competition with migrants when they are primed to pay attention to their countries' and industries' economic decline.

Although we find that the larger economic environment interacts with sectoral patterns to shape evaluations about immigration, it is not the case that industry-level exposure to immigrants has systematic effects on people's views about immigration's cultural impact. Though individuals may feel a heightened sense of economic vulnerability during the crisis, being exposed to immigrant co-workers in their sector does not appear to influence how natives feel about the cultural ramifications of immigration. Thus, in Europe, predictions of extreme increases in xenophobia are not borne out in survey data.

Instead, most natives seem to differentiate between the economic threat of labor market competition and the distinct question of how culturally threatening migration is. Though we do not dispute that cultural concerns matter in the production of anti-immigrant sentiment, the evidence presented in this chapter demonstrates that while the broader economic context decisively influences how exposure to immigration at the workplace affects evaluations about immigration, it does not lead to noticeable changes in the stabler patterns of perceptions of cultural threat. The Great Recession has thus significantly shaped individual responses to immigration. Despite small changes in average attitudes toward immigration, the last few years have seen sharp changes in the relationship between sectoral conditions and attitudes, suggesting that as the crisis deepens, we may see sectoral and economic concerns play a larger role in the politics of immigration.

We proceed by first discussing how the economic crisis may influence opinions about immigration, paying particular attention to developments at the industry level. We next present the opinion and sectoral data we use, and then display and discuss the results of statistical models based on that data. In addition to examining the political implications of sectoral exposure to immigration in varying economic times, we investigate whether the economic crisis has affected how individuals who are typically characterized as "globalization losers"—the less-skilled, older workers, and men—feel about immigration.[4] The chapter concludes with thoughts about the broader political implications of our findings for attitudes and public policy toward immigration.

Sectoral Exposure to Immigrants in Times of Crisis

The sharp drop in economic activity associated with the global economic crisis put pressure on politicians to devise job-saving measures; many of whom responded by restricting employment opportunities for immigrants. Soon after the crisis hit, governments across Europe began to consider policies that would reduce the inflow of immigrants. On September 8, 2008, two British MPs announced the formation of the Cross-Party Group on Immigration (Balanced Migration 2008a). A week later the group released a statement arguing that because immigration continued despite rising unemployment, the government should develop a policy aimed at reducing net migration to zero. Though Gordon Brown's government resisted these calls (despite the fact that many Labour back-benchers were sympathetic), the new coalition has moved to limit immigration sharply. The policies they have proposed include a targeted effort to restrict immigrant employment in sectors such as hotels and restaurants (BBC News 2011) complementing a larger effort to reduce the number of non-EU immigrants to a much lower level.[5]

Similar arguments played out in Spain, where, in 2008, the Socialist government implemented a "pay-to-go" scheme in which migrants were offered cash payments to leave the country (Plewa 2009).[6] Indeed, across Europe, governments promoted the voluntary return of migrants (OECD 2011a). Such actions are reminiscent of (largely unsuccessful) measures enacted in the 1970s, when governments offered cash incentives to make return migration more attractive in the face of economic downturns. In some countries, such as in Germany, return policies specifically targeted declining industries (e.g., mining and steel) that had employed high numbers of immigrants (Dancygier 2010).

Are these policies driven by public demands? Are natives who work in industries that employ immigrants more likely to view immigration in a negative light? If so, are these negative assessments more pronounced during the economic crisis? Previous work has shown that economic evaluations matter in shaping preferences over immigration, though little work thus far has focused specifically on the role of industries.[7] Citrin and colleagues (1997), for instance, have shown that pessimism about the state of the economy leads Americans to endorse restrictive immigration policies. More recently, in a comparison of two North Carolina counties that differ in the size of their migrant populations, O'Neil and Tienda (2010) have found that U.S. natives who feel economically insecure are more likely to perceive immigration as a problem, but this effect is at work only where immigrants are present locally. Opposition to immigration is thus conditional on how economic insecurity interacts with local immigration contexts. In a similar vein, we argue that when public confidence in the economy ebbs, as it did during the crisis, exposure to immigrants in one's sector of employment is associated with restrictionist attitudes.

Why the Economic Crisis Triggers Hostility

Economic theory indeed suggests that natives who are exposed to immigrant workers at the industry level will suffer wage losses owing to immigration.

According to the specific-factors model, as immigrants enter a sector natives who possess skills similar to those of incoming migrant labor will see their wages decline. One important assumption underlying this model is that movement across sectors is associated with some costs.[8] For example, a worker employed in the food processing industry cannot easily switch to a job in the retail trade, even if the two jobs require the same level of skills.

This assumption is particularly relevant during economic downturns. When the economy contracts, native workers have fewer outside options and may feel locked into their sectors. Moreover, given the geographic clustering of many industries, changing jobs across industries may require costly relocation. Especially in the context of the global economic crisis, which was in large part fueled by the collapse of the housing market, such relocation likely represents a substantial financial burden. Lastly, entering a new sector may be associated with nonmonetary costs, such as anxiety and stress (Lee and Wolpin 2006), particularly during times of economic uncertainty. In light of these heightened costs to intersectoral mobility during economic downturns, we hypothesize that exposure to immigrants at the industry level provokes negative responses to immigration when economic conditions deteriorate.

Moreover, we argue that sectoral exposure to immigrants matters in shaping opinions about immigration during the crisis because the crisis provided natives with salient economic frames. Although the public debate about immigration has taken a cultural turn in many European countries, the global economic downturn served to highlight immigration's costs to domestic economies. The crisis thus helped frame immigration as a primarily economic issue. As Kinder (1998, 172) notes on the importance of framing, "how citizens understand an issue—which features of it are central and which are peripheral—is reflected in how the issue is framed."[9] Economic framing, we argue, leads to a tighter association between economic interests and attitudes toward immigration.

Even though natives may sustain wage losses because of the inflow of immigrants into their industries when economies are expanding, they may lack the relevant information and cognitive frameworks to connect these two phenomena. Additionally, in prosperous times natives may simply pay less attention to their own economic situation and to how the immigrant presence may or may not affect their economic welfare. During the crisis, however, policy makers highlighted immigration as an issue that hurt native workers and domestic economies as a whole. In Italy, for example, the government statistics agency publicly pinned the blame for the country's increasing unemployment rate on immigrants (Papademetriou, Sumption, and Somerville 2009). In neighboring Switzerland, high-ranking officials called on businesses to give preferential treatment to native workers when making hiring decisions.[10]

For these reasons, we argue that native workers who are employed in industries that hire substantial numbers of immigrant workers will be more likely to perceive their migrant co-workers as unwelcome competitors when economic prospects are bleak, and they will express negative views about immigration as a result. By contrast, industry-level exposure should not shape opinions about the economic merits of immigrants when economies are doing better, and it should not influence how natives evaluate immigration's cultural impact.

Data

The economic crisis could have been a massive shock to immigration attitudes, but a cursory examination of such attitudes suggests that its effects are mixed. To see this, we examine attitudes using data from all five rounds of the European Social Survey (ESS). The most obvious place to look for the effects of the crisis is in responses to two questions:

> Would you say it is generally bad or good for [country]'s economy that people come to live here from other countries?
> (W)ould you say that [country]'s cultural life is generally undermined or enriched by people coming to live here from other countries?

These questions distinguish, to the extent possible, between cultural and economic concerns. Figure 6.1 shows that during the crisis (beginning with round 4 of the ESS)[11] there is not a sharp change in beliefs about the *economic impact* of immigration in most countries. This is true regardless of the depth of the economic downturn they experienced, as measured by change in GDP from 2008 to 2010.[12] Similarly, Figure 6.2 shows that the crisis appears to have no effect on average beliefs about the *cultural impact* of immigration.

Figure 6.3 displays the average support on a four-point scale for open immigration policies toward poor immigrants. The fieldwork for rounds 4 and 5 took place during the financial crisis, and yet the average support for immigration does not sharply deviate from previous rounds. Similarly, Figure 6.4 shows there is no sharp deviation when the relevant immigrant

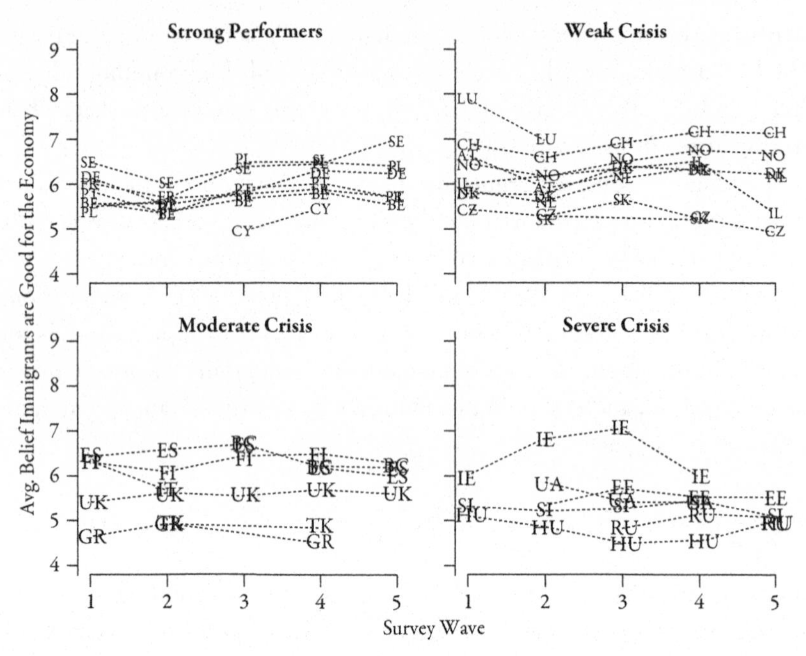

FIGURE 6.1 The Economic Impact of Immigration.

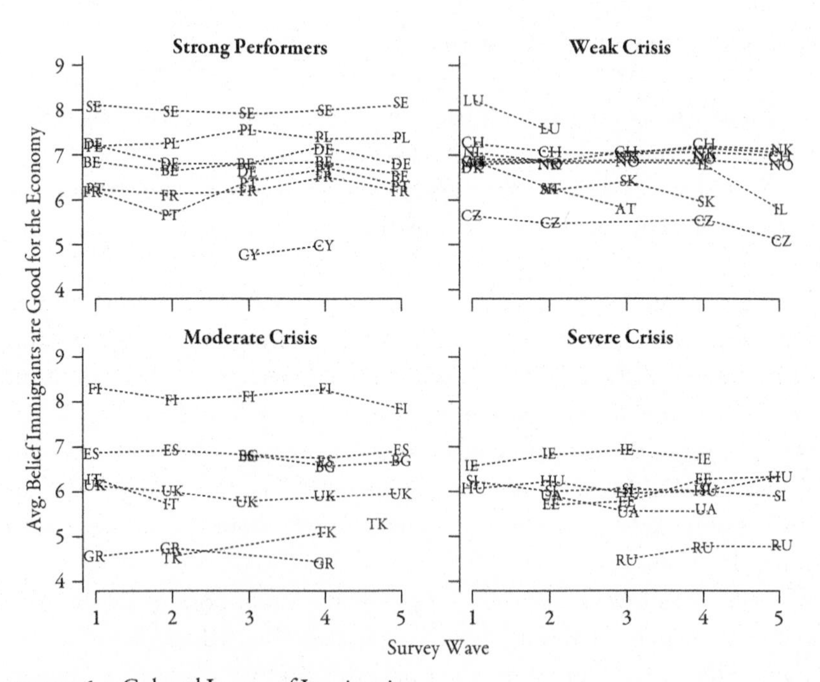

FIGURE 6.2 Cultural Impact of Immigration.

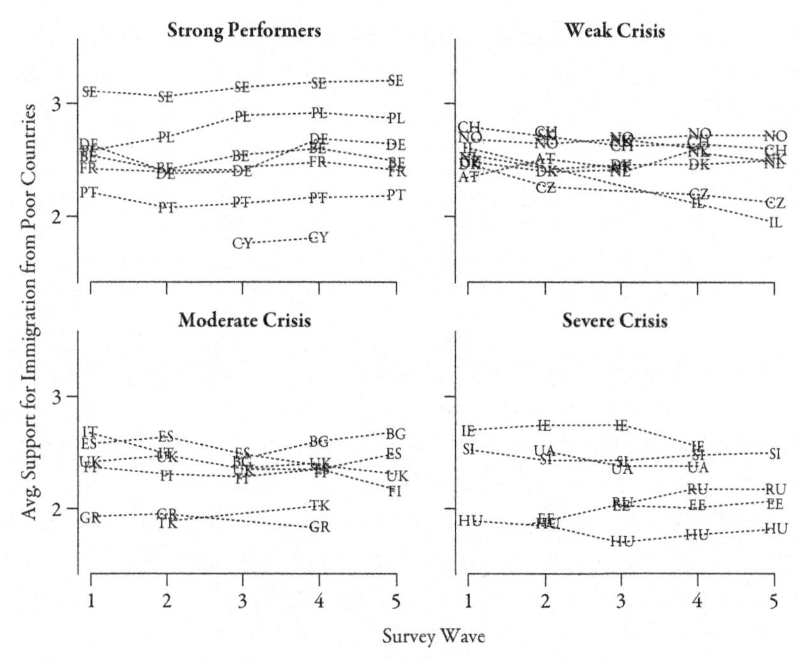

FIGURE 6.3 Immigration from Poorer Countries.

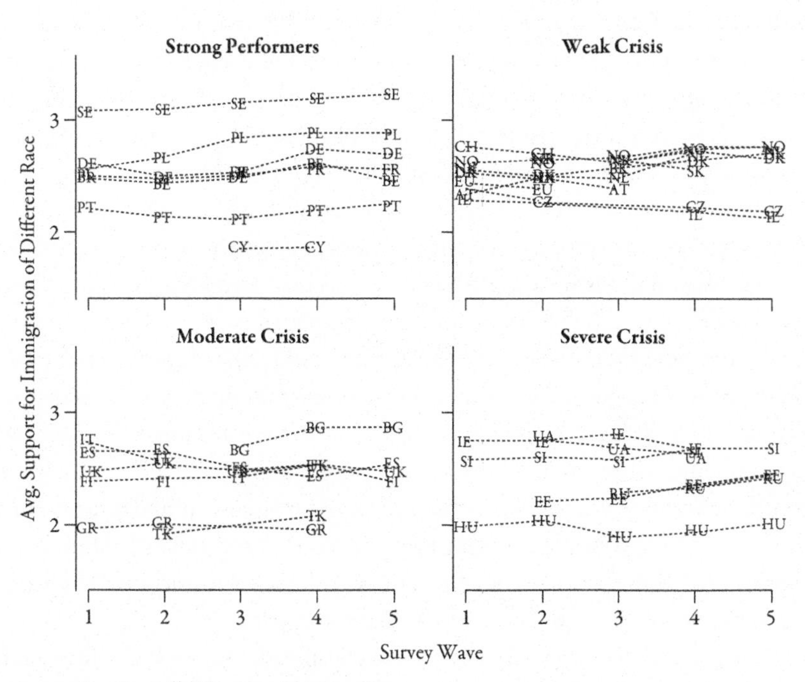

FIGURE 6.4 Racially Distinct Immigration.

group is ethnically or racially distinct from natives. To measure attitudes toward immigrants of specific sorts, the ESS asks respondents these questions:

> Now, using this card, to what extent do you think [country] should allow people... to come and live here?
> How about people from the poorer countries outside Europe?
> How about people of a different race or ethnic group from most [country] people?

After each question, respondents were given a card containing the options (1) "Allow many to come and live here," (2) "Allow some," (3) "Allow a few," and (4) "Allow none." Differences on policy questions can be interpreted as functions of both economic and cultural factors, but we believe that by including the word *poorer* the third question best taps the economic dimension, while the fourth best taps cultural attitudes. Together, the aggregate data tell a mixed story: the impact of the crisis on immigration attitudes varies across countries, across time, and across the type of immigration attitude under consideration.

The overall distribution of attitudes depicted in these figures does not suggest that the crisis represents a major turning point with respect to immigration opinions among the public at large. However, the effects of the crisis may be disguised by aggregating across groups with different reactions. Do these overall patterns hold when we investigate groups of natives who may be particularly exposed to immigrants?

The downturn may change what kinds of economic groups support open immigration policies. In order to test this possibility, we examine two measures of economic interest on the basis of sectors. Since our theory proposes that sector-level forces interact with national forces to shape attitudes, we require a sectoral classification scheme that is consistent across countries and over time. Using the definitions of sector provided by the Classification of Economic Activities in the European Union (NACE), we constructed a categorization of economic sectors that harmonizes two-digit codes from across two revisions (Rev. 1.1 and Rev. 2). NACE codes are a standard measure of sectoral employment across Europe, but since the revisions differ, obtaining accurate measures of changes within sectors over time required a new set of thirty-one sector codes, accounting for approximately 98 percent of European employees.[13] These sectors range from the very large ("Education" or "Health and social services") to the very small ("Air transportation").

Next, using data from Eurostat, we estimated, for each country-year, the proportion of employees in each sector who were born in the relevant country, born in the EU, or born outside the EU, as well as the total number of employees. Immigrant Proportion, which uses only non-EU migrants, allows us to measure the extent to which natives working in that sector are exposed to competition with migrants who are likely to be ethnically distinct and to accept lower wages for similar work. It varies widely across sectors, countries, and time. Table 6.1 gives some examples, and Figure 6.5 shows the distribution of Immigrant Proportion. The high bar on the left shows that about 20 percent of our sample works in a sector where the proportion of employees born outside the current EU is less than 1 percent. A large number of individuals work in sectors with 1 to 10 percent, and a tiny number work in sectors beyond 15 percent.[14]

Given this distribution, most European natives are not likely to encounter immigrants at the workplace. It makes sense, therefore, that aggregate opinions about immigration do not appear to be too sensitive to the recession. By the same token, in industries where foreign-born labor tends to concentrate we might expect bad economic times to influence how native workers feel about additional immigrant co-workers. Indeed, after the onset of the crisis, many sectors continued to add large numbers of immigrants, despite shedding jobs overall, as immigrants replaced natives.[15] For instance, in 2008 in

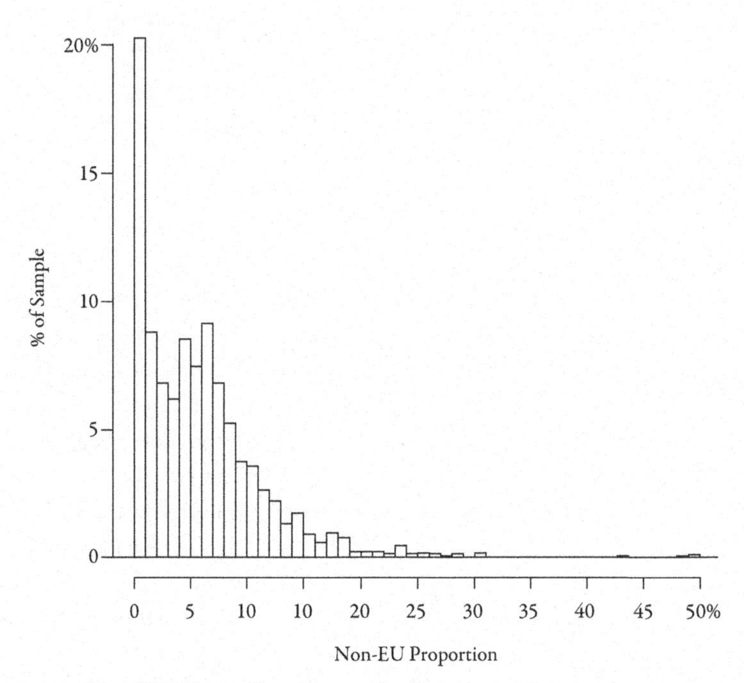

FIGURE 6.5 Non-EU Migrant Employment by Sector.

Table 6.1 Distribution of Non-EU Immigrants Across Industries (2002–2008).

	Non-EU Immigrants in Employment (%)	Major Industries with the Smallest Shares of Non-EU Employees (%)	Major Industries with the Largest Shares of Non-EU Employees (%)
Austria	11.0	Agriculture/fishing/logging (1. 9)	Construction (14.6) Accommodation and food (22.2) Other business (13.7)
Belgium	5.9	—	Retail (5.5) Other business (7.3) Accommodation and food (15.6) Food manufacturing (6.7)
Bulgaria	0.0	—	—
Cyprus	11.2	—	Construction (15.8) Accommodation and food (16.6) Agriculture/fishing/logging (11.4) Household goods and services (94.5)
Czech Republic	0.0	—	—
Denmark	0.0	—	—
Estonia	14.7	—	Land transportation (21.0)
Finland	0.0	—	—
France	7.9	Agriculture/fishing/logging (2.7) Food manufacturing (4.6)	Construction (9.1) Other business (11.0) Accommodation and food (14.9) Household goods and services (11.2)
Greece	7.2	Public administration (0.7)	Construction (26.5) Accommodation and food (10.4) Manufacturing, consumer goods (10.67) Food manufacturing (8.2) Manufacturing, natural resources (8.5)

Table 6.1 (Continued)

	Non-EU Immigrants in Employment (%)	Major Industries with the Smallest Shares of Non-EU Employees (%)	Major Industries with the Largest Shares of Non-EU Employees (%)
Hungary	0.0	—	—
Ireland	3.3	—	Health and social services (6.2) Other business (3.8) Accommodation and food (11.0) Food manufacturing (5.7)
Italy	0.0	—	—
Luxembourg	5.5	—	Construction (6.5) Other business (8.2) Accommodation and food (16.8)
Netherlands	8.8	Agriculture/fishing/logging (3.8)	Other business (11.2) Manufacturing, consumer goods (10.5) Accommodation and food (14.3) Manufacturing, natural resources (10.6)
Poland	0.0	—	—
Portugal	0.1	—	—
Norway	4.3	Agriculture/fishing/logging (0.3)	Health and social services (5.2) Other business (4.9) Accommodation and food (14.8) Land transportation (6.5) Food manufacturing (6.4)
Slovenia	0.1	—	—
Slovakia	0.0	—	—

(*Continued*)

Table 6.1 (Continued)

	Non-EU Immigrants in Employment (%)	Major Industries with the Smallest Shares of Non-EU Employees (%)	Major Industries with the Largest Shares of Non-EU Employees (%)
Spain	10.3	Public administration (1.59)	Construction (16.0) Accommodation and food (20.7) Agriculture/fishing/logging (11.9) Household goods and services (43.1) Food manufacturing (9.4)
Sweden	8.3	Agriculture/fishing/logging (1.4)	Health and social services (8.9) Other business (8.6) Accommodation and food (23.9) Land transportation (10.6)
Switzerland	11.6	Public administration (6.4) Agriculture/fishing/logging (2.3)	Construction (13.8) Accommodation and food (24.7) Manufacturing, natural resources (16.4)
UK	7.5	Construction (3.6)	Health and social services (9.7) Accommodation and food (14.6) Land transportation (9.7)

Note: "Non-EU Immigrants in Employment (%)" measures the percentage of the employed labor force in a given country that is born outside of the European Union. "Major Industries with the Smallest (Largest) Shares of Non-EU Employees" include industries with more than 2% of total employment that are in the bottom (top) quintile with respect to their share of non-EU employees, with measures of the percentage of non-EU employees in these sectors. All measures are based on annual figures, averaged over the period 2002 to 2008.

the United Kingdom, employment in accommodation and food declined by more than 1.5 percent, while the number of immigrants increased by a similar magnitude. Together, these changes increased the proportion of employees in the sector born outside the EU from 15 to more than 17 percent. The replacement of natives by immigrants during times of economic crisis and uncertainty—when employers need to cut costs and workers are especially concerned about job security—might well produce support for tighter immigration restrictions among native workers.

In the analyses below, we use a dichotomized variable, Sector Growth, which is coded 1 for sectors that have more total employees than they did the previous year and 0 otherwise. Here, we provide some detail on the distribution of growth across time. Figure 6.6[16] shows the evolution of sectoral employment growth before and during the crisis. The arrival of the crisis led to a sharp downturn in employment, as the average respondent was employed in a sector that shrank by 1 percent (2008) to 2.5 percent (2009) per year. This collapse in employment was mirrored by a rise in unemployment at the EU level, which moved from 6.7 percent in early 2008 to 9.6 percent in 2010 (OECD 2011b). This upheaval was widely covered in the media, and such macro-level economic outcomes shaped how individuals thought about politics and society (Anderson and Hecht, Chapter 2 of this volume). Midrange measures of economic problems may be less likely to enjoy coverage in the mass media, but they are also more observable to individuals in their daily lives. A worker employed in the construction sector in Spain in 2009 would certainly recognize when that sector lost 24 percent of its jobs compared to

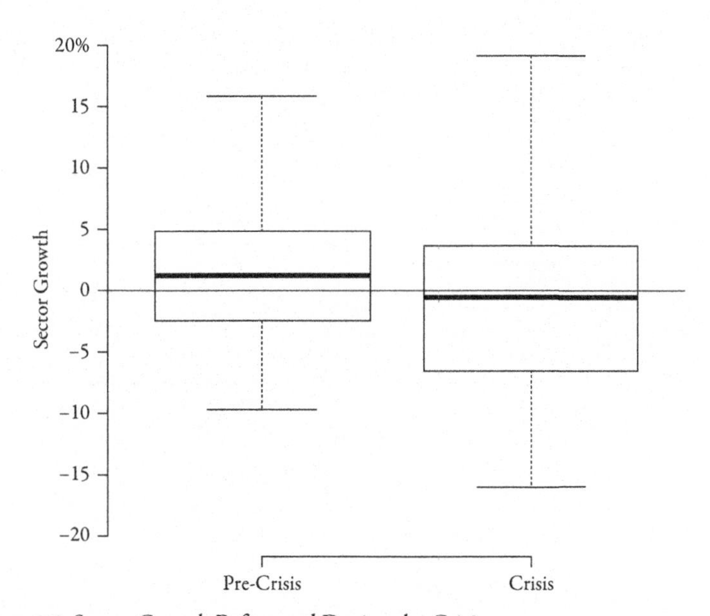

FIGURE 6.6 Sector Growth Before and During the Crisis.

the previous year.[17] Such a decline is likely to be highly salient, since it may well include an individual's own firm and almost certainly includes similar firms that are subject to the same kinds of economic forces.

Estimating the effects of the crisis on the relationship between sectoral and attitudinal variables requires a measure of the crisis. We use two variables to measure this effect. First, we subset the data by economic Outlook, which allows us to compare across countries and time and consists of a national average response to a question about the "expected change in the general economic situation over the next 12 months" (OECD 2011c). We take this variable, which is measured every month and harmonized across countries by Eurostat,[18] as an indicator of the macro-level economic climate, and we divide the sample into high- and low-confidence country-months on the basis of the sample median.[19] It fits our theory better than more objective measures of economic performance, such as the unemployment rate, because perceptions of future economic performance are closely related to beliefs about intersectoral mobility.

Second, we also examine the impact of changes in the unemployment rate (OECD 2011b). This is measured as the annual change in the OECD Harmonized Unemployment Rate. Figures 6.7 and 6.8 display the distribution of Outlook and Unemployment Rate Increase for our sample before and during the crisis. Clearly, the crisis had begun by the time these respondents

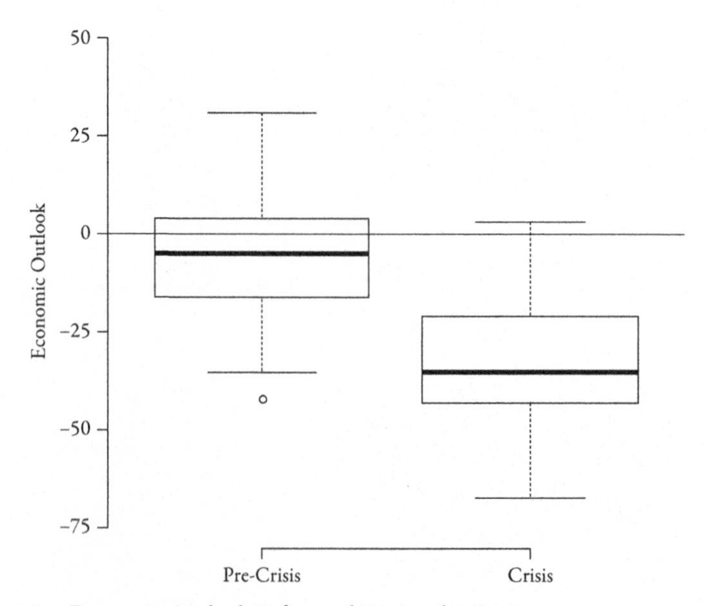

FIGURE 6.7 Economic Outlook Before and During the Crisis.

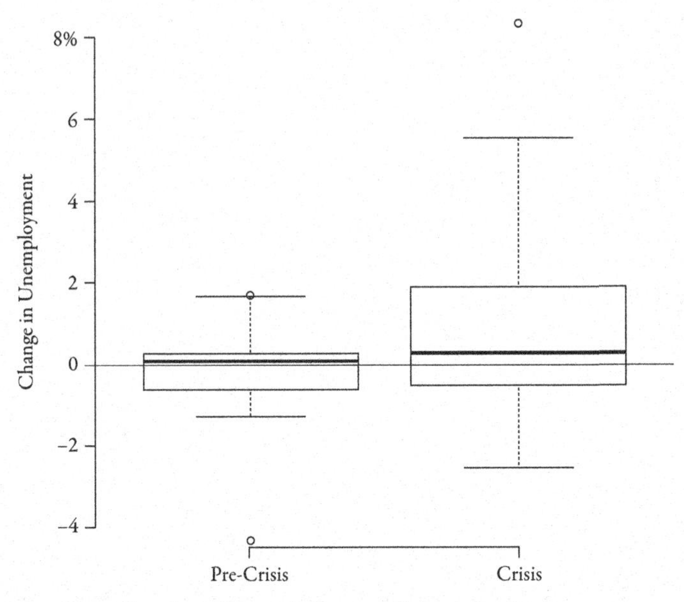

FIGURE 6.8 Unemployment Change Before and During the Crisis.

were sampled. Although the depth and length of the crisis had not yet become clear, both our subjective and objective measures of the crisis suggest rough economic times ahead.

Our analysis of immigration opinions focuses on these sectoral and macroeconomic variables, but we also include a number of additional control variables, among them age, gender, and union membership at the individual level and percentage foreign-born, social security spending, and GDP per capita at the country-year level. Table 6.2 displays descriptive statistics for these variables in our sample, which excludes individuals with no sectoral data and those who are retired. We control for education because it may be related both to sectoral economic variables and to attitudes. This is particularly problematic for us if education's effect on attitudes is primarily ideational, rather than based on skill-driven economic interests (see Hainmueller and Hiscox 2007). Similarly, Age and gender (Male) may be related to attitudes about immigration and to economic interests. Our data indicate that the less-educated, older people, and males tend to work in declining sectors. These groups of workers have also often been found to hold ethnocentrist views and to oppose immigration for cultural reasons. Without controlling for these demographic characteristics, any relationship we found between sectoral growth and attitudes toward immigrants might therefore be driven by these underlying differences. By the same token, we are interested in testing

Table 6.2 Descriptive Statistics.

Variable	N Obs.	Unit	Description	Mean	Std. Dev.	Source
Sectoral Immigrant Proportion	84,643	Proportion	Proportion of non-EU workers in a sector's workforce	0.06	0.05	OECD (2009)
SectorGrowth	85,365	Dichotomous	1 if the number of workers employed in a sector has increased in the last year	0.57	0.50	Author's calculations
Unemployment Rate Increase	86,809	Percentage points	Annual change	0.16	1.33	OECD (2011b)
Education	86,263	Years	Years of formal education	12.81	3.78	ESS
Age	86,516	Years	—	40.97	13.07	ESS
Male	86,791	Dichotomous	—	0.48	0.50	ESS
Union Member	86,523	Dichotomous	Currently in a trade union or similar organization	0.28	0.45	ESS
GDP per Capita	86,809	Thousands of 2000 USD	—	21.82	10.98	OECD (2011b)
Percentage Foreign Born	86,809	Percentage	Percentage of a country's population born outside that country	9.59	5.56	United Nations (2011)
Social Benefits (% of GDP)	86,809	Percentage of GDP	Social transfers, including unemployment, pensions, and other direct transfers	14.26	2.71	OECD (2011b)

whether the economic crisis shapes how skill, age, and gender relate to views about immigration after accounting for industry-level growth and exposure to immigration. If the impact of these demographic variables is reduced by controlling for sectoral variables, then we can conclude that the sectoral differences between demographic groups account for part of the apparent group differences.

Lastly, trade union membership may have differential effects on immigration policy preferences depending on the economic climate. Being a union member may be associated with opposition to immigration if union leaders emphasize the importance of restricting the labor supply in order to raise wages. Alternatively, unions may encourage members to take left-leaning political positions or feel solidarity with immigrants, especially during times of economic hardship when the salience of class-based politics may rise.[20]

We control for GDP per Capita (in 2000 U.S. dollars) because richer societies may be more tolerant, and if richer societies also take in more non-EU immigrants or have sectors that are more likely to grow, our results below might be suspect. Similarly, if migrants tend to go to tolerant societies and tolerant societies tend to have growing sectors, we would expect to find more non-EU immigrants in sectors found within tolerant societies. Therefore, we control for the percentage of a society that is born outside the relevant country (Percentage Foreign Born). Finally, a number of scholars have raised the possibility that a major driver of opposition to immigration is a fear that migrants will serve as a drain on the welfare state (Hanson, Scheve, and Slaughter 2007; Facchini and Mayda 2009). If sectoral developments are closely related to welfare state provisions, our results might be biased. Thus we control for the percentage of a country's GDP spent by the government on Social Benefits.

Results

Table 6.3 demonstrates that there is, in fact, a strong relationship between the proportion of employees in a respondent's sector who are born outside the EU and her belief that immigration hurts the economy. The negative and statistically significant coefficient on Immigrant Proportion in Model 2 suggests that, at times of relatively weak economic performance, a change of one standard deviation in Immigrant Proportion is associated with a 0.05 drop on Economic Impact. This is a modest effect, since Economic Impact is measured on an eleven-point scale, but according to this model it is about a third of the effect of one year of education. Given the importance of education to the literature on beliefs about immigration, we consider this a moderate,

Table 6.3 Economic Impact of Immigration.

	(1)	(2)	(3)	(4)
	Positive Outlook	Negative Outlook	Positive Outlook	Negative Outlook
Sector Growth	0.0433	0.0675*	0.0266	0.0531
	(0.0315)	(0.0310)	(0.0285)	(0.0300)
Immigrant Proportion	−0.240	−0.945**	−0.144	−0.930**
	(0.346)	(0.334)	(0.339)	(0.340)
ESS 2	−0.166***	0.035	−0.109	−0.151*
	(0.038)	(0.060)	(0.065)	(0.068)
ESS 3	0.040	0.179*	0.058	−0.206
	(0.039)	(0.080)	(0.118)	(0.106)
ESS 4	−0.179	0.103	0.207	−0.244*
	(0.106)	(0.054)	(0.120)	(0.108)
Years of Education	0.150***	0.139***	0.151***	0.140***
	(0.004)	(0.005)	(0.004)	(0.005)
Age	0.00668***	0.00253*	0.00677***	0.00258*
	(0.00113)	(0.00121)	(0.00113)	(0.00121)
Male	0.298***	0.280***	0.301***	0.279***
	(0.028)	(0.031)	(0.027)	(0.031)
Union Member	0.004	0.089*	0.001	0.083
	(0.029)	(0.043)	(0.028)	(0.043)
Unemployment Rate Increase	—	—	−0.119**	−0.085**
			(0.038)	(0.026)
GDP per Capita (in thousands)	—	—	−0.086	0.126**
			(0.044)	(0.041)
% Foreign Born	—	—	−0.0353	0.0890**
			(0.0284)	(0.0262)
Social Benefits (% of GDP)	—	—	−0.140	−0.009
			(0.036)	(0.027)
Constant	2.934	3.546	8.161	−0.499
	(0.136)	(0.143)	(1.747)	(1.290)
Country Fixed Effects	Yes	Yes	Yes	Yes
N	43,595	37,058	43,595	37,058

* $p < 0.05$, ** $p < 0.01$, *** $p < 0.001$.

Note: OLS coefficients with robust standard errors, clustered on country-sector, in parentheses.

but important, effect. Model 1 shows that the same effect does not appear among individuals living in better economic climates. This difference is statistically insignificant at conventional levels (p-value.11)[21] but consistent with our expectations. We argued that when the economic Outlook is positive, respondents have good outside options and should not feel pressure from immigrants. This suggests that the Great Recession has led some European citizens—particularly those in high-immigrant sectors—to believe that immigrants are bad for the economy.

A similar pattern appears with Sector Growth, which is clearly related to beliefs about the impact of immigration when the overall economic climate is bad, but less clearly related under better conditions.[22] When the economy is suffering, being in a sector that is growing leads individuals to evaluate the effect of immigration more positively by about half the effect of a year of education. On the other hand, we cannot be as confident that there is a strong association between Sector Growth and beliefs about immigration when the economy is doing well.

Models 3 and 4 show that these patterns hold even when we control for four country-level variables that we might expect to be related to both sectoral economic conditions and beliefs about immigration. The addition of the controls only makes the comparisons already mentioned stronger. The effect of Immigrant Proportion in Model 3 is statistically different from its effect in Model 4 (p-value .08), reinforcing our argument that the economic climate matters for the relationship between meso-level economic variables and beliefs about immigration. It seems, then, that sectoral concerns shape attitudes about immigration, and that this effect is clearest during a downturn.

The coefficient on Unemployment Rate Increase suggests that even for individuals in sectors whose employment growth has stayed constant, the economic crisis is likely to make individuals less likely to believe that immigration is good for the economy. In the United Kingdom, for example, the unemployment rate increased from 5.1 percent to 7.5 percent in the year leading up to April 2008. The predicted change in beliefs about the Economic Impact of immigration associated with the onset of the crisis, then, is about three-tenths of a point on the eleven-point scale. Though this difference is dwarfed by some of the cross-national differences displayed in Figure 6.1, it is about twice the effect of two years of education. We take this to be a large effect and conclude from these estimates that examining macroeconomic changes is crucial to understanding the politics of immigration.

We turn now to Table 6.4, which shows that the same patterns do not appear when the dependent variable is Cultural Impact—the respondent's belief that

Table 6.4 Cultural Impact of Immigration.

	(1)	(2)	(3)	(4)
	Positive Outlook	Negative Outlook	Positive Outlook	Negative Outlook
Sector Growth	0.0375	0.0576	0.0323	0.0455
	(0.0329)	(0.0337)	(0.0324)	(0.0333)
Immigrant	0.220	−0.446	0.230	−0.455
Proportion	(0.342)	(0.348)	(0.341)	(0.350)
ESS 2	−0.138***	−0.017	0.014	−0.019
	(0.035)	(0.062)	(0.060)	(0.071)
ESS 3	−0.208***	0.028	0.075	0.046
	(0.046)	(0.057)	(0.114)	(0.091)
ESS 4	−0.278***	−0.018	0.253*	0.074
	(0.057)	(0.050)	(0.119)	(0.100)
Years of Education	0.152***	0.131***	0.152***	0.132***
	(0.005)	(0.006)	(0.005)	(0.006)
Age	−0.00157	−0.00279*	−0.00147	−0.00282*
	(0.00117)	(0.00135)	(0.00117)	(0.00134)
Male	−0.137***	0.000	−0.136***	−0.000
	(0.031)	(0.031)	(0.031)	(0.031)
Union Member	0.107*	0.116*	0.105**	0.114*
	(0.034)	(0.044)	(0.034)	(0.044)
Unemployment	—	—	−0.088*	−0.118***
Rate Increase			(0.041)	(0.029)
GDP per Capita	—	—	−0.125**	−0.075
(in thousands)			(0.041)	(0.038)
% Foreign Born	—	—	−0.0662*	0.0460
			(0.0311)	(0.0273)
Social Benefits	—	—	−0.0235	0.0181
(% of GDP)			(0.0397)	(0.0263)
Constant	3.505	4.269	7.892	5.135
	(0.129)	(0.153)	(1.618)	(1.140)
Country Fixed Effects	Yes	Yes	Yes	Yes
N	43,890	36,987	43,890	36,987

* $p < 0.05$, ** $p < 0.01$, *** $p < 0.001$

Note: OLS coefficients with robust standard errors, clustered on country-sector, in parentheses.

immigration is beneficial for her country's culture. Across both bad and good economic climates (Models 1 and 2), the coefficient on Immigrant Proportion is insignificant. The coefficient on Sector Growth is significant (p-value .09) in Model 2, but none of the coefficients on Immigrant Proportion attain significance, suggesting that sectoral variables have little effect on cultural attitudes, if any. This is consistent with our argument above that cultural concerns, though important, are not as likely to be activated by economic factors as are more distinctly economic concerns. Note, however, that an increase in the unemployment rate does make respondents more doubtful about the cultural merits of immigration. Views about the cultural desirability of immigrants are thus not impervious to economic trends, but they appear to be less systematically related to changes in economic conditions at the industry level and at the national level than are opinions about immigration's economic impact. In other words, the Great Recession does not appear to have spilled over into xenophobia among those exposed to immigrants in the workplace, despite leading them to fear the economic impact of migration.

Tables 6.5 and 6.6 demonstrate that these effects play out in a similar manner when respondents are asked not to evaluate the effects of immigration but rather to express a policy preference. Presumably, policy preferences are driven by a mix of concerns about a wide range of effects and principles, but we argue that when responding to a question about individuals of a different race or ethnicity, cultural concerns are likely to be predominant, while questions about immigrants from a poor country are likely to also prime concerns about economics. In Model 2 of Table 6.5, we see that when the economy is doing poorly, the coefficient on Sector Growth is marginally statistically significant (p-value .11). This suggests that being in a growing sector has about half the effect of a year of education, though this effect is noisily estimated and is not robust to the inclusion of macro-level controls (Model 4). In Models 1 and 3—estimated on respondents living in economically good times—the effect of Sector Growth is not statistically distinguishable from zero, and the point estimate is much smaller than in Models 2 and 4.

The effect of Immigrant Proportion is statistically significant and quite large in Model 2. Since a standard deviation of Immigrant Proportion in this sample is a little over .055, a change of one standard deviation would have an effect about half the size of the effect of one year of education. In Model 4, this effect is slightly weaker but remains significantly different from zero. In Models 1 and 3, we cannot detect an effect of Immigrant Proportion. This strengthens our case that responses to a question about migrants from poor countries are influenced by economic concerns. Since the extent to which

Table 6.5 Immigration from Poor Countries Outside of Europe.

	(1) Positive Outlook	(2) Negative Outlook	(3) Positive Outlook	(4) Negative Outlook
Sector Growth	0.0152	0.0246	0.0104	0.0296
	(0.0156)	(0.0153)	(0.0153)	(0.0150)
Immigrant Proportion	−0.0363	−0.369*	0.011	−0.324
	(0.176)	(0.171)	(0.173)	(0.170)
ESS 2	−0.053**	0.011	−0.042	−0.012
	(0.018)	(0.024)	(0.030)	(0.027)
ESS 3	−0.070**	−0.086**	−0.064	−0.149***
	(0.019)	(0.029)	(0.054)	(0.042)
ESS 4	−0.088**	−0.028	0.023	−0.080
	(0.028)	(0.022)	(0.060)	(0.041)
Years of Education	0.0560***	0.0494***	0.0565***	0.0495***
	(0.0023)	(0.0021)	(0.0022)	(0.0021)
Age	−0.00687***	−0.00532***	−0.00686***	−0.00531***
	(0.00054)	(0.00058)	(0.00054)	(0.00058)
Male	−0.065***	0.017	−0.065***	0.017
	(0.015)	(0.016)	(0.015)	(0.016)
Union Member	0.025	0.058**	0.024	0.058**
	(0.016)	(0.019)	(0.016)	(0.019)
Unemployment Rate Increase	—	—	−0.0213	−0.0208
			(0.0186)	(0.0125)
GDP per Capita (in thousands)	—	—	−0.00902	0.0367*
			(0.0204)	(0.0169)
% Foreign Born	—	—	−0.0341*	−0.0076
			(0.0156)	(0.0123)
Social Benefits (% of GDP)	—	—	−0.0303	0.0004
			(0.0180)	(0.0108)
Cutpoint 1	−0.824	−0.647	−2.084	0.147
	(0.065)	(0.059)	(0.797)	(0.484)
Cutpoint 2	0.381	0.547	−0.878	1.342
	(0.064)	(0.059)	(0.794)	(0.481)
Cutpoint 3	1.725	1.819	0.467	2.614
	(0.066)	(0.063)	(0.797)	(0.483)
Country Fixed Effects	Yes	Yes	Yes	Yes
N	43,880	37,328	43,880	37,328

* $p < 0.05$, ** $p < 0.01$, *** $p < 0.001$.

Note: Ordered probit coefficients with robust standard errors, clustered on country-sector, in parentheses.

sectoral patterns are associated with these responses depends on the level of economic optimism in a country, it seems reasonable to suppose that these are economic relationships.

Table 6.6 demonstrates that responses to a very similar question that does not prime economic concerns about migrants of a different race or ethnicity—in other words, those who would be most likely to be culturally distinct from natives—do not seem to be influenced by sectoral economic concerns. This holds both for Sector Growth and for Immigrant Proportion. The small size and lack of significance for these coefficients suggests that if cultural xenophobia is being activated by a poorly performing economy, it is not doing so differentially across sectors with different levels of performance or different levels of immigrant employment.

Demographic Effects During the Crisis

We now examine whether the economic crisis matters in how various types of individuals view immigration. Specifically, we may think that globalization losers—the less-skilled, older, and male workers—should be particularly concerned about immigration during the downturn given their already more precarious economic situation. But is this the case once we control for the well-being of their industries?

We first turn to the effect of skill, measured in years of education. Being exposed to immigrants in their sector of employment may be more unsettling to low-skilled natives (who generally face more economic insecurity than natives with higher skills)[23] during the recession, which can activate economic concerns. Further, if the specific factors model of immigration is correct, any effect of Immigrant Proportion on attitudes toward immigration should be concentrated among low-skilled natives. We assume that non-EU immigrants generally compete more with low-skilled natives than with high-skilled natives in the labor market, both because they have lower skills to begin with and because many of their qualifications may not be recognized in receiving countries. We code respondents as high-skilled if they have more years of formal education than the median in their country and low-skilled if they have the same number as the median or fewer.[24]

Table 6.7 displays the results of OLS models similar to those in Table 6.3 but across subsamples based on skill. Model 1 shows that we cannot detect an effect of competition from immigrants among low-skilled individuals when the economic climate is good. Model 3 reveals the same lack of an effect among high-skilled individuals. However, Models 2 and 4, which focus on

Table 6.6 Immigrants of a Different Race or Ethnicity.

	(1)	(2)	(3)	(4)
	Positive Outlook	Negative Outlook	Positive Outlook	Negative Outlook
Sector Growth	0.0093	0.0150	0.0056	0.0094
	(0.0156)	(0.0152)	(0.0154)	(0.0148)
Immigrant Proportion	−0.217	−0.223	−0.157	−0.137
	(0.177)	(0.159)	(0.173)	(0.153)
ESS 2	0.040**	0.060*	0.052	0.043
	(0.015)	(0.024)	(0.029)	(0.028)
ESS 3	0.020	−0.045	0.043	−0.111**
	(0.017)	(0.030)	(0.050)	(0.043)
ESS 4	0.051*	0.023	0.156**	−0.040
	(0.025)	(0.025)	(0.058)	(0.043)
Years of Education	0.0677***	0.0578***	0.0681***	0.0579***
	(0.0023)	(0.0022)	(0.0023)	(0.0022)
Age	−0.00545***	−0.00427***	−0.00543***	−0.00426***
	(0.00056)	(0.00057)	(0.00056)	(0.00057)
Male	−0.022	0.040***	−0.021	0.039**
	(0.016)	(0.015)	(0.016)	(0.015)
Union Member	0.035*	0.043*	0.035*	0.043*
	(0.016)	(0.020)	(0.016)	(0.020)
Unemployment Rate Increase	—	—	0.0001	−0.0126
			(0.0200)	(0.0127)
GDP per Capita (in thousands)	—	—	0.0022	0.0630***
			(0.0180)	(0.0183)
% Foreign Born	—	—	−0.0555***	−0.0382**
			(0.0165)	(0.0125)
Social Benefits (% of GDP)	—	—	−0.0225	0.0044
			(0.0168)	(0.0114)
Cutpoint 1	−0.507	−0.474	−1.632	0.634
	(0.064)	(0.058)	(0.699)	(0.509)
Cutpoint 2	0.704	0.726	−0.420	1.835
	(0.064)	(0.059)	(0.696)	(0.505)
Cutpoint 3	2.071	2.041	0.948	3.152
	(0.067)	(0.066)	(0.698)	(0.509)
Country Fixed Effects	Yes	Yes	Yes	Yes
N	44,005	37,381	44,005	37,381

* $p < 0.05$, ** $p < 0.01$, *** $p < 0.001$.

Note: Ordered probit coefficients with robust standard errors, clustered on country-sector, in parentheses.

Table 6.7 Economic Impact of Immigration, by Outlook and Skill.

	Low Skill		High Skill	
	(1) Positive Outlook	(2) Negative Outlook	(3) Positive Outlook	(4) Negative Outlook
Sector Growth	0.0111	0.0604	0.0392	0.0669
	(0.0382)	(0.0431)	(0.0365)	(0.0363)
Immigrant Proportion	−0.308	−0.936*	−0.145	−1.087*
	(0.401)	(0.382)	(0.439)	(0.517)
ESS 2	−0.152	−0.119	−0.064	−0.188*
	(0.088)	(0.093)	(0.094)	(0.090)
ESS 3	−0.028	−0.144	0.110	−0.285*
	(0.154)	(0.142)	(0.177)	(0.130)
ESS 4	0.247	−0.159	0.149	−0.337*
	(0.177)	(0.138)	(0.168)	(0.136)
Years of Education	0.0495***	0.0816***	0.157***	0.140***
	(0.0106)	(0.0112)	(0.0062)	(0.0079)
Age	0.00185	−0.00067	0.00941***	0.00394**
	(0.00146)	(0.00175)	(0.00150)	(0.00150)
Male	0.279***	0.213***	0.320***	0.360***
	(0.037)	(0.042)	(0.035)	(0.043)
Union Member	0.040	0.12	−0.031	0.053
	(0.041)	(0.063)	(0.036)	(0.049)
Unemployment Rate Increase	−0.153**	−0.073	−0.095	−0.103***
	(0.048)	(0.043)	(0.053)	(0.029)
GDP per Capita (in thousands)	−0.085	0.124*	−0.092	0.129*
	(0.055)	(0.055)	(0.067)	(0.051)
% Foreign Born	−0.048	0.056	0.002	0.122***
	(0.038)	(0.043)	(0.042)	(0.030)
Social Benefits (% of GDP)	−0.144**	−0.011	−0.133*	0.014
	(0.045)	(0.035)	(0.056)	(0.035)
Constant	9.677	0.558	7.601	−1.220
	(2.121)	(1.459)	(2.657)	(1.746)
Country Fixed Effects	Yes	Yes	Yes	Yes
N	20,734	18,008	22,861	19,050

* $p < 0.05$, ** $p < 0.01$, *** $p < 0.001$.

Note: OLS coefficients with robust standard errors, clustered on country-sector, in parentheses.

times when the public confidence in the economy is low, show large and statistically significant relationships between the presence of non-EU immigrants in a sector and the extent to which workers in that sector think immigration helps the economy. The direction and magnitude of the effect do not seem to vary across skill groups, suggesting that this cannot be a simple self-interest story, at least not among the high-skilled. That high-skilled native workers respond to the sectoral inflow of mostly low-skilled immigrants in a manner similar to low-skilled natives suggests that individuals take into account the well-being of their sector as a whole, not simply the effect that immigration might have on their own wages.[25]

Table 6.8 shows that these patterns do not hold when the question at hand is the effect of immigrants on the culture of the receiving country. High- and low-skilled workers, in good and bad economic times, seem to ignore the presence or absence of immigrants in their sectors when deciding whether immigration is good or bad for their national culture. Interestingly, there is some evidence for a relationship between sector growth and cultural attitudes in Model 2, which is estimated on low-skilled workers in bad economies. Given that this coefficient cannot be statistically distinguished from its counterpart in Model 4,[26] which focuses on high-skilled workers in bad economies, our results do not suggest that high- and low-skilled workers are reacting to downturns differently.

The fact that sector-level economic concerns are not concentrated among the low-skilled could be the result of at least two patterns. The first is that individuals care about their fellow workers—defined either at the sectoral or at the firm level. This is consistent with arguments about sociotropic voting (as opposed to pocketbook voting; see Kinder 1998 and the debate that followed), though rather than focusing on the national economy, it focuses on a middle level between the individual and the nation. The second possible mechanism is that sectoral developments are the best source of information about overall economic performance available to workers. This might be especially true during the economic crisis, when workers likely paid more attention to developments in their industries. We do not have the space or data to distinguish these mechanisms here, but future research should explore whether one, the other, or both are at work.

We now turn to a brief examination of how globalization "losers" differ from other natives before and during the economic crisis. Many previous analyses suggest that males are more likely to suffer from globalization than females. The existence of gender differences in attitudes toward immigration—one aspect of globalization—has, however, not been as clearly

Table 6.8 Cultural Impact of Immigration, by Outlook and Skill.

	Low Skill		High Skill	
	(1) Positive Outlook	(2) Negative Outlook	(3) Positive Outlook	(4) Negative Outlook
Sector Growth	0.0217	0.0878*	0.0478	0.0291
	(0.0417)	(0.0432)	(0.0400)	(0.0438)
Immigrant Proportion	0.226	−0.390	−0.034	−.881
	(0.394)	(0.387)	(0.477)	(0.561)
ESS 2	−0.126	−0.053	0.173*	0.046
	(0.095)	(0.091)	(0.080)	(0.106)
ESS 3	−0.136	0.137	0.255	−0.065
	(0.171)	(0.134)	(0.148)	(0.125)
ESS 4	0.164	0.126	0.327*	0.002
	(0.198)	(0.141)	(0.159)	(0.130)
Years of Education	0.0600***	0.0600***	0.155***	0.141***
	(0.0098)	(0.0131)	(0.0070)	(0.0075)
Age	−0.00530***	−0.00447**	0.00001	−0.00437**
	(0.00152)	(0.00173)	(0.00142)	(0.00166)
Male	−0.125**	−0.012	−0.148***	0.039
	(0.041)	(0.044)	(0.037)	(0.041)
Union Member	0.119**	0.104	0.086*	0.131**
	(0.046)	(0.060)	(0.041)	(0.050)
Unemployment Rate Increase	−0.152**	−0.096*	−0.037	−0.151***
	(0.058)	(0.046)	(0.050)	(0.033)
GDP per Capita (in thousands)	−0.065	−0.069	−0.196***	−0.074
	(0.059)	(0.056)	(0.054)	(0.047)
% Foreign Born	−0.108**	0.001	0.004	0.092**
	(0.040)	(0.042)	(0.042)	(0.030)
Social Benefits (% of GDP)	0.044	−0.003	−0.088	0.079*
	(0.053)	(0.037)	(0.050)	(0.032)
Constant	6.852	6.735	9.898	3.393
	(2.201)	(1.488)	(2.122)	(1.553)
Country Fixed Effects	Yes	Yes	Yes	Yes
N	20,820	17,826	23,070	19,161

* $p<0.05$, ** $p<0.01$, *** $p<0.001$

Note: OLS coefficients with robust standard errors, clustered on country-sector, in parentheses.

established. Mayda (2006) shows that males are more likely to support open immigration policies than females, though the difference is not always statistically significant. Hainmueller and Hiscox (2007) show that females are more opposed to immigration than males are when the sending country is rich. Our results add temporal variation to this work, highlighting the importance of economic context. They also suggest the importance of distinguishing between the various underlying dimensions of support or opposition. We see that the choice of dependent variable and the overall economic context lead to very different results. In Tables 6.3 and 6.7, for which the dependent variable is Economic Impact, we see that males are more likely to believe that immigrants are good for the economy once we account for sectoral differences between genders. On the other hand, in Tables 6.4 and 6.8, for which the dependent variable is Cultural Impact, our results suggest that males are less likely to believe that immigrants are good for the culture, at least when the economy is doing well.

Similarly, Tables 6.5 and 6.6, which focus on policy questions, suggest that the relative position of males is more positive during times of economic crisis than during good times. Model 1 of Table 6.5 shows that males are less likely to support immigration from poor countries than are similar females when the economic Outlook is positive, but there is no detectable difference in Model 2, which focuses on bad economic times (this difference is statistically significant). Model 2 of Table 6.6 shows that women are less supportive of immigration by ethnic minorities in bad times than are similar males, but in good times (Model 1) this difference, if any, is in the opposite direction. Overall, these results suggest that gender interacts with immigration opinions in complex ways, a conclusion that is consistent with previous research (Mudde 2007).

Disaggregating across contexts and immigration opinions also reveals that the impact of Age is conditional on these factors. Most previous public opinion analyses have suggested that older individuals are consistently less friendly to immigrants than their younger counterparts (O'Rourke and Sinnott 2006; Mayda 2006; Hainmueller and Hiscox 2007). Instead, our results highlight the need, once again, to differentiate between various dimensions of anti-immigrant beliefs and preferences. On policy and cultural questions, older individuals do appear to take the anti-immigrant position, but they are also more likely to believe that immigration is good for the economy. This effect is found primarily among high-skilled individuals (see Table 6.7). Though we cannot be sure of the mechanism driving this result from our data, this is consistent with the theory that well-educated older individuals see immigration as a way to ease the burden on European pensions systems, even if this does not carry through to their policy preferences.[27]

A more consistent effect is the difference between union members and nonmembers. Across Tables 6.3 through 6.8, union members take more immigrant-friendly positions than similar nonmembers.[28] This is inconsistent with the assumption that unions desire to restrict the supply of labor, but it is in line with more recent work highlighting some ways in which unions might benefit from immigration (Haus 2002; Watts 2002).[29] These potential benefits include the recruitment of immigrants into unions, the complementarity of relatively skilled labor market insiders (including union members) and outsiders (including migrants), and the likelihood that immigrants will, along with union members, vote for left parties. It may also be that unions, as key players in the organized left, are strongly committed to the core program of left ideologies. This would explain the surprisingly strong results in Tables 6.4 and 6.6, suggesting that, across a variety of economic contexts, union members are much less likely to express attitudes that we might associate with xenophobia than are nonmembers. Unlike its effect on cultural attitudes, union membership's effect on economic attitudes does seem to vary across economic contexts, appearing stronger during economic downturns. This pattern also suggests that union membership is more than simply an economic identity. The economic aspect of union membership responds to economic changes, while the more broadly political effects of union membership do not vary on the basis of the Economic Outlook.

Those groups that are most often cited as being negatively affected by globalization did not respond to the economic crisis by becoming relatively more anti-immigrant, once we account for sector-level differences. Males, if anything, are less anti-immigrant than females during periods of low Economic Outlook, and union members become relatively more positive, while there are no (or mixed) differences across contexts for skill and age. This suggests a need for the literature on globalization to reexamine the definition of "losers" in light of the crisis and the role of developments in workers' industry of employment. This reexamination could help shed some light on the culture versus economics debate in the immigration literature. This is particularly important for researchers hoping to understand the effect of the economic crisis on existing political coalitions, as a change in the attitudes toward a central issue in European politics, such as immigration, could presage a change in the abilities of parties and other actors to mobilize certain groups of voters.

Conclusion

The Great Recession has altered the dynamics of immigration politics in Europe, but it has done so rather subtly. Most countries have not seen dramatic shifts in beliefs about the impact of immigration or in preferences for immigration policies. Instead, this chapter documents a shift in the types of individuals who believe immigration is good for the economy and who prefer to allow immigrants from poor countries to enter. When the economy is doing well, sectoral patterns have little impact on how workers see immigration. When it is doing poorly, such factors rise in salience and play a larger role in shaping these attitudes.

We have also shown that cultural attitudes, though clearly related to macro-level economic conditions, are less well associated with sectoral variables than economic attitudes. This pattern suggests that even if there may be some connection between cultural concerns and economic performance, the connection between economic concerns and economic performance is much tighter. The public may not know much about the relationship between immigration and economics, but it does seem to respond to economic concerns in a predictable and theoretically coherent fashion.

These results raise two questions. First, how large are these effects? That is, are the changes in the distribution of support for immigration sufficiently large to shape politics? We believe they are. Clearly, the magnitudes of the effects detected here are not as large as some of the cross-country differences displayed in Figure 6.1, but they are only a bit smaller than the effects of a year of education or the difference between union members and nonmembers. If we think those differences are large enough to shape politics, then we should conclude that sectoral economic concerns, at least in troubled economic times, have shaped the politics of immigration. Certainly, some politicians have responded to rather small aggregate opinion changes with new policies, and this may be because they recognize the tighter links between sectoral interests and attitudes. If these links make it easier for politicians to target restrictions to voters who are likely to respond, we should expect to see an increase in sectoral restrictions on non-EU migration to complement broader, macro-level responses.

The second important question, and one about which we have less information, is whether these relationships continue to matter as the economic crisis goes on. Public optimism rebounded rather quickly after the initial shock of the economic crisis, but the recent troubles of the eurozone, combined with falling exports and shrinking public sectors in many countries, have kept the economy at the top of the political and media agenda. Since we have argued that the differences across good and bad economic times are driven by the salience of the economy and the confidence individuals feel about their prospects, our results suggest that economic concerns, including sectoral growth or decline and sectoral immigrant employment, will continue to shape immigration attitudes.

Notes

1. For recent scholarship on cultural effects, see, for example, Sides and Citrin (2007), Sniderman and Hagendoorn (2007), Hainmueller and Hiscox (2007), and Brader, Valentino, and Suhay (2008).
2. See, for instance, Scheve and Slaughter (2001), Mayda (2006), Dancygier (2010), and Malhotra, Margalit, and Mo (2013).
3. Similar claims were made by, for example, the EU Agency for Fundamental Rights (2009); Frank Elbers, of the Human Rights Education Association (DARE-HREA 2009); and Dominique Moisi, of the *Guardian* (2009).
4. On globalization losers, see, for example, Kriesi et al. (2008), Walter (2010), and Walter and Maduz (2009).
5. The Tory Party's 2010 manifesto called for "steps to take net migration back to the levels of the 1990s—tens of thousands a year, not hundreds of thousands" (Conservative Party 2010). Given the institutional constraints on policies regarding EU immigration, this implies a sharp reduction in the number of migrants from outside the EU.
6. For a broad comparison of such policies, see Black, Collyer, and Somerville (2011). Plewa (2009) highlights some similarities between the Spanish approach and policies implemented in the wake of the first oil crisis (1973–74) in France.
7. For two recent exceptions, see Malhotra et al. (2013) and Hainmueller, Hiscox, and Margalit (2011).
8. The Heckscher-Ohlin model, by contrast, assumes no costs to factor mobility. This allows the impact of immigration to be shared across the whole set of natives with skills similar to those of immigrants.
9. See also Hopkins (2010), who argues that the national media's framing of immigration interacts with local demographic changes to influence native reactions toward immigration across U.S. localities.
10. *Das Handelsblatt*, "Schweizer Offenheit stößt an ihre Grenzen." December 9, 2009.
11. The surveys were in the field 2008–09 for round 4 (Ireland's fieldwork extended into 2010) and 2010–11 for round 5. All of the surveys are weighted to most closely match population distributions. The sampling frame is all adult residents. See http://ess.nsd.uib.no/ for more information. The sample sizes range from 995 to

3,031, with relatively low rates of missing data for most of the immigration-related variables. Margins of error for the means presented in Figures 6.1–6.4 are therefore quite small, typically around +/-.04 on the four category variables and +/-.12 on the eleven category variables.

12. See http://ec.europa.eu/employment_social/eie/graphs/download/Chap1_Graph_5.jpg. Note that this choice of time period leads to Greece being categorized as having a "moderate crisis." This would surely change if we used a more recent time period. However, since there is no Greek survey in the fifth round (2010–11), we believe the classification is accurate for our purposes.
13. Table A2 in Dancygier and Donnelly (2013) provides a list of which NACE codes are counted in which sector.
14. We have run all of the models below excluding individuals in sectors in which non-EU migrants make up more than 30 percent of the workforce. The substantive results are similar to those presented here.
15. The mean annual change in immigrant employment in a respondent's sector in the fourth round of the ESS is essentially zero, while, as shown in Figure 6.6, the average sector lost jobs over that same time period.
16. Here and below, the whiskers on the box plots extend 1.5 times the distance between the 75th and 25th percentiles. Any observations outside that range are displayed as dots.
17. All of these values are based on our calculations from Eurostat data. A similar number for Spanish construction was reported in Figure 5 of ILO (2010), which is also based on Eurostat data.
18. The Norwegian data on economic outlook do not come from Eurostat and have not been harmonized. In addition, they are an aggregate of multiple questions. The substantive results presented below are robust to dropping Norway.
19. In our data, the sample median is -12, and we group those at the median with those below.
20. Donnelly (2011) shows that union members are more pro-immigrant than similar nonmembers and posits a solidarity-based mechanism.
21. Here and below, the comparisons across subgroups are calculated using Seemingly Unrelated Regression comparisons. Using an interaction term between Immigrant Proportion and Outlook rather than subsets produces results of a similar magnitude and stronger significance. We use subsets for ease of presentation and interpretation, and because other control variables may interact with Outlook in unexpected ways.
22. This difference is not statistically significant at conventional levels.
23. See Rehm et al. (2012, 390), who note, "Across all the countries and domains of economic risk that we examine, we find none in which economically advantaged citizens face greater risk of loss on average."
24. About 57 percent of our survey respondents are coded as having low skills.

25. For more on the sociotropic nature of sectoral economic concerns in the context of immigration, see Dancygier and Donnelly (2013).
26. The p-value on a Seemingly Unrelated Regression comparison of these coefficients is .31.
27. The positive relationship between Age and Economic Impact is robust to including retired individuals in the sample and to including a quadratic term for Age (within the range of a normal human life).
28. None of the coefficients on Union Membership in Table 6.7 are statistically significant; but in Tables 6.3–6.6 and 6.8 this relationship is quite strong.
29. For a more detailed analysis of the relationship between union membership and attitudes toward immigration using a similar data set, see Donnelly (2011).

References

Balanced Migration. 2008a. "First Cross Party Group on Immigration Calls for Balanced Migration." http://www.balancedmigration.com/2008/09/first-cross-party-group-on-immigration-calls-for-balanced-migration/.

Balanced Migration. 2008b. "Statement from Frank Field MP and Nicholas Soames MP, Co-Chairmen of the Cross Party Group on Balanced Migration, on Today's Unemployment Figures." http://www.balancedmigration.com/2008/09/statement-from-frank-field-mp-and-nicholas-soames-mp-co-chairmen-of-the-cross-party-group-on-balanced-migration/

BBC News. 2011. *UK Takeaway Jobs Ban for Immigrants from Outside EEA*, March 28, 2011. Available from http://www.bbc.co.uk/news/uk-12733899. Accessed March 16, 2011.

Black, Richard, Michael Collyer, and Will Somerville. 2011. *Pay-to-go Schemes and Other Noncoercive Return Programs: Is Scale Possible?* Washington, DC: Migration Policy Institute.

Brader, Ted, Nicholas A. Valentino, and Elizabeth Suhay. 2008. "What Triggers Public Opposition to Immigration? Anxiety, Group Cues, and Immigration Threat." *American Journal of Political Science* 52(4): 959–978.

Conservative Party. 2010. "Invitation to Join the Government of Britain: The Conservative Manifesto 2010." http://www.media.conservatives.s3.amazonaws.com/manifesto/cpmanifesto2010_lowres.pdf.

Citrin, Jack, Donald P. Green, and Cara Wong. 1997. "Public Opinion Toward Immigration Reform: The Role of Economic Motivations." *Journal of Politics* 59(3): 858–881.

Dancygier, Rafaela. 2010. *Immigration and Conflict in Europe*. New York: Cambridge University Press.

Dancygier, Rafaela, and Michael Donnelly. 2013. "Sectoral Economies, Economic Contexts and Attitudes Toward Immigration." *Journal of Politics* 75(1): 17–35.

DARE-HREA. 2009. "Economic Crisis Could Result in Increase in Xenophobia in Europe." http://www.hrea.org/index.php?doc_id=981.

Donnelly, Michael. 2011. "Competition and Solidarity: Union Members and Immigration in Europe." Working Paper. http://www.princeton.edu/~mdonnell/pdfs/CompetitionandSolidarity.pdf.

EU Agency for Fundamental Rights. 2009. "Leading European Rights Agencies Warn That Economic Crisis Fuels Racism and Xenophobia." http://fra.europa.eu/en/press-release/2010/leading-european-rights-agencies-warn-economic-crisis-fuels-racism-and-xenophobia.

Facchini, Giovanni, and A. Mayda. 2009. "Does the Welfare State Affect Individual Attitudes Toward Immigrants? Evidence Across Countries." *Review of Economic and Statistics* 9(12): 295–314.

van Genugten, Saskia and Erik Jones. 2009. "The far-right cherishes this crisis." *The Guardian*. http://www.guardian.co.uk/commentisfree/2009/apr/13/global-economy-globalrecession.

Global Migration Group. 2009. *Fact-Sheet on the Impact of the Economic Crisis on Discrimination and Xenophobia*. Bangkok: UNESCO.

Hainmueller, Jens, and Michael J. Hiscox. 2007. "Educated Preferences: Explaining Attitudes Toward Immigration in Europe." *International Organization* 61(2): 399–442.

Hainmueller, Jens, Michael Hiscox, and Yotam Margalit. 2011. "Do Concerns About Labor Market Competition Shape Attitudes Toward Immigration? New Evidence from U.S. Workers." Paper presented at the Annual Meeting of the American Political Science Association, Seattle, Washington, September 1–4.

Hanson, Gordon H., Kenneth F. Scheve, and Matthew J. Slaughter. 2007. "Public Finance and Individual Preferences over Globalization Strategies." *Economics and Politics* 19(1): 1–33.

Haus, Leah. 2002. *Unions, Immigration, and Internationalization: New Challenges and Changing Coalitions in the United States and France*. New York: Palgrave Macmillan.

Hopkins, Daniel J. 2010. "Politicized Places: Explaining Where and When Immigrants Provoke Local Opposition." *American Political Science Review* 104(1): 40–60.

ILO. 2010. "Spain." *G20 Statistical Update*. Prepared for the meeting of labour and employment ministers, Washington D.C., April 20–21. http://www.dol.gov/ilab/media/events/G20_ministersmeeting/G20-spain-stats.pdf

Kinder, Donald R. 1998. "Communication and Opinion." *Annual Review of Political Science* 1: 167–197.

Kriesi, Hanspeter, Edgar Grande, Romain Lachat, Martin Dolezat, Simon Bornschier, and Timotheos Frey. 2008. *West European Politics in the Age of Globalization*. Cambridge: Cambridge University Press.

Lee, Donghoon, and Kenneth I. Wolpin. 2006. "Intersectoral Labor Mobility and the Growth of the Service Sector." *Econometrica* 74(1): 1–46.

Malhotra, Neil, Yotam Margalit, and Cecilia Hyunjung Mo. 2013. "Economic Explanations for Opposition to Immigration: Distinguishing Between Prevalence and Conditional Impact." *American Journal of Political Science* 57(2): 391–410.

Mayda, Anna Maria. 2006. "Who Is Against Immigration? A Cross-Country Investigation of Individual Attitudes Toward Immigrants." *Review of Economics and Statistics* 88(3): 510–530.

Moisi, Dominique. 2009. "Is it 1929 or 1989?" *The Guardian*. http://www.guardian.co.uk/commentisfree/2009/mar/20/credit-crunch-economy.

Mudde, Cas. 2007. *Populist Radical Right Parties in Europe*. Cambridge: Cambridge University Press.

OECD. 2009. *International Migration Outlook*. Paris: OECD.

OECD. 2011a. *International Migration Outlook*. Paris: OECD.

OECD. 2011b. *Quarterly National Accounts*. http://stats.oecd.org/, accessed April 27, 2011.

OECD. 2011c. "Sources and Definitions: Consumer Opinion Surveys." Main Economic Indicators. http://stats.oecd.org/mei/.

O'Neil, Kevin, and Marta Tienda. 2010. "A Tale of Two Counties: Natives' Opinions Toward Immigration in North Carolina." *International Migration Review* 44(3): 728–761.

O'Rourke, Kevin, and Richard Sinnott. 2006. "The Determinants of Individual Attitudes Towards Immigration." *European Journal of Political Economy*, 22(4): 838–861.

Papademetriou, Demetrios, Madeleine Sumption, and Will Somerville. 2009. "Migration and the Economic Downturn: What to Expect in the European Union." Washington, DC: Migration Policy Institute.

Plewa, Piotr. 2009. "Voluntary Return Programmes: Could They Assuage the Effects of the Economic Crisis?" Working Paper No. 75. Centre on Migration, Policy and Society, Oxford University.

Rehm, Philipp, Jacob S. Hacker, and Mark Schlesinger. 2012. "Insecure Alliances: Risk, Inequality, and Support for the Welfare State." *American Political Science Review* 106(2): 386–406.

Scheve, Kenneth, and Matthew J. Slaughter. 2001. "Labor Market Competition and Individual Preferences over Immigration Policy." *Review of Economics and Statistics* 83(1): 133–145.

Sides, John, and Jack Citrin. 2007. "European Opinion About Immigration: The Role of Identities, Interests and Information." *British Journal of Political Science* 37(3): 477–504.

Sniderman, Paul M., and Louk Hagendoorn. 2007. *When Ways of Life Collide*. Princeton: Princeton University Press.

United Nations. 2011. *International Migrant Stock: The 2008 Revision*. http://esa.un.org/migration/index.asp?panel=1.

Walter, Stefanie. 2010. "Globalization and the Welfare State: Testing the Microfoundations of the Compensation Hypothesis." *International Studies Quarterly* 54(2): 403–426.

Walter, Stefanie, and Linda Maduz (2009). "How Globalization Shapes Individual Risk Perceptions and Policy Preferences. A Cross-national Analysis of Differences Between Globalization Winners and Losers." *WCFIA Working Paper* 09-0015. Cambridge: Harvard University.

Watts, Julie. 2002. *Immigration Policy and the Challenge of Globalization: Unions and Employers in Unlikely Alliance*. Ithaca, NY: Cornell University Press.

7

Ideology and Retrospection in Electoral Responses to the Great Recession

Larry M. Bartels

THE GLOBAL ECONOMIC crisis triggered by the financial meltdown of 2008 provides a dramatic setting in which to explore perennial questions of democratic accountability. Dozens of incumbent governments around the world faced their voters under conditions of significant economic distress. How did voters respond to these opportunities to help steer the ship of state through the squall? Did electorates evaluate the performance of their elected leaders on the basis of sober-minded assessments of the economic situation? Did they compare the proposals of "ins" and "outs" and communicate meaningful preferences regarding the future course of public policy? Was there a global shift of ideological views to the left or to the right in response to a broadly shared understanding of the nature of the crisis and appropriate governmental responses? Or did voters simply and uncritically punish incumbents wherever and whenever times were hard?

In this chapter I attempt to shed some light on these questions by providing a broad comparative analysis of forty-two elections in twenty-eight OECD countries in the period just before, during, and after the Great Recession. By focusing on common patterns across these diverse electoral settings, I of course ignore much important detail regarding economic conditions, policy choices, party strategies, and voting behavior in individual countries. My hope is that this inevitably superficial comparative analysis will provide a useful starting point for more detailed studies, which may in turn suggest modifications and elaborations of the empirical generalizations proposed here. In the meantime, I offer a few brief case studies of specific elections; they are intended not as evidence in their own right but as illustrations of the empirical generalizations—and of some of the additional complexities shaping specific election outcomes.

Ideology or Retrospection?

In the past half-century, political scientists have developed two distinct models of electoral accountability. In the first of these models, voters are supposed to weigh the ideological commitments and policy platforms of competing parties or candidates and vote so as to further their own policy preferences (for example, see Downs 1957; Enelow and Hinich 1984; for a critique, Stokes 1963). The notion that elections provide meaningful judgments on the ideologies and policies of democratic governments is an enduring—and, for many citizens and political observers, reassuring—tenet of democratic faith. Thus analysts called on to explain or interpret specific election outcomes often do so in ideological terms. The fall of a left-wing government is taken to imply that the electorate has shifted to the right; conversely, its reelection is interpreted as evidence of a continued attachment of the masses to the principles and policies of socialism.

Although this way of thinking about electoral politics is common among sophisticated political observers in modern democracies, it may be less compelling than it seems. As Philip Converse (1964, 219) put it in a classic essay challenging the empirical veracity of the model, "While it may be taken for granted among well educated and politically involved people that a shift from a Democratic preference to a Republican one probably represents a change in option from liberal to conservative, the assumption cannot be extended very far into the electorate as a whole."

An alternative model of electoral accountability dispenses with the arguably unrealistic assumption that voters are attentive to ideological commitments and policy promises; instead, they are merely expected to assess the general performance of the incumbent government, decide whether it is satisfactory or unsatisfactory, and vote accordingly to retain or replace the incumbents (for example, see Key 1966; Fiorina 1981; for a critique, Achen and Bartels 2002). This so-called *retrospective voting* model is generally less prominent in sophisticated political discourse than the *ideological* model; however, it has come to play an increasingly prominent role in scholarly analyses of electoral politics. For example, in a recent paper on the 2009 German election, Robert Rohrschneider, Rüdiger Schmitt-Beck, and Franziska Jung

(2010, 18) wrote that voters in competitive party systems "have been socialized to change governments when they are unhappy with the economic performance of a party because they (rightly or wrongly) have come to believe that this will in due course help to improve the economy under a new set of governing parties." David Mayhew (2002, 161) put it more succinctly: "academics have tended to dismiss campaign slogans of the past like 'the full dinner pail' and 'a chicken in every pot' on the grounds that something deeper must have been going on in these elections. But perhaps it wasn't."

These two alternative models of electoral accountability have both received substantial scholarly attention, but they have less often been considered in juxtaposition. As a result, it is easy for observers to mistake one sort of electoral response for the other. Thus, for example, Christopher Achen and I (Achen and Bartels 2005) suggested that the American electorate's response to the Great Depression in the 1930s was much less ideological than is often supposed. Employing state-level data on income growth, we showed that Franklin Roosevelt's historic landslide in 1936—the pivotal electoral event in what came to be called the New Deal era—was heavily concentrated in areas where incomes happened to be growing in the year of the election. If the recession of 1938 had occurred two years earlier, this analysis suggests, Roosevelt would probably have been a one-term president and the "New Deal era" would have amounted to a brief interlude in American political history.

In support of this interpretation, Achen and I noted "the impressive consistency with which electorates around the world deposed incumbent governments during the worst days of the Depression, regardless of their ideologies." Thus, "what looks to the American eye like a triumph of both democratic responsiveness and Democratic ideology may instead be an illusion produced by a specific configuration of election dates, partisan alterations, and economic vicissitudes in a world where policies are, in fact, largely irrelevant and voters are blindly and myopically retrospective" (2005, 2).

Maria Victoria Murillo, Virginia Oliveros, and Milan Vaishnav (2010) offered a parallel reinterpretation of the rise of the left in Latin America in the first decade of the new millennium. They argued (87–88) that the "rising tide of leftist political movements across Central and South America" discerned by "journalists, policy makers, and academics" was primarily due not to "structural conditions, such as poverty and inequality," "globalization and disenchantment with neoliberal market reforms," or a "crisis of representation" but to "the disenchantment of voters with underperforming right-wing governments." Analyzing the outcomes of 106 elections in eighteen countries over a period of three decades (1978–2008), they found that voters routinely punished incumbents of both the right and the left for high levels of price inflation. Moreover, the estimated sensitivity of voters to economic performance was fairly symmetric; a tenfold increase in prices in the year before the election was associated with a decline of about eight percentage points in the expected vote share of left-wing governments and with a decline of about five percentage points in the expected vote share of right-wing governments.

The impact of economic conditions on election outcomes has been a prime focus of investigation by scholars of retrospective voting, first in the United States (Kramer 1971; Tufte 1978) and more recently in a wide variety of other countries (Lewis-Beck 1988; Anderson 1995; Duch and Stevenson 2008). Economic conditions have the virtue of being (relatively) easy to measure, and their impact has proved to be sufficiently large and consistent to provide powerful leverage for explaining and predicting election outcomes (Rosenstone 1983; Hibbs 2006).

Although the general importance of economic voting is widely recognized by scholars of electoral politics and public opinion, the precise nature and normative significance of the phenomenon are matters of debate. At one extreme, theorists have developed elaborate models of economic voting in which voters make sophisticated calculations regarding the implications of observed economic performance for their future utility streams (Hibbs 2006). For example, Raymond Duch and Randolph Stevenson (2008, 339) posited, "Voters observe shocks to the macro-economy but cannot observe the mix of exogenous and competence components that comprise these shocks. Voters do, however, know the variances of the distributions of these different kinds of shocks and so are able to solve a well-defined signal-extraction problem that produces a competence signal." At the opposite extreme, scholars have suggested that retrospective voting is often short-sighted (Achen and Bartels 2004; Bartels 2008, chapter 4) and that voters routinely punish incumbents for such uncontrollable "failures" as droughts, shark attacks, and lost football games (Achen and Bartels 2002; Healy, Malhotra, and Mo 2010). Analyses like these raise the question of whether elections provide meaningful retrospective accountability, much less ideological or policy "mandates."

The Impact of Economic Conditions

To what extent have electoral responses to the Great Recession been directly shaped by economic conditions? Table 7.1 lists forty-two parliamentary elections conducted in twenty-eight OECD countries between 2007 and 2011. For each election, the table records the ideological profile of the incumbent

Table 7.1 Elections in OECD Countries, 2007–2011.

Country	Election Date	Incumbent Party	Incumbent Ideology	GDP Growth	Vote Gain/Loss
Estonia	4 March '07	Reform/Centre	Center/ Right	9.1	+10.81
Finland	18 March '07	Centre/Social Dem	Center/Left	5.0	−4.61
Iceland	12 May '07	Independence (SSF)	Right	3.2	+2.96
Ireland	24 May '07	Fianna Fáil	Center	6.7	+0.08
France	17 June '07	UMP	Right	2.6	+0.91
Turkey	22 July '07	Justice and Devlp	Right	3.6	+12.38
Greece	16 Sept '07	New Democracy	Right	4.2	−3.52
Poland	21 Oct '07	Law and Justice	Center	6.3	+5.12
Denmark	13 Nov '07	Liberal (Venstre)	Right	1.5	−2.77
Spain	9 March '08	Socialist (PSOE)	Left	3.1	+0.60
Italy	14 April '08	Democratic (PD)	Left	0.4	+1.90
Slovenia	21 Sept '08	Slov Dem (SDS)	Right	4.9	+0.18
Austria	28 Sept '08	Soc Dem/ People's	Center	2.1	−14.43
Canada	14 Oct '08	Conservative	Right	0.7	+1.38
United States	4 Nov '08	Republican	Right	−0.6	−1.68
New Zealand	8 Nov '08	Labour	Left	−0.6	−7.11
Israel	10 Feb '09	Kadima/Labor	Center/Left	2.0	−4.68
Iceland	25 April '09	Independence (SSF)	Right	−5.4	−12.94
Japan	30 Aug '09	Liberal Dem	Right	−6.5	−9.09
Norway	14 Sept '09	Labour (DNA)	Left	−2.3	+2.68
Germany	27 Sept '09	CDU/SPD	Center	−6.2	−12.59
Portugal	27 Sept '09	Socialist (PS)	Left	−3.5	−8.47
Greece	4 Oct '09	New Democracy	Right	−3.5	−8.36
Chile	13 Dec '09	Concert (CPD)	Left	−0.8	−7.41

(*Continued*)

Table 7.1 (Continued)

Country	Election Date	Incumbent Party	Incumbent Ideology	GDP Growth	Vote Gain/Loss
Hungary	25 April '10	Socialist (MSZP)	Left	−0.3	−23.91
United Kingdom	6 May '10	Labour	Left	1.2	−6.19
Netherlands	9 June '10	Chr Dem/ Labour	Center	0.3	−14.46
Slovak Republic	12 June '10	Direction–Soc Dem	Left	4.9	+5.66
Australia	21 Aug '10	Labor	Left	3.0	−2.58
Sweden	19 Sept '10	Moderate	Right	5.3	+3.83
United States	2 Nov '10	Democratic	Left	3.5	−8.16
Ireland	25 Feb '11	Fianna Fáil	Center	0.1	−24.11
Estonia	6 March '11	Reform	Right	6.0	+0.74
Finland	17 April '11	Centre/Nat Cltn	Center	5.3	−9.23
Canada	2 May '11	Conservative	Right	2.9	+1.97
Portugal	5 June '11	Socialist (PS)	Left	−0.6	−8.51
Turkey	12 June '11	Justice and Dvlpt	Right	10.9	+3.25
Denmark	15 Sept '11	Liberal (Venstre)	Right	1.3	+0.47
Poland	9 Oct '11	Civic Platform	Right	4.0	−2.33
Spain	20 Nov '11	Socialist (PSOE)	Left	0.8	−14.71
New Zealand	26 Nov '11	National	Right	1.4	+2.38
Slovenia	4 Dec '11	Social Democrats	Left	−0.2	−20.42

party, total real GDP growth in the four quarters leading up to the election, and the increase or decrease in the incumbent party's vote share by comparison with the previous election.[1] In most cases the "incumbent party" is the largest party in the government; however, in seven cases where coalition governments included two roughly equal partners I have totaled the vote gains or losses for both major incumbent parties.[2]

The elections in Table 7.1 provide the primary data for my analysis. The basic relationship between economic growth and the outcomes of these elections is displayed in Figure 7.1. For each election, the figure shows how changes in the incumbent party or coalition's electoral support from the

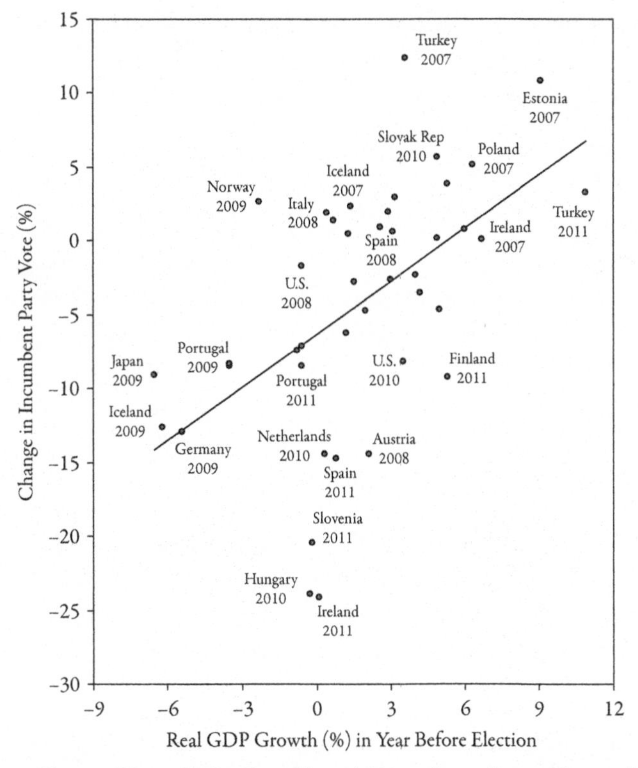

FIGURE 7.1 Election-Year GDP Growth and Incumbent Party Electoral Support, 2007–2011.

previous election varied with the rate of GDP growth in the year leading up to the election.[3]

The relationship between economic conditions and election outcomes evident in Figure 7.1 is represented statistically in the first column of Table 7.2, which reports the results of a bivariate linear regression of changes in incumbent party vote shares on real GDP growth in the four quarters leading up to the election; the corresponding regression line is plotted in Figure 7.1. These results imply that each additional percentage point of real GDP growth was associated with an increase of about 1.2 percent in the incumbent party's expected vote share.

The second column of Table 7.2 reports the results of a regression model including two distinct economic variables: real GDP growth in the year leading up to the election and real GDP growth in the year before that (cumulating growth in quarters five through eight before the quarter in which the election occurred). This model does a better job of accounting for election outcomes, reducing the standard error of the regression by about 5 percent. The results

Table 7.2 Economic Conditions and Changes in Incumbent Vote Shares, 2007–2011.

	1	2	3	4	5	6
ΔGDP(1–4Q)	1.20 (.30)	1.02 (.29)	—	.75 (.37)	1.05 (.29)	.95 (.24)
ΔGDP(5–8Q)	—	.56 (.24)	—	.42 (.36)	.42 (.25)	.26 (.21)
Relative ΔGDP(1–4Q)	—	—	1.61 (.53)	.75 (.65)	—	—
Relative ΔGDP(5–8Q)	—	—	.38 (.42)	−.02 (.54)	—	—
Unemployment	—	—	—	—	−.44 (.30)	—
Intercept	−6.33 (1.22)	−7.10 (1.20)	−5.75 (1.15)	−6.92 (1.24)	−3.31 (2.89)	−5.20 (1.06)
Adjusted R^2	.27	.35	.29	.34	.36	.33
Std error of reg	7.12	6.75	7.05	6.80	6.66	5.51
N	42	42	42	42	42	39[a]

Notes: Ordinary least squares regression parameter estimates (with standard errors in parentheses).

[a] Excluding countries where incumbents lost more than 20 percentage points (Hungary 2010, Ireland 2011, Slovenia 2011).

suggest that voters probably attached significant weight to economic performance over a two-year horizon. However, the estimated weight attached to earlier economic growth is only a little more than half the estimated weight attached to election-year growth, suggesting that voters significantly discounted earlier growth in favor of growth in the quarters immediately preceding the election (Achen and Bartels 2004; Bartels 2008, chapter 4). This relationship is presented graphically in Figure 7.2.[4]

The third and fourth columns of Table 7.2 present the results of additional regression analyses probing the impact on election outcomes of *relative* economic growth rates. I calculated *relative* GDP growth by subtracting from each country's growth rate in each quarter the OECD-average growth rate in the same quarter. This would be a more appropriate measure of economic conditions if voters in each country were comparing their own economy's performance against that of other OECD economies—in effect, making rough allowance for the impact of global economic forces on national performance

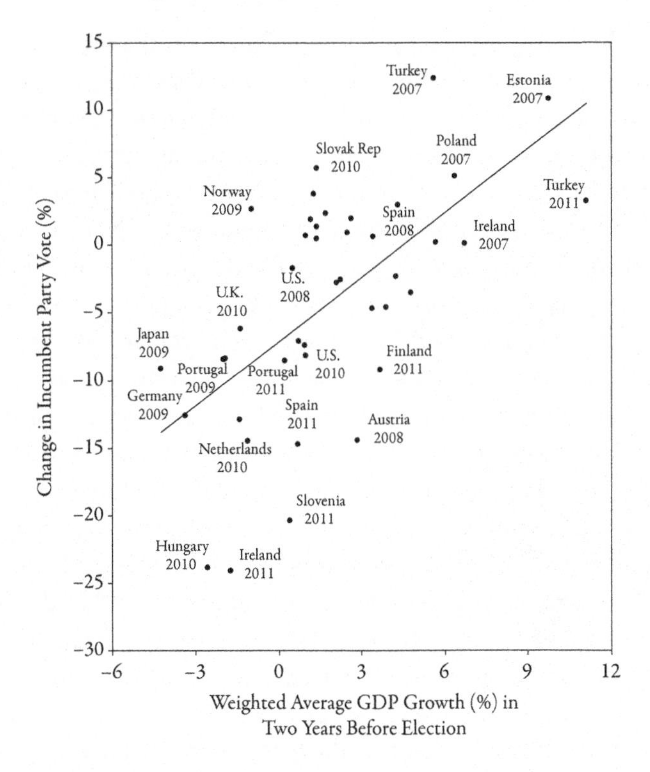

FIGURE 7.2 Cumulative Growth and Election Outcomes in OECD Countries, 2007–2011.

(Kayser and Peress 2012). However, the statistical results provide little evidence that voters did use the global economic climate as a benchmark in assessing the performance of their own governments. The regression analysis employing relative GDP growth rates (reported in the third column of Table 7.2) accounts for election outcomes rather less well than the analysis (in the second column) employing unadjusted growth rates. Even the analysis reported in the fourth column, which includes both relative and absolute growth rates, does not improve on the fit of the simpler model employing only absolute growth rates. Though the parameter estimates for the more complex specification are too imprecise to rule out the possibility that relative economic performance had some independent impact on election outcomes, the weight of the evidence—such as it is—clearly suggests that absolute growth rather than relative growth is what mattered to voters.[5]

The analysis presented in the fifth column of Table 7.2 adds another measure of economic performance, the unemployment rate at the time of the election.[6] The estimated effect of unemployment on the incumbent party's vote share is negative, but rather modest, and incorporating it does little to improve the statistical fit of the model. Additional analyses (not shown) failed to uncover any greater effect of unemployment among the sixteen cases with left-of-center governments, which might be more likely than right-of-center governments to be punished for high unemployment.[7] Nor did *changes* in unemployment in the year leading up to each election have any reliable electoral impact, once GDP growth was taken into account.[8]

The sixth column of Table 7.2 reports regression results for the same model as in the second column, but excluding the three biggest outliers in Figures 7.1 and 7.2: the elections in Hungary in 2010 and Ireland and Slovenia in 2011. In the first two cases, the effects of poor economic performance were compounded by draconian austerity programs and by major political scandals, producing disastrous electoral losses for the incumbent parties, the Socialist Party (MSZP) in Hungary (−23.9 percent) and Fianna Fail in Ireland (−24.1 percent). In Slovenia, a no-confidence vote in the National Assembly triggered an early election, and the incumbent Social Democrats lost two-thirds of their previous electoral support (−20.4 percent) to a brand new party, Positive Slovenia, led by the popular mayor of Ljubljana. Excluding these cases from the analysis reduces the estimated impact of GDP growth in the year before the election by 7 percent, while the estimated impact of GDP growth in the preceding year is cut in half; nevertheless, it is clear from these results that the apparent impact of economic conditions on election outcomes is not simply an artifact of rare conjunctions of economic and political crises.[9]

Taken as a whole, the regression analyses in Table 7.2 provide empirical support for a rather simple model of retrospective voting. Citizens in OECD countries generally rewarded their governments when their economies thrived and punished their governments when economic growth slowed.[10] The magnitude of these rewards and punishments was substantial, with differences in expected vote shares of 24 percentage points over the observed range of GDP growth.

Hanspeter Kriesi's analysis in Chapter 10 of this volume underlines the consistency of the relationship between economic conditions and incumbent support over the course of the Great Recession. Despite the fact that Kriesi looks at a rather different set of countries[11] using other statistical models,[12] his findings likewise suggest that "incumbent parties were severely punished for the negative economic consequences of the crisis."

Of course, the statistical relationship between economic conditions and election outcomes leave a great deal of electoral politics unaccounted for.

Much of this residual variation presumably reflects the impact of a wide array of other considerations voters brought to the polls: social concerns, wars and international crises, evaluations of the competence and charisma of party leaders, stirring speeches, scandals, and on and on. In addition, the impact of economic conditions themselves may have varied significantly from one election to another because of variation in "the extent of political (or electoral) control of the economy; the concentration and distribution of policy-making responsibility over parties; and the pattern of contention among the parties for future policy-making responsibility" (Duch and Stevenson 2008, 338), among other factors. Those variations are beyond the scope of the rudimentary analysis presented here. Nevertheless, it is clear even from rudimentary analysis that elections in the wake of the Great Recession were significantly influenced by voters' consistent inclination to reward or punish incumbent governments on the basis of economic growth rates in the months leading up to an election.

Accidents of Timing: Spain and Portugal

One important implication of the results presented in Table 7.2 is that incumbent governments are, to a significant degree, at the mercy of the electoral calendar. A reelection campaign in the midst of an economic boom may provide a convenient opportunity for an incumbent government to renew its popular mandate; conversely, facing the voters in the midst of an economic downturn is likely to be hazardous to an incumbent government's survival, even if the downturn is global in scope.

The political significance of electoral timing may be illustrated by comparing the likely fate of a government presiding over typical (OECD-average) economic conditions in early 2007, before the onset of the Great Recession, with the likely fate of an otherwise similar government presiding over typical economic conditions at the bottom of the recession, in the spring of 2009. Applying the regression parameter estimates in the second column of Table 7.2 to the average OECD growth rates in the first case suggests that a typical incumbent OECD government facing the voters in early 2007 might have expected its vote share to decline by a modest 2.3 percentage points. In contrast, an incumbent government facing the voters with an OECD-average growth trajectory in the spring of 2009 could expect its vote share to decline by a disastrous 11.2 percentage points.

The contrasting electoral fates of the Socialist governments of Spain and Portugal during the period covered by my analysis provide a more concrete illustration of the political ramifications of election timing. The Spanish government led by Socialist Workers' Party (PSOE) Prime Minister José Luis Rodriguez Zapatero faced the voters in March 2008, just before slowing economic growth in Spain (and in the OECD as a whole) slid into full-blown recession. The Portuguese Socialist government of José Sócrates was less fortunate; its four-year mandate expired in September 2009, just months after the Great Recession reached its nadir in Portugal (and in the OECD as a whole). The result in Spain was a slight *increase* in the governing party's vote share, while the Portuguese Socialists suffered a substantial loss—and the loss of their parliamentary majority.

In Spain, the governing PSOE began the three-month campaign period leading up to the March 2008 election with a small—but dwindling—lead in the polls over the conservative People's Party. According to a report in the *Times* of London:

> The economy expanded rapidly during Mr Zapatero's four-year term in office, extending an uninterrupted, 15-year growth spurt. But dark clouds are forming on the horizon, something the Opposition is doing its best to exploit. Inflation is picking up, hurting household budgets; house prices are also starting to slip after a decade-long boom.[13]

The dark clouds on the horizon were not enough to derail the Socialist government in the election. The opposition People's Party gained 1.1 percent of the vote, but with an erosion of support for minor parties the PSOE also gained slightly (.6 percent), producing a 4.5 percent popular vote margin. The PSOE gained 5 seats in the 350-seat Congress of Deputies, maintaining a narrow plurality that allowed Zapatero to continue as prime minister for up to four more years. Nevertheless, the shadow hanging over the Socialists' reelection was evident in a morning-after report in the *Economist*, which noted that Zapatero "must turn his attention to the mounting economic problems facing Spain.... Inflation is running at 4.3 percent, a housing boom has bust, unemployment is growing and once robust growth is slowing rapidly.... And with global financial turmoil adding to Spain's woes, the difficult bit is just starting."[14]

For the Zapatero government, the "difficult bit" was indeed "just starting." Spain's economy was stagnant in the first quarter following the election; it then experienced six consecutive quarters of declining real GDP and steadily escalating unemployment.[15] Had an election been held in the fall of 2009, when voters in Portugal went to the polls, the statistical analysis reported in the second column of Table 7.2 suggests that the deterioration in economic conditions since early 2008 would have cost the PSOE an additional 8.8 percent of the vote—more than enough to doom the Socialist government.

The narrow window of political survival for the Spanish Socialists is evident in opinion surveys conducted by the Centro de Investigaciones Sociológicas (CIS) in Madrid. In July 2008—just four months after the election—CIS's "vote estimate" showed the PSOE and the People's Party in a dead heat. By October 2009 the People's Party held a slim (3.3 percent) lead. By early 2011 that lead had swelled to ten percentage points.[16]

With Zapatero's popularity having "plummeted close to historic lows for a Spanish head of government," the prime minister first announced that he would step down on completion of his term, and then he acceded to mounting pressure to call an early election despite the likelihood that the PSOE would lose its parliamentary majority.[17] In the November 2011 election the party's vote share declined by almost fifteen percentage points, resulting in the loss of 59 of its 169 seats in the Congress of Deputies. The People's Party won an absolute majority of seats. Nevertheless, the Socialist government had had forty-four months of its original forty-eight-month term in which to attempt to engineer an economic rebound before facing the verdict of the electorate.

The electoral calendar was less kind to the Socialist government of Portugal, which had to face the voters in September 2009, just as the Portuguese economy was emerging from a year-long recession in which real GDP contracted by 4 percent. Economic conditions in Portugal were no worse—indeed, they were somewhat less bad—than elsewhere at this point in the global economic downturn.[18] Thus, voters assessing the incumbent government's performance in comparative context might have been inclined to reward the Socialists for preventing a worse downturn. But that is not what happened. The Socialist Party's vote share declined by 8.5 percent from 2005 to 2009, producing a loss of 24 seats—and majority status—in the 230-seat Assembly.

Most of the votes lost by the Socialists did not go to the opposition Social Democrats, but to two smaller parties: the Left Bloc and the People's Party, a conservative Christian democratic party. These results suggest that there was no consistent ideological basis for the turn against the Socialists, but a general disaffection with the party in power when the economy plunged.

Only the Socialists' substantial cushion of electoral support (reflected in a 16 percent vote margin over the Social Democrats in the 2005 parliamentary election) allowed Sócrates to carry on as prime minister for another eighteen months, albeit without a majority in the Assembly. In March 2011, when none of the five opposition parties proved willing to support the austerity program demanded by the European Union in exchange for a bailout—the last in a yearlong series of austerity measures in response to Portugal's burgeoning debt crisis—Sócrates was forced to resign and an early election was scheduled for June 2011.

The Socialists' 8.5 percent loss in the 2009 Portuguese election nearly matches the expected loss of 10.3 percent implied by the statistical results presented in the second column of Table 7.2. However, the same statistical results suggest that if the Socialist government had faced the voters in early 2008, as the Zapatero government did in Spain, it probably would have lost only one or two percentage points, and its absolute majority in the Assembly would have been comfortably preserved for another four years—long enough to adopt prime minister Sócrates's austerity program and, perhaps, begin to see its effects before the next election.

Instead, Portuguese voters went to the polls once again in June 2011 with their economy stagnant, unemployment rising, and a steady diet of painful austerity measures on the horizon. The Socialists garnered only about 28 percent of the vote—another 8.6 percent loss on top of the 8.5 percent loss they had suffered in 2009. Sócrates conceded defeat halfway through the vote counting, and the Social Democratic leader, Pedro Passos Coelho, prepared to lead a new center-right coalition government including the conservative People's Party. One voter, a social worker quoted by the *New York Times*,

> said that he continued to feel "ideologically on the left," but had voted for the first time for the Social Democrats on Sunday. "When you have hit the wall like our economy has, you have to accept that it's time to gamble on a change of direction and give somebody new a chance," he said.[19]

Ideology: A Turn to the Right?

A variety of political observers have seemed surprised by the fact that the Great Recession did not produce substantial gains in electoral support for parties of the political left (Lindvall 2012). For example, the *Economist* observed that in elections to the European Parliament in June 2009, at the bottom of the economic downturn, parties of the left had "failed to capitalise on an economic crisis tailor-made for critics of the free market."[20] Two years (and more than a dozen national elections) later, the prominent American political consultant Stanley Greenberg wrote:

> During this period of economic crisis and uncertainty, voters are generally turning to conservative and right-wing political parties, most notably in Europe and Canada. It's perplexing. When unemployment is high, and the rich are getting richer, you would think that voters of average means would flock to progressives, who are supposed to have their interests in mind—and who historically have delivered for them.

Instead, he suggested, "many voters in the developed world are turning away from Democrats, Socialists, liberals and progressives."[21]

Greenberg's perplexity is understandable if one supposes that voters are animated by the same ideological understandings that are commonplace among political elites, including most journalists, political scientists, and activists. However, if average voters are mostly inattentive to the manifestos of "critics of the free market" and skeptical of assertions about which parties "historically have delivered for them," it may not be so surprising to find them behaving in ways that confound conventional ideological expectations.

One virtue of systematic comparative electoral analysis is that it can help to suggest alternative explanations for observed election outcomes. Table 7.3 reports the results of a variety of statistical analyses intended to test whether voters in OECD countries in the midst of the Great Recession displayed any consistent shift in support for left-wing or right-wing governments. I classify the incumbent government in each country as Left (+1), Center (0), or Right (−1), or (in a few cases of coalition governments) Center/Left (+.5) or Center/Right (−.5). This simple classification is not intended to reflect the absolute ideological position of each government, but to characterize its relative position in the political context of its own country.[22]

The results presented in the first column of Table 7.3 indicate that, on average, left-wing governments did do less well at the polls than right-wing governments over the period covered by my analysis.[23] However, adding the GDP growth variables from Table 7.2 to the analysis (in the second column of Table 7.3) produces a considerably smaller ideological difference, suggesting that much of the apparent effect of ideology in the simpler regression analysis reflected worse economic conditions at election time under left-wing governments than under right-wing governments. Omitting the three most significant outlier elections—Hungary (2010), Ireland (2011), and Slovenia (2011)—from the analysis in the third column further reduces the apparent impact of ideology. Limiting the analysis to the thirty-five cases in which a single party governed alone or was clearly a senior coalition partner (in the fourth column) leaves the results essentially unchanged.

Table 7.3 Ideology and Changes in Incumbent Vote Shares, 2007–2011.

	1	2	3	4	5	6
Government	−3.42	−2.05	−1.45	−1.89	−.18	−2.12
Left-Ideology	(1.38)	(1.22)	(1.03)	(1.27)	(2.61)	(1.30)
Left-Ideology ×	—	—	—	—	−.65	—
Year					(.81)	
Left-Ideology ×	—	—	—	—	—	.07
ΔGDP(1–4Q)						(.40)
ΔGDP(1–4Q)	—	.97	.92	1.01	.95	1.00
		(.29)	(.24)	(.33)	(.29)	(.33)
ΔGDP(5–8Q)	—	.45	.19	.41	.48	.46
		(.24)	(.21)	(.26)	(.24)	(.24)
Intercept	−4.45	−6.98	−5.18	−6.20	−6.86	−7.00
	(1.22)	(1.18)	(1.05)	(1.29)	(1.19)	(1.20)
Adjusted R^2	.11	.38	.35	.34	.37	.36
Std error of reg	7.87	6.59	5.44	6.69	6.62	6.68
N	42	42	39[a]	35[b]	42	42

Notes: Ordinary least squares regression parameter estimates (with standard errors in parentheses).

[a] Excluding countries where incumbents lost more than 20 percentage points (Hungary 2010, Ireland 2011, Slovenia 2011).

[b] Excluding coalition governments (Estonia 2007, Finland 2007, Austria 2008, Israel 2009, Germany 2009, Netherlands 2010, Finland 2011).

Taken together, these results imply that the Great Recession produced surprisingly little overall change in the ideological proclivities of voters—and that retrospective voting was a stronger and more consistent factor than ideology in accounting for observed shifts in electoral behavior in OECD countries. Parties of the left certainly "failed to capitalise" on the crisis in most countries, but voters do not seem to have been "generally turning to conservative and right-wing political parties," either—except in times and places where a left-wing party presided over a significant economic downturn. This interpretation of voting patterns is quite consistent with the more direct evidence from European survey data (summarized in Figure 1.6 of Chapter 1), which showed only minor changes in ideological views in most countries, and no overall shift to the left or to the right.

The analyses reported in the fifth and sixth columns of Table 7.3 test two alternative specifications representing slightly subtler ways in which ideology might influence voters' responses to the crisis. The interaction between Government Left-Ideology and the timing of each election (measured in years elapsed since the beginning of 2007) allows for the possibility that ideological preferences gradually shifted in favor of left-wing (or right-wing) governments as the economic crisis evolved. For example, Johannes Lindvall (2012, 514) argued that "the political consequences of the Great Recession and the Great Depression were remarkably similar: in the first phase of both crises, right-wing parties did significantly better than left-wing parties; after approximately three years, left-wing parties began to recover." This pattern would be reflected by a larger negative coefficient for Government Left-Ideology in the fifth column of Table 7.3 (reflecting the "significantly better" performance of right-wing parties early in the crisis), and a *positive* coefficient for the interaction between Left-Ideology and Year (reflecting the recovery of left-wing parties with the passage of time). In fact, the temporal pattern here turns out to be the opposite of Lindvall's—left-wing governments did *worse* in later elections than in earlier ones, holding economic conditions constant—though the statistical results are far too imprecise to be reliable.

Finally, the interaction between Government Left-Ideology and GDP growth over the year leading up to the election, in the sixth column of Table 7/3, allows for the possibility that voters' sensitivity to economic conditions was greater for left-wing governments than for right-wing governments or vice versa. However, there is no evidence in the data for this possibility either.

On the whole, the statistical results reported in Table 7.3 provide little evidence that voters reacting to the Great Recession made any meaningful ideological distinctions between left-wing and right-wing governments. Of course, this is not to say voters did not bring ideological values to bear in casting their votes. For one thing, the distribution of durable ideological commitments in each country's electorate was presumably already reflected in the previous vote share of the incumbent party or parties, which serves as a baseline for my analysis of *shifts* in vote shares from one election to the next. Moreover, cross-national analysis of the sort presented here can only detect a *consistent* shift in ideological predilections across the diverse set of countries included in my analysis. If some electorates shifted to the left in response to the crisis while others shifted to the right, there may be no clear ideological pattern in the cross-national data—as there *is* no clear ideological pattern in the statistical results reported in Table 7.3. More detailed analysis of specific elections in specific countries might nevertheless provide evidence of consequential ideological shifts.

Germany: Diffusion of Responsibility

Germany held a federal election on September 27, 2009—the same day as Portugal. As in Portugal, the timing looked inauspicious for the incumbent government, a "grand coalition" pairing Chancellor Angela Merkel's Christian Democratic Union (and its Bavarian sister party, the Christian Social Union) with its largest competitor, the Social Democratic Party (SPD). Economic conditions in Germany at the time of the election were in some respects even worse than in Portugal; real GDP had declined by a disastrous 5.6 percent over the previous year, and the OECD consumer confidence index stood at 95.7, well below the European and OECD averages at the time.

At first glance, the German election outcome was exactly what might have been expected given these dire economic conditions. The governing parties lost a combined 12.6 percent of the popular vote, putting the outcome right on the regression lines in Figures 7.1 and 7.2. However, the two coalition partners did not share equally in this electoral rout. The SPD's vote share declined by 11.2 percent (from 34.2 percent in 2005 to 23.0 percent), while the CDU/CSU vote share declined by only 1.4 percent (from 35.2 percent to 33.8 percent). Chancellor Merkel jettisoned her chastened left-wing partner in favor of a new governing coalition with the smaller, center-right Free Democratic Party (FDP)—precisely the result she had angled for during the campaign.

This result seems puzzling from either of the perspectives considered here. If Germans were simply engaging in retrospective voting, as the close fit with the overall patterns in Figures 7.1 and 7.2 might suggest, why did they choose to punish the SPD but not the CDU/CSU for the country's economic distress? On the other hand, if they were voting for an ideological shift to the right, spurning the SPD and endorsing the FDP as a new coalition partner, what basis did they have for thinking that the new coalition's economic policies would be any more successful than the old coalition's policies had been?

The puzzle is reinforced by survey data suggesting that Germans were less in the mood to punish their leaders than might have been expected given the dire economic situation. In a cross-national opinion survey conducted by WorldPublicOpinion.org in May—just four months before the election—only 27 percent of Germans said that their own country's economic policies contributed "a lot" to the economic downturn.[24] Germans were less likely than citizens in any other country except China and India to say that their own government's efforts to address the crisis did not go far enough. This relative satisfaction with the government's handling of the crisis is striking in light of the fact that Germany's GDP had declined by 6.8 percent in the year leading up to the survey.

Responses to some other questions in the same survey shed some additional light on this seemingly anomalous German popular response to the crisis. Whereas only 27 percent of Germans said that Germany's economic policies contributed "a lot" to the economic downturn, 68 percent (more than in any country other than South Korea) said the economic policies of the United States contributed a lot; 78 percent blamed their own country's bankers' taking excessive risks; and 88 percent (more than in any other country in the survey) blamed international bankers' taking excessive risks. These results suggest that citizens in Germany, perhaps more than anyplace else in the developed world, interpreted the economic downturn as symptomatic of an external financial shock rather than a domestic political failure.

The concrete impact of the crisis on citizens was ameliorated by the existing German welfare state, and also by a variety of extraordinary measures intended "to ease workers' pain ahead of the election. The government launched a $116 billion stimulus package, subsidized the wages of workers on short hours, boosted welfare payments, and instituted a popular cash-for-clunkers program to spur auto production and purchases. Employers privately admit to business publications that they've held off on mass layoffs prior to the election."[25] Thus, even though the proportion of Germans who said that national economic conditions were "bad" peaked at almost 50 percent in March 2009, the proportion who said *their own* economic circumstances were bad "fluctuated between 10 and 15 percent ... through the ups and downs of the greatest economic crisis since the Great Depression" (Anderson and Hecht 2012, 9).

For his part, the leader of the SPD, Foreign Minister Frank-Walter Steinmeier, launched his party's election campaign by promising new policies to address the crisis, including raising the top tax rate, bolstering the minimum wage, and supporting the struggling German carmaker Opel. However, the dissonance between this platform and the policies the SPD had been supporting as part of the grand coalition generated swift simultaneous attacks from the right and from the left. The general secretary of the CDU "dubbed Steinmeier 'Wobbly Walter' and said that the SPD 'shift to the left is now a done deal.'" The SPD's prospective coalition partner on the left, the Greens, responded equally critically: "What the SPD is proposing today is the opposite of what they did during four years in the grand coalition. So we have to ask them: 'Are you really serious?' "[26] Perhaps as a result, though only 40 percent of respondents in a pre-election survey trusted Merkel to handle the continuing economic crisis, vastly fewer—a mere 9 percent—expressed similar confidence in Steinmeier.[27]

The "awkward yoking" of "historically bitter rivals" in the grand coalition clearly created a strategic dilemma for the SPD, but it also seems to have made for a campaign devoid of drama.[28] According to one press report, the CDU and SPD "tended to defend their government's record rather than challenge one another. A televised debate September 13 found Merkel and Steinmeier agreeing more often than not."[29] "Despite the difficult issues and choices that lie ahead," another said, "the race has largely steered clear of substantive discussion and debate." Chancellor Merkel's high approval ratings "have encouraged her to play it safe and sedate in the campaign" while hoping that the pro-business Free Democratic Party would gain enough support to emerge as a feasible coalition partner.[30]

The reality of German coalition politics produced yet another barrier to electoral accountability. A voter disinclined to support either of the current governing parties would be forced to choose among a variety of minor parties, the largest of which (FDP, the Left, and the Greens) had received less than 10 percent of the vote in the last election. But, as Christopher Anderson and Jason Hecht (2012, 11) noted, "whichever of the smaller parties such a voter chose would inevitably be forced into a coalition with one of the existing governing parties, given the necessity to achieve a majority in parliament to form a government." Thus one or the other of the partners in the grand coalition—Merkel or Steinmeier—would be the next chancellor regardless of what German voters thought of the coalition's performance over the previous four years.

In short, as Anderson and Hecht (2012, 5) put it, "several factors mitigated against strong economic voting effects: voters did not experience much personal economic hardship, the problems produced by the crisis were not homemade, and the alternatives to the incumbent government [were] muddled." Nevertheless, their detailed analysis of voting behavior, based on data from the German Longitudinal Election Study (GLES), found that voters' assessments of how their own economic circumstances had changed over the past two years did have a significant impact on which party they supported—though not on which of the *governing* parties they supported. Voters who said they had fared badly during the recession were slightly more likely to choose the SPD over the CDU; but they were much more likely to choose the FDP or (especially) the Left Party over *either* of the coalition partners (Anderson and Hecht 2012, 13). As the authors put it (16), "voters who personally had suffered during the crisis deserted the two governing parties in almost equal measure."

The fact that voters directly affected by the Great Recession seem to have punished both governing parties similarly at the polls—and defected to smaller parties in both directions, to the left and the right—suggests that retrospective voting in this instance was, to a good approximation, ideologically neutral. However, the fact remains that the SPD's vote share fell much more precipitously than the CDU/CSU's. Anderson and Hecht's analysis leaves the striking asymmetry unaccounted for. Perhaps it reflected a preference among German voters for the tax cuts and labor market reforms promised by the CDU/CSU (and FDP) over the conventional leftist policies proposed by the SPD?

Another analysis of the GLES survey data sheds additional light on the relative electoral fortunes of the two partners in Germany's grand coalition. Robert Rohrschneider, Rüdiger Schmitt-Beck, and Franziska Jung (2010, 23, 22) argued that because the coalition between the two largest parties "precluded a campaign that offered clear choices" on policy grounds, voters were "particularly prone to rely on simple shortcuts such as candidate personality to arrive at decisions"—and that these simple shortcuts strongly favored Merkel over Steinmeier. The authors' statistical analysis (2010, table 1) provided support for their interpretation. Voters' choices were most strongly influenced by their preferences for Merkel or Steinmeier as chancellor, and somewhat less affected by evaluations of the CDU/CSU and SPD. Once these personal and party evaluations were taken into account, vote choices were seen to be virtually unaffected by ideological self-placements, specific policy positions, or other political values.

This analysis suggests that the "muddle" of accountability produced by Germany's grand coalition resulted in a personal victory for Chancellor Merkel rather than an ideological mandate. In the days after the election, the *Economist* suggested hopefully that the outcome would allow Merkel to "escape from the cage of the 'grand coalition'" and pursue "many of the reforms that Germany needs, including to its tax and welfare systems, and to health care and the labour market."[31] However, the *New York Times* was a good deal more cautious, noting that German voters had "shown little appetite for drastic change in the midst of the economic crisis."[32]

Policy Choices and Their Electoral Impact

The statistical analyses reported in Table 7.3 provide little evidence of any consistent ideological shift in voting behavior in the wake of the Great Recession. But the notion that voters should have "flock[ed] to progressives," as Greenberg put it, is predicated on the assumption that parties of the left "who historically have delivered for them" might be expected do so again. In the midst of a global financial and economic crisis, most governments regardless of their own ideological values faced substantial pressures from powerful economic and political interests, including lenders and supernational organizations such as the EU and the World Bank, to pursue fiscal austerity and structural reform. Thus broad ideologies may not be indicative of the specific policies adopted by incumbent governments in response to the economic crisis. If left-of-center governments did not pursue conventional left-of-center policies such as Keynesian fiscal stimulus measures—or, for that matter, if

Table 7.4 Ideology, Economic Conditions, and Policy Responses to the Crisis.

	Incremental Debt (2008–2010)	Cyclical Deficit (2009)	Discretionary Stimulus (2009)	Bailouts and Nationalizations (2009)
Government Left-Ideology	.51 (3.39)	−.20 (.28)	−.58 (.96)	1.21 (1.01)
ΔGDP (2008:I–2009:I)	.58 (.86)	−.51 (.11)	.49 (.39)	.38 (.40)
GDP/capita (US $1000s, 2007)	−.000 (.001)	−.077 (.037)	.156 (.126)	.142 (.132)
Total debt (% GDP, 2007)	.097 (.087)	−.028 (.009)	.042 (.032)	.003 (.033)
Intercept	15.42 (6.06)	6.95 (1.35)	−4.18 (4.60)	−.50 (4.82)
Adjusted R^2	−.10	.46	−.06	−.02
Std error of reg	15.04	1.09	3.72	3.89
N	27[a]	20[b]	20[b]	20[b]

Notes: Ordinary least squares regression parameter estimates (with standard errors in parentheses).

[a] Including only countries with OECD debt data.

[b] Including only countries with OECD spending data.

centrist and right-of-center governments *also* pursued those policies, as seems to have been the case in Germany—then voters might have little reason to be swayed one way or the other by conventional ideological labels.

The statistical analyses reported in Table 7.4 explore the relationship between broad ideologies and specific policy choices in response to the Great Recession. As it turns out, the relationship is very modest, revealing almost no connection between the ideological postures of incumbent governments and the policies they pursued. Indeed, the statistical analyses suggest that major policy choices in the wake of the economic crisis were mostly unrelated to a variety of fundamental political and economic indicators, among them ideology, wealth, prior indebtedness, and the severity of the recession in each country.

The regression analysis reported in the first column of Table 7.4 focuses on government debt.[33] The cumulative growth in central government debt from 2007 to 2010 exceeded 40 percent of GDP in Iceland (58.1 percent), Britain, Greece, and Ireland. The United States, Japan, Spain, and Portugal saw increases in debt ranging from 20 to 26 percent of GDP. Debt increased by 5–15 percent of GDP in most other OECD countries, with the exception of Sweden and Israel, which slightly *reduced* their outstanding debt.

The parameter estimates in Table 7.4 indicate that left-wing governments accumulated only slightly more debt over the course of the economic crisis than right-wing governments did—an additional 1 percent of GDP, other things being equal.[34] Nor is there any evidence that incremental debt was driven by the depth of the recession in a given country (the estimated effect of 2008 GDP growth is actually positive, though quite imprecise) or its level of economic development (as measured by GDP per capita in 2007). Finally, the expectation that debt accumulation might be constrained by existing indebtedness is confounded by a modest (and also quite imprecise) *positive* coefficient on prior debt (as measured by total debt in 2007 relative to GDP).

The regression analyses reported in the remaining columns of Table 7.4 focus on three more specific aspects of governments' fiscal policies at the height of the crisis, in 2009: (1) cyclical deficits resulting from declines in tax revenues and increased spending on "automatic stabilizers" such as unemployment insurance; (2) discretionary stimulus spending; and (3) other discretionary spending such as bailouts and nationalizations.[35] Here, too, there is surprisingly little evidence of systematic connections between ideologies and economic conditions on one hand and policy choices in response to the Great Recession on the other.

Cyclical deficits were substantial in every OECD country, ranging from 3 percent of GDP in the United States to 8.7 percent in Sweden. Some of this variation no doubt reflects differences in the structure of welfare states resulting from durable ideological differences among countries (as the examples of the United States and Sweden suggest). However, the ideological complexion of the incumbent government in each country seems to have had little or no bearing on the magnitude of the cyclical deficit it incurred in 2009. Rather, the statistical results presented in the second column of Table 7.4 suggest that the magnitude of each country's cyclical deficit mostly reflected the severity of its recession—as we would expect if this spending was an *automatic* response to the downturn rather than a fiscal policy *choice*. There is also some evidence that preexisting debt moderated cyclical responses to the recession, with an 18 percent increase in 2007 indebtedness (roughly, the difference between a typical country like Germany or Britain and a low-debt country like Canada or New Zealand) counterbalancing an additional 1 percent decline in GDP.

Discretionary stimulus programs were smaller in magnitude, ranging from less than 1 percent of GDP in Italy, Switzerland, France, and Portugal to 4.5 percent in Japan—though in Hungary, Iceland, and Ireland draconian austerity programs produced substantial *declines* in discretionary spending (ranging from 6.5 percent to 7.7 percent of GDP) in 2009. Again, the results in Table 7.4 reveal no consistent relationship between the ideological complexion of a country's government and its fiscal policy; if anything, left-wing governments may have spent slightly *less* on stimulus programs than right-wing governments did, other things being equal. However, once cases of significant fiscal contraction are set aside, there is some indication that ideology influenced the relationship between GDP growth and discretionary stimulus spending, with left-wing governments spending more in countries with mild recessions and right-wing governments spending more in countries with more severe downturns.[36]

Other discretionary spending also varied substantially across OECD countries, with major bailouts in all of the English-speaking democracies (ranging from 4.5 percent of GDP in the United States to 8.8 percent in the United Kingdom). Here, too, the statistical analysis (summarized in the fourth column of Table 7.4) suggests that the cross-national differences are not easily explained by differences in ideology or economic circumstances. Richer countries and those with left-wing governments may have been slightly more prone to bailouts, other things being equal, but the differences are fairly small and statistically unreliable.

Table 7.5 Policies and Changes in Incumbent Vote Shares, 2009–2011.

	1	2	3	4	5	6
Incremental government debt (% GDP, 2008–2010)	−.24 (.11)	−.14 (.12)	−.10 (.12)	—	—	—
Cyclical deficit (% GDP, 2009)	—	—	—	−.93 (1.00)	−.51 (1.21)	—
Discretionary stimulus (% GDP, 2009)	—	—	—	1.36 (.40)	2.39 (1.66)	2.21 (1.48)
Bailouts and nationalizations (% GDP, 2009)	—	—	—	−.77 (.42)	−.02 (.79)	—
ΔGDP(1–4Q)	—	.77 (.44)	.78 (.37)	1.00 (.45)	1.05 (.51)	1.01 (.44)
Intercept	−2.82 (2.34)	−5.27 (2.63)	−4.72 (2.37)	−2.70 (6.11)	−10.21 (8.50)	−12.40 (4.19)
Adjusted R^2	.15	.22	.21	.54	.10	.24
Std error of reg	7.90	7.56	6.30	5.70	5.99	5.49
N	25[a]	25[a]	22[c]	17[b]	14[c]	14[c]

Notes: Ordinary least squares regression parameter estimates (with standard errors in parentheses).

[a] Including only countries with OECD debt data and elections after 2008.

[b] Including only countries with OECD spending data and elections after 2008.

[c] Excluding countries with major austerity programs (Iceland 2009, Hungary 2010, Ireland 2011).

Did voters reward or punish their political leaders for engaging in Keynesian fiscal policies in response to the Great Recession? The regression analyses reported in Table 7.5 explore the electoral impact of the policy choices of incumbent governments. Since the OECD spending data employed here are projections for 2009, the analyses are limited to elections from 2009 through 2011.

The regression analyses reported in the first three columns of Table 7.5 focus on the electoral impact of government debt. The simple bivariate regression of incumbent electoral performance on incremental debt, presented in the first column of the table, suggests that every additional percentage point of debt accumulated by a government over the three years of the crisis (2008, 2009, and 2010) reduced the incumbent government's vote share by a quarter of a percentage point.[37] This is a fairly strong relationship, suggesting, for example, that the ballooning debts of Greece, Ireland, and the United Kingdom depressed electoral support for their incumbent governments by as much as 10 percentage points. However, part of the relationship is spurious, reflecting the fact that governments in worse economic circumstances were more likely to resort to substantial increases in debt. When real GDP growth rates in the year leading up to each election are added to the analysis (in the second column of Table 7.5), the apparent effect of incremental government debt is cut almost in half. This estimate implies that the debt increases in Greece, Ireland, and the United Kingdom probably cost their incumbent governments five or six percentage points at the polls, while a typical accumulation of debt—about 12 percent of GDP—would have cost an incumbent government only one or two percentage points. Excluding the three countries that pursued stringent austerity programs—Hungary, Iceland, and Ireland—from the analysis (reported in the third column of Table 7.5) reduces the apparent electoral impact of debt still further.

The regression analyses reported in the last three columns of Table 7.5 focus on the electoral impact of specific aspects of governments' fiscal policies at the height of the recession, in 2009. The analysis in the fourth column relates each incumbent party's vote share (in the seventeen countries with elections after 2008 for which the relevant data are available) to the magnitude of the cyclical deficit, discretionary stimulus spending, and bailouts and nationalizations. This analysis suggests that, even after allowing for the electoral impact of overall GDP growth, discretionary stimulus spending had a significant electoral payoff—while cyclical deficit spending and bailouts and nationalizations, if they had any effect at all, were probably harmful to incumbents' electoral prospects.

The parameter estimate for discretionary spending suggests that ambitious stimulus programs in Japan, Sweden, Australia, Denmark, Germany, Finland, and New Zealand (ranging from 3.0 to 4.5 percent of GDP) probably netted incumbent governments an extra four to six percentage points at the polls, whereas severe retrenchments in Iceland, Hungary, and Ireland (ranging from 6.5 percent to 7.7 percent of GDP) cost the incumbent governments in those countries nine or ten percentage points when they stood for reelection. Analyses excluding the three countries with stringent austerity programs—in the fifth and sixth columns of Table 7.5—suggest an even larger

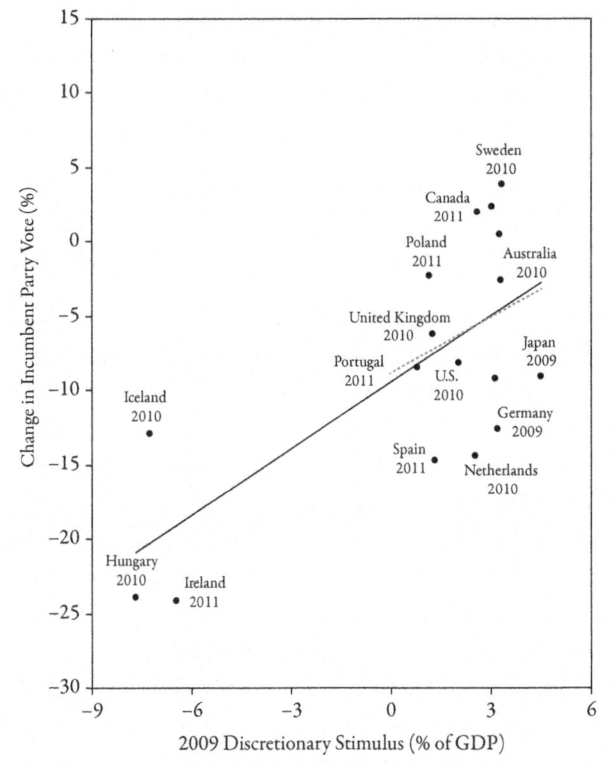

FIGURE 7.3 Discretionary Stimulus Spending and Incumbent Party Electoral Support, 2009–2011.

electoral impact of stimulus spending, though the parameter estimates are much less precise.

The apparent impact of discretionary stimulus spending provides the strongest evidence I have found of a significant electoral response to governments' fiscal policy choices during the Great Recession. However, even this evidence is unavoidably fragile, given the limitations of the data on which it is based. The basic relationship between incumbents' vote shares and discretionary stimulus spending is displayed in Figure 7.3. Although the relationship is clearly positive (and the slope of the bivariate regression closely matches the corresponding parameter estimate in the fourth column of Table 7.5), the disparity in policies between the fourteen countries with modest stimulus programs and the three with severe austerity programs provides rather little statistical leverage for assessing the electoral effects of less drastic policy differences. However, excluding the three austerity cases leaves the bivariate relationship between stimulus spending and election outcomes (represented by the dotted line in Figure 7.3) virtually unchanged. Thus it seems likely—though by no means certain—that voters did punish incumbent governments for austerity and rewarded them for stimulating their economies in a period of crisis.

The United States: A Rejection, But of What?

Barack Obama's historic victory in the 2008 U.S. presidential election was portrayed by enthusiastic pundits as a "rebirth of American liberalism" and "the culmination of a Democratic realignment that began in the 1990s." The atmosphere of crisis in which Obama took office reinforced expectations of swift action on an ambitious and, presumably, popular progressive legislative agenda. One prominent political observer, John Judis, argued not only that "liberal views have re-emerged... with a vengeance" but also that those views "can be expected to shift further leftward—especially on economic questions—in the face of coming recession." Comparisons with Franklin Roosevelt and the famous first one hundred days of the New Deal era abounded.[38]

However, as with many new political orders proclaimed by pundits, America's "New Liberal Order" (as *Time* magazine dubbed it) proved to be remarkably short-lived. A slow rebound of economic growth, high unemployment, and partisan rancor drove Obama's popularity steadily lower through most of his first two years in office. When his Democratic allies in Congress faced the voters in November 2010 they suffered a substantial defeat, losing 8.4 percent of the popular vote and 63 seats in the 435-seat House of Representatives—an even worse showing than might have been expected given the state of the U.S. economy at the time. With the Republican opposition back in control of the House, Americans faced a return to "divided government" and legislative gridlock.

Unlike the 2009 federal election in Germany, the 2010 midterm election in the United States was widely interpreted as an adverse judgment by voters on the policies of the incumbent government. In the *New York Daily News*, for example, the election result was presented as "a stinging rebuke to President Obama."[39] In his election night victory speech, the new Speaker of the House John Boehner argued that the American people had sent an "unmistakable message" to the president, "and that message is: 'change course'. We hope President Obama will now respect the will of the people, change course, and commit to making the changes they are demanding." According to Boehner, voters had rejected "the spending sprees, the bailouts, the backroom deals, the takeovers and all the nonsense" in favor of cutting spending, reducing the size of government, and "helping small businesses get people back to work."[40]

In his own postelection press conference, Obama resisted the notion that voters had rejected his policies, preferring to interpret the outcome as merely a reflection of economic frustration. Voters, the president said,

> are not satisfied with the outcomes. If right now we had 5 percent unemployment instead of 9.6 percent unemployment, then people would have more confidence in those policy choices. The fact is, is that for most folks, proof of whether they work or not is, has the economy gotten back to where it needs to be. And it hasn't.... And ultimately, I'll be judged as President as to the bottom line, results.[41]

In a television interview the next day, Obama was pressed once again regarding the meaning of the election. He replied by ticking off a variety of popular policy initiatives and then added a grudging concession that voters might have misinterpreted his administration's responses to the economic crisis as reflecting an ideological agenda. "I think that what happened over the course of two years," he said,

> was that we had to take a series of big, emergency steps quickly. And most of them in the first six months of my administration. Each of them had a big price tag. You got intervention in the banks. You've got the auto bailout. You've got a stimulus package. Each one with a lot of zeroes behind it. And people looked at that and they said, 'Boy, this feels as if there's a huge expansion of government.'[42]

A national survey of voters leaving their polling places seemed to bolster the notion that the election outcome was shaped not only by adverse economic conditions but also by adverse assessments of the policies and priorities of the Obama administration. For example, 56 percent of the exit poll respondents said the government was "doing too much," and they supported Republican candidates by a margin of almost four to one; on the other hand, 38 percent said the government "should do more," and they supported Democratic candidates by about the same margin. Similarly, 58 percent said the "highest priority" for the next Congress should be reducing the deficit (40 percent) or cutting taxes (18 percent); they voted Republican by a 67–30 margin, while the 37 percent who said the highest priority should be "spending to create jobs" supported Democratic candidates by a 68–30 margin.[43]

Results like these suggest that voters on both sides were animated by policy concerns related to the government's response to the economic crisis—and that many more of them were animated to *oppose* the policies of the president and the Democratic majority in Congress than to *support* those policies. However, a different—and perhaps more reliable—way to assess the political significance of specific policy choices in the American setting is to estimate the direct electoral impact of major roll call votes on the electoral fortunes of individual members of Congress (Jacobson 1996). In this spirit, Eric McGhee (2010) estimated the electoral cost to Democratic incumbents of supporting each of four controversial bills: the 2008 Troubled Assets Relief Program (TARP); the $787 billion stimulus package passed a few weeks after President Obama took office; a cap-and-trade energy bill that later died in the Senate; and the Affordable Care Act, which substantially reformed the American health care system. His estimates suggest that the cost of supporting TARP was "small and insignificant," while the cost of supporting the stimulus package was 2.8 percent, cap-and-trade 2.1 percent, and health care reform 4.5 percent. The cap-and-trade and health care votes seem to have been more ideologically charged, with Democratic supporters punished much more in more Republican districts, while support for the stimulus "seems to [have] hurt everyone." A simulation based on these estimates suggested that, if every vulnerable Democrat had refrained from supporting the cap-and-trade and health care bills, the party would have lost twenty-four fewer seats, bringing the election outcome into close agreement with forecasts based primarily on the state of the economy.[44]

McGhee's estimates of the effects of Democratic support for cap-and-trade (2.1 percent) and health care reform (4.5 percent) are just large enough (bearing in mind that only about half the districts in the country had Democratic incumbents who supported those bills running for reelection) to account for the discrepancy between the Democrats' aggregate vote loss (8.4 percent) and their expected vote loss on the basis of the statistical relationship in Figure 7.3 (5.2 percent). Although the exactness of this correspondence is no doubt coincidental, it does suggest that the Democrats' apparent underperformance in the 2010 election may have been attributable to policy choices largely unrelated to the economic crisis.

Individual Democrats in Congress seem to have been punished for supporting health care reform and cap-and-trade legislation, but their support for legislative initiatives more directly related to the economic crisis probably bolstered their electoral support. Even if we accept McGhee's estimate that supporting the Obama stimulus package cost Democratic incumbents

2.8 percent of the vote, this electoral penalty was almost certainly more than offset by the political benefit of improved economic conditions resulting from the implementation of the stimulus program. Economists Alan Blinder and Mark Zandi (2010, table 9) estimated that the stimulus package added 1.3 percent to real GDP in 2009 and 1.9 percent in 2010.[45] Combining those estimates with my own estimates of electoral responses suggests that the economic benefit of the stimulus package probably reduced the Democrats' national vote loss by somewhere between 2.7 percent and 4.9 percent—enough to offset the direct electoral cost to specific Democratic incumbents who voted for the stimulus bill, while leaving the party as a whole distinctly better off.[46]

Thus, even though many observers interpreted the 2010 election outcome as a rejection by American voters of the president's response to the economic crisis, the truth of the matter is that the stimulus program almost certainly staved off an even worse electoral debacle—because it staved off an even worse economic debacle. If Obama and his party overreached, it was in other areas—most notably, by forcing through Congress an historic overhaul of health care reform and by trying but failing to pass a major energy bill. By rebuking Democrats for what may have felt like "a huge expansion of government" in these areas, voters also *seemed* to be rejecting the huge expansion of government that forestalled a much longer and deeper Great Recession. The ironic result, as one observer noted, was that "the electorate has now restored to power in the House the same crowd they repudiated only two years ago—and whose policies, by any honest reckoning, wrecked the economy."[47]

Conclusion

Interpreting election outcomes is not merely a scholarly pursuit. Specific understandings of what voters had in mind, individually and collectively, in casting their ballots can shape practical political thought, discourse, and action for better or worse (Grossback, Peterson, and Stimson 2006). American political culture in the twentieth century was significantly shaped by the conventional belief that the 1936 election constituted a referendum on the New Deal and, more broadly, on the role of the federal government in the American economy and society. More recently, the notion that the outcome of the 2010 midterm election represented "a stinging rebuke to President Obama" and that the American people had sent an "unmistakable message" to "change course" has seemed to alter the political standing and strategies of both the president and his Republican opponents.

When understandings of this sort are mistaken, political trouble may ensue. For example, British Conservative Party leader David Cameron interpreted his party's 2010 election victory as a mandate for "new economic management" and "the most radical decentralization of power this country has seen for generations."[48] However, polls at the time found solid majorities of Britons in favor of aiding troubled major industries and companies, significantly increasing government spending, and even providing financial support to troubled banks.[49] And a detailed study of British public opinion found that "public satisfaction with health and education improved dramatically" under the Labour government, "leaving the researchers asking why Labour did not fight the election on its social policy record—and warning that the [Conservative-led] coalition is now risking a significant backlash against its reforms and cuts to public services that people are happy with."[50]

Placing the outcome of any particular election in a broader comparative perspective may help to restrain the tendency of election observers—and especially of election winners—to overinterpret the ideological significance of the result. Americans in the Great Depression repudiated Herbert Hoover and then reelected Franklin Roosevelt in a landslide; but voters in other democracies in the same period repudiated left-wing governments when times were bad and reelected right-wing governments when economic conditions improved. By the same token, John Boehner and David Cameron led conservative opposition parties to significant victories at the polls in the wake of the Great Recession, but they—and we—might do well to bear in mind that, at the same time, conservative governments in countries as diverse as Iceland and Japan were even more decisively repudiated after presiding over significant economic downturns.[51] In periods of economic crisis, as in more normal times, voters have a strong tendency to support any policies that seem to work, and to punish leaders regardless of their ideology when economic growth is slow.

Acknowledgements

I am grateful to Christopher Achen, Christopher Anderson, Nancy Bermeo, Mark Kayser, Johannes Lindvall, Markus Prior, Steven Rogers, and participants in the Oxford conference on "Popular Reactions to the Great Recession" and the Vanderbilt Political Behavior Workshop for helpful discussions and comments on early versions of this chapter. The work reported here was supported by the Princeton Institute for International and Regional Studies and by Vanderbilt University's May Werthan Shayne Chair in Public Policy and Social Science.

Notes

1. Election results are for the lower house of each country's national parliament. In presidential systems, I treat the president's party as the incumbent party. I exclude elections in Belgium in 2007 and 2010 (a prolonged constitutional crisis produced a series of caretaker governments), the Czech Republic in 2010 (an interim government of experts nominated by both major parties had replaced the previous incumbent government fourteen months before the election), Korea in 2008 (partisan turnover in a presidential election four months earlier blurred responsibility), and Switzerland in 2007 and 2011 (all major parties participated in a plural executive). Election data are from NSD European Election Database, supplemented with various national sources for non-European countries.
2. Parallel analyses focusing solely on vote gains or losses for the prime minister's party produce results generally similar to those reported here. Coalition governments include Estonia in 2007 (the Centre Party received 25.4 percent of the vote in the preceding election, while the Reform Party received 17.7 percent but included the incumbent prime minister), Finland in 2007 (Centre Party with 24.7 percent and Social Democrats with 24.5 percent), Austria in 2008 (Social Democratic Party with 35.3 percent and People's Party with 34.3 percent), Israel in 2009 (Kadima with 22.0 percent and Labor with 15.1 percent), Germany in 2009 (CDU/CSU with 35.2 percent and SPD with 34.2 percent), Netherlands in 2010 (Christian Democrats with 26.5 percent and Labour with 21.2 percent), and Finland in 2011 (Centre Party with 23.1 percent and National Coalition Party with 22.3 percent).
3. "Quarterly Growth Rates of real GDP, change over previous quarter," seasonally adjusted, OECD (http://stats.oecd.org). I sum the quarterly growth rates over the four quarters preceding each election.
4. "Weighted GDP growth" in Figure 7.2 combines growth in quarters 1–4 before the election and growth in quarters 5–8 before the election, each weighted by the associated parameter estimate in the second column of Table 7.2: $(1.02\times(\Delta GDP(1\text{-}4Q))+.56\times(\Delta GDP(5\text{-}8Q)))/(1.02+.56)$.
5. I also looked for effects of relative economic performance within the narrower confines of the Euro area (using the average growth of Euro-area economies over the same period as the relevant benchmark) and among the "old OECD" economies (excluding the United States) studied by Mark Kayser and Michael Peress (2012). In both cases, election results were more strongly related to absolute economic performance than to relative economic performance.
6. "Labour Force Statistics (MEI): Harmonized Unemployment Rates and Levels (HURs)," quarterly data seasonally adjusted, OECD (http://stats.oecd.org).
7. The estimated effect of unemployment was – .53 (with a standard error of .44).
8. The estimated effect of the *change* in unemployment was –.93 (with a standard error of.81).

9. Omitting these three outliers from the analysis of relative growth reported in the third column of Table 7.2 reinforces the conclusion that *relative* growth matters less than *absolute* growth. The adjusted R^2 statistic falls from .29 to .15, whereas the comparable statistic for the analysis of absolute growth falls only from .35 (in the second column of Table 7.2) to .33 (in the sixth column). The absolute growth model clearly fits these data better than the relative growth model.
10. The parameter estimates in Table 7.2 imply that real GDP growth of about 4.5 percent per year would be required for an incumbent government to maintain its vote share. The average real GDP growth rate in OECD countries before the onset of the Great Recession (in 2005, 2006, and 2007) was a bit less than 3 percent. This discrepancy suggests that, even in normal economic times, incumbent governments are likely to experience a gradual erosion of electoral support.
11. Of the forty-two elections analyzed here, twenty also figure in Kriesi's analysis. He excludes elections in OECD countries outside Europe (Australia, Canada, Chile, Israel, Japan, New Zealand, Turkey, and the United States) and those held in 2007 and early 2008, while including several elections in countries outside the OECD (Bulgaria, Cyprus, Latvia, Lithuania, Malta, and Romania) and three omitted here for structural reasons set out in note 2 (Belgium and the Czech Republic in 2010, and Switzerland in 2011).
12. Kriesi reports separate analyses of the electoral effects of GDP growth, unemployment, and deficits in three distinct sets of countries: Western European majoritarian systems, Western European nonmajoritarian systems, and Central and Eastern European systems. Given the resulting small sample sizes, most of the parameter estimates are not "statistically significant" by conventional standards; nevertheless, they are comparable in magnitude to those reported here. For example, the estimated effect of GDP growth on incumbents' vote shares (averaging Kriesi's separate estimates for prime ministers' parties and all cabinet parties in majoritarian, nonmajoritarian, and Central and Eastern European systems in Table 10.3 of Chapter 10) is 1.04, only slightly smaller than the estimate of 1.20 reported in the first column of Table 7.2 above.
13. Thomas Catan, "Spain Gets March Election as Zapatero Struggles to Stay in Office," *Sunday Times*, January 15, 2008 (http://www.timesonline.co.uk/tol/news/world/europe/article3187271.ece).
14. "Spain's Election: Back for More," *The Economist*, March 10, 2008 (http://www.economist.com/node/10833787).
15. The unemployment rate doubled in the eighteen months following the election, from 9.4 percent to 18.9 percent, and subsequently increased even further, reaching 23 percent by the time of the November 2011 election.
16. Centro de Investigaciones Sociológicas, "Indicadores Electorales" (http://www.cis.es/cis/opencms/EN/11_barometros/Indicadores_PI/electorales.html); "Estimación de Voto" (http://www.cis.es/cis/opencms/-Archivos/Indicadores/documentos_html/sB606050020.html).

17. Raphael Minder, "Spanish Premier Says He Won't Seek a New Term," *New York Times*, April 4, 2011, page A11. Raphael Minder, "Spanish Premier, Under Pressure, Calls Election for November," *New York Times*, July 30, 2011, page A5.
18. Portugal's real GDP grew by .8 percent in the second quarter of 2009, while the rest of the Euro area was still contracting. The cumulative decline in real GDP over the two years leading up to the election amounted to 2.3 percent in Portugal, 3.8 percent in the Euro area, and 3.5 percent in the OECD as a whole. Portuguese unemployment stood at 11.1 percent at the time of the election—slightly higher than the Euro-area average of 10 percent, but far below the 18.9 percent level in neighboring Spain.
19. Raphael Minder, "Social Democrats Claim a Strong Victory in Portugal," *New York Times*, June 6, 2011, page A9.
20. "The European Elections: Swing Low, Swing Right." *The Economist*, June 11, 2009 (quoted by Lindvall 2011).
21. Stanley B. Greenberg, "Why Voters Tune Out Democrats," *New York Times*, July 31, 2011, page SR1.
22. Since my interest is in economic ideology, I classify governing parties on the basis of that dimension. For example, Poland's Law and Justice Party and Civic Platform Party are classified as centrist and right-wing, respectively, despite the fact that the former is more conservative on social issues. See Ben Stanley, "Party Placement in Two-Dimensional Issue Space, 2011," at Polish Party Politics (http://polishparty-politics.com/2012/03/23/party-placement-in-two-dimensional-issue-space-2011/).
23. The average vote losses for Left and Right incumbents were 6.9 percent and .6 percent, respectively.
24. "Public Opinion on the Global Economic Crisis," July 21, 2009 (http://www.worldpublicopinion.org/pipa/pdf/jul09/WPO_FinCrisis_Jul09_quaire.pdf).
25. Folko Mueller and Lee Sustar, "The Left in the German Elections," SocialistWorker.org, September 25, 2009 (http://socialistworker.org/2009/09/25/left-german-elections).
26. "Steinmeier Determined to Topple Merkel in German Elections," *Deutsche Welle*, April 19, 2009 (http:// www.dw-world.de/dw/article/0,,4190864,00.html).
27. Nicholas Kulish, "Before Election, Not a Voter Was Stirring," *New York Times*, August 20, 2009, page A6.
28. Henry Chu, "German Election a Yawner for Voters," Los Angeles Times, September 27, 2009 (http://articles.latimes.com/2009/sep/27/world/fg-germany-election27).
29. Mueller and Sustar, "The Left in the German Elections."
30. Chu, "German Election a Yawner for Voters."
31. "Merkel's Moment," *The Economist*, October 1, 2009 (http://www.economist.com/node/14548863).
32. Nicholas Kulish, "Merkel's Party Claims Victory in Germany," *New York Times*, September 27, 2009 (http://www.nytimes.com/2009/09/28/world/europe/28germany.html).

33. "Central Government Debt: Total central government debt (% GDP)," OECD (http://stats.oecd.org). I have tabulated the growth in outstanding debt from 2007 to 2010 (extrapolating Japan in 2010).
34. Allowing for a statistical interaction between ideology and the severity of the recession suggests that left-wing governments may have been more sensitive to economic conditions in accumulating debt than right-wing governments were; but this difference is far from being statistically "significant," and it mostly reflects the anomalous case of Greece, where a substantial debt crisis coincided with a relatively modest decline in GDP in 2008.
35. Projected spending data from OECD June 2009 Economic Outlook tabulated by Ansell (2012, Table 11.8).
36. Altering the regression model in the third column of Table 7.4 to include an interaction between ideology and GDP change produces a coefficient of 1.16 (with a standard error of 1.78) for the main effect of ideology and a coefficient of .42 (with a standard error of .35) for the interaction term. Excluding the three cases with substantial fiscal contractions—Hungary, Iceland, and Ireland—the corresponding parameter estimates are.60 (with a standard error of .42) and .30 (with a standard error of.09). The latter estimates suggest that a mild recession like Norway's (GDP growth of − 1.1 percent) would produce an expected discretionary stimulus amounting to 2.3 percent of GDP under a left-wing government and 1.8 percent under a right-wing government, while a more severe downturn like Germany's (−6.8 percent) would produce an expected stimulus of only .8 percent under a left-wing government but 3.7 percent under a right-wing government.
37. Kriesi's corresponding estimates of the electoral impact of budget deficits in Table 10.5 of Chapter 10 are even larger, ranging from .33 for Central and Eastern Europe to .85 for majoritarian countries in Western Europe. However, this difference in magnitudes is unsurprising in light of the fact that Kriesi's analysis focuses on budget deficits in the single year before each election, whereas mine focuses on the total accumulation of government debt over three years, 2008–2010.
38. Peter Beinart, "The New Liberal Order," *Time*, November 13, 2008. John B. Judis, "America the Liberal," *New Republic*, November 19, 2008. The cover of the post-election issue of *Time* magazine in which Beinart's story appeared featured a portrait of Obama as FDR, complete with fedora and cigarette holder, and a title proclaiming "The *New* New Deal."
39. Thomas M. DeFrank, "Midterm Election Results Show Voters Unhappy with President Obama's Leadership," *New York Daily News*, November 3, 2010.
40. "Midterms 2010: John Boehner's Victory Speech in Full." *The Telegraph*, November 3, 2010 (http://www.telegraph.co.uk/news/worldnews/us-politics/8106711/Midterms-2010-John-Boehners-victory-speech-in-full.html).
41. "Press Conference by the President, November 03, 2010" (http://www.whitehouse.gov/the-press-office/2010/11/03/press-conference-president).

42. "Transcript: President Barack Obama, Part 1. '60 Minutes' Correspondent Steve Kroft Interviewed the President Nov. 4, 2010" (http://www.cbsnews.com/stories/2010/11/07/60minutes/main7032276.shtml?tag=contentMain;contentBody).
43. "U.S. House: National Exit Poll, 17,504 Respondents" (http://www.cnn.com/ELECTION/2010/results/polls/#val=USH00p1).
44. A similar analysis by Brady, Fiorina, and Wilkins (2011) focused only on the cap-and-trade and health care votes; their results implied that by opposing these bills Democrats could have saved somewhere between twenty-two and forty seats, "strongly suggesting that the votes in question cost the Democrats their majority" (249).
45. More broadly, Blinder and Zandi (2010, Table 4) estimated that the entire portfolio of policy responses to the Great Recession by the Federal Reserve, Congress, and the Bush and Obama administrations boosted real GDP by 4.9 percent in 2009 and 6.6 percent in 2010.
46. On the basis of parameter estimates reported in the second column of Table 7.2, the combined effect of an additional 1.9 percent real GDP growth in 2010 and an additional 1.3 percent growth in 2009 would be to increase the Democratic vote share in the 2010 election by 2.7 percent. The analysis presented in the fourth column of Table 7.5 implies that the direct effect of a stimulus amounting to $309 billion (approximately 2.2 percent of GDP) in 2009 would be to increase the Democratic vote share by about 3 percent, while the additional impact of greater overall GDP growth would increase the Democratic vote share by an additional 1.9 percent.
47. DeFrank, "Midterm Election Results."
48. David Batty, "David Cameron Launches Election Campaign with Economy Pledge," *The Guardian*, January 2, 2010 (http://www.guardian.co.uk/politics/2010/jan/02/david-cameron-election-campaign-economy).
49. Britons favored "financial support to troubled major industries and companies" by a margin of 73 percent to 23 percent, "significantly increasing government spending" by a margin of 60 percent to 35 percent, and "financial support to troubled banks" by a margin of 55 percent to 42 percent. "Global Poll Shows Support for Increased Government Spending and Regulation," September 13, 2009 (http://www.worldpublicopinion.org/pipa/pdf/sep09/BBCEcon_Sep09_rpt_final.pdf).
50. Polly Curtis, "Britain 'More Thatcherite Now Than in the 80s' Says Survey," *The Guardian*, December 13, 2010 (http://www.guardian.co.uk/education/2010/dec/13/social-survey-thatcherite-britain).
51. Iceland and Japan experienced declines in real GDP of 6.1 percent and 7.0 percent, respectively, in the run-ups to their 2009 elections; their right-of-center governments suffered vote losses of 12.9 percent and 9.1 percent.

References

Achen, Christopher H., and Larry M. Bartels. 2002. "Blind Retrospection: Electoral Responses to Droughts, Floods, and Shark Attacks." Annual Meeting of the American Political Science Association, Boston (http://www.unc.edu/polisci/aprg/pdfs/Achen%20APRG%20Talk.pdf).

Achen, Christopher H., and Larry M. Bartels. 2004. "Musical Chairs: Pocketbook Voting and the Limits of Democratic Accountability." Annual Meeting of the American Political Science Association, Chicago (https://my.vanderbilt.edu/larrybartels/files/2011/12/musical-chairs.pdf).

Achen, Christopher H., and Larry M. Bartels. 2005. "Partisan Hearts and Gall Bladders: Retrospection and Realignment in the Wake of the Great Depression." Annual Meeting of the Midwest Political Science Association, Chicago (https://my.vanderbilt.edu/larrybartels/files/2011/12/partisan-hearts.pdf).

Anderson, Christopher J. 1995. *Blaming the Government: Citizens and the Economy in Five European Democracies*. Armonk, NY: Sharpe.

Anderson, Christopher J., and Jason D. Hecht. 2012. "Voting When the Economy Goes Bad, Everyone Is in Charge, and No One Is to Blame: The Case of the 2009 German Election." *Electoral Studies 31*:1, 5–19.

Ansell, Ben W. 2012. "Crisis as Political Opportunity? Partisan Politics, Housing Cycles, and the Credit Crisis." In Nancy Bermeo and Jonas Pontusson, eds., *Coping with Crisis: Government Reactions to the Great Recession*, pp. 327–360. New York: Russell Sage Foundation.

Bartels, Larry M. 2008. *Unequal Democracy: The Political Economy of the New Gilded Age*. New York and Princeton, NJ: Russell Sage Foundation and Princeton University Press.

Blinder, Alan S., and Mark Zandi. 2010. "How the Great Recession Was Brought to an End." Princeton University and Moody's Analytics (http://www.economy.com/mark-zandi/documents/End-of-Great-Recession.pdf).

Brady, David W., Morris P. Fiorina, and Arjun S. Wilkins. 2011. "The 2010 Elections: Why Did Political Science Forecasts Go Awry?" *PS*, April, 247–250.

Converse, Philip E. 1964. "The Nature of Belief Systems in Mass Publics." In David E. Apter, ed., *Ideology and Discontent*, pp. 206–261. New York: Free Press.

Downs, Anthony. 1957. *An Economic Theory of Democracy*. New York: Harper & Brothers.

Duch, Raymond M., and Randolph T. Stevenson. 2008. *The Economic Vote: How Political and Economic Institutions Condition Election Results*. New York: Cambridge University Press.

Enelow, James M., and Melvin J. Hinich. 1984. *The Spatial Theory of Voting: An Introduction*. Cambridge: Cambridge University Press.

Fiorina, Morris P. 1981. *Retrospective Voting in American National Elections*. New Haven, CT: Yale University Press.

Grossback, Lawrence J., David A. M. Peterson, and James A. Stimson. 2006. *Mandate Politics*. Cambridge: Cambridge University Press.

Healy, Andrew J., Neil Malhotra, and Cecilia Hyunjung Mo. 2010. "Irrelevant Events Affect Voters' Evaluation of Government Performance." *Proceedings of the National Academy of Sciences 107*:29, 12804–12809.

Hibbs, Douglas A., Jr. 2006. "Voting and the Macroeconomy." In Barry R. Weingast and Donald A. Wittman, eds., *The Oxford Handbook of Political Economy*, pp. 565–586. Oxford: Oxford University Press.

Jacobson, Gary C. 1996. "The 1994 House Elections in Perspective." *Political Science Quarterly 111*:2, 203–223.

Kayser, Mark Andreas, and Michael Peress. 2012. "Benchmarking Across Borders: Electoral Accountability and the Necessity of Comparison." *American Political Science Review 106*:3, 661–684.

Key, V. O., Jr. 1966. *The Responsible Electorate: Rationality in Presidential Voting, 1936–1960*. Cambridge, MA: Harvard University Press.

Kramer, Gerald H. 1971. "Short-Term Fluctuations in U.S. Voting Behavior, 1896–1964." *American Political Science Review 71*:1, 131–143.

Lewis-Beck, Michael S. 1988. *Economics and Elections: The Major Western Democracies*. Ann Arbor: University of Michigan Press.

Lindvall, Johannes. 2012. "The Political Consequences of the Great Depression and the Great Recession: Remarkably Similar." *Swiss Political Science Review 18*:4, 514–517.

Mayhew, David R. 2002. *Electoral Realignments: A Critique of an American Genre*. New Haven, CT: Yale University Press.

McGhee, Eric. 2010. "Which Roll Call Votes Hurt the Democrats?" *Monkey Cage*, November 9 (http://themonkeycage.org/blog/2010/11/09/which_roll_call_votes_hurt_the/).

Murillo, Maria Victoria, Virginia Oliveros, and Milan Vaishnav. 2010. "Electoral Revolution or Democratic Alternation?" *Latin American Research Review 45*, 87–114.

Rohrschneider, Robert, Rüdiger Schmitt-Beck, and Franziska Jung. 2010. "Short-Term Factors versus Long-Term Values: Testing Competing Explanations of Electoral Choice." German 2009 Election Conference, Lawrence, Kansas (http://www.dgfw.eu/dok/papers/rohr_schm_jung.pdf).

Rosenstone, Steven J. 1983. *Forecasting Presidential Elections*. New Haven, CT: Yale University Press.

Stokes, Donald E. 1963. "Spatial Models of Party Competition." *American Political Science Review 57*:2, 368–377.

Tufte, Edward R. 1978. *Political Control of the Economy*. Princeton, NJ: Princeton University Press.

8

Crisis Perceptions and Economic Voting Among the Rich and the Poor

THE UNITED KINGDOM AND GERMANY

Raymond M. Duch and Iñaki Sagarzazu

ONE ASPECT OF the Great Recession of 2008–2010 that will dominate historical accounts of the crisis is its dramatic effects on the average citizen in countries troubled by these events. Given the unique magnitude of the economic shocks experienced by many economies, this important historical event provides a unique opportunity to study how such economic shocks affect the attitudes and voting behavior of the average citizen. Unlike with the Great Depression, we now have extensive survey data on the attitudes and behavior of average citizens from a variety of countries. This essay leverages extensive survey data collected during this period in order to understand whether individuals, who are from distinct economic circumstances and who might have been differentially affected by the Recession, respond similarly or not to these economic shocks. We believe that the analysis presented in this essay will make an important contribution to the historical record by helping understand how voters were affected by, and responded to, the Great Recession.

The principal puzzle addressed here is how the economic shocks of the Great Recession affected the average citizen's attitudes and political behavior. The literature on how the economy shapes political behavior constitutes an important foundation for understanding the political ramifications of the Great Recession. In one characterization, economic shocks are shared "events" that are, for the most part, experienced rather uniformly by citizens. Certainly when we examine aggregate-level economic attitudes, on the whole, citizens seem quite astute when it comes to assessing and anticipating macroeconomic outcomes (Duch and Stevenson 2011; MacKuen, Erikson, and Stimson 1992). An important contributing factor here is the role of the media in shaping national attitudes about the economy (Duch and Stevenson 2011; Duch, Palmer, and Anderson 2000; MacKuen et al. 1992; Hetherington 1996).

In another characterization, these macroeconomic events are expected to affect groups in the population very differently: for some citizens the shocks have very negative consequences, while for others their effects are relatively moderate. For example, much of the political economy literature on labor markets focuses on how macroeconomic "events" affect various occupations quite differently. Some occupations are more at risk than others in economic hard times. Understanding differences in perceived risk associated with one's employment or occupation may help explain preferences over policies that have redistributive consequences (preferences over marginal tax rates, for example). Implicit in this characterization is the notion of considerable heterogeneity in how certain groups perceive economic events, in how these events shape their political preferences, and finally in their impact on vote choices.

Our contention is that these two perspectives on how the economy shapes political behavior have very different implications for the political legacy of the Great Recession. In one perspective the Great Recession is a homogeneously shared economic experience that is essentially defined and framed by the media. And the political response to these shocks could have been fairly uniform across income groups in society. On the other hand, the economic shocks could have quite different effects on the rich and poor in society, they could have been perceived quite differently by them, and they could have resulted in opposing political preferences for, and behavior by, the rich and poor. This chapter explores these two distinct portrayals of the economic and political consequences of the recent Great Recession. The macroeconomic events of central concern in our analysis are real economic growth, unemployment, and inflation. We describe how voters responded to the economic crisis of 2008–2010 drawing on data from two panel studies conducted during the 2009 German Federal election and the 2010 UK Parliamentary election.

Our empirical analysis addresses these questions: (1) Is there evidence that the crisis affected poor and rich people differently? (2) Were perceptions of the national macroeconomic events disparate across income groups? (3) Did poor and rich people perceive differences in how their personal finances were affected? (4) Did the rich and poor have opposed preferred policy responses to these macroeconomic events? and (5) Did these policy responses or perceptions of economic outcomes (personal or national) weigh more heavily in the vote functions of the poor than those of the rich? We evaluate these differences between the rich and the poor by dividing the participants in our studies on the basis of their self-reported income level; those in the top two quartiles are classified as rich, while those in the bottom two quartiles are classified as poor. [1]

Two Perspectives on Macroeconomic Shocks

Although many chronicles of the Great Recession assume that its economic shocks would have important political ramifications, it remains unclear precisely how these events should be expected to shape economic attitudes and behavior. In order to provide some insights here, we propose building on the classic literature on the economy and voting behavior that treats voters as instrumentally rational actors. Downs (1957) introduced the notion that individuals make vote choices according to their comparison of expected utilities for each of the competing parties. The notion of voters as utility-maximizing political "consumers" was a significant deviation from widely accepted explanations for vote choice that borrowed from the social-psychological literature (Berelson, Lazarsfeld, and McPhee 1954; Campbell et al. 1960). But it was Kramer's efforts (1971) to "test the Downsian rationality hypothesis" by exploring the link between economic outcomes and U.S. election results that inspired early economic voting research. Kramer in effect argued for the importance of economic well-being in the voter utility function introduced by Downs. Fair (1978) took this argument a step forward by presenting a formal statement of how economic performance enters the voter utility. This was an important theoretical advance because it established a foundation for modeling vote choice from a rational utility maximization perspective that included economic well-being in the utility function.

These models are the foundation for our effort to understand the political implications of the Great Recession. They suggest that voters should punish incumbents for negative economic shocks. However, a fundamental presumption here is that macroeconomic shocks register in a reasonably similar fashion with most voters. It is true that we are in some sense collective spectators of macroeconomic events; we watch them unroll on BBC, Fox News, and CNN. But the macroeconomic events, and government policy responses to them, have distributional consequences. But there will be economic winners and losers; highly leveraged unemployed homeowners in Spain may respond quite unlike highly paid German engineers working in Munich. The losers, who are likely to be the poor, may have much different evaluations and reactions to macroeconomic events.

First, one might expect heightened attention to economic shocks—or more negative responses—on the part of the poor relative to the rich. It is true that the rich and the poor are at least potentially exposed to the same media narrative regarding these macroeconomic events, and hence we might expect homogeneous evaluations. But the poor are typically more negatively affected, which might elicit more negative assessments of macroeconomic performance. In particular, certain segments of the labor markets may be exposed to significant shocks linked to declining trade barriers, increased global trade, structural changes in the labor force (in some cases imposed by governmental authorities), and the exporting of jobs to low-wage regimes. Any number of aspects of individuals' economic attitudes might be affected by these shocks, so we focus on three of them: policy preferences, personal economic evaluations, and national economic assessments.

Economic policy preferences. Many expected the Great Recession to be a catalyst for more aggressive government redistributive policies. The assumption was that certain sectors of the economy and certain types of employees were more exposed than others to the shocks resulting from the Great Recession. For example, with the collapse of the housing market and with a dramatic decline in construction, individuals working in construction-related occupations and industries were, in many countries, exposed to high unemployment risk.

Differential risk exposure was expected to affect voters' preferences for redistribution. Rehm (2011) defines risk exposure in terms of income expectations and suggests that it affects policy and partisan preferences. Rehm operationalizes risk exposure in terms of level of unemployment in an individual's occupational category. Other scholars have conceptualized risk exposure differently; examples are factor endowments, trade exposure of the sector in which an individual is employed, the tradeability of sectors (Mayda and Rodrik 2005), foreign direct investment by multinational enterprises (Scheve and Slaughter 2004), job "off-shore-ability" (Walter 2010), and skill specificity (Iversen and Soskice 2001). What is common to these treatments is the notion that voters acquire information on risk exposure, use this information to calibrate their personal risk exposure, and make appropriate calculations regarding the extent to which existing policies (in particular, government redistributive measures) insure them against these risks.

To the extent that rich and poor voters respond in a self-interested fashion to economic shocks, the poor will favor redistributive policies that moderate the negative impact of the economic shocks on the less fortunate, while the rich should be less enthusiastic about such policies. As it turns out, the evidence for a relationship between economic status and policy preferences is mixed, at best. The politics of inequality suggests that the redistributive policy preferences of the poor and the rich may not conform to such a simple characterization. Considerable evidence suggests that countries with unequal distributions of income redistribute less than those with more equitable distributions of income (Bradley et al. 2003; Iversen and Soskice 2009). Explanations for why redistributive policies do not more closely conform to classical theoretical expectations typically focus on institutional and electoral factors that intervene between the voter and policy outcomes (Pontusson and Rueda 2010; Pontusson and Lupu 2011).

Casual observation of the media and political rhetoric associated with macroeconomic shocks suggests additional reasons for redistributive policy preferences not lining up neatly along income lines. There is widespread acceptance during crises of "no pain, no gain" theories of the macroeconomy—claims that without radical measures (such as reduced government spending) that typically affect the poor negatively, economic recovery is impossible. Surprisingly, the poor often favor these policies and give considerable weight to them in deciding how to vote. This is consistent with other public opinion evidence suggesting, for example, that poor voters favor policies that make taxes less progressive (Bartels 2005).

Another possibility, typically unexplored, is simply that the redistributive preferences of poor and rich voters do not differ, perhaps because voters do not perceive significant income inequalities (Kenworthy and McCall 2008; Page and Jacobs 2009). The context of a serious financial shock provides an opportunity to explore whether the redistributive preferences of the poor and rich do in fact diverge in a situation most likely to produce such polarization.

National economic attitudes. Major political fallout of the Great Recession had it that a number of incumbent governments were defeated in elections during this period—for example, Prime Minister Brown in Britain, President Sarkozy in France, and the ruling Spanish Socialist Party. This is not surprising given the extensive literature on economic voting, which unambiguously confirms the existence of an empirical connection between the economy and vote choice—though, as Duch and Stevenson (2008) point out, the magnitude of the connection can vary significantly cross-nationally and within particular countries over time. And there clearly were incumbents, such as President Obama in the United States, who dodged the economic-vote bullet.

This chapter is concerned with two empirical foundations for the connection. First, voters are assumed to be attentive to fluctuations in the macroeconomy and to have a pretty accurate collective sense of macroeconomic conditions and trends.[2] A common theme in this literature is that voters increasingly are exposed, via various media, to considerable information about macroeconomic events, which accounts for both the relative accuracy of their evaluations and the homogeneity of those evaluations (Hetherington 1996).

Second, and likely following from this observation, national aggregate economic outcomes are assumed to play a particularly important role, compared to personal economic circumstances, in voter's utility functions. Classic economic voting models typically focus on the effects of collectively experienced macroeconomic events. And there is evidence from the United States suggesting that even in the face of the recent economic shocks and the diverging economic fortunes of the rich and poor, these income groups share very similar assessments of macroeconomic fluctuations (Hopkins 2012).

But there is an alternative narrative to this classic rational choice characterization of voters responding in a homogeneous fashion to economic shocks. In particular there is evidence that the poor are typically less attentive to the media and that this might result in biased evaluations of the real economy (Bartels 1996; Krause 1997; Duch, Palmer, and Anderson 2000) or in a more moderate economic vote (Gomez and Wilson 2001; Singer 2011).

Personal economic attitudes. The rich and the poor might have quite similar evaluations of aggregate macroeconomic outcomes but quite dissimilar assessments of how their personal finances are faring. Voters who are more negatively affected by local economic conditions or who belong to segments of the economy that experience more negative economic shocks do seem to register more negative evaluations of the economy (Ansolabehere, Meredith, and Snowberg. 2011).

The Great Recession is one in which the personal economic circumstances of many voters were subject to significant shocks; but it was also, in every country, a national economic event that played out very prominently in the traditional media and, increasingly, in social networks. Hence this offers a unique opportunity to evaluate how these two dimensions of economic evaluation—assessment of personal finances and evaluation of the national economy—evolve over the course of a severe economic downturn.

Economic attitudes and policy preferences. Are the politics of the Great Recession simply based on valence issues? Are voters simply punishing the incumbent for what they perceive as poor economic outcomes? Given the magnitude of the economic shocks and their differential impact on less affluent segments of society, we would expect this to have an effect on the public's policy preferences. In particular, perceived economic shocks should affect preferences for redistribution such as redistributive taxation. Given that the poor are likely to be disproportionately affected, they should be the most supportive of redistributive policies.

The assumption here is that economic shocks result in support for policies that have significant redistributive consequences. However, empirical support for the conjecture that self-interest conditions support for these policy responses is mixed. For example, Scheve and Slaughter (2004) and Hays, Ehrlich, and Peinhardt (2005) have found that support for policy responses to trade shocks is tied to economic self-interest. However, Bechtel, Hainmueller, and Margalit (2012), examining German public support for international financial bailouts in the aftermath of the recent eurocrisis, concluded that support is not related to conventional measures of economic self-interest, but rather with measures of other-regardingness and cosmopolitanism.

Economic attitudes in the vote utility function. Ultimately, we are interested in economic attitudes—and how they vary between the rich and the poor—because they shape vote choices and hence can affect policy responses to economic shocks such as the recent financial crisis. Again, there is a debate in the literature regarding the relative importance of economic attitudes for the voting decisions of the rich and the poor. Of particular concern is which economic perceptions shape the vote choice of the rich and the poor. In the case of the U.S. electorate, Bartels (2008) demonstrates that by favoring national economic evaluations over personal financial outcomes in their vote decision, the rich and the poor both effectively reward incumbents who make the rich better off. In a sense, he suggests that Republican presidents get widespread support from low-income voters despite implementing macroeconomic policies that favor the rich because low-income voters vote sociotropically. (The argument is a little more complicated, but this is the bare-bones version). In a similar vein, Gomez and Wilson (2006) have argued that higher political sophistication (which correlates with income and education) prompts citizens to vote their own pocketbooks.

Redistributive policy preferences in the vote utility function. Redistributive policies typically take center stage during serious macroeconomic shocks. Again, which policies enter into the vote-utility function of the rich and poor and the relative weight accorded different policies may have implications for how all these voters fare in the aftermath of the crisis. In the context of a severe economic crisis, the poor may accord greater weight to redistributive policies in their vote choice than is the case for the rich. But given the considerable evidence that the poor in fact exhibit redistributive preferences at odds with their self-interest, it would not be surprising if the poor and rich allocated similar importance to redistributive policy preferences in their vote decision.

We assume, although it bears demonstrating, that in this particular crisis macroeconomic shocks had a more negative impact on the poor than on the rich. We would expect the poor and the rich to differ in their preferred policy responses to these macroeconomic events—particularly to the extent that the policy responses have redistributional consequences. And to the extent this is the case, self-interested poor voters are likely to be more negative in their evaluations of these shocks. We would expect to see economic evaluations enter into the vote-utility function of the poor in a fashion that does not undermine their economic self-interest; they should not, for example, give less weight than the rich to these shocks.

The Economic Crisis

We begin our empirical analysis by characterizing changes in objective economic conditions in the two countries included in our study, Germany and

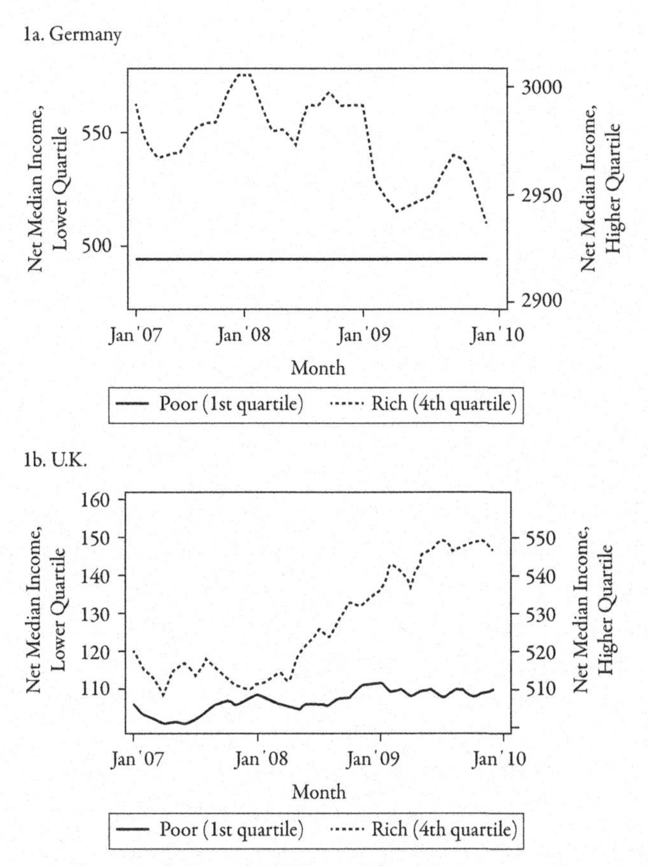

FIGURE 8.1 Evolution of Smoothed Net Median Income in Germany and UK, 2007–2009.

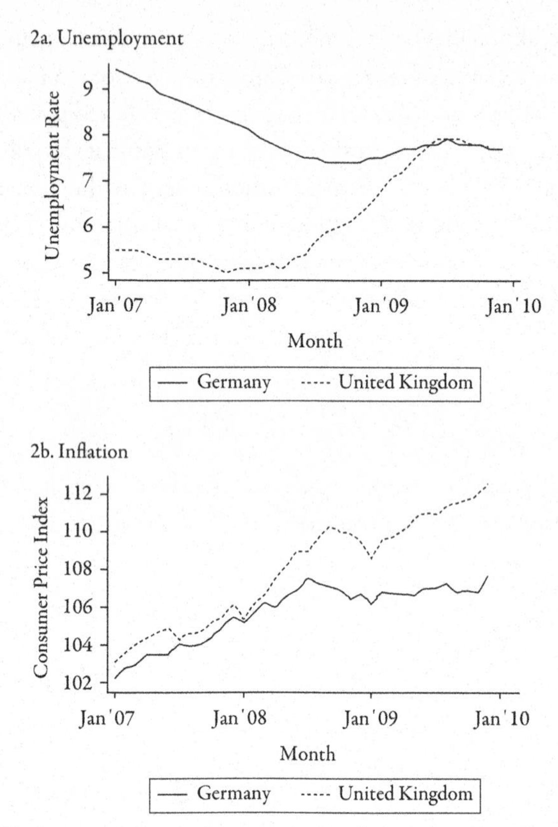

FIGURE 8.2 Evolution of Unemployment and Inflation Rates in Germany and UK, 2007–2009.

the UK. Real disposable income (RDI) declined from 2008 through 2009 in both countries, and one might expect the magnitude of those declines to be greater for people in the lower levels of the income distribution. Figure 8.1 shows the evolution of net median income for the lowest- and highest-income quartiles in both Germany and the UK.[3] In Germany the weekly income of the highest quartile dropped from its pre-crisis levels, while in the UK the income of this group actually increased. In both countries however, the income of the lowest quartile experienced little or no change in either direction.

Similarly, Figure 8.2 shows how unemployment rates and inflation evolved over the course of the crisis.[4] In terms of unemployment (Figure 8.2a), Germany barely felt the effects of the financial crisis. The decline in unemployment that occurred from 2007 to 2008 stopped midway through 2008; but instead of climbing back up to its 2007 level, unemployment held steady. In fact, Germany experienced a remarkably low level of unemployment throughout the crisis, one not seen in decades. In contrast, unemployment in the UK had been relatively low and constant from 2007 to 2008, five percentage points lower than in Germany; however, after the first quarter of 2008 it quickly climbed from about 5 percent to 8 percent. The contrasting nature of the economic crisis in the two countries can also be seen with regard to levels of inflation (Figure 8.2b). Before the crisis, in these two countries the levels were similar; starting in 2008 prices in the UK increased at a faster pace than those in Germany.

National Subjective Measures

Clearly, both the UK and Germany experienced economic shocks of a significant magnitude in the aftermath of the recent financial crisis. We now explore how this crisis was perceived by citizens, what effects it had on their policy preferences, and how it affected voters' choices. Our analysis is based on data from two panel surveys, one carried out in the UK from 2008 to 2010 and the other carried out in Germany in 2009.

The 2008–2010 British Cooperative Campaign Project (BCCAP) was a six-wave panel study of 10,000 respondents. The survey waves were conducted by the internet survey firm Polimetrix YouGov in December 2008, May and October 2009, and January, May, and June 2010. The 2009 German Cooperative Campaign Project (DeCCAP) was a four-wave panel study of six thousand respondents, likewise conducted by Polimetrix YouGov in June, August, September, and October 2009. The surveys were conducted online and were approximately twenty minutes long; every attempt was made to retain all respondents throughout all the waves of each panel.[5]

Waves 2 to 6 of the BCCAP survey included questions measuring perceptions of the economy, changes in consumption habits, and policy preferences. Similar questions were included in the four waves of the DeCCAP. Regarding the national economy, respondents were asked:

1. Would you say that OVER THE PAST YEAR the nation's economy has…
2. What about the next 12 months? Do you expect the economy, in the country as a whole, to…
3. Would you say that OVER THE PAST YEAR, inflation has…
4. Would you say that OVER THE PAST YEAR, the level of unemployment in the country has…

National economic evaluations in both countries were remarkably negative but improved rapidly over the course of the study. In December 2008—at the peak of the financial crisis and ensuing recession—essentially the entire sample thought things were getting worse; 75 percent of the UK respondents

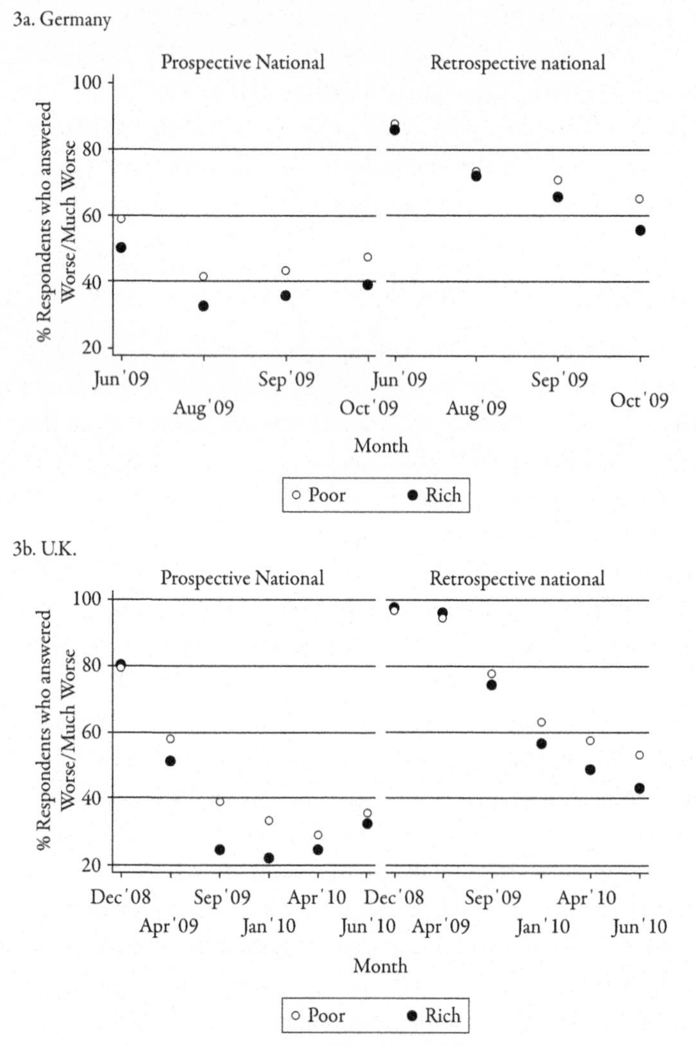

FIGURE 8.3 "Worse"/"Much Worse" Perceptions of National Economic Conditions.

answered "much worse." This persisted until the beginning of 2010, when the balance of sentiment about the UK economy shifted from negative to positive. Given the dramatic shock to the global economy, the negative assessments in both countries in early 2009 are unsurprising. However, the rapid rate of improvement in national retrospective economic evaluations in both countries over the relatively brief periods covered by our panel studies is more surprising, certainly in comparison to the rather modest changes in actual macroeconomic indicators over these periods.

Figure 8.3 presents the evolution of the "worse" and "much worse" national economic evaluations for both Germany and the UK by income group. With

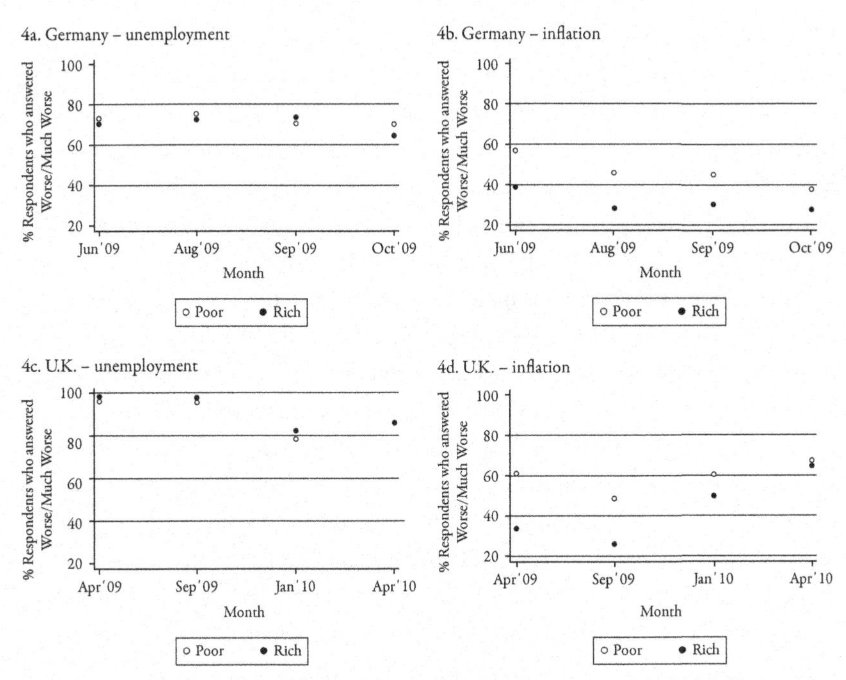

FIGURE 8.4 "Worse"/"Much Worse" Perceptions of Unemployment and Inflation.

respect to these national economic evaluations, the poor and rich exhibit very similar patterns. In the UK, for instance, in December 2008 97 percent of the low- and high-income respondents alike had "worse" or "much worse" retrospective evaluations. By April 2010, the corresponding figures were 58 percent and 49 percent, respectively. The high-income respondents were somewhat less negative, but not dramatically so. In the case of prospective economic evaluations, the proportion of high-income respondents with "worse" or "much worse" evaluations went from 80 percent to 25 percent, while the proportion of low-income respondents with "worse" or "much worse" evaluations dropped from 80 percent to 39 percent. Hence, both the rich and the poor became increasingly less pessimistic and guardedly more optimistic over the sixteen months of the panel survey.

For the most part, respondents who thought the economy was performing poorly in the first panel wave in December 2008 either remained pessimistic in subsequent waves or changed to perceiving the economy as being the "same." However, respondents were generally much less pessimistic in their assessments of the future than in their assessments of the previous twelve months. Finally, and most importantly for our purposes, Figure 8.3 shows that the improvements in national perceptions over the course of our panel study were roughly parallel across income levels. Likewise for Germany, retrospective and prospective evaluations for the low- and high-income respondents were very similar, although with a less dramatic drop.

Additional questions in the surveys permit some insight into what specific macroeconomic concerns were driving these general economic evaluations. Recall from Figure 8.2 that unemployment was declining or stable in Germany but rising in the UK, while both countries were experiencing a rising rate of inflation. Figure 8.4 presents British and German retrospective assessments specifically of unemployment and inflation over the preceding year. Negative evaluations of the employment situation resemble the levels we saw for retrospective national evaluations: more than 80 percent of UK respondents and almost 80 percent of German respondents reported "worse" or "much worse" perceptions (see Figures 8.4a and 8.4c). We would not expect the Germans to be as pessimistic as the British, given that unemployment was declining prior to 2009 and remained stable in 2009, compared to quite significant rises in unemployment in the UK after the financial crisis. Again, we suspect that this high level of employment pessimism in Germany is a result of media stories concerning threats to employment resulting from the global economic shock. Finally, once again, there is no evidence here that the rich and poor had differing subjective evaluations; both groups were extremely pessimistic about the employment situation.

As we would expect, given the relatively low levels of inflation in both countries, Figure 8.4b and 8.4d indicate that assessments of inflation were much less negative than was the case for unemployment. The British respondents over the course of the two-year panel exhibited rising concern with price increases—a concern that ultimately proved prescient on their part. But of particular concern here are the differences between the rich and poor respondents; the poor were significantly more likely to have negative retrospective evaluations of inflation.

We began this chapter by sketching two visions of how citizens experience macroeconomic events such as the recent financial crisis. In one, economic experience is collective and heavily shaped by mediated representations of economic outcomes. In the other, citizens are sensitive to how economic shocks affect their particular occupational or socioeconomic niche—hence we would expect quite different evaluations on the part of the rich and poor. Our analysis of subjective evaluations of the national economy indicates that the former is by far the more accurate characterization of how attitudes about the economy are shaped during financial crises. Though there were some indications of difference between the rich and poor—particularly with respect to inflation—they were generally relatively minor.

Table 8.1 Economic Circumstances of Rich and Poor Respondents in Germany and UK.

	Germany		UK	
	Poor	Rich	Poor	Rich
Made more than four changes in consumption	32%	20%	14%	15%
Bad time to make big purchases	49%	22%	35%	23%
Petrol prices are higher	97%	97%	91%	85%
Worried over ability to get loans	55%	26%	50%	28%
Concerned about ability to pay for housing	72%	39%	62%	36%
Affected by the economy	64%	43%	71%	49%

Crisis in Personal Finances?

Macroeconomic events have real implications for household and personal finances. And it is a reasonable conjecture that the poor are affected differently from the rich. One would anticipate, or at least we do, that shocks to personal finances are not something experienced collectively or shaped by the media. Our expectation is that these economic shocks are likely to generate much more significant differences in how the poor and the rich evaluate their own financial situations.

We begin with a measure of respondents' own finances based on responses to a series of questions about their personal economic circumstances. The battery of questions included respondents' assessment of whether it is a good time to make major purchases (such as furniture, kitchen appliances, and televisions), of changes in oil and housing prices, and of their ability to make monthly payments or their need to make consumer behavior changes to achieve this goal. Table 8.1 shows how the poor and the rich in both Germany and the UK felt the financial crisis. It is interesting to note that in both countries there are significant differences in most categories between the responses of the poor and the rich. Specifically, we see this in how the economic crisis affected citizens, in the concern respondents expressed regarding their ability to get a loan or pay for their house, and in their personal assessments of how the economy had affected them.

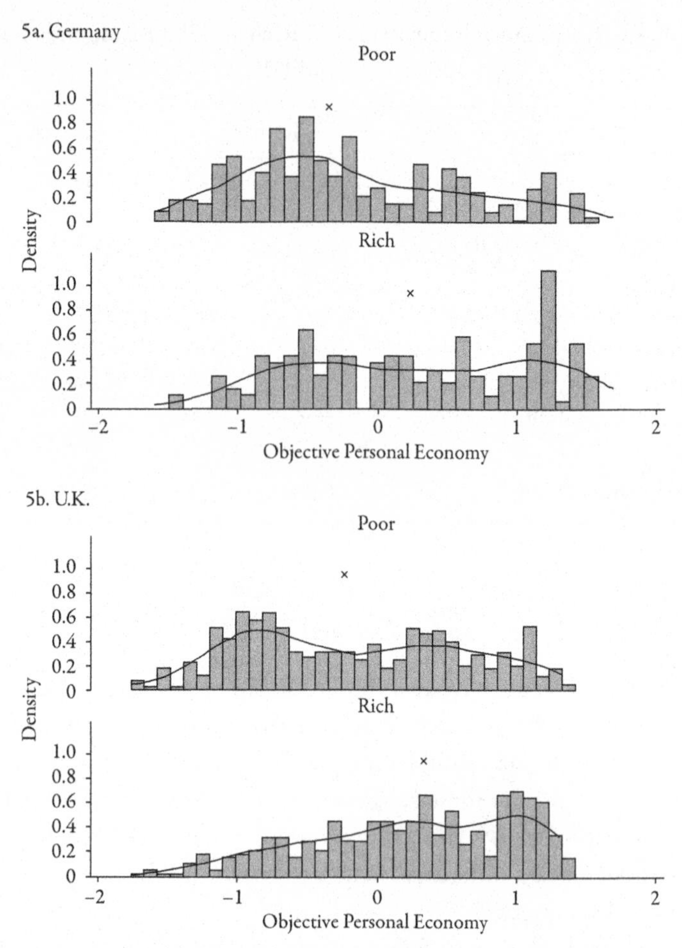

FIGURE 8.5 Distributions of Summary Scores for Personal Economic Circumstances.

From the responses to this battery of questions, we created a measure of how much each respondent's own economic circumstances were affected by the economic crisis.[6] Figure 8.5 shows the distribution of scores for the summary measure of Personal Economic Circumstances for respondents at a number of income levels for the April 2009 wave in the UK and the June 2009 wave in Germany. Positive values indicate a better personal economic situation, and negative values indicate a worse personal economic situation. Note that the distribution of responses for the rich is skewed in the positive direction, while the opposite is the case for the poor. As expected, the poor have a more negative assessment of their personal financial situation. This is particularly noticeable if we look at the mean score (marked as an x in the figure) for respondents in each category. The means differ in both Germany and the UK, with the rich being on average more positive and the poor more negative.

We also measured respondents' retrospective and prospective evaluations of their personal finances more generally. Respondents in both the UK and Germany were much more positive about their own personal financial situations than they were about national economic conditions. Roughly 40 percent of British and German respondents in each panel wave had negative prospective evaluations of personal finances; about 50 percent in each group reported negative retrospective evaluations.

Figure 8.6 presents the evolution of the percentage of respondents who reported "worse" or "much worse" retrospective and prospective evaluations of personal finances, broken down by income level. In both cases there are

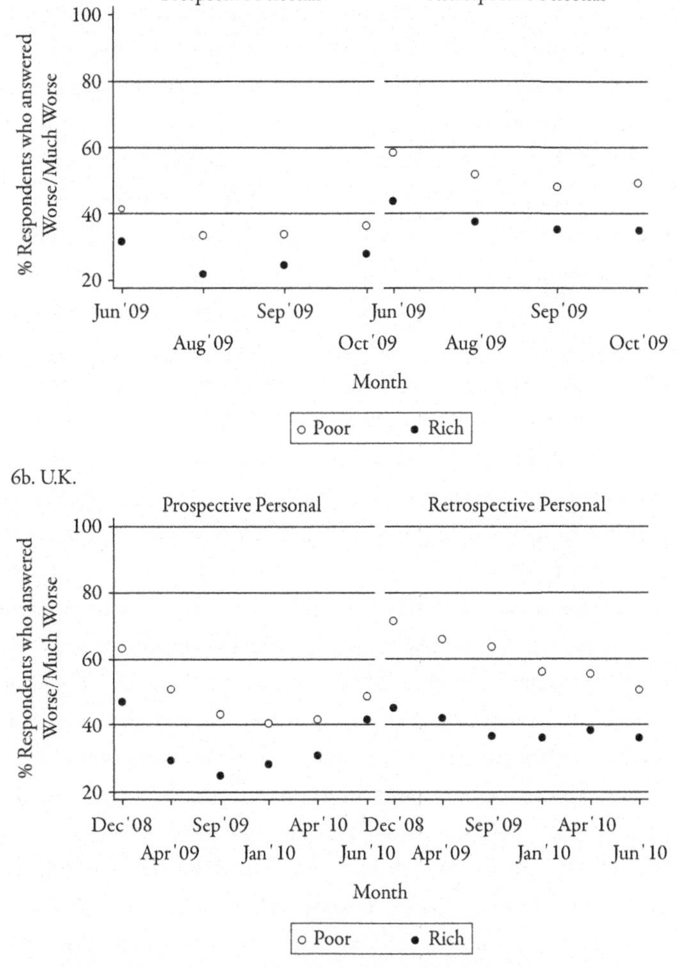

FIGURE 8.6 "Worse"/"Much Worse" Perceptions of Personal Financial Situations.

significant income differences between retrospective and prospective evaluations, these are greater in the UK sample. First, almost three-fourths of the low-income respondents in the December 2008 wave reported that their personal financial situation had gotten "worse" or "much worse," compared to just under half of the high-income respondents. And we see similar, although somewhat more modest, income differences in December 2008 for prospective assessments of personal finances. Over the course of a relatively short period of time—eighteen months—these income differences changed quite significantly. Between December 2008 and April 2010, UK retrospective evaluations of personal finances in general became less negative. Among the lowest income quartile we actually see a slight improvement in their conditions, an increase of almost 4 percent in the proportion of respondents who saw their retrospective personal finances as getting "better" or "much better," as opposed to a *decrease* of almost 3 percent for the highest income quartile.

With regard to prospective evaluations, Figure 8.6 shows a 15 percent decrease in the percentage of respondents who see their retrospective personal finances as getting "worse/much worse" (as opposed to a decrease in 6 percent for the highest income quartile). The net effect of these shifts is to make the low-income group look more similar to the high-income group in terms of retrospective evaluations of their personal finances. The prospective personal financial evaluations of both high- and low-income groups become somewhat more positive (or significantly less negative) between December 2008 and April 2010.

Thus Figure 8.6 suggests that the poor perceived their personal finances to have been much more negatively affected than the rich by the economic shocks of 2008. And even though we see an improvement over the course of the subsequent sixteen months in the economic evaluations of the poor, they remain significantly more negative about their personal financial situation than is the case for the rich.

Our expectation was that there would be much more heterogeneity in citizens' perceptions of how their own financial situations were affected by the financial crisis than in their perceptions of how their national economies were affected. This expectation is borne out in the analysis. The poor were significantly more pessimistic about their personal finances than the rich, and in the UK this difference became more evident in the later waves of the panel survey.[7] This breach between the evaluations of poor and rich presumably reflects the fact that the disposable income of the rich held up better than that of the poor over the course of the economic crisis, especially in the UK, where the rich saw their income increase while the income of the poor remained steady (before inflation) after the 2008 crisis.

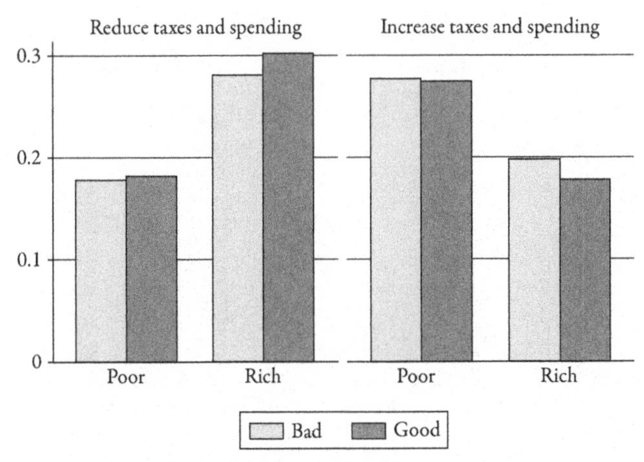

FIGURE 8.7 Tax Increases vs. Health Spending, UK.

Note: For the purposes of this figure, and given the stability in responses across waves, we used the answers provided in wave 5 given that it has a larger number of respondents compared to waves 3 and 4, where this question was also fielded.

Preferred Policy Responses

Most governmental responses to the financial crisis have implied a reduction or moderation of redistributive programs. These initiatives have negative effects on the income of the poor. From the perspective of the self-interested voter, then, we might expect to see poor-rich differences emerge with respect to government spending and taxation policies. We test this expectation using two sets of questions administered in the British BCCAP survey that measure redistributive policy preferences.

The BCCAP survey included a series of questions concerning government spending in the context of the economic crisis. In particular, the survey asked whether it is better to increase taxes to pay for higher health spending or not to raise taxes and as a consequence not increase health spending.[8] We are particularly interested in whether these preferences varied with respondents' perception of the national economic situation and with their own income level. Using data from the fifth wave of the BCCAP survey, we compare those who said they preferred an increase in spending and taxes to those who said they preferred a decrease.

For respondents at the lowest and highest income quartiles, Figure 8.7 compares the percentages favoring an increase in taxes (and spending) with those favoring a decrease. Clearly there are strong differences between the rich and poor categories. However, these differences were relatively unaffected by perceptions of how the national economy had performed. Among

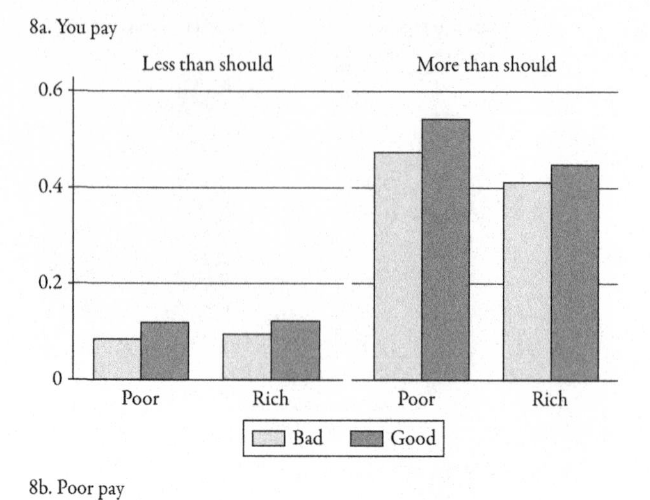

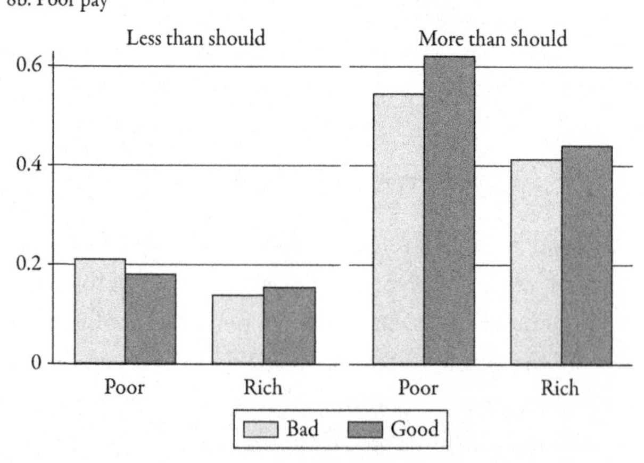

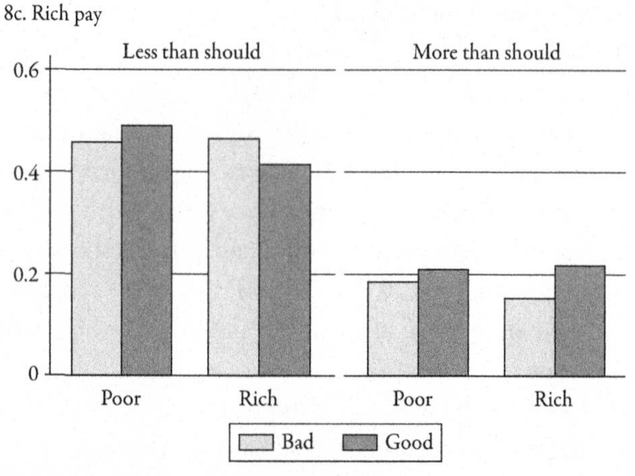

FIGURE 8.8 Redistributive Tax Preferences, UK.

Note: For the purposes of this figures, and given the stability in responses across waves, we used the answers provided in wave 1 given that it has a larger number of respondents.

poor respondents, regardless of whether they perceived the national economy positively or negatively, 28 percent preferred an increase in taxes and spending while 18 percent preferred a reduction. The preference orderings were reversed for respondents in the highest income quartile, who were more likely to prefer lower taxes and lower social spending; but these preferences too were relatively insensitive to perceptions of national economic performance: 30 percent of rich respondents who perceived the national economy positively and 28 percent of those who perceived the national economy negatively preferred a reduction in taxes and spending, while 18 percent of the first group and 20 percent of the second group preferred an increase in taxes and spending.

In the battery of questions related specifically to tax preference, respondents were asked whether they think they pay too much in taxes, pay the right amount, or pay too little. In addition, they were asked similar questions about the taxes paid by the rich and by the poor.[9] Figure 8.8 presents the taxation results for these questions. There is considerable agreement on the part of the rich and poor regarding inequities in the tax system. Not surprisingly, most of the respondents believe that their tax burden is too high (paying more than they should). On average, across all four waves 57 percent of poor respondents thought they were paying too much in taxes, while 18 percent thought they were paying too little. Similarly, 43 percent of rich respondents thought they were paying too much, while 13 percent thought they were paying too little. It is interesting to note that the poor and rich respondents agreed that, overall, the rich are paying less in taxes than they should (49 percent and 43 percent) and the poor are paying more taxes than they should (57 percent and 43 percent), regardless of their own economic situation. It may be the case—although this would require much more careful investigation—that there is rough agreement among all income levels in the UK (and elsewhere) as to what an appropriate overall level of redistributive taxation is.

An Economic Vote?

There is little evidence that the poor in some sense have misaligned subjective assessments of the economic shocks in the post-2008 period. And in the case of their personal finances, there is strong evidence to suggest that they reacted more negatively to the economic shocks than was the case for the more affluent segments of the population. Ultimately, of course, what matters politically is how these economic attitudes shape vote choice. In the highly stylized political economy models described earlier, poor voters who are more negatively affected by the crisis will make vote choices that have consequences for redistribution that in some sense compensate them for the fallout from these negative shocks. And subject to the income profile of the median voter, this redistribution may or may not take place. As pointed out earlier, the self-interested nature of the economic vote can depend on which economic evaluations enter into the vote utility function. In particular, given the results reported above, poor voters could undermine their economic vote if it was entirely based on national economic evaluations rather than personal financial circumstances. A poor economic vote that gave insignificant weight to personal financial circumstances could undermine the financial interests of the poor.

Over the course of this two-year period we have the opportunity to assess the extent to which the economy shapes vote preferences—and in particular the relative importance of evaluations of personal financial conditions compared to evaluations of the performance of the national economy. Again, our interest here is in characterizing how segments of the population respond, politically, to the shocks associated with this economic crisis. And our principal concern is whether the nature of these responses is consistent with what we typically consider to be in the financial self-interest of socioeconomic segments of the population. As we pointed out earlier, one can imagine political responses that are likely to exaggerate or moderate economic inequalities resulting from this economic crisis.

Using the data from the preelection waves of both the BCCAP (waves 2 through 5) and DeCCAP (waves 1 through 3) surveys, we estimated the economic vote for the party of the prime minister (Labour in the UK and CDU/CSU in Germany). Of particular interest were the differences in the effect of the economic vote between the rich and the poor. We use two measures to obtain the effect of the economic vote: retrospective subjective assessments of the national economy, and retrospective subjective assessments of the personal economy. Both variables are five-scale items that range from 1 (much better) to 5 (much worse). We also include our measure of Personal Economic Circumstances to see whether or not it influences the vote choices of the rich or the poor differently. This variable takes on values from −1.5 to 2, with more positive values signaling a better personal economic situation and more negative values signaling a worse economic situation. In the model we control for respondents' Left-Right ideological self-identification (0 Left to 10 Right), education level (in quartiles), satisfaction with democracy (1 to 4 scale), union membership (1 yes, 0 no), and age.[10]

We estimate separate economic voting models for rich and poor respondents.[11] Table 8.2 reports the results for the logistic model of UK vote choice (Labour versus other parties). Of particular concern here is whether the poor are employing economic evaluations differently from the rich in making

Table 8.2 Logistic Regression Analysis of Votes for the Incumbent (Labour) Party, UK.

	April 2009		September 2009		January 2010		April 2010	
	Poor	Rich	Poor	Rich	Poor	Rich	Poor	Rich
Personal Economic	0.113	−0.064	0.265	−0.153	0.092	−0.198	−0.093	0.052
Circumstances	(0.136)	(0.134)	(0.153)	(0.156)	(0.139)	(0.14)	(0.101)	(0.102)
Retrospective	−0.439***	−0.931***	−0.514***	−0.517***	−0.690***	−0.525***	−0.711***	−0.701***
National	(0.137)	(0.145)	(0.114)	(0.11)	(0.107)	(0.1)	(0.075)	(0.075)
Retrospective	−0.05	−0.114	−0.033	−0.337*	−0.096	−0.292*	−0.318***	−0.12
Personal	(0.124)	(0.121)	(0.149)	(0.161)	(0.148)	(0.14)	(0.101)	(0.101)
Left-Right Self ID	−0.414***	−0.414***	−0.472***	−0.479***	−0.524***	−0.576***	−0.397***	−0.522***
	(0.051)	(0.047)	(0.061)	(0.057)	(0.056)	(0.054)	(0.038)	(0.037)
Education	−0.219*	−0.321***	−0.096	−0.05	−0.299*	−0.293*	−0.269***	−0.226**
	(0.111)	(0.11)	(0.131)	(0.136)	(0.124)	(0.118)	(0.086)	(0.087)
Satisfaction with	−0.961***	−0.921***	−1.015***	−0.940***	−0.875***	−0.790***	−0.721***	−0.698***
Democracy	(0.118)	(0.113)	(0.141)	(0.136)	(0.125)	(0.12)	(0.087)	(0.087)
Union Member	0.372	0.351	0.511*	0.068	0.418	0.581***	0.464***	0.527***
	(0.212)	(0.189)	(0.238)	(0.217)	(0.222)	(0.195)	(0.159)	(0.141)
Age	−0.008	0.003	−0.002	0.006	−0.004	0.007	0.001	0.007
	(0.007)	(0.007)	(0.008)	(0.009)	(0.008)	(0.008)	(0.005)	(0.005)
Constant	6.523***	8.430***	5.892***	6.281***	7.222***	6.745***	6.359***	5.380***
	(0.876)	(0.937)	(0.915)	(0.904)	(0.833)	(0.802)	(0.574)	(0.547)
N	813	922	719	818	802	918	1752	2098
Log likelihood	−395.863	−418.727	−290.283	−313.506	−324.059	−382.056	−675.266	−722.856

Table 8.3 Logistic Regression Analysis of Votes for the Incumbent (CDU/CSU) Party, Germany.

	June 2009		August 2009		September 2009	
	Poor	Rich	Poor	Rich	Poor	Rich
Personal Economic Circumstances	0.068	0.014	−0.129	0.278	0.404	−0.088
	(0.139)	(0.118)	(0.197)	(0.172)	(0.286)	(0.238)
Retrospective National	−0.106	−0.313***	−0.229	−0.075	−0.078	−0.585*
	(0.117)	(0.111)	(0.172)	(0.146)	(0.247)	(0.232)
Retrospective Personal	−0.074	0.082	0.028	0.152	−0.016	−0.205
	(0.126)	(0.122)	(0.201)	(0.2)	(0.265)	(0.289)
Left-Right Self ID	−0.679***	−0.801***	−0.783***	−0.710***	−0.856***	−0.646***
	(0.122)	(0.13)	(0.173)	(0.157)	(0.241)	(0.225)
Education	0.176***	0.062	0.215***	0.125*	0.119	0.061
	(0.042)	(0.042)	(0.061)	(0.057)	(0.087)	(0.084)
Satisfaction with Democracy	−0.255**	−0.093	0.041	−0.169	0.18	−0.13
	(0.099)	(0.085)	(0.143)	(0.121)	(0.208)	(0.17)
Union Member	−0.042	−0.072	−0.142	−0.045	−0.079	−0.119
	(0.068)	(0.059)	(0.106)	(0.085)	(0.146)	(0.118)
Age	−0.011	−0.013	−0.015	0.006	0.001	−0.004
	(0.007)	(0.007)	(0.011)	(0.01)	(0.015)	(0.013)
Constant	2.042*	3.153***	2.184	0.75	1.347	4.630***
	(0.806)	(0.737)	(1.125)	(0.966)	(1.611)	(1.53)
N	617	681	300	330	151	183
Log likelihood	−367.187	−417.327	−168.47	−202.802	−84.725	−105.719

9a. Retrospective national

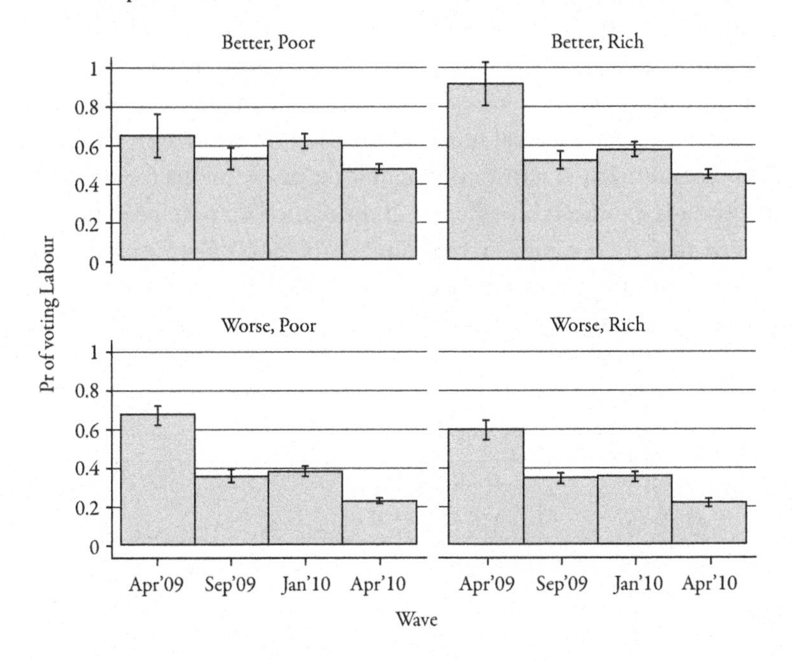

9b. Retrospective personal

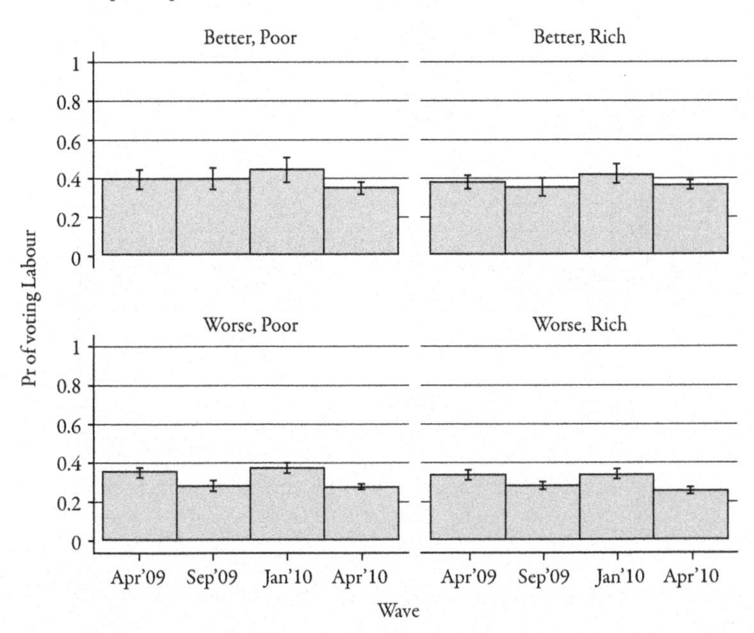

FIGURE 8.9 Predicted Probability of Voting for Prime Minister's Party (Labour), UK.

Note: These estimates come from a multinomial logit model that considers vote for each party. The results are similar to those of the logistic model.

their vote decision. We do see a difference. Both rich and poor are employing national retrospective evaluations in their vote choice decision, and the coefficient sizes suggest they are giving these evaluations relatively similar importance; but there is some evidence that the rich are more likely to give importance to their personal financial situation. In two waves, the personal economic evaluation is statistically significant in the model for rich respondents, but it is significant in only one of the models for poor respondents.

Given that the incumbent coalition in the 2009 German federal election consisted of the country's two largest parties, our expectation is that

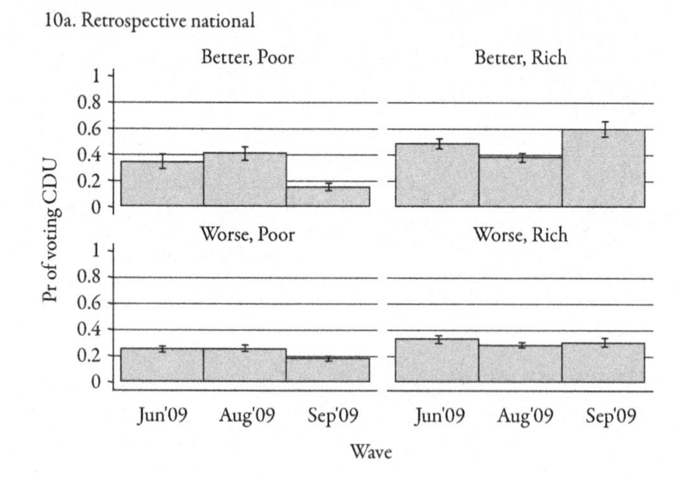

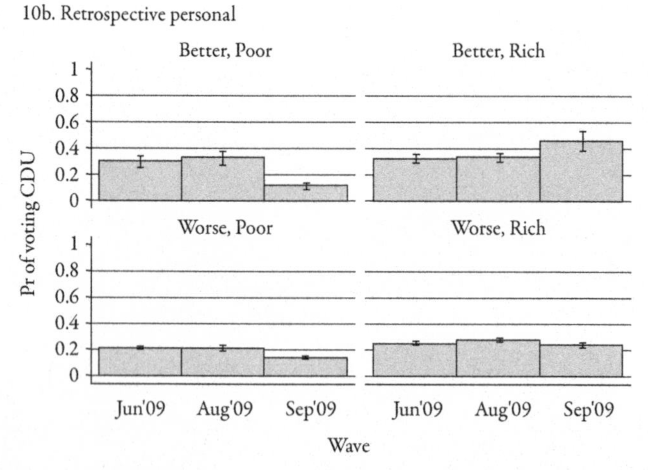

FIGURE 8.10 Predicted Probability of Voting for Prime Minister's Party (CDU/CSU), Germany.

Note: These estimates come from a multinomial logit model that considers vote for each party. The results are similar to those of the logistic model.

the economic vote for the prime minister's party would be weak (Duch and Stevenson 2008). And as Table 8.3 indicates, this is essentially the case. Overall, the coefficients on both national and personal economic evaluation variables are not statistically significant.

Based on the results of this model of the economic vote, Figure 8.9a presents the probability of voting for the incumbent Labour Party, for those who have a better or worse evaluation of the national economy, both rich and poor. Results are presented for all four waves used in the analysis. Retrospective economic evaluations get worse as we move from the top row to the bottom, as we would expect; average probabilities of voting Labour decline quite significantly. By moving across the columns, we can get a sense of whether the economic vote varies by income group—whether the poor are less, or more, likely to exercise an economic vote than the rich. There is no evidence here that the probabilities vary by income group. Figure 8.9b repeats the same analysis for retrospective personal evaluations. Here we see considerably less difference as we move down the rows; retrospective personal finances seem to matter less for vote choice. Differences across income groups are not obvious, either. Figures 8.10a and 8.10b replicate the analysis for Germany and again find no income group differences.

On balance, there is little heterogeneity in the economic vote estimated during this period of financial crisis and economic shock. Generally, evaluations of the national economy weigh most heavily in the vote utility functions of both the rich and poor. Assessments of personal financial conditions are reasonably important for the richer members of the electorate, but they get little weight in the vote decisions exercised by poor voters. Since poorer voters, in both Germany and the UK, have much more negative assessments of personal finances than is the case for richer voters, underweighting of personal evaluations in their vote-choice decision might moderate the redistributional signal of the poor vote (here we are simply treating this as the magnitude of the economic vote). In this particular financial crisis the macroeconomic shocks were such that it's not clear that focusing on personal versus national economic outcomes would be of much consequence for the policy signal of the poor (or rich) economic vote. This is not to say that the poor and rich do not vary on the specific policy responses to these economic shocks—a theme we address in the next section.

A Redistributive Policy Vote?

The final step in the analysis is to assess the effect that redistributive policy preferences had on the vote function. Our measure of redistributive preferences is the question asking UK respondents whether they prefer increases

Table 8.4 Logistic Regression Analysis of Votes for the Incumbent (Labour) Party, UK.

	April 2009		September 2009		January 2010		April 2010	
	Poor	Rich	Poor	Rich	Poor	Rich	Poor	Rich
Personal Economic Circumstances	0.196	−0.052	0.238	−0.11	0.096	−0.198	−0.087	0.038
	(0.153)	(0.15)	(0.155)	(0.159)	(0.14)	(0.14)	(0.102)	(0.103)
Retrospective National	-0.515***	-0.929***	-0.498***	-0.532***	-0.668***	-0.511***	-0.682***	-0.676***
	(0.149)	(0.162)	(0.115)	(0.113)	(0.108)	(0.1)	(0.075)	(0.075)
Retrospective Personal	0.025	-0.092	-0.064	-0.297	-0.09	-0.277*	-0.310***	-0.099
	(0.14)	(0.134)	(0.151)	(0.164)	(0.148)	(0.14)	(0.103)	(0.101)
Tax and Health Policy	0.694***	0.336	0.546*	0.410*	0.438*	0.189	0.291*	0.259*
	(0.195)	(0.185)	(0.217)	(0.204)	(0.205)	(0.181)	(0.127)	(0.122)
Left-Right Self ID	-0.361***	-0.410***	-0.425***	-0.448***	-0.485***	-0.563***	-0.372***	-0.493***
	(0.058)	(0.054)	(0.062)	(0.06)	(0.058)	(0.056)	(0.039)	(0.039)
Education	-0.204	-0.353***	-0.119	-0.021	-0.280*	-0.290*	-0.252***	-0.234**
	(0.124)	(0.122)	(0.132)	(0.138)	(0.124)	(0.118)	(0.087)	(0.087)
Satisfaction with Democracy	-1.000***	-0.815***	-0.970***	-0.935***	-0.873***	-0.779***	-0.724***	-0.700***
	(0.132)	(0.124)	(0.141)	(0.139)	(0.125)	(0.12)	(0.088)	(0.087)
Union Member	0.39	0.432*	0.515*	0.033	0.438*	0.584***	0.467***	0.507***
	(0.234)	(0.207)	(0.238)	(0.22)	(0.223)	(0.195)	(0.16)	(0.142)
Age	-0.004	-0.001	-0.004	0.006	-0.006	0.006	0	0.005
	(0.008)	(0.008)	(0.008)	(0.009)	(0.008)	(0.008)	(0.005)	(0.005)
Constant	4.628***	7.577***	4.574***	5.111***	6.029***	6.217***	5.517***	4.683***
	(1.072)	(1.159)	(1.037)	(1.067)	(0.967)	(0.921)	(0.673)	(0.635)
N	703	797	712	809	797	911	1702	2042
Log likelihood	-326.903	-345.38	-286.067	-304.682	-320.683	-379.196	-660.098	-711.703

in taxes and health spending or decreases in both taxes and health spending. This is the one policy item available that exhibits considerable heterogeneity in preferences: the rich prefer lower taxes and spending while the poor favor more taxes and more spending on health services. The tax and health policy variable consists of the mean answer to the question across the three waves in which it is asked. High values indicate support for taxation and spending on health services. The correlation between the mean and each of the wave values is extremely high (0.8) and as such it provides a good measure of the long-term preference of respondents, allowing us to incorporate this item in vote-choice models for waves 2 through 4.

Results of this UK analysis are reported in Table 8.4. Generally, those who favor more taxation and more spending on health services have a higher probability of voting for the Labour incumbent. And this is a reasonably robust result given the controls we include here, such as left-right self-identification. Our interest here is whether the rich and poor differ in terms of the weight they accord redistributional preferences in their vote decision. If anything, these results suggest that the poor give somewhat more weight to redistributional preferences than the rich. For poor respondents, the health-policy preference variable is consistently significant across all waves, and its effect (not shown here) is typically larger than for rich respondents. And note that in two of the waves the coefficient for the rich is not statistically significant. Hence, on balance there is certainly no evidence here that the poor underweight redistributional preferences in their vote decision—indeed, there is some evidence that these play a more important role than is the case for rich voters. In fact, for the poor, going from lower taxes and less health spending to more taxes and more spending increases the probability of voting for Labour by 0.2 in April 2009 and by 0.1 in the other three waves. That is, the poor are 10 percent more likely to vote for Labour if they prefer more redistribution. With regard to the rich, however, the difference is about 0.05, which means the electoral impact of preferences for redistribution is twice as large for the poor as for the rich.

Conclusion

There is widespread agreement that macroeconomic events such as the recession that resulted from the 2008 financial crisis can have important political ramifications. This chapter is an attempt to identify how these economic shocks affect voter attitudes and in turn shape electoral outcomes. We sketched out two visions of how citizens experience macroeconomic events such as the recent financial crisis. One perspective suggests these events are collective experiences, and as such economic attitudes will be heavily shaped by media representations of the macroeconomy. A second perspective suggests that these events affect groups in the population differently (occupational groups, for example); as such citizens will differ in how they experience the crisis; and as a result their evaluations will depend on the nature of their exposure. In this chapter, we focus on whether the rich and poor perceived this economic crisis quite differently and whether this in turn had implications for their policy preferences and voting behavior.

The analysis is based on panel studies conducted in the UK (BCCAP) and Germany (DeCCAP). Our analysis of subjective evaluations of the national economy suggest that voter attitudes were strongly affected by the economic shocks, but we found very small differences in the evaluations of the national economy by the rich and the poor. This suggests that rich and poor respondents' attitudes regarding macroeconomic circumstances were similar—perhaps not unexpectedly, since they were exposed to the same mediated representations of macroeconomic events.

Although voters are dependent on mediated representations of macroeconomic events in order to form attitudes about macroeconomic performance, their personal finances are by definition not a collective experience. Hence, our expectation was that rich and poor respondents' perceptions of their personal finances in the aftermath of the financial crisis would differ much more than their national economic evaluations. We found that the poor were significantly more pessimistic about their personal finances than the rich; in the UK, this became more evident in the later waves of the panel survey. This difference in poor and rich evaluations may reflect the fact that the disposable income of the rich was less affected by the economic crisis. This is particularly true of the UK, where the rich saw their disposable income increase while the real disposable income of the poor remained stagnant.

Having looked at how the crisis was perceived at both the national and personal levels, we set out to understand its implications. We were particularly interested in the extent to which economic evaluations shaped vote choices. In terms of the economic vote, the rich and poor responded very similarly to the macroeconomic shocks: they had similar evaluations of macroeconomic performance and they weighed those evaluations similarly in their vote choices. However, there is some evidence that the poor were less likely to take their own personal finances into consideration when casting an economic vote. This difference would likely have important political consequences, since the poor clearly had much more negative assessments of their personal finances than the rich.

There is no evidence that the economic vote of the rich and poor would favor redistributive responses to the economic shocks generated by the financial crisis. But government responses to these macroeconomic shocks are not simply reactions to the economic vote. Poor voters can hold redistributive preferences that are quite distinct from those of the rich. We found that the poor do prefer more redistributive policies, favoring higher taxes together with higher social spending, while the rich favor lower taxes and lower social spending. Our model of the relationship between these redistributive preferences and vote choice suggests that these policy preferences of the poor should have political consequences: first, those preferring redistributive measures are more likely to vote for the center-left Labour Party; and second there is some evidence that these redistributive policy concerns weigh more heavily in the vote-utility function of the poor compared to the rich.

Our evidence suggests that in the aftermath of the Great Recession the economic vote of the rich and that of the poor were quite similar. Hence there is little to suggest from these two cases that the valence component of Great Recession politics differed for the rich and poor. There is evidence, though, that the redistributive preferences of the rich and poor differed. Moreover, these redistributive preferences seemed to have played some nontrivial role in the decisions of the British voters during the General Elections that followed the 2008 financial crisis.

Appendix

The data employed in our analyses are from the German (DeCCAP) and British (BCCAP) CCAP surveys. Information on the recruitment of participants, the resulting samples, and their characteristics is available at http://ccap.nuff.ox.ac.uk. These internet panel surveys included a series of questions regarding respondents' own economic situations. This appendix explains how we used responses to those questions to construct a summary measure of Personal Economic Circumstances for each respondent.

The following questions were asked of British respondents in BCCAP waves 2, 3, 4, and 5, and of German respondents in all four DeCCAP waves. (To avoid any postelectoral effect, we use only the preelection waves, 2 through 5 in the UK and 1 through 3 in Germany.)

> How concerned are you about being able to pay your housing costs (e.g., mortgage or rent payments)? (1) Very concerned; (2) Somewhat concerned; (3) Not very concerned; (4) Not at all concerned; (5) Don't know.

Table 8.A1 Factor Analysis of Personal Economic Circumstances: DeCCAP.

	June 2009	August 2009	Sept 2009
Number of observations	1915	1715	1002
Retained factors	2	2	2
Number of parameters	11	11	11
$X^2(15)$	1524.7	1550.33	1707.43
Factor1	1.27122	1.3545	1.36709
Factor2	0.04348	0.02233	0.03031
Factor3	−0.02151	−0.0224	−0.0269
Factor4	−0.05012	−0.07399	−0.06663
Factor5	−0.1421	−0.13238	−0.11417
Factor6	−0.20517	−0.18784	−0.20397

	June 2009	August 2009	Sept 2009
Factor 1			
Paying House	0.6325	0.6098	0.6660
Affected by Crisis	0.5688	0.6188	0.5858
Loans Difficulty	0.4221	0.4345	0.4523
No. of Changes	0.5049	0.5436	0.5171
Big Items	−0.2436	−0.2423	−0.2084
Energy Prices	−0.2351	−0.2382	−0.2546
Uniqueness			
Paying House	0.5999	0.628	0.5564
Affected by Crisis	0.6764	0.6167	0.6523
Loans Difficulty	0.8153	0.8108	0.7952
No. of Changes	0.7399	0.7033	0.7301
Big Items	0.9248	0.935	0.9470
Energy Prices	0.9289	0.9294	0.9214

Thinking about the money you owe on credit cards and loans (NOT including your mortgage), would you say you…(1) Owe a lot more than you can afford; (2) Owe a little more; (3) Owe about what you can afford; (4) Owe a little less; (5) Owe much less than you can afford; (6) Not applicable—I don't have any credit cards or loans; (7) Don't know.

Table 8.A2 Factor Analysis of Personal Economic Circumstances: BCCAP.

	April 2009	Sept 2009	Jan 2010	April 2010
Number of observations	2237	2008	2222	4725
Retained factors	1	2	2	3
Number of parameters	6	11	11	15
$X^2(15)$	1524.7	1550.33	1707.43	3258.71
Factor1	1.40161	1.49847	1.48526	1.40912
Factor2	−0.00564	0.01108	0.08917	0.01625
Factor3	−0.01765	−0.00636	−0.04615	0.00933
Factor4	−0.04	−0.04632	−0.06833	−0.05703
Factor5	−0.12757	−0.11055	−0.13164	−0.14616
Factor6	−0.20034	−0.2209	−0.20677	−0.20517

	April 2009	Sept 2009	Jan 2010	April 2010
Factor 1				
Paying House	0.6479	0.6643	0.6664	0.6040
Affected by Crisis	0.5906	0.6137	0.6155	0.5775
Loans Difficulty	0.5123	0.5185	0.4990	0.5026
No. of Changes	0.5232	0.5539	0.5677	0.5921
Big Items	−0.2233	−0.2461	−0.1931	−0.2374
Energy Prices	−0.2168	−0.2105	−0.232	−0.2264
Uniqueness				
Paying House	0.5802	0.5587	0.5524	0.6334
Affected by Crisis	0.6512	0.621	0.6206	0.6638
Loans Difficulty	0.7376	0.7291	0.7454	0.7421
No. of Changes	0.7263	0.6919	0.6701	0.6474
Big Items	0.9501	0.9348	0.9306	0.9377
Energy Prices	0.9530	0.9549	0.9065	0.9409

Which, if any, of the following changes have you made to your spending? (*Multiple choice*) (1) Delayed or cancelled plans to buy a new home or make major home improvements; (2) Delayed or cancelled plans to buy a new car; (3) Delayed or cancelled plans to make a major purchase for your household, such as a computer or appliance; (4) Cut back on planned spending for going on holiday; (5) Adjusted your plans for retirement; (6) Changed the way your money is saved or invested; (7) Eaten out at restaurants less often; (8) None of these.

How much have you been affected personally by the downturn in the economy? (1) Very affected; (2) Somewhat affected; (3) Not very affected; (4) Not at all affected; (5) Don't know.

About the big things people buy for their homes—such as furniture, kitchen appliances, televisions, and things like that. Generally speaking, do you think now is a good or a bad time for people to buy major household items? (1) Good

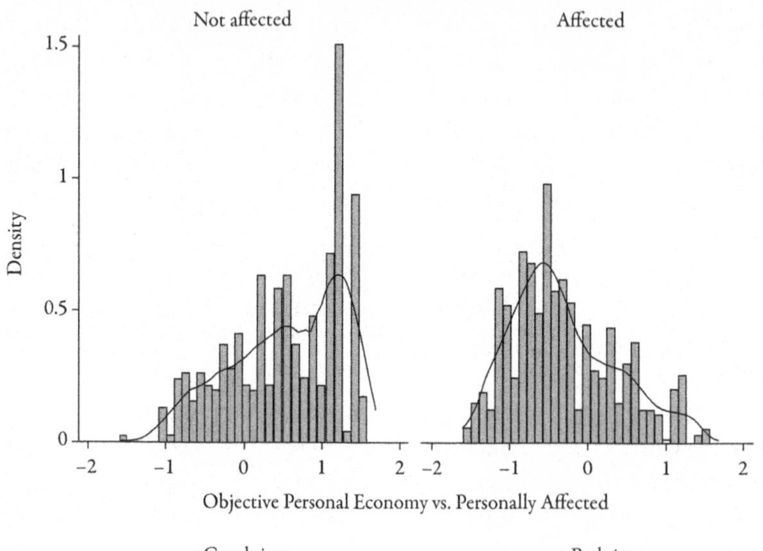

FIGURE 8.A1 Distributions of Components of Personal Economic Circumstances: DeCCAP.

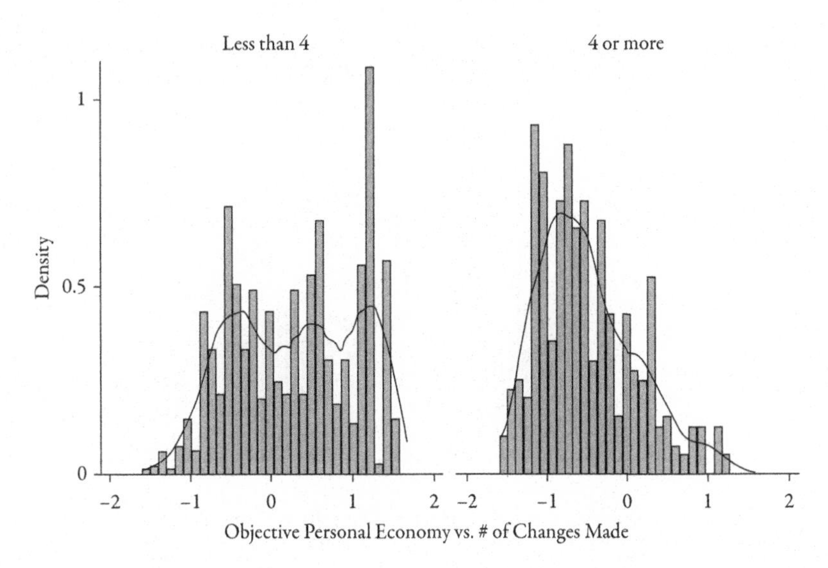

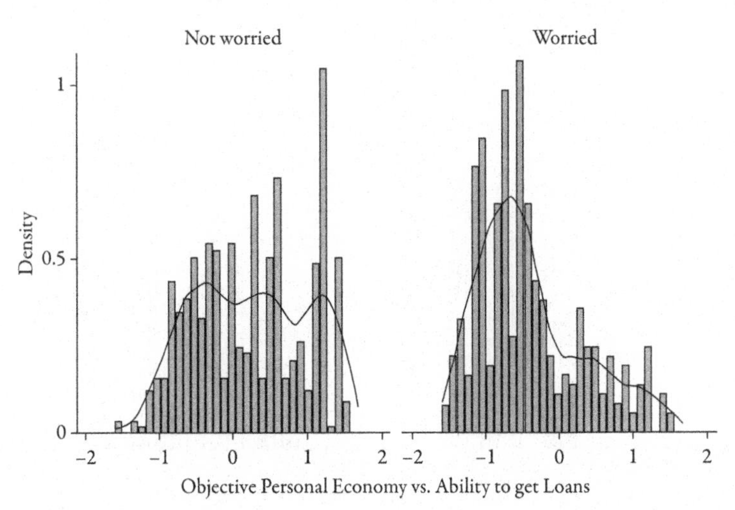

FIGURE 8.A1 (Continued)

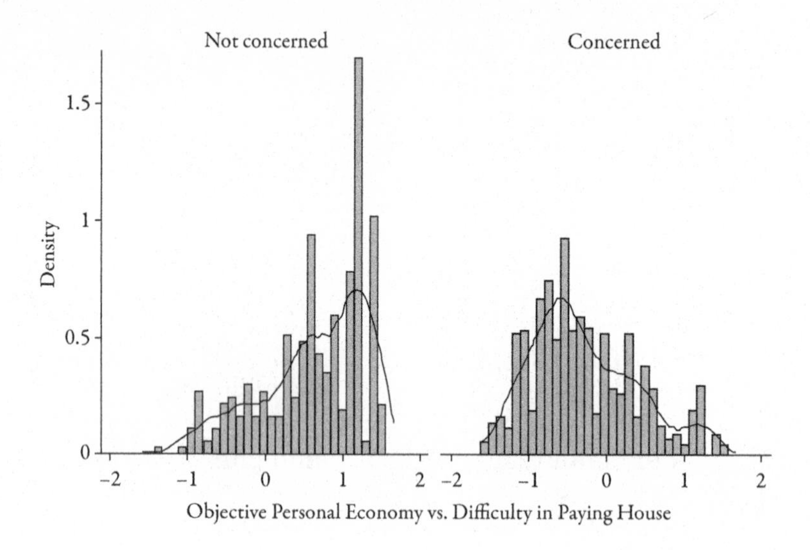

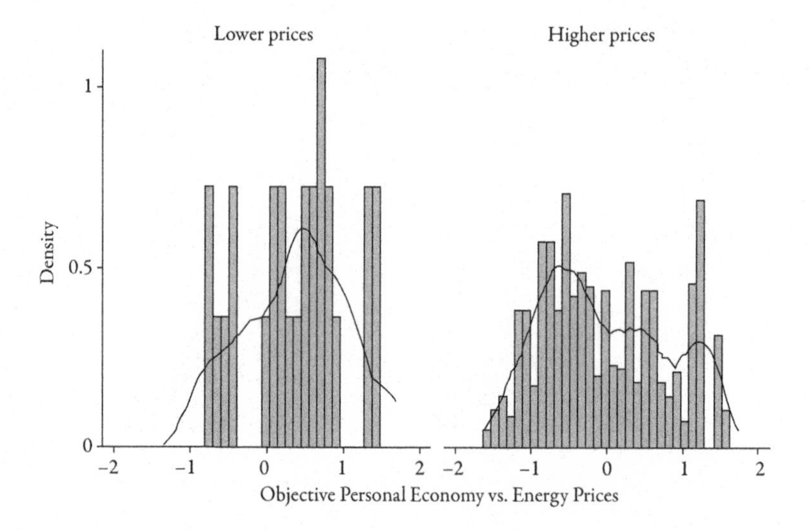

FIGURE 8.A1 (Continued)

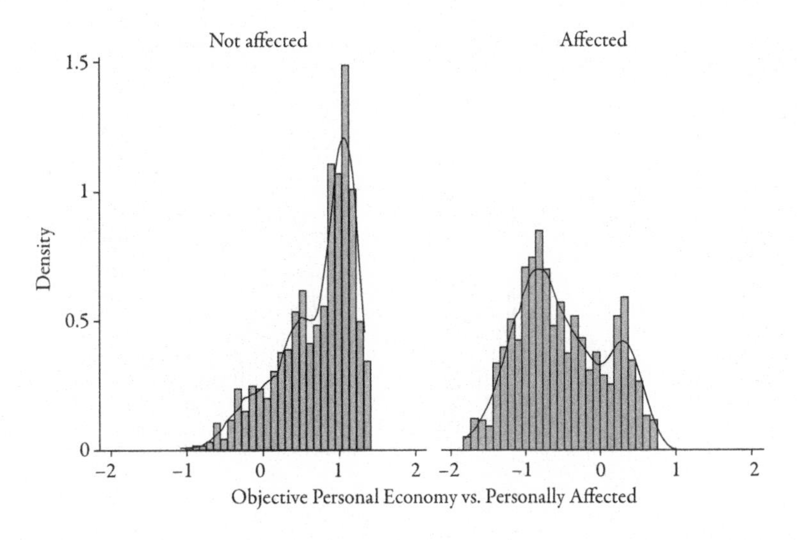

FIGURE 8.A2 Distributions of Components of Personal Economic Circumstances: BCCAP.

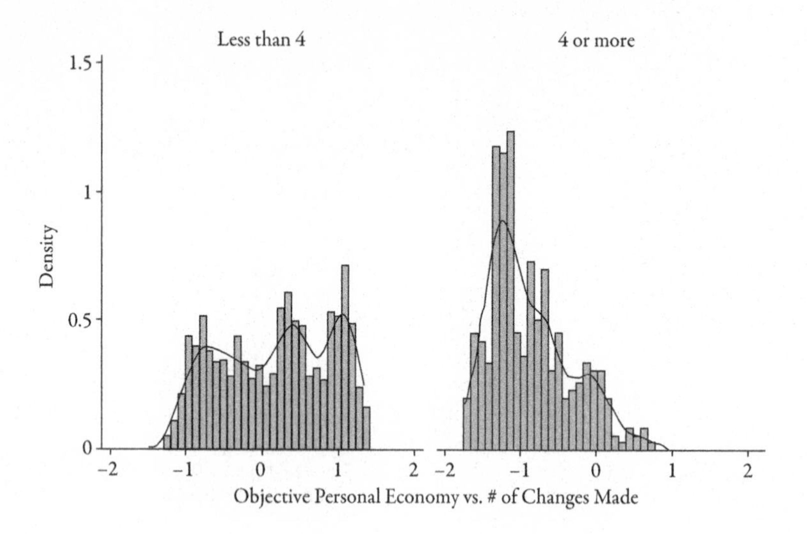

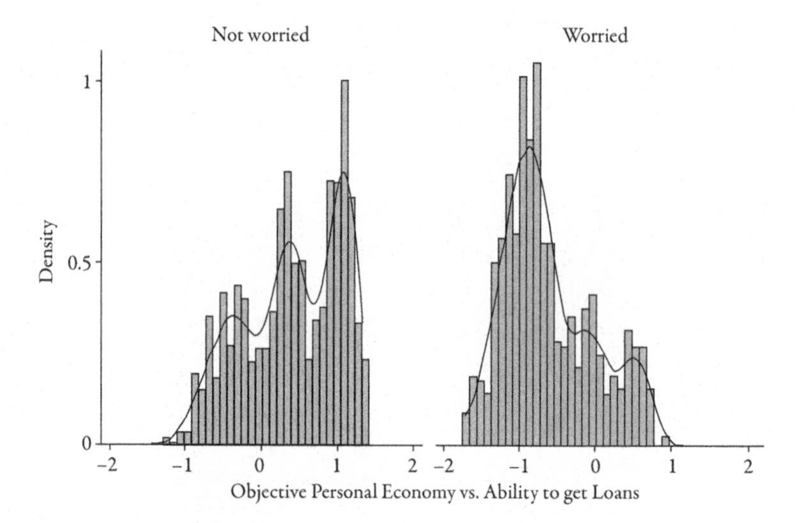

FIGURE 8.A2 (Continued)

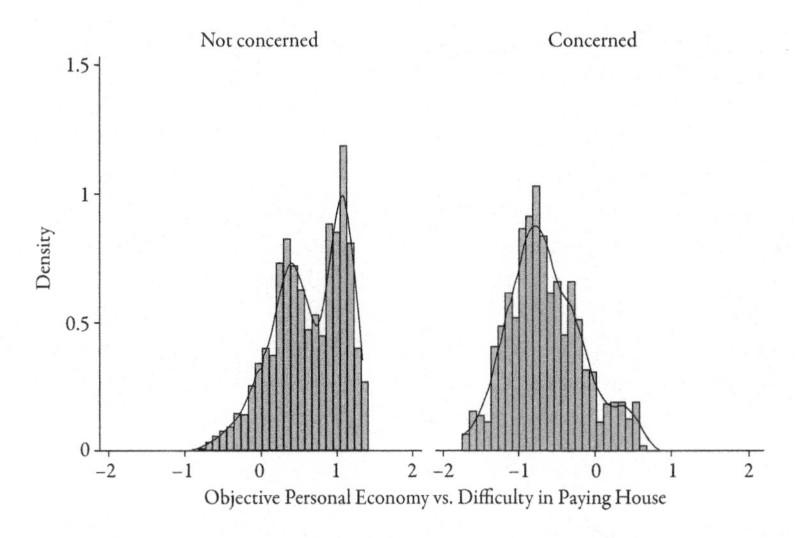

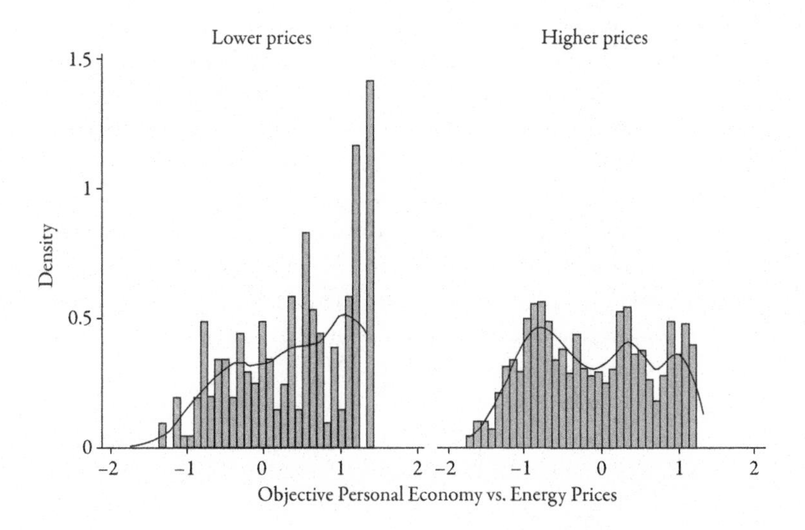

FIGURE 8.A2 (Continued)

time to buy; (2) Bad time to buy; (3) Neither good nor bad time to buy; (4) Don't know.

Generally, would you say that energy prices in this country are…(1) Rising a lot; (2) Rising somewhat; (3) Staying about the same; (4) Falling somewhat; (5) Falling a lot; (6) Don't know.

We used responses to these questions to create a summary measure of Personal Economic Circumstances. The summary measure is based on the first factor retained from a factor analysis including all the respondents in each country in each wave who answered all the questions (and who did not answer "don't know"). As can be seen in figures A1 and A2, this summary measure of Personal Economic Circumstances is consistently a good mixture of the various indicators we used to measure a number of aspects of respondents' economic situations.

Notes

1. In Germany, the median income for those classified as poor is between €18,000 and €24,000 (roughly $24,000–$32,000) per year, while the median income for those classified as rich is between €42,000 and €48,000 ($56,000–$64,000) per year. In the UK, the median income for those classified as poor is between £20,000 and £24,999 ($31,000–$39,000) per year and the median income for those classified as rich is between £50,000 and £59,999 ($77,000–$93,000) per year.
2. A classic empirical account of how well voters are able to anticipate macroeconomic events is MacKuen, Erikson, and Stimson (1992). More recently, Duch and Stevenson (2011) find that price expectations in a sample of European countries anticipate subsequent fluctuations in prices, although with considerable cross-national variation in accuracy.
3. The data are from the German Socio Economic Panel and the UK Labour Workforce Survey.
4. The data are from the OECD Consumer Price Index (MEI) dataset.
5. A more detailed description of these surveys and an explanation of subject recruitment and panel representativeness are available at http://ccap.nuff.ox.ac.uk/.
6. A detailed description of the questions and the creation of the summary measure are presented in the Appendix.
7. This result is consistent with Hopkins's finding (2012) that poor respondents in the U.S. ANES survey data were consistently more pessimistic than rich respondents about their personal financial situations.
8. The specific question asked was: "Suppose the government had to choose between the three options below. Which do you think it should choose? (1) Reduce taxes and spend less on health, education and social benefits; (2) Keep taxes and

spending on these services at the same level as now; (3) Increase taxes and spend more on health, education and social benefits."

9. (1) "Do you feel you are asked to pay more than you should in income taxes, about the right amount, or less than you should?" (2) "What about rich people? Do you feel rich people are asked to pay more than they should in income taxes, about the right amount, or less than they should?" (3) "What about poor people? Do you feel poor people are asked to pay more than they should in income taxes, about the right amount, or less than they should?"
10. (1) "If there were a General Election tomorrow, which party would you vote for?" (2) "In politics, people sometimes talk about parties and politicians as being on the left or right. Using the 0 to 10 scale on this card, where the end marked 0 means left and the end marked 10 means right, where would you place yourself on this scale?" (3) "On the whole, are you very satisfied, fairly satisfied, a little dissatisfied, or very dissatisfied with the way that democracy works in this country?" (4) "Are you now a member of a trade union or staff association?"
11. Although we specifically refer to the poor as the lowest-income quartile and the rich as the highest, for analytical purposes we used the two lower-income quartiles for the poor model and the two highest quartiles for the rich model. The results are no different from the models using only the lowest and highest income quartiles, and thus we decided to report these models as they include all available observations in the dataset.

References

Ansolabehere, Stephen, Marc Meredith, and Erik Snowberg. 2011. "Mecro-Economic Voting: Local Information and Micro-Perceptions of the Macro-Economy." http://www.sas.upenn.edu/~marcmere/workingpapers/HeterogenousEconomicVoting.pdf.

Bartels, Larry M. 1996. "Uninformed Votes: Information Effects in Presidential Elections." *American Journal of Political Science 40*: 194–230.

Bartels, Larry M. 2005. "Homer Gets a Tax Cut: Inequality and Public Policy in the American Mind." *Perspectives on Politics 3*: 15–31.

Bartels, Larry M. 2008. *Unequal Democracy: The Political Economy of the New Gilded Age*. New York and Princeton, NJ: Russell Sage Foundation and Princeton University Press.

Bradley, David, Evelyne Huber, Stephanie Moller, François Nielsen, and John D. Stephens. 2003. "Distribution and Redistribution in Postindustrial Democracies." *World Politics 55*: 193–228.

Bechtel, Michael M., Jens Hainmueller, and Yotam M. Margalit. 2012. "Sharing the Pain: Explaining Public Opinion Towards International Financial Bailouts." April 1. MIT Political Science Department Research Paper No. 2012-5. http://ssrn.com/abstract=2032147.

Berelson, Bernard, Paul Lazarsfeld, and William McPhee. 1954. *Voting*. Chicago: University of Chicago Press.

Campbell, Angus, P. E. Converse, W. E. Miller, and D. E. Stokes. 1960. *The American Voter*. Hoboken, NJ: Wiley.

Downs, Anthony. 1957. *An Economic Theory of Democracy*. New York: Harper and Row.

Duch, Raymond M., Harvey D. Palmer, and Christopher J. Anderson. 2000. "Heterogeneity in Perceptions of National Economic Conditions." *American Journal of Political Science 44*: 635–649.

Duch, Raymond M., and Randy Stevenson. 2008. *The Economic Vote: How Political and Economic Institutions Condition Election Results*. Cambridge: Cambridge University Press.

Duch, Raymond M., and Randy Stevenson. 2011. "Context and Economic Expectations: When Do Voters Get it Right?" *British Journal of Political Science 41*: 1–31.

Fair, Ray C. 1978. "The Effect of Economic Events on Votes for President." *Review of Economics and Statistics 60*: 159–178.

Gomez, Brad T., and J. Matthew Wilson. 2001. "Political Sophistication and Economic Voting in the American Electorate: A Theory of Heterogeneous Attribution." *American Journal of Political Science 45*: 899–914.

Gomez, Brad T., and J. Matthew Wilson. 2006. "Cognitive Heterogeneity and Economic Voting: A Comparative Analysis of Four Democratic Electorates." *American Journal of Political Science 50*: 127–145.

Hays, Jude C., Sean D. Ehrlich, and Clint Peinhardt. 2005. "Government Spending and Public Support for Trade in the OECD: An Empirical Test of the Embedded Liberalism Thesis." *International Organization 59*: 473–494.

Hetherington, Marc J. 1996. "The Media's Role in Forming Voters' Retrospective Economic Evaluations in 1992." *American Journal of Political Science 40*: 372–395.

Hopkins, Daniel. 2012. "Whose Economy? Perceptions of National Economic Performance During Unequal Growth." *Public Opinion Quarterly 76*: 50–71.

Iversen, Torben, and David Soskice. 2001. "An Asset Theory of Social Policy Preferences." *American Political Science Review 95*: 875–895.

Iversen, Torben, and David Soskice. 2009. "Distribution and Redistribution: The Shadow of the Nineteenth Century." *World Politics 61*(3): 438–486.

Kenworthy, Lane, and Leslie McCall. 2008. "Inequality, Public Opinion, and Redistribution." *Socio-Economic Review 6*: 35–68.

Kramer, Gerald H. 1971. "Short-term Fluctuations in U.S. Voting Behavior, 1896–1964." *American Journal of Political Science 23*: 495–527.

Krause, George A. 1997. "Voters, Information Heterogeneity, and the Dynamics of Aggregate Economic Expectations." *American Journal of Political Science 41*: 1170–1200.

MacKuen, Michael B., Robert S. Erikson, and James A. Stimson. 1992. "Peasants or Bankers? The American Electorate and the U.S. Economy." *American Political Science Review 86*: 597–611.

Mayda, Anna Maria, and Dani Rodrik. 2005. "Why Are Some People (and Countries) More Protectionist Than Others?" *European Economic Review 49*: 1393–1430.

Page, Benjamin I., and Lawrence R. Jacobs. 2009. *Class War? What Americans Really Think About Economic Inequality*. Chicago: University of Chicago Press.

Pontusson, Jonas, and David Rueda. 2010. "Politics of Inequality: Voter Mobilization and Left Parties in Advanced Industrial States." *Comparative Political Studies 43*: 675–705.

Pontusson, Jonas, and Noam Lupu. 2011. "The Structure of Inequality and the Politics of Redistribution." *American Political Science Review 105*: 316–336.

Rehm, Philipp. 2011. "Risk Inequality and the Polarized American Electorate." *British Journal of Political Science 41*(2): 363–387.

Scheve, Kenneth, and Matthew J. Slaughter. 2004. "Economic Insecurity and the Globalization of Production." *American Journal of Political Science 48*: 662–674.

Singer, Matthew M. 2011. "Who Says 'It's the Economy'?" Cross-National and Cross-Individual Variation in the Salience of Economic Performance." *Comparative Political Studies 44*: 284–312.

Walter, Stefanie. 2010. "Globalization and the Welfare State: Testing the Microfoundations of the Compensation Hypothesis." *International Studies Quarterly 54*: 403–426.

9

The Electoral Impact of the Crisis on the French Working Class

MORE TO THE RIGHT?

Nonna Mayer

THIS CHAPTER EXPLORES the electoral impact of the 2008 financial crisis in France. It focuses in particular on the reactions of the working class, the social group most affected by the economic fallout from the crisis.[1] Using survey data spanning the past three decades, I argue that the current economic crisis has mainly amplified a preexisting electoral trend: the shift of the working class to the far Right of the political spectrum.[2]

This is quite a paradox for a class that used to be the stronghold of the Communist and Socialist Left, and it matters because the working class continues to carry substantial, if diminished, electoral weight. The group still represents roughly a quarter of the economically active population, and far more if one takes into account familial connections with the working class—having a working-class parent or spouse—as Michelat and Simon (1977) did in their pioneering study. At the time of the 2007 presidential election, 56 percent of the voters had at least one working-class link, meaning they were either working class themselves or the child of at least one working-class parent.

In the 1970s, the density of a person's working-class connections predicted the probability of voting for the Left, and especially for the Communists. Today, it predicts the probability of voting for the extreme Right.[3] This development is not specific to France. The transition to a postindustrial society, with the numerical decline of the industrial working class, the transformation of social democratic parties into middle-class parties (Przeworski, 1985), and the expansion of the service sector and the salaried middle classes have loosened the links between workers and the Left, and fueled a debate about the death of "class voting" (Clark, Lipset, and Rempel 1993; Evans 1999) and more generally "cleavage voting" based on group identity (Franklin et al. 2009). The dealignment of the working class, however one measures it, is by now a well-acknowledged process; only its timing and intensity differ from one country to another.

In the wake of the dealignment debate, a second debate has started about the growing support of the working class for right-wing populist parties (Betz 1994; Kitschelt and McGann 1995; Kriesi et al. 2008; Oesch 2008). For Kriesi and his colleagues, the globalization process is giving birth to a new party cleavage. Opening economic borders, making society more diverse, and reducing the prerogatives of the nation-state, globalization has opened a political space for antiglobalization, and more specifically in Europe, anti-EU parties appealing to the "globalization losers"—workers and small business owners who feel directly threatened by the process because they do not have the necessary skills to compete. Far-right populist parties such as the French National Front were the first to occupy this space, promoting identity politics with a nationalist, protectionist, and anti-immigrant line. These "cultural" issues are gradually mixing with, if not prevailing over, traditional economic issues such as state intervention and public expenditure (Van der Waal, Achterberg, and Houtman, 2008; Bornschier 2010). And on such issues, educational cleavages are becoming more important than the traditional class cleavages. Globalization and the rising relative importance of educational rather than class cleavages help explain working-class voting in the 2012 presidential election, the first "postcrisis" national ballot in France.

The first section of this chapter analyses the socioeconomic effects of the 2008 financial crisis in France, with particular emphasis on the French working class. The second section focuses on the electoral effects of the crisis, especially rising working-class support for the National Front in four electoral contests between 2008 and 2012. The third section places these post-2008 voting patterns in historical context, portraying them as a continuation of longstanding trends of working-class dealignment with the Left and realignment with the Right and far Right. Rather than provoking a massive swing to the extreme Right or the extreme Left, the crisis led to the modest reinforcement of trends that began years ago. Increasing working-class support for Marine Le Pen, who became president of the National Front in January 2011, also contributed to boosting the party's vote, as did the weakness of Le Pen's competition on the center Right and Left.

The Shock of the 2008 Financial Crisis in France

The Economic Shock

The 2008 financial crisis triggered an economic recession in France,[4] resulting in a dramatic rise in unemployment, which disproportionately affected the working class, and particularly unskilled workers. France has been troubled by mass unemployment since the oil shocks of 1973–1979, with rates climbing from some 3 percent of the gainfully employed in 1975 to above 10 percent in 1993–1999, with another peak at 9.5 percent in 2006. As Figure 9.1 shows, the rates had been steadily declining for two years when the financial crisis sent them up again in 2009. In 2010, the average level of unemployment (ILO definition) was 9.2 in metropolitan France, a little above the EU-27 rate of 9 percent. In November 2011 unemployment reached its highest level in twelve years, with almost thirty thousand additional people registered as job applicants in one month, for a total of 2.8 million.[5]

A more nuanced picture appears if one takes into account gender, ethnicity, age, and occupation.[6] The recession affected men first, because they are overrepresented in the most exposed sectors (construction, manufacturing, and interim work). As a result, for the first time since 1975, the male rate of unemployment at the end of 2009 exceeded the female rate (at 9.7 and

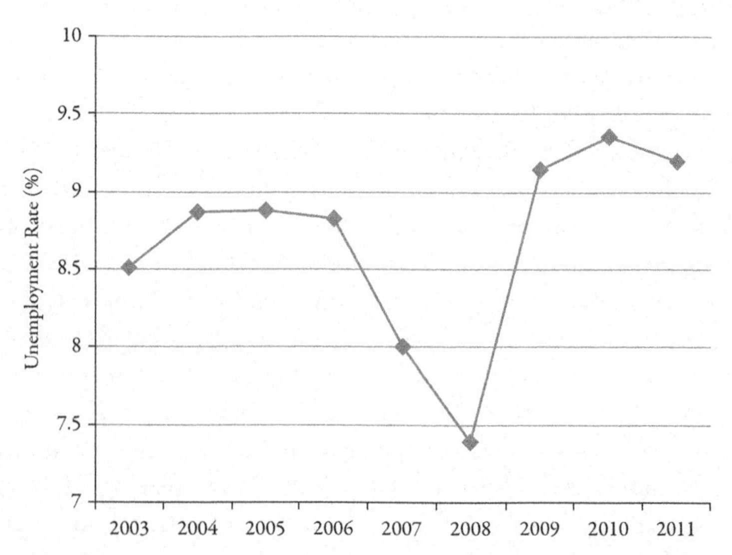

FIGURE 9.1 The Evolution of Unemployment Rates in Metropolitan France, 2003-2011.
Source: Yearly data for metropolitan France, INSEE Employment surveys, unemployment rate as defined by ILO.

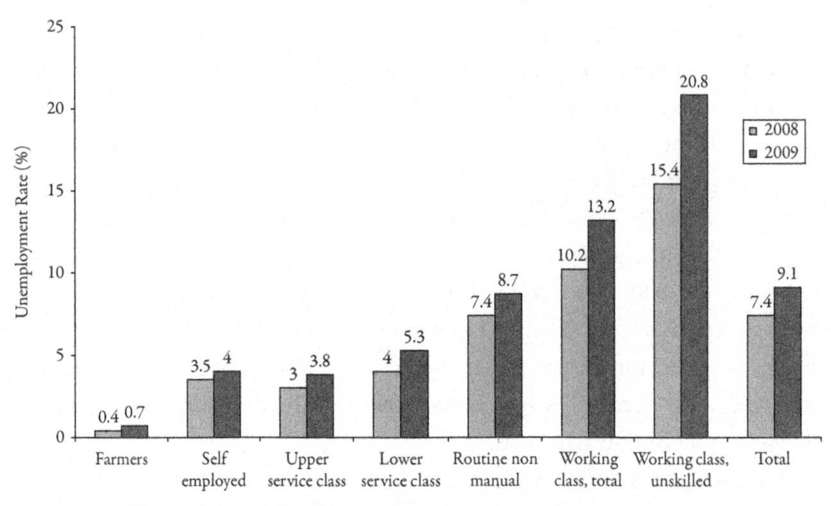

FIGURE 9.2 Unemployment by Occupation, 2008–2009.

9.4 percent, respectively). The rates of unemployment were double among foreigners (17.9 percent among men and 17.5 percent among women, compared with 8.3 and 8.9 percent for French citizens), and almost triple among the young (23.7 percent for those between fifteen and twenty-four years old). As Figure 9.2 shows, the unemployment rates varied considerably across occupation groups, from 4–5 percent among the self-employed and the higher- and lower-level service classes to almost 9 percent among routine nonmanual employees, 13 percent among workers, and almost 21 percent among unskilled manual workers. The last figure represented an increase of more than five percentage points between 2008 and 2009.

The Psychological Impact of the Crisis

The psychological impact of the crisis can be seen in the answers to survey questions posed immediately after the collapse of Lehman Brothers in September 2008. Asked "when you think about the financial crisis, would you say you are personally worried or not worried?" 77 percent of a sample representative of the adult French population expressed worry, a proportion that went up to 83 percent among the low-income respondents (versus 68 percent among the well-off) (Teinturier 2009, 16). Almost 70 percent of low-income respondents said the crisis concerned them personally (versus 57 percent of the well-off).

Meanwhile unemployment and purchasing power rose in the hierarchy of the public's preoccupations (over 73 percent in December, versus 57 percent in June 2008 ranking them first). More generally, the feeling that life had become more difficult was predominant. A frequently asked question is, "Looking at the last five years, would you say that people like you live better, or less well?" In 1966, at the time of the "Trente Glorieuses" (the thirty glorious years of economic growth), only 28 percent of the French chose the answer "less well." By 1981, when the Left won the presidential election, 50 percent chose this response. In the midst of the 1993 recession, 60 percent made this choice, while in June 2010 71 percent of all respondents felt they lived less well, with 74 percent of working-class respondents drawing this conclusion (Michelat and Simon 2011, 141–142).

A survey of reactions to inequality and social justice conducted just after the beginning of the recession, in the fall of 2008, shows that 42 percent of manual workers and routine nonmanual employees felt disadvantaged as far as unemployment and precariousness were concerned (versus 34 percent of respondents overall). These same groups were also more likely to feel disadvantaged as far as their incomes were concerned, with 64 percent of workers feeling disadvantaged versus 51 percent of respondents overall (Forsé and Galland 2011, 54).

Another useful indicator is the Annual Barometer of the DREES.[7] The survey responses presented in Table 9.1 show that since 2007 the French public has massively come to feel that inequalities are increasing, that inequalities will continue to increase in the coming years, and that France is an "unfair" rather than a "fair" society. The proportions expressing these views were generally higher among the working class until 2010, when the feeling of unfairness became general. It is also among the working class that the demand for a "radical change" was greatest; "revulsion" with the socioeconomic situation rose to 64 percent in 2011, 16 percentage points above the sample average (Figure 9.3).

The Electoral Impact of the Crisis

To what extent have anger and perceived injustice influenced voting within the French working class, the group most affected by unemployment and job insecurity? Did workers punish incumbents? If so, did they favor the Left-wing opposition? Or revitalize the extreme Right?

The three midterm elections that took place between the time the recession hit France and the spring of 2011 provide a first set of clues. European

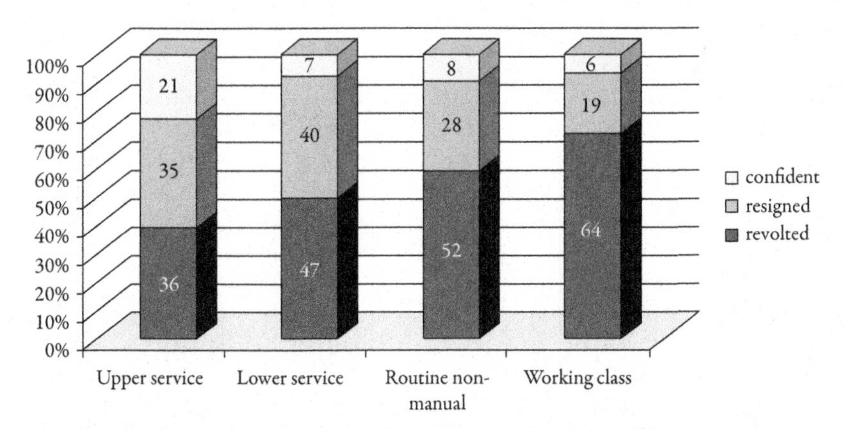

FIGURE 9.3 Feeling About France's Social and Economic Situation by Occupation.

Table 9.1 Perceptions of Inequality and Social Justice, 2007–2010.

% Agreeing with Following Statements	2007	2008	2009	2010	Increase
France is an unfair society (*among working class*)	69 (*75*)	71 (*74*)	73 (*79*)	78 (*78*)	+9 (*+3*)
Inequalities have been rising in the last five years (*among working class*)	77 (*78*)	80 (*82*)	85 (*87*)	87 (*88*)	+10 (*+10*)
Inequalities will be rising in the coming five years (*among working class*)	72 (*74*)	78 (*80*)	81 (*82*)	84 (*86*)	+12 (*+12*)
Which of These Statements Do You Most Agree with:					
One should radically change French society (*among working class*)	19 (*21*)	22 (*29*)	22 (*27*)	23 (*28*)	+5 (*+7*)
One should reform it on certain points while keeping most of it (*among working class*)	76 (*73*)	71 (*64*)	72 (*66*)	72 (*68*)	−4 (*−5*)
One should keep French society as it is (*among working class*)	5 (*5*)	6 (*6*)	5 (*7*)	4 (*4*)	−1 (*−1*)

Source: DREES/Ministry of Health, Annual Barometer surveys done every October–November by the polling Institute BVA on samples of 4,000 people representative of adults living in metropolitan France.

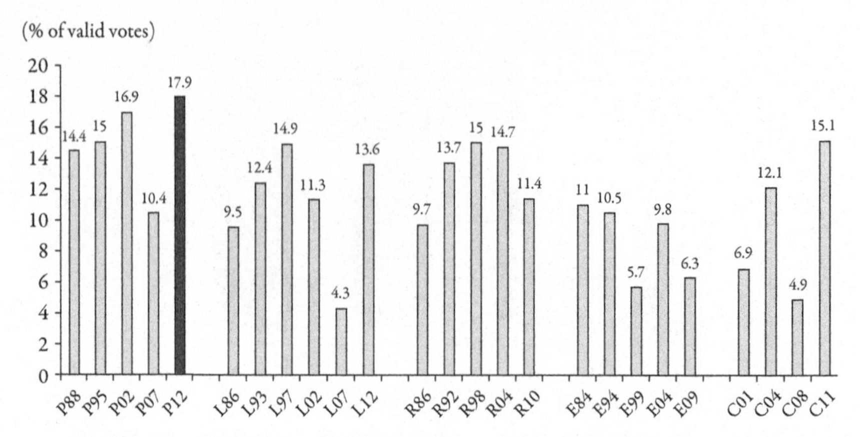

FIGURE 9.4 Votes for the National Front Since 1984 (% of Valid Votes).

Parliamentary elections were held in June 2009, regional elections were held in April 2010, and local (cantonal) elections were held in March 2011. Figure 9.4 compares the electoral performance of the National Front in each of these elections with its performance in similar elections since 1984.

In spite of a very low turnout of around 40 percent,[8] incumbent president Nicolas Sarkozy's party, the UMP, was the winner of the 2009 European elections with 28 percent of the valid votes, far ahead of the Socialist party (16.8 percent), the Greens (who experienced a spectacular rise, to 16.2 percent), and the centre-Modem (8.5 percent). The National Front won 6.3 percent of the vote, just two percentage points more than in the previous parliamentary elections.

The year after the EU elections brought two major changes. First, the Left swept the regional elections, dominated by the issues of employment and purchasing power, with 54 percent of the valid votes in the second round and victories in twenty-one of the twenty-two metropolitan regions. The second change came on the extreme Right. Le Pen's party attracted 11.4 percent of the votes in the first round, clearing the bar of 10 percent required to compete in the second round in twelve regions. A survey done between the two rounds of the election confirmed the popularity of the National Front among the working-class electorate. Twenty-two percent of the workers who cast ballots voted for the National Front, twice the average proportion for the electorate as a whole. But the survey also showed that a majority of workers (54 percent) voted for the Left or for Green lists—the same proportion as among nonworkers. Workers withdrew their support from the president's

UMP party (18 percent versus 26 percent on average),[9] despite the fact that in 2007 Sarkozy had won an impressive 26 percent of their votes, as much as the Socialist candidate, Ségolène Royal.

A year later, in 2011, the cantonal elections brought both further punishment for the president's party on the Right and the comeback of the National Front. In the 2026 cantons where the general council was to be renewed, the National Front drew 15.1 percent of the votes in the first round, the most votes it ever garnered in such an election. In the second round, the number of National Front voters increased substantially in the four hundred cantons where it could maintain its candidates (from 620,000 votes in the first round to 915,000). The National Front attracted the most votes in working-class cantons of northern and eastern France (where the working class represents between 33 and 40 percent of the local population), drawing 43.4 percent of the second-round votes in Noyon (Oise), 42 percent in Condé sur l'Escaut (Nord), and 40.9 percent in West-Montbéliard (Doubs), (Mergier and Fourquet 2011, 14).

The pattern of punishment seen in the 2011 cantonal elections continued the following year. In the first round of the 2012 French presidential election, the vote support for the National Front reached an historic high of 17.9 percent. Marine Le Pen surpassed her father's record support in the 2002 election by 1.6 million votes and one percentage point.[10] Although she did not qualify for the second round as her father had, Martine Le Pen's performance clearly indicated that the National Front was on an ascending trajectory,

An Extremist Reaction to Economic Crisis?

Though the recession that began in 2008 contributed to the expansion of the National Front's popularity, the party's boost in support should not be seen as simply an extremist reaction to the economic crisis. The National Front's expanded support represents the continuation of a longstanding trend toward right-wing voting among French workers. This trend was modestly accelerated by three other factors: the vulnerability of the incumbent Center-Right party (due only partially to the recession), the shortcomings of Left-wing alternatives, and Marine Le Pen's appeal to new sectors of the working class.

The Dealignment from the Left

Class voting has declined in most postindustrial democracies, whether measured with a simple distinction between manual and nonmanual

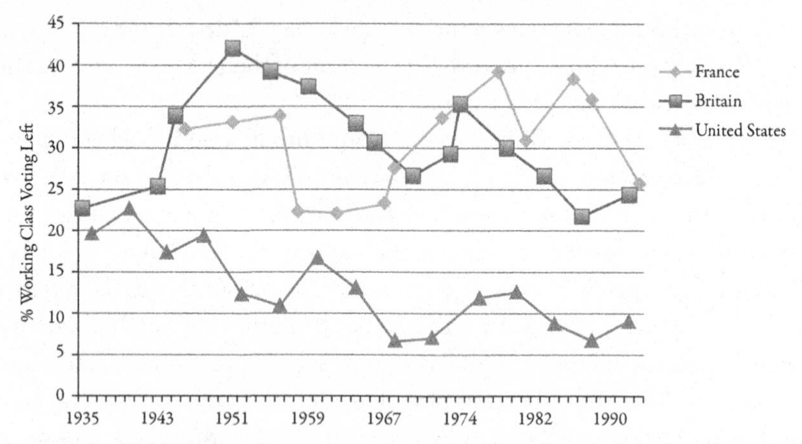

FIGURE 9.5 Class Voting in France, Britain, and the United States, (1935–1993).

workers or assessed with more refined categories and indices (Manza, Hout, and Brooks 1995; Nieuwbeerta and de Graaf 1999; Weaklien and Heath 1999). The shift is not linear, and its timing and intensity vary from one country to another according to the political context. Figure 9.5 provides a summary of trends in class voting in three countries—France, Great Britain, and the United States.[11] In France, the first years of the Fifth Republic—a time when class voting had practically disappeared in the United States and was beginning a sharp decline in Great Britain—saw an increase in class voting, due to political polarization between the Gaullist Right and the Union of the Socialist and Communist Left (involving the signing of a Common Government Program in 1972). In spite of the rupture of the Union of the Left, class voting continued, reaching its peak in the 1978 parliamentary elections, and almost allowing the Left to win the elections in the first round. Three years later, after twenty-three years of right-wing domination, the Socialist François Mitterrand was elected president of the Republic and four Communist ministers entered the government.

During this period working-class support for the Left increased, especially among the "baby boom" generations that reached voting age at a time of economic growth (les Trente Glorieuses), when the Communist party was the "party of the working class" and when the dynamic of the Union of the Left bred hope to change the world (Gougou 2011; Gougou and Mayer 2012). In the first round of the 1978 parliamentary elections, 69 percent of working-class voters supported the candidates of the Left. In the first round of the presidential election of 1981, the comparable figure was still 66 percent, with half supporting the Communist George Marchais and half the Socialist Mitterrand. It is only after the Left came into office that the support of the working class started to decline.

The first drop in the proportion of workers supporting the Left appeared in the European elections of 1984, followed by the parliamentary elections of 1986 (Gougou 2007; Gougou and Roux 2013). The second and bigger drop took place in the 1990s. In 1993, for the first time in a parliamentary election, the Left lost the majority of the votes among the working class in parliamentary elections, and in 1995 it duplicated that loss in the presidential election. The Left never recovered this majority again. Between the presidential elections of 1981 and 2007, the proportion of working-class votes for the Left dropped by nearly half, from 68 percent to 37 percent (Figure 9.6).

These figures make sense only when compared to the average support for the Left in the electorate as a whole. If one computes the odds ratios of the workers' (versus nonworkers') votes for the Left (versus non-Left), the picture is even clearer; these odds ratios are presented in Figure 9.7. In the 1970s, workers were more than two-and-a-half times more likely to vote for the Left than nonworkers. In 1988, the odds ratio dropped to one and a half, and by

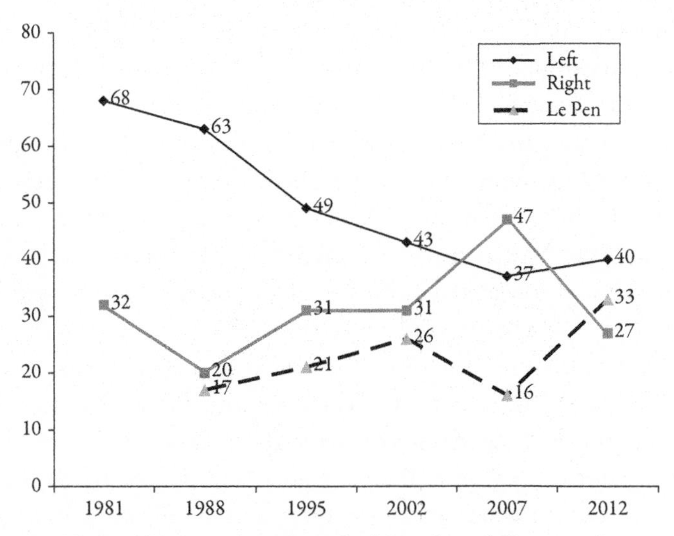

FIGURE 9.6 Workers' Votes in First Round of Presidential Elections Since 1981 (% of Valid Votes).

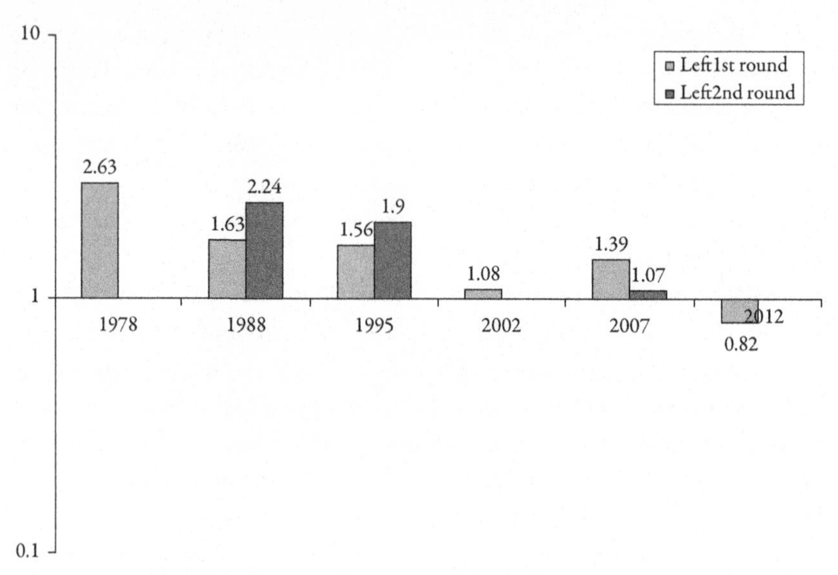

FIGURE 9.7 Odds Ratios of Workers' Votes for the Left (1978–2012).

2002 there was no difference at all. The slight rise in the first round of the 2007 presidential election, owing to the mobilization around the Socialist candidate Royal, disappeared in the second round.

The causes of working-class disaffection include disappointment with the policies of the socialists—disapproving of their economic austerity policies after 1982, of participation in the first Gulf War on the side of the United States in 1990, and finally of the 1992 Treaty of Maastricht accelerating European integration (Mayer 2002, 107–108). They also include the gradual decline of the Communist party, the "working-class" party par excellence, reluctantly trapped in its alliance with the Socialist party. Then there was the slow demise of the communist dream, from the first revelations of the crimes of Stalinism to the fall of the Berlin Wall and the collapse of the Soviet Union. Lastly, there were structural changes linked to the transition to a postindustrial economy and accelerated by the end of economic growth brought about by the two oil shocks of 1973 and 1979.

The working class was the group hardest hit by unemployment and labor precariousness. The number of workers, especially unskilled workers in the industrial sector, declined after 1973, and the first large-scale strikes of unskilled workers began that very year. The big plants (automobile, mines, steel and iron manufacturing), where workers were unionized and enjoyed job security, housing, and social advantages, began closing down. By 1990, two workers out of five were employed in service activities (storage, transportation, cleaning), where the sense of solidarity and group belonging generated in the industrial sector was less likely (Chenu 1993; Cézard 1996).

Workers' class consciousness and the sense of shared identity that held the class together has long been evaporating. In 1966, in response to an open-ended question asking, "Do you have the feeling you belong to a social class? And if so, which one?" almost a quarter of the French population said they belonged to the working class. The proportion ranged between 12 percent for those with no working-class attributes and 51 percent for those with two. In 2010, only 6 percent of the sample declared themselves as belonging to the working class, and among those with two working-class attributes the percentage rose only to 17 (Michelat and Simon 2011, 139). The political fragmentation of the group reflects its social fragmentation and polarization, with the most skilled workers moving upward and eventually out of the class, to positions of foreman or technician, while the unskilled are confined to precarious and underpaid jobs.

The Attraction of the Extreme Right

The dealignment of the working class generally benefited the Right, which has attracted a majority of the workers' votes in the first round of every presidential election since 1995 (Figure 9.6). The National Front, the extreme right anti-immigrant party then headed by Jean-Marie Le Pen, reaped the most dramatic benefits from these trends. Even in 2007, when Sarkozy captured a large share of Le Pen's 2002 votes, workers were the National Front's most faithful adherents.[12]

The National Front was created in 1972 with the aim of federating all the components of the French Extreme Right and reintegrating them into the parliamentary game, on the model of the Italian fascist party, the MSI (Movimento Sociale Italiano). For ten years this strategy was a complete failure, attracting less than 1 percent of the valid votes, whatever the election. The turning point was the arrival of the Left in office in 1981. After local successes in by-elections in 1983, the 1984 European elections marked the national emergence of the National Front, which drew 11 percent of the valid votes. Since then, the party has been a constant on the French electoral scene, with its ups (as in the 2002 presidential election, when Le Pen beat the socialist candidate in the first round and qualified for the second) and its downs (as in 2007, when he drew only 10 percent in the first round of the presidential election and only around 4 percent in the first round of parliamentary elections; Figure 9.4).

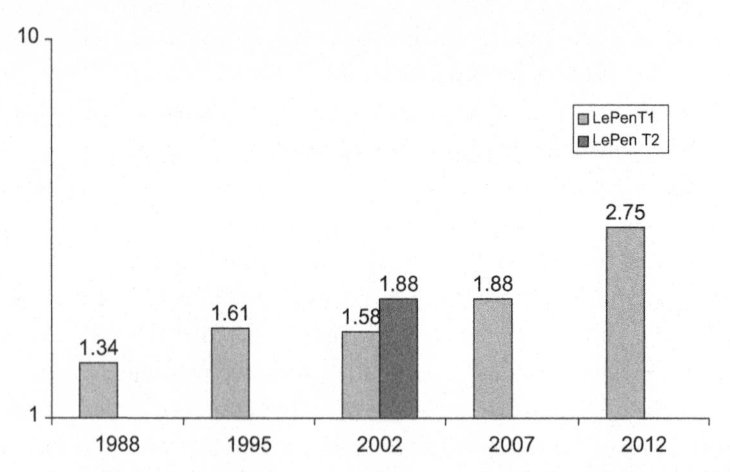

FIGURE 9.8 Odds Ratios of Workers' Votes for National Front Presidential Candidates (1988–2012).

National Front candidates have been attracting a growing share of the working-class vote since the presidential election of 1988, coming ahead of all candidates for this group in 1995. Even in 2007, when Le Pen drew hardly more than 10 percent of the votes in the first round of the presidential elections, it was still among French workers that he found the most support, 16 percent (Table 9.2). The odds ratios of the working-class vote for Le Pen presented in Figure 9.8 show this clearly. Since 2002, workers have been almost twice as likely as non workers to vote for the extreme right in presidential elections. By 2012, the odds are getting close to three. And if one computes the odds ratios of votes for the extreme right versus the moderate right (Gougou 2011), it is clear that the realignment dynamic plays in favor of the former. Since 1988, workers have been about twice as likely as the average French voter to prefer the extreme right candidate in the first round of presidential elections.

The main sociodemographic variables predicting support for Jean-Marie Le Pen from 1988 to 2007 were not the usual suspects, class and religion, the "variables lourdes" as one calls them in France, but gender and education (Perrineau 1997; Mayer 2002). Jean-Marie Le Pen did best among less-educated voters (Table 9.2), for they were most receptive to the simple and tough solutions he advocated for solving the complicated issues of politics, targeting immigrants as the only cause of all the problems of France. And until very recently, women were always more reluctant than men to support the National Front, with its traditional vision of gender relations and an aura of violence.

Table 9.2 Sociodemographic Profile of Le Pen Voters in French Presidential Elections (% of Valid Votes).

	1988	1995	2002	2007	2012
Total sample	15	15	17	11	*18*
Gender					
Men	18	19	20	12	*19*
Women	11	12	14	9	*17*
Age					
18–24 years	14	18	13	10	*23*
25–34 years	15	20	17	10	*23*
35–49 years	15	16	18	11	*18*
50–64 years	14	14	20	12	*21*
65 years and older	16	10	15	9	*10*
Respondent's occupation					
*Farmer	10	10	22	10	—
Self-employed (shopkeeper, artisan)	19	19	22	10	*20*
Upper service class	14	4	13	7	*8*
Lower service class	15	14	11	5	*12*
Routine nonmanual	14	18	22	12	*23*
Working class	17	21	23	16	*33*
Degree					
Primary	15	17	24	13	*26*
Secondary, vocational	17	20	21	13	*31*
Baccalaureate (end high school)	13	12	15	8	*18*
Baccalaureate + 2	10	13	11	3	*13*
College and beyond	9	4	7	4	*7*
Religion					
Regularly practicing Catholic	13	8	12	5	15
Occasionally practicing	13	13	18	10	17
Nonpracticing	16	19	20	12	21
No religion	10	14	15	12	20
Size of town					
Less than 2,000 inhabitants	12	14	19	11	20
Paris and suburbs	17	14	11	5	12

Note: * Including retired and unemployed workers, coded according to the last occupation they held.

Source: CEVIPOF postelection surveys, French Electoral Panels 2002 and 2007 (wave 1 pre-electoral), TNS-Sofres/TriElec survey "Voting Day", April 22, 2012.

If one turns to motivations and attitudes, Le Pen voters stand out for their high level of intolerance toward immigrants, foreigners, and "others," combined with an authoritarian and repressive vision of society. Contrary to the vote for the Left and the moderate Right, the best predictor of the Le Pen vote was not economic liberalism but ethnocentrism-authoritarianism. "Cultural" issues were more important than purely "economic" issues (Van der Waal et al. 2008; Van der Waal et al. 2010).

Support for the National Front among workers, in particular, was based in part on cultural anxieties grounded in the fear of downward mobility. Camille Peugny's work on the political effects of downward social mobility shows that among the working class, and more generally among the downwardly mobile, fear of falling below one's class is a most powerful ingredient of support for the National Front:

Because they are employees and workers in subordinate positions, they virulently reject economic liberalism and call for a strong and protective state. Because their social trajectory is downward, they rationalise it and develop a particularly violent discourse against the "assisted" who are, in their eyes individuals unfairly exempted from work (unemployed, minimum wagers). Now the platform of the FN clearly conciliates the claimed willingness to defend the little man, with the violent critique of the culture of assistance provided by the welfare state (Peugny 2009, 150).

The recession will likely breed even more fear of downward mobility, and this may be even more important than actual descent. A study by Olivier Schwartz (2009) of bus drivers in Marseille tells a similar story. These are workers who have some skills and some property. They are at the boundary of the working class and the lower middle class, the "petits moyens" (small middle ones) described by Cartier et al. (2008). They drive the already "fallen" in their buses every day and do not want to become like them. As Schwartz explains, the working class of the past had a simple, dual vision: "the have-nots" against "the haves," the top versus the bottom. Today they have a "triangular consciousness": they define themselves against the bottom as much as against the top. And the National Front gives them arguments to distinguish themselves from the bottom, the scum, the lazy, who do not work and cheat the social security office. This more complex vision gives them an identity that replaces their lost class identity.

Table 9.3 presents a summary of views related to ethnocentrism and the National Front in various occupational groups, based on survey data from

Table 9.3 Ethnocentrism and Agreement with Ideas of the National Front, by Occupation.

	Not Feeling at Home in France Anymore	Too Many Immigrants	Too Many Rights for Islam/ Muslims	Get Rid of the Euro	Restore Death Penalty	National Preference for Jobs	Agree with Ideas of National Front
Petty bourgeoisie	43%	67%	62%	32%	27%	17%	34%
Upper service class	22%	31%	38%	9%	15%	9%	8%
Lower service class	30%	44%	47%	27%	20%	12%	18%
Routine non manual	48%	56%	55%	43%	35%	20%	22%
Working class	**60%**	**70%**	**68%**	**50%**	**42%**	**30%**	**34%**
Total sample	*43%*	*53%*	*53%*	*34%*	*30%*	*20%*	*22%*
Working class – Total sample	**+17%**	**+16%**	**+15%**	**+16%**	**+12%**	**+10%**	**+12%**

Source: TNS-Sofres/*Le Monde*, Canal +, France Inter, face-to-face interviews, January 3–4, 2011, N = 1,000; not weighted.

early 2011. Working-class people were significantly more likely than others to say they do not feel at home in France anymore, there are too many immigrants and too many rights for Islam and Muslims, and they agree with the ideas of the National Front. These attitudes seem to have intensified in the wake of the financial crisis. For example, the annual Barometer survey on racism, anti-Semitism, and xenophobia for the National Commission for Human Rights (CNCDH), conducted in January 2011, showed that intolerance toward immigrants, foreigners, and Muslims, which had been declining consistently since 1990 (Mayer, Michelat, and Tiberj 2010), was increasing.[13] Between October 2009 and January 2011, the proportion of respondents who thought there are "too many immigrants in France" went up by eight percentage points, and the feeling "one does not feel as at home as before in France" by seven percentage points. Support for these ideas among working-class voters reached new highs, with approval rates sixteen and seventeen points above the sample average.[14] Additional analysis indicates that anti-Islam feelings and anti-immigrant attitudes both played important roles in bolstering support for the program of the National Front.

Cultural concerns thus account for part of the distinctive appeal to workers of the National Front. They are predominantly male (83 percent in 2008, according to INSEE). Fewer than 20 percent hold a baccalaureate or its equivalent (compared to 37 percent in the French population age fifteen or more), and they display the highest level of ethnocentrism and authoritarianism because of their low level of education and difficult work conditions. However, not all workers are equally receptive to extreme Right ideas.

One variable explaining differences in receptivity to the National Front among working-class voters is political leaning. The most inclined to vote for the National Front are the right-wing workers, the "conservative blue collars," or the "neither-nor-ers," those who define themselves as "neither right wing nor left-wing," the politically disaffected. One should not forget that even in the golden age of the "class vote" there always was a sizeable minority of the working class voting for the Right, either because of the traditions of the region where they lived[15] or for individual reasons (including anticommunism rooted in Catholicism, property ownership, or upward mobility).[16] At the beginning of the Fifth Republic, one-third of workers regularly voted for Charles de Gaulle, a proportion rising to 42 percent in the first round of the 1965 presidential election, just one point below the general's national score (Charlot 1970, 75). And if one looks at the workers who declared an intention to vote for Le Pen on the eve of the first round of the 2007 presidential election, 43 percent defined themselves as "somewhat right wing,"

41 percent "neither left wing nor right wing" or refused to answer. Only 16 percent claimed to be "somewhat left wing," contrary to other workers, where the respective proportions were 24, 35, and 41 percent (CEVIPOF French Electoral Panel 2007, wave 1, see Appendix 2).

Support for the extreme Right among working-class voters also varies significantly across generations. The cohorts born during the baby boom, who reached voting age in a period of growth and employment that stabilized the economic and social condition of blue-collar workers, helped bring the Socialist and Communist parties into office and remained faithful to the parties of the Left. Younger cohorts, who were hard-hit early in their working lives by deindustrialization and mass unemployment, turned to the Right or the extreme Right or just stopped going to the polls.[17]

The relative importance of generation as an explanatory factor suggests an apparent paradox, because the younger generations of workers have the same pro-state economic attitudes as the older ones, and they are far less ethnocentric and less authoritarian than the older ones. Yet the paradox is resolved when we look at the respective impact of these two attitudes on the vote, by cohort and by election. The older cohorts are more likely to vote for the Left because they attach more importance to economic issues at the moment of voting, even though they are more ethnocentric than average. Among the post–baby boomers, the cultural dimension outweighs the economic one; anti-immigrant sentiments trump economic considerations and drive them toward the xenophobic Right (Gougou and Mayer 2012, table 4).[18]

The Weakness of the Incumbent and the Left-wing Opposition

The extreme Right benefited from the weakness of the incumbent president as well as the established trends summarized above. Sarkozy was elected on the promise "Work more, to gain more," but the recession shattered the dream, bringing about unemployment, insecurity, and anger. The economic crisis hurt the incumbent party deeply, but discontent with Sarkozy's government was fueled by other factors as well. The "fiscal shield," which reduced the income tax of the rich so that no one had to pay more than 50 percent of his or her annual income in tax, was widely unpopular. The pension reform bill, seen as unfair for the working classes and for women, sent millions of demonstrators into the streets (September and October 2010), and several scandals related to embezzlement and favoritism tarnished the image of the political class. By September 2011, a survey showed that a record 72 percent of the French population agreed with the statement "the political class is somewhat corrupt" (19 percent found them honest). The proportion rose to 65 percent among workers and 89 percent among National Front sympathizers.[19] As for Sarkozy, his popularity hit a record low. By December 2011, barely 29 percent of the French public trusted him to solve the country's problems, while 68 percent did not (TNS-Sofres/Figaro Magazine monthly Popularity Barometer). Among workers, 81 percent distrusted the president, while only 18 percent trusted him.

The Socialist Party was likely to benefit from this discontent. The open primaries in October 2011 were a real success, attracting the attention of the media and mobilizing 2.7 million people in the first round and 2.9 million in the second. But the winner, François Hollande, had less support than his challenger, Martine Aubry, within the working class and more generally among low-income voters. Hollande has a more middle-class image that some thought might be a liability for attracting workers' and poorer people's votes. The odds ratios of voting probabilities for workers versus nonworkers (using data from the TriElec survey of July 2011) revealed that workers were indeed less likely to vote for Hollande than nonworkers were (Figure 9.7). Dividing respondents by level of household income reveals that the higher the income, the greater the likelihood of voting for Hollande, while for Marine Le Pen this pattern was reversed.[20]

On the extreme Left, the probability of attracting working-class and lower-income votes also seemed problematic. The New Anticapitalist Party (NPA), founded by Olivier Besancenot, fell into crisis, hindered by the new Party of the Left, launched by the socialist Jean-Luc Mélenchon in 2008 and by the insignificance of its presidential candidate, Philippe Poutou.

The weakness of Sarkozy, the middle-class aura of Hollande, the organizational weakness of the extreme Left, and workers' dealignment with the traditional Left might have expanded the political space for an antisystem party even without an economic crisis, but the coincidence of these factors with the Great Recession was certainly advantageous to the National Front.

Marine Le Pen's Appeal

Marine Le Pen was well positioned to take advantage of the opportunities this troubled situation afforded. Polls of voting intentions for 2012 illustrated her personal appeal shortly after she was elected chair of the National Front at the Congress of Tours in January 2011. Her potential presidential scores rose sharply from 13 percent in July 2010 to 20 percent in May 2011.[21] They even surpassed the voting intention scores for Sarkozy[22] until the summer of 2011, when she fell back to third position. Still, in December 2011, the voting intentions in her favor were much higher than her father's ever were at the same distance from the first round, with an average score from mid-November through mid-December 2011 of 17 percent, compared to 25.8 percent for Sarkozy and 30 percent for the Socialist Hollande.[23]

As for the working class, its support for Marine Le Pen was higher than in any other occupational group and higher than ever before. Table 9.4 tracks support for Le Pen from 2010 through 2011 among various occupational groups. Her support among working-class voters peaked in April 2011 at 42 percent, more than twice her national support at the time. Similarly, in our TriElec survey of July 2011, we presented respondents with a list of potential candidates and asked them to estimate the chance of their voting for her in 2012, on a scale from zero to ten; whereas 15 percent of all respondents rated the likelihood of voting for Le Pen at 50 percent or greater, the corresponding proportion among workers was nearly twice as large—28 percent. Though support for Marine Le Pen varied from poll to poll, it was always higher among workers than among the population as a whole. Though one must be cautious with opinion polls, these data show an undeniable electoral dynamic for Marine Le Pen in the months before the 2012 election.

The election itself proved these predictions to be accurate. Marine Le Pen's record high number of votes was attributed, by some, to her strategy of "de-demonization"— that is, her attempt to soften the National Front's image and make it credible on issues other than immigration in order to diversify its

Table 9.4 Voting Intentions for Marine Le Pen (2010–2011).

	June–Oct. 2010	Feb–March 2011	April 2011	Nov.–Dec. 2011
Self-employed	13.5%	21%	19%	20%
Upper service	6.5%	12%	14%	12%
Lower service	19%	16%	14%	20%
Routine nonmanual	18.5%	34.5%	28%	27%
Working class	**25.5%**	**37.5%**	**42%**	**35%**
Total sample	*13.5%*	*37.5%*	*20.5%*	*20%*

Source: Pooling of seven IFOP surveys, N = 2,000, access panel, from which members are selected by quota sampling (in Mergier and 2011, 15, data updated for fall 2011). I am very grateful to Jérôme Fourquet, who provided the data from the November–December 2011 wave.

electoral support. Yet a survey carried out on the day of the first round of the presidential election shows a more complex picture.[24]

Working-class occupation was a significant predictor of support for Le Pen even after controlling for the effects of age, gender, monthly income (divided by the number of people in the household), and education. It is important to note, however, that education cancels the effect of social class. Because cultural issues have become central, education counts more than class per se in predicting the National Front vote, and support for the extreme Right goes beyond the boundaries of the traditional working class.

As Table 9.2 illustrates, Marine Le Pen's voters still appeared ideologically and socially very similar to her father's. Despite the economic crisis, she did not manage to extend her influence among middle- and upper-class voters. Her support, like her father's, was heavily concentrated in the ranks of the poorly educated. Indeed, her 2012 vote support nearly quadruples as one moves from people with a university degree to those who did not go beyond primary school—a ratio even higher than her father's. And, in keeping with past trends, she got her lowest level of support among teachers, students, and people working in advertising, arts, and information.[25]

Though she did not build new support among the educated, Marine Le Pen did succeed in broadening the National Front's support among her father's traditional constituency. She succeeded in attracting even more working-class voters than her predecessor, with a record score of 33 percent. She also succeeded in narrowing the gender gap that had hampered even higher working-class support in the past. Under Jean-Marie Le Pen, women were systematically less inclined to vote for National Front candidates. Yet in the first round of the 2012 presidential election, not only did the gap between men and women's support narrow to two percentage points but a logistic regression controlling step by step for gender, age, education, religion, and left-right placement shows that gender no longer had a significant independent impact on the likelihood of voting for the National Front (Table 9.5).

As Table 9.6 shows, support for Marine Le Pen was still at its highest level among working-class men (37 percent, 15 points above women), but her support was now higher with women than men among routine nonmanual employees, especially salespeople and shop assistants (25 percent, 9 points above men). The gender difference is even more striking if, instead of including retired and unemployed respondents classified according to their latest occupation, one takes into account only the

Table 9.5 Regression Analysis of Marine Le Pen Votes, 2012, by Gender, Sociodemographic and Political Variables.

	B	Standard Error	Exp(B)
Gender (men)	.100	(.235)	1.105
Education			
No degree	**1.303** **	(.564)	3.682
Primary school	**2.224** ***	(.518)	9.243
Secondary general	**1.564** ***	(.559)	4.778
Secondary vocational	**1.939** ***	(.377)	6.955
Bac vocational	**1.104** **	(.464)	3.016
Bac. general	.910 *	(.479)	2.484
Bac + 2	.472	(.451)	1.604
Religion			
Regularly practicing Catholic	−1.041 **	(.496)	.353
Occasionally practicing	−.857 **	(.365)	.425
Nonpracticing	−.378	(.283)	.686
Other religion	−1.151 **	(.561)	.316
Age			
18–24	**1.823** ***	(.502)	6.191
25–34	**1.772** ***	(.457)	5.880
35–49	**1.245** ***	(.408)	3.472
50–64	**1.254** ***	(.380)	3.505
Left-Right scale			
1	−2.642 ***	(.507)	.071
2	−3.500 ***	(.769)	.030
3	−2.509 ***	(.423)	.081
4	−2.099 ***	(.437)	.123
5	−1.073 ***	(.324)	.342
6	−.465	(.372)	.628
Constant	−2.567 ***	(.579)	.077

Note: *** p <.01; ** p <.05; * p <.10.

gainfully employed. Support for Marine Le Pen rises to 30 percent among economically active females who are routine nonmanual employees, compared to 10 percent among their male counterparts. Among economically active working-class men, support for Marine Le Pen reaches a record level of 43 percent.

Table 9.6 Le Pen Votes Among Working Class and Routine Nonmanual Employees by Gender, 2007 and 2012 Presidential Elections (% Valid Votes).

	2007		2012	
	Men	Women	Men	Women
Routine nonmanual employees	12% (13%)	12% (13%)	16% (10%)	25% (30%)
Manual workers	18% (18%)	13% (16%)	37% (43%)	22% (22%)

Note: Retired and unemployed classified by occupation of origin; proportion of Le Pen votes among the gainfully employed only shown in parentheses.

Conclusion

The National Front's latest advances among French workers in general and among women in particular are surely due in some measure to the economic crisis. Workers were among the first hit by the economic crisis, the most exposed to unemployment and precariousness, and the most discontented with Sarkozy's policies. Marine Le Pen's popularity among women, and especially among routine nonmanual employees, is also attributable, at least in part, to the economic crisis. The economic recession that hit France in 2008 first affected the industrial sector and therefore mostly men, but it has now extended to women, already overrepresented in jobs with part-time and temporary contracts and, as a consequence, less covered by the welfare system and more susceptible to poverty (Milewski and Cochard 2011).

This said, it is important to point out that the economic crisis beginning in 2008 has thus far not had a dramatic effect on electoral support for the far Right. The vulnerability of wage workers in general is the result of long-term structural trends that predate the crisis. Even the closing of the gender gap is, in large part, the result of trends that began decades ago. The overrepresentation of women in the unskilled service proletariat (Oesch 2006) and the rise of women's participation in service sector jobs, which can be as precarious and "lousy" as industrial jobs, began long before 2008.

More important, however, is the very modest scope of the electorate's move to extremism. Though voting workers have, in fact, moved "more to the Right" in the aftermath of the crisis, they have not done so in massive numbers or at an unprecedented rate. The National Front failed to reach historic highs in three out of five post-2008 elections. And though Marine Le Pen attracted a record number of supporters for her presidential bid, the vast majority of French voters—even the majority of working-class voters—chose moderate candidates instead.

One should, however, be careful in discussing the electoral behavior of the working class in 2012. The very notion of "working class" needs careful scrutiny because of the transformations the group is undergoing. A large body of literature has outlined the segmentation of the labor market, the rise of an unskilled service proletariat, and a dualization process opposing insiders to outsiders (Emmenegger et al., 2012). The latter are less skilled, less well paid, and more often on short-term contracts, with fewer chances of career advancement and little or no social protection, especially in a "continental" or Bismarckian welfare system such as France's, organized on the basis of occupational categories and linking social advantages to employment status. Among the outsiders, women, young, and immigrants are overrepresented.

Several authors thus call for a redefinition of class boundaries, considering the standard classifications such as Goldthorpe and Erikson's class schema (1992) as obsolete (Oesch 2006a, 2006b). In France, the traditional separation between manual workers (*ouvriers*) considered in this chapter and manual routine employees (*employés*), made by the standard occupation classification (INSEE) and used by opinion polls, is being questioned. Two workers out of five are employed in the service sector (transportation, cleaning, storage) while a growing proportion of employees do unskilled repetitive subordinate tasks not so different from manual workers on the production line. Amossé and Chardon (2006; Jauneau, 2009) suggest that a new social class of "unskilled workers" is emerging, representing some 20 percent of the gainfully employed: unskilled blue-collar workers on the one side, mostly men, and unskilled employees on the other, mostly women (cashiers at the supermarket, hotel cleaning women). They share difficult working conditions, long hours, low wages, social precariousness, and isolation. They form a class without class awareness, fragmented, socially and politically isolated, as shown by the large-scale survey "Histoire de vie/Life story" conducted by INSEE (National Institute of Statistic and Economic Studies) in 2003.

Compared to skilled workers, these unskilled workers and employees are less likely to declare a party identification (27 and 31 percent versus 35 and 47 percent), and less likely to be (or to have been) connected with a party, a political movement, or a union (17 and 14 versus 20 and 23 percent; Amossé and Chardon 2006, 212). At the same time, because they lack class identification, they put more weight on the defense of their nonclass identity, with the immigrant-born insisting on their religion and its transmission to their children and nonimmigrants defining themselves above all as "French." Such lines of cleavage breed a "racism of resentment" (ibidem, 223; Michelat and Simon 2004) that could fuel support for the extreme right, in France as in other European countries such as Switzerland, Denmark, and Austria (Oesch 2008), whether or not the present economic crisis continues.

Appendix 1: Correspondence Between the Class Scheme of Goldthorpe and Erikson (1992) and the French Classification of Occupations (INSEE)

Goldthorpe and Erikson (1992)	Groupe Socioprofessionnel de l'INSEE
Self-employed	Agriculteurs, commerçants, artisans, chefs d'entreprise
Upper service class	Cadres, professions intellectuelles supérieures
Lower service class	Professions intermédiaires
Routine nonmanual employees	Employés de commerce et de bureau
Skilled workers	Ouvriers qualifiés
Unskilled workers	Ouvriers non qualifiés

Appendix 2: Survey Data

This chapter employs four primary sources of survey data.

1. CEVIPOF French National Elections Surveys 1978–2007, including the 2002 and 2007 French Electoral Panels (funded by the French Home Office), on large samples (N ≥ 4,000), representative of registered voters in metropolitan France. Quota sampling based on census data and political regions (available on the website of the Centre for sociopolitical data of Sciences Po (CDSP), http://cdsp.sciences-po.fr/enquetes.php?lang=ANG&idRubrique=enquetesFR&idTheme/).
2. TNS-Sofres survey on the image of the National Front just before the Congress of Tours. TNS-Sofres/*Le Monde,* Canal +, France Inter, face-to-face interviews conducted January 3–4, 2011, with a sample of 1,000; not weighted.
3. First wave of the TriElec network[26] electoral survey. Telephone interviews by TNS-Sofres, July 6–7, 2011, with a sample of 1,009 people representative of the registered voters in metropolitan France. Quota sampling based on census data and political regions. Instead of voting intentions, the survey asked about voting probabilities for each potential candidate separately: "What are the chances of your voting for the following personalities if they are candidates for the 2012

presidential election? 0 means there is no chance you vote for her/him, 10 that there are very strong chances, and between these two scores you can nuance your answer."

4. TNS-Sofres/TriElec electoral survey "Voting Day," April 22, 2012. Telephone interviews with a sample of 1,500 people representative of the registered voters in metropolitan France. Quota sampling based on census data and political regions.

Notes

1. I use the term *working class* to refer to skilled and unskilled manual workers, not only in manufacturing and production but also in transportation, construction, services, and crafts, as defined by the French Census Office, Group 6 in the INSEE (National Institute for Statistics and Economic Studies) Classification of Professions and Socioprofessional Categories (2003). Appendix 1 relates this classification scheme to that developed by Erikson and Goldthorpe (1992).
2. The various surveys employed in this chapter are described in Appendix 2.
3. For instance, in the first round of the 2002 presidential election the proportion of Le Pen voters went from 16 percent among those who had no links with the working class to 26 percent if they were workers themselves and so were their fathers (Mayer 2002, 344). In 2007 (French Electoral Panel, wave 2), it rises from 8 percent among those who have no links to over 16 percent among workers whose father and mother were also working class.
4. France's GDP fell by 1.2 percent between the second and third quarters of 2008, and by 1.2 percent again between the last quarter of 2008 and the first quarter of 2009.
5. Ministry of Labor, December 2011. This is the figure for people with no job whatsoever. Including those who had reduced activity, the total of job applicants amounted to 4.5 million, a rise of 5.6 percent in one year.
6. INSEE (National Institute of Statistics and Economic Studies) Employment Surveys, average of the four quarters of 2009.
7. The DREES is the Department of Research, Evaluation, and Statistics of the Ministry of Labor, Employment, and Health. I am very grateful for the invaluable help of Pierre Fleutiaux, who provided me with the cross-tabulations by occupation.
8. The three midterm elections following the beginning of the recession all showed increased abstention rates compared to the last similar elections: +2.2 percent in the European elections of 2009, +14.5 percent in the regional elections of 2010, and +19.6 percent in the cantonal elections of 2011. Survey data suggest that abstention rates reached a maximum among the working class, ten, fifteen, and eleven points above the national rates in these elections respectively. Abstention

rates are from TNS-Sofres surveys conducted June 7, 2009, and March 19–20, 2010, and Ipsos-Logica, March 14–18, 2011.

9. TNS-Sofres telephone survey for Logica/Radio France/*Le Monde*, March 19–20, 2010. The survey was based on a national quota sample of fifteen hundred people representative of the French adult population.
10. She even exceeded by 700,000 votes the combined score of the two National Front candidates in 2002, Jean-Marie Le Pen and the dissident Bruno Mégret.
11. I am very grateful to Anthony Heath and David Weaklien, who provided the data for Figure 9.5 (Weaklien and Heath 1999).
12. The French Electoral Panel data (first wave) show that the switchers from Le Pen in 2002 to Sarkozy in 2007 were less working-class than the faithful Le Pen voters, more likely to be women, elderly people, Catholics, and small shopkeepers and artisans, and less to the right (Mayer 2007).
13. Similar levels of intolerance appeared in another survey conducted at the same time (TNS-Sofres/*Le Monde*, Canal +, France Inter, January 3–4, 2011, N = 1000).
14. The corresponding differences in previous surveys were around ten points.
15. See, for instance, the interesting typology of working-class constituencies (left, right, new right) established by Gougou (2011), part of a Ph.D. dissertation at Sciences Po on working-class votes in France and Germany since World War II.
16. See Capdevielle and Mouriaux (1983), *The Conservative Worker*, echoing Goldthorpe et al.'s *The Affluent Worker* (1969), or more recently Groux and Lévy (1993) on the effect of working-class home ownership.
17. In the first round of the presidential election of 2002, the most popular "working-class party"—ahead of any other electoral choice—was abstention, with 31 percent.
18. Gougou and Mayer's analysis (2012) draws on Gougou's exceptional dataset (2011) combining 25,880 observations from eight postelection studies covering more than forty years of French electoral history, from 1962 to 2007, including 6,106 workers (INSEE Group 6, with retired and unemployed people coded according to their last occupation).
19. TNS-Sofres/Matinale de Canal + survey, face-to-face interviews, September 23–26, 2011, N = 1,000 people representative of the French adult metropolitan population. These are the highest proportions recorded in these groups since the measure started in 1977.
20. The variable is monthly income divided by number of consumption units in household in quartiles. The potential vote for Marine Le Pen goes from 19.5 in the lower quartile to 9.3 in the upper, the vote for Martine Aubry from 41 to 33 percent, and the vote for François Hollande from 34 to 40 percent.
21. Survey TNS-Sofres/*Nouvel Observateur*/I-Télé, "Présidentielle 2012: Intentions de vote," four waves (August 20–21, 2010; November 19–20, 2010; February 18–19, 2011; and May 20–21, 2011), national samples representative of the French

population of voting age (N = 1,000), quota sampling. We computed the average of the voting intentions tested with different lists of candidates.

22. With 23 percent of voting intentions versus 21 percent for Martine Aubry and Nicolas Sarkozy, according to an online survey by Harris Interactive for *Le Parisien/Aujourd'hui en France*, March 5–6, 2011 (sample of 1,347 individuals drawn from the *access panel* Harris Interactive, representative of the French population of voting age, quota sampling).
23. http://www.sondages-en-france.fr/sondages/Elections/Présidentielles2012/archive, accessed on December 28, 2011.
24. Election Day telephone survey (N = 1,515), April 22, 2012, by TNS Sofres/Sopra Group/TriÉlec-Sciences-Po Bordeaux, Grenoble et Paris/TF1, Métro. See the TriElec website, http://www.pacte-grenoble.fr/blog/resultats-du-sondage-tns-sofres-avec-trielec-du-22-avril-2012/.
25. Nevertheless, Marine Le Pen, like her father, has attracted academics, intellectuals, and upper-class voters. There is an elite, sophisticated, and ideologically coherent version of this vote (Mayer 2002, 84–86; Lubbers and Tolsma 2011). On "elite" xenophobia, see Wodak and Van Dijk (2000).
26. TriElec associates three teams of researchers from the Centre Emile Durkheim (Sciences Po Bordeaux), the Centre d'études européennes (Sciences Po Paris) and PACTE (Sciences Po Grenoble). It coordinates several pre- and postelection surveys with methodologies focused on the presidential and parliamentary elections of 2012. Additional information is available from the TriElec website, http://www.trielec2012.fr/.

References

Amossé, Thomas, and Olivier Chardon. 2006. "Les travailleurs non qualifies: une nouvelle classe sociale?" *Economie et statistique 393–394*: 203–227.

Betz, Hans-Georg. 1994. *Radical Right-wing Populism in Western Europe*. New York: St. Martin's Press.

Bornschier, Simon. 2010. *Cleavage Politics and the Populist Right: The New Cultural Conflict in Western Europe*. Philadelphia: Temple University Press.

Capdevielle, Jacques, and René Mouriaux. 1983. *L'ouvrier conservateur*. Nantes: Les Cahiers du LERSCO, 6.

Cartier, Marie, Isabelle Coutant, Olivier Masclet, and Yasmine Siblot. 2008. *La France des petits-moyens*. Paris: La Découverte, coll. "Textes à l'appui/Enquêtes de terrain."

Cézard, Michel. 1996. *"Les ouvriers."* Paris: INSEE Première,455.

Charlot Jean. 1970. *Le phénomène gaulliste*. Paris: Fayard.

Chenu, Alain. 1993. "Une *classe ouvrière en crise*." *Données Sociales*, INSEE, 476–485.

Clark, Terence, Seymour M. Lipset, and Michael Rempel. 1993. "The Declining Political Significance of Social Class." *International Sociology 8*: 293–316.

Emmeneger, Patrick, Silja Haüsermann, Bruno Palier, and Martin Seeleib-Kaiser (eds.). 2012. *The Age of Dualization: The Changing Face of Inequality in De-Industrializing Societies* Oxford: Oxford University Press.

Erikson, Robert, and John H. Goldthorpe. 1992. *The Constant Flux: A Study of Class Mobility in Industrial Societies*. Oxford: Oxford University Press.

Evans, Geoffrey (ed.). 1999. *The Decline of Class Politics? Class Voting in a Comparative Context*. Oxford: Oxford University Press.

Forsé, Michel, and Olivier Galland (eds.). 2011. *Les Français face aux inégalités et à la justice sociale*. Paris: Armand Colin.

Franklin, Mark, et al. 2009 [1992]. *Electoral Change: Response to Evolving Social and Attitudinal Structures in Western Countries*. Colchester: ECPR Press.

Goldthorpe, John H., David Lockwood, Frank Bechhofer, and Jennifer Platt. 1969. *The Affluent Worker in the Class Structure*. Cambridge: Cambridge University Press.

Gougou, Florent. 2007. "Les mutations du vote ouvrier sous la Vème République." Paris: *Nouvelle Fondation 1*(5): 1–10.

Gougou, Florent. 2011. "La droitisation du vote des ouvriers: entre désalignement électoral et redéploiement d'un réalignement." In Jean-Michel De Waele, Michel Hastings and Mathieu Vieira (eds.). *Une droitisation de la classe ouvrière en Europe*, 142–172. Paris: Economica.

Gougou, Florent, and Nonna Mayer. 2012. "The Class Basis of Extreme Right Voting in France: Generational Replacement and the Rise of New Cultural Issues (1984–2007)." In J. Rydgren (eds.), *Class Politics and the Radical Right*, 156–172. London: Routledge.

Gougou, Florent, and Guillaume Roux. 2013. "Political Change and Cleavage Voting in France: Class, Religion, Political Appeals, and Voter Alignments (1962–2007)." In G. Evans and N. D. de Graaf (eds.), *Political Choice Matters: Explaining the Strength of Class and Religious Cleavages in Cross-National Perspective*, 244–276. Oxford: Oxford University Press.

Groux, Guy, and Catherine Lévy. 1993. *La possession ouvrière Du taudis à la propriété. XIX–XXème siècle*. Paris: Editions de l'Atelier, Editions ouvrières.

Jauneau, Yves. 2009. "Les employés et ouvriers non qualifies." *INSEE Première*, N° 1250: 1–4.

Kitschelt, Herbert, and Anthony McGann. 1995. *The Radical Right in Western Europe: A Comparative Analysis*. Ann Arbor: University of Michigan Press.

Kriesi, Hanspeter, Edgar Grande, Romain Lachat, et al. 2008. *West European Politics in the Age of Globalization*. Cambridge: Cambridge University Press.

Lubbers, Marcel, and Jochem Tolsma. 2011. "Education's Impact on Explanations of Radical Right-wing Voting," http://cream.conference-services.net/resources/952/2371/pdf/MECSC2011_0218_paper.pdf. Accessed on August 20, 2013.

Manza, Jeff, Michael Hout, and Clem Brooks. 1995. "Class Voting in Capitalist Democracies Since World War II: Dealignment, Realignment, or Trendless Fluctuation?" *Annual Review of Sociology 21*: 137–162.

Mayer, Nonna. 2002. *Ces Français qui votent Le Pen*. Paris: Flammarion.

Mayer, Nonna. 2007. "Comment: Nicolas Sarkozy a rétréci l'électorat de Le Pen." *Revue française de science politique 57*: 429–445.

Mayer, Nonna, Guy Michelat, and Vincent Tiberj. 2010. "Le racisme à l'heure de la crise." In Commission nationale consultative des droits de l'homme, *La lutte contre le racisme et la xénophobie. Année 2009*, 102–123. Paris: La Documentation française.

Mergier, Alain, and Jérôme Fourquet. 2011. *Le point de rupture*. Paris: Fondation Jean Jaurès.

Michelat, Guy, and Michel Simon, 1977. *Classe, religion et comportement politique*. Paris : Presses de la FNSP/Editions sociales.

Michelat, Guy, and Michel Simon. 2004. *Les ouvriers et la politique*. Paris: Presses de Sciences Po.

Michelat, Guy, and Michel Simon. 2011. "Inquiétudes, dynamiques idéologiques, attitudes politiques: quoi de neuf?" In TNS-Sofres, *L'état de l'opinion,* 137–164. Paris: Seuil.

Nieuwbeerta, Paul, and Nan Dirk de Graaf. 1999. "Traditional Class Voting in Twenty Post-war Societies." In Evans Geoffrey (ed.), *The End of Class Politics? Class Voting in a Comparative Context,* 23–56. Oxford: Oxford University Press.

Oesch, Daniel. 2006. *Redrawing the Class Map: Stratification and Institutions in Britain, Germany, Sweden and Switzerland.* New York: Palgrave Macmillan.

Oesch, Daniel. 2008. "Explaining Workers' Support for Right-wing Populist Parties in Western Europe: Evidence from Austria, Belgium, France, Norway, and Switzerland." *International Political Science Review 29*: 349–373.

Perrineau, Pascal. 1997. *Le symptôme Le Pen*. Paris: Fayard.

Peugny, Camille. 2009. *Le déclassement*. Paris: Grasset.

Przeworski, Adam. 1985. *Capitalism and Social Democracy*. New York: Cambridge University Press.

Schwartz, Olivier. 2009. "Vivons nous encore dans une société de classes?" www.laviedesidees.fr, September 22, 2009.

Teinturier, Brice. 2009. "Peurs et attentes des Français" TNS-Sofres, *L'état de l'opinion 2008*. Paris, 11–26.

Van der Waal, Jeroen, and Peter H. Achterberg, Dick Houtman. 2008. "Class Is Not Dead! It Has Been Buried Alive." *Politics and Society, 35*(3): 403–426.

Van der Waal, Jeroen, et al. 2010. "Some Are More Equal Than Others: Economic Egalitarianism and Welfare Chauvinism in the Netherlands." *Journal of European Social Policy* 20: 350–363.

Weaklien, David, and Anthony Heath. 1999. "Class Voting in Britain and the United States: Definitions, Models, and Data." In Geoffrey Evans (ed.), *The Decline of Class Politics? Class Voting in a Comparative Context*, 281–307. Oxford: Oxford University Press.

Wodak, Ruth and Teun A. van Dijk.2000. *Racism at the Top: The Investigation, Explanation andCountering of Xenophobia and Racism.* Klagenfurt, Austria: Drava.

10

The Political Consequences of the Economic Crisis in Europe

ELECTORAL PUNISHMENT AND POPULAR PROTEST

Hanspeter Kriesi

THE ECONOMIC FALLOUT of financial crises tends to be "nasty, brutish, and long," as Robin Wells and Paul Krugman (2010) put it (see also Reinhart and Rogoff 2009). The economic consequences of the Great Recession have certainly not played out fully yet, and thus it is still too early to tell how the economy will eventually get through the destabilization caused by the Great Recession and what its consequences will eventually be for European politics. However, some economic implications of the crisis for European countries have already become clear. European governments responded to the crisis by bailing out their financial sectors and by stimulating their economies with fiscal packages. The most important long-term economic consequence of these measures is that most governments got themselves heavily into debt. In the countries hardest hit by the crisis, the increasing public debt rapidly proved to be unsustainable, and bailouts by the IMF (or jointly by the EU and the IMF) followed. Governments across Europe took austerity measures in an attempt to rebalance their budgets. Over time, the unsustainable indebtedness of some countries began to threaten the viability of the entire European monetary system.

This chapter explores the political reactions of Europe's citizens to the economic crisis and to its repercussions on government finances. It is a first, exploratory cut at a very complex question. The unit of analysis is

Note: I am grateful to Nancy Bermeo, Larry Bartels, and Swen Hutter for their very helpful comments on earlier versions of this chapter.

countries—the member states of the European Union and three nonmembers (Iceland, Norway, and Switzerland). My perspective is that of a comparativist who asks how the political and economic context is shaping the political aftermath of the crisis.

In democratic regimes, the political response is, first of all, an electoral one. It is, however, my contention that we should not exclusively focus our attention on the electoral arena when trying to understand the political impact of financial and economic crises. Contentious reactions in the direct-democratic arena and the protest arena are equally important and closely related to the public's electoral response. I shall first discuss some theoretical concepts for the analysis of both electoral and protest mobilization in reaction to an economic crisis. Next, I shall present some systematic evidence for the electoral outcome of the crisis, before presenting four individual cases chosen to illustrate the interaction between electoral reactions and protest mobilization.

The Interaction of Convention and Contention: Electoral and Protest Mobilization

The literature on social movements teaches us that political mobilization depends on the combination of three sets of factors: grievances, organization, and opportunity. Grievances constitute the starting point; an exogenous shock such as a financial and economic crisis creates a tremendous amount of popular discontent. People with grievances seek to express them, and they do so by raising their voice or by exiting (Hirschman 1970). They raise their voice to the extent that they are organized and have an opportunity to do so—in the electoral arena as well as in the direct-democratic and protest arenas.

In democratic societies, citizens have the right to vote and they have the opportunity to express their grievances as voters. As Piven and Cloward (1977, 15) noted long ago, "ordinarily, defiance is first expressed in the voting booth simply because, whether defiant or not, people have been socialized within a political culture that defines voting as the mechanism through which political change can and should properly occur." Accordingly, one of the first signs of popular discontent is a sharp shift in voting patterns.

Economic Voting

The vast literature on economic voting provides us with more precise ideas about how the crisis may have played out in electoral terms. This literature is based on the assumption of instrumentally rational voters, who will reward incumbents with their vote when the economy is good and punish them when the economy is bad. Much of this literature conceives of economic voting specifically in terms of changes in electoral support for the chief executive, but some also focuses on changes in support for the government coalition as a whole. According to this literature, it is not the voter's personal financial situation that is decisive for the economic vote, but her perception of the national economy (Lewis-Beck and Stegmaier 2007; Duch and Stevenson 2008). Empirical studies of economic voting make it clear that economic voting is both pervasive and variable, depending on the economic and political context. According to Duch and Stevenson's overall estimates (2008, 65), economic voting is at least as important as issue voting or ideological voting (indicated by left-right placement, or postmaterialism). Their results are obtained by analyzing a large number of "normal" elections. On the basis of the work of Singer (2011), who showed, among other things, that the economy is more likely to dominate other issue concerns under conditions of economic recession, we would expect a much greater average impact of economic voting in elections which take place after an economic disaster like the one we are focusing on here.

The variability of economic voting as a function of context was first demonstrated in Powell and Whitten's landmark study (1993) documenting that the *clarity of political responsibility* conditions economic voting: voters' assessment of the government's economic performance plays a role only if the institutional context allows voters to clearly attribute responsibility for economic performance to the government. Duch and Stevenson's much more detailed results (2008, chap. 9) confirm this evidence. In line with these results, we can expect that the government or the chief executive will be electorally punished for the economic crisis, above all in countries where the responsibility for the government's economic performance can clearly be identified by the voters and where they can hold governments accountable for the country's economic performance.

Economic voting may also be reduced by *factors that constrain the government's maneuvering space.* Voters may hold governments less accountable for an economic disaster if they understand that the government could not do very much about it. Duch and Stevenson (2008) show that voters are attentive to the constraining implications of economic openness for the government's economic policy choices, and that, accordingly, economic voting is less pronounced in situations where the government's competence in economic policy making is constrained by economic openness. Similarly, Hellwig and

Samuels (2007) provide empirical support for their *"government constraint" hypothesis,* which suggests that greater exposure to the world economy reduces electoral accountability. They also find that voters in more open economies are less likely to evaluate incumbents on the basis of fluctuations in economic growth.

Expanding on this argument, we could distinguish aspects of the recent economic crisis on the basis of the differing ability of governments to affect them. For example, voters in European countries may understand that the government's hands are tied with respect to the shock experienced by their country's economy, but they may not buy the government's excuse that it had no choice in bailing out the banking sector to avoid a general economic meltdown. In line with this argument, van der Brug, van der Eijk, and Franklin (2007) showed that the consequences of economic conditions for party preferences and party choice are very different for economic growth, unemployment, and inflation.

The economic voting literature has largely failed to account for the kind of parties that voters turn to when punishing the governing parties (van der Brug et al. 2007, 18ff.; Tucker 2006, 4ff.). As a matter of fact, depending on the party system, disaffected voters may have several options. They may turn to established opposition parties that habitually blame the government for the country's economic misfortune. However, confronted with increasing unemployment and stagnating or even diminishing incomes as a result of the austerity measures taken in the aftermath of the crisis, discontented voters may nurture resentment against all the mainstream parties, the established political elites, or the "political class" (la "casta" or de "regenten"). Accordingly, they may turn to new challengers in the party system—provided such challengers are available—that typically mobilize with populist appeals, claiming the people have been betrayed by those in charge and *they* will redeem the people once they are in power (Mény and Surel 2002, 11ff.).

In Western Europe, the most important recent challengers of the mainstream parties have been parties of the new populist right. (See Mayer's Chapter 9 in this volume for a discussion of the rise of the populist right in France.) The rise of these challengers is not directly linked to the crisis, but they may have benefited from it. In the less institutionalized and much more volatile party systems of Central and Eastern Europe, new parties enter into the electoral competition at almost every new election. In these countries, populist mobilization is a sort of generalized strategy of the opposition. Finally, disaffected voters may also turn against political parties altogether. Thus a more radical *"exit" hypothesis* suggests that discontented voters may turn against all existing parties by supporting independents or "anti-parties" opposing, and sometimes ridiculing, all the established parties, or by abstaining.

Protest Mobilization Outside the Electoral Arena

The electoral arena is, of course, not the only institutionalized arena for mobilizing protest against government decisions. If mobilization in the electoral arena is the most obvious choice, in many countries there are other institutionalized channels. Thus, *direct-democratic institutions* are available for the articulation of protest in an increasing number of countries. As comparative analysis of new social movements in Western Europe has shown, such institutions are readily used by social movements when they are available (Kriesi et al. 1995). In particular, these institutions may also be used by opposition parties to mobilize protest against the government. Other institutional channels for protest include litigation in courts, as well as appeal to other governmental institutions such as the head of state, who may have some constitutional rights to exercise control over the government.

In the absence of immediately available options in the institutionalized arenas, discontented groups of citizens are likely to resort to the protest arena, attempting to force concessions from political elites by directly appealing to the general public. This is Schattschneider's idea (1960) of the "expansion of conflict." Public protest is designed to unleash a public debate, to draw the attention of the public to the grievances of the actors in question, to create controversy where there was none, and to obtain the support of the public for the actors' concerns. Discontented citizens are all the more ready to resort to protest, since protest mobilization has become increasingly conventional, at least in Western Europe, although not yet to the same extent in Central and Eastern Europe. Western European countries have become "movement societies," in the apt term coined by Meyer and Tarrow (1998). As this term suggests, political protest has become an integral part of these countries' way of life: protest behavior is no longer used as a last resort only but is employed with greater frequency, by more diverse constituencies, to represent a wider range of claims than ever before. We observe the "normalization of the unconventional" (Fuchs 1991). Professionalization and institutionalization are changing social movement into instruments of conventional politics, and social movement organizations become rather like interest groups. However, while protest becomes conventional across Western Europe, the typical action repertoire of protest may still vary from one country to another. Thus, in Southern Europe combinations of strikes and large demonstrations constitute a core element of the protest repertoire, while citizens in Northern Europe are much less likely to combine demonstrations with strikes.

As a result of its routinization, the protest repertoire loses some of its news value, its surprise effect, and its impact on the general public. If grievances are pressing and a response to more or less conventional protest is not forthcoming, however, challengers, even in democracies, may be tempted to step up their protest, to radicalize, and to *create a political crisis* through massive use of disruption (Keeler 1993). A political crisis can create a sense of urgency predicated on the assumption that already serious problems will be exacerbated by inaction. In addition, a political crisis can create a sense of genuine fear predicated on the assumption that inaction may endanger lives and property, or even result in a revolution or coup d'état. If either of these mechanisms comes into play, the government may feel propelled to adopt reform measures.

Dynamics of Convention and Contention

The electoral arena observes its own rhythm, and electoral punishment of governments in countries hit by the economic crisis may be impossible in the short run—at least at the national level, which is where the important economic policy decisions are made. Alternatively, electoral punishment of the national government may be meted out in elections at other levels—local, regional, or European—that happen to be on the political agenda in the short run. These "secondary elections" may serve as referendums on national politics, and their outcome may put pressure on the national government to accommodate the voters. Thus it is well known that second-order elections provide voters with low-cost opportunities to voice their dissatisfaction with government parties (e.g., Schmitt 2005, 651).

Even if there are no opportunities for direct electoral punishment, the electoral cycle may interact with the ongoing process of political mobilization in complex ways. Protest mobilization influences election campaigns and election outcomes (see McAdam and Tarrow 2010), but protest mobilization and accompanying public debate also put pressure on the government in between elections (see Goldstone 2003, 8ff.). This pressure strengthens the opposition and other allies of the protesting groups in the political system, which may be the main reason opposition parties support or even create such protest in the first place. The controversial public debates that result from the expansion of conflict by protest mobilization increase the legitimacy of speakers and allies of protest movements with journalists and decision makers who tend to closely follow the public debates (Gamson and Meyer 1996, 288). Wolfsfeld's "principle of political resonance" (1997, 47) formulates this relationship in a concise way: challengers who succeed in producing events that resonate with the professional and political culture of important news media can compete with much more powerful adversaries.

In the context of the Great Recession, the most likely triggers for grievances to express themselves in protest mobilization were (1) adoption of austerity measures and (2) spending cuts by governments to meet their financial obligations to bond holders and the international community (represented by the "Troika" of the EU commission, the European Central Bank, and the IMF; see Beissinger and Sasse, Chapter 11, this volume). Accordingly, I expect the mobilizing agents to include not only opposition parties but also the organizations of the groups most directly targeted by the spending cuts (labor unions in general and the unions of public employees in particular, as well as pensioners' and students' organizations) and by the liberalization measures (associations of farmers, small businessmen such as truckers or taxi drivers, and professional associations such as notaries or pharmacists).

The stronger the pressure exerted from below, the more likely it is that the government will be forced to make some concessions. To accommodate this pressure, incumbent parties may above all resort to procedural concessions: they may change their leadership, reshuffle the cabinet, call for early elections, or cede responsibility to a caretaker government composed of technocrats, which will manage the consequences of the crisis until the regularly scheduled elections. As a result of the pressure, internal tensions in the incumbent parties may lead to the replacement of the party leader, to the expulsion of some disloyal members of parliament, or even to a split in the party. Early elections may be imposed by the attempt of some (minority) coalition members to save themselves by leaving the government and by putting the blame on the prime minister's party for the economic disruptions. Handing over the government to technocratic caretakers may be a measure imposed by the necessity to restore the confidence of international organizations and "the market."

Procedural concessions are more likely than substantive ones, given the general predicament of European governments today. As a result of the financial and economic crisis, governments all over Europe find themselves between the proverbial rock (international pressure) and a hard place (domestic expectations). The situation of governments in the countries hardest hit by the crisis proves to be particularly uncomfortable in this respect. Not only are they likely to be exposed to domestic pressure in the streets, but they also face international pressure from a series of international stakeholders who expect them to act responsibly—to execute the measures deemed necessary by "the market." The predicament of these governments is that adoption of the required measures, which amount to a more or less severe austerity program, inevitably reduces their responsiveness to the national public and increases the likelihood that the pressure exerted by domestic protest mobilization will increase. This dilemma serves as a perfect illustration of the general situation of the "growing gap between responsibility and responsiveness" in European party systems that Peter Mair (2009) sketched in one of his last papers.

Against the background of these assumptions, the interaction between contention and convention may be expected to play out according to a predictable scenario. At the first possible occasion, the voters will punish incumbents as predicted by models of economic voting. In countries most severely hit by the crisis, discontented groups will mobilize against austerity measures even before the first elections, in an active attempt to signal their discontent to the incumbents (in secondary elections), or to bring them down (in national elections). In response to the protest mobilizations, the incumbents will make some procedural concessions, especially if the protest is voiced in institutionalized, direct-democratic channels or by institutional allies of the protesters. But the incumbents will not succeed in satisfying the discontented voters, who will severely punish them in the first national elections after the crisis. In these elections, Western European voters are likely to turn to established opposition parties, while Central and Eastern European voters may turn to newly created challenger parties.

Once in charge of the government, however, the former opposition will hardly be able to adopt any other policy than that of the previous government, given the economic constraints imposed by the legacy of the former government and conditions imposed by the rescuers (IMF and EU) and by "the market." The voters are bound to notice that the new government is forced to take just the same measures as its predecessors whom they had voted out of office, and they may resort to punishing the mainstream parties as a whole in the following (secondary) elections—by turning to new challengers, in line with the "populist" hypothesis, or by exiting from the established electoral channel altogether.

It is hard to predict what will happen next. Eventually, protest may subside—not because the discontented population starts to trust the government, but because it loses faith in the effectiveness of protest or because it is forced to acknowledge the constraints imposed on the government. Given these constraints, resigned acceptance of the inevitable may replace contention.

Alternatively, protest may escalate, and radicalization may produce a political crisis of extraordinary proportions, which may lead to electoral realignments and policy innovations that profoundly change economic and social policies.

The Electoral Impact of the Crisis

Here, I explore the electoral impact of the recent economic crisis by analyzing electoral outcomes at the aggregate level. More specifically, in each country I compare the electoral outcome of the first national parliamentary election after the outbreak of the crisis with the last national parliamentary elections before the onset of the crisis. The defining date for the outbreak of the crisis is a matter of debate. Often, it is taken to be the crash of Lehman Brothers in September 2008. But already in spring 2008, the fall of Bear Stearns was a serious warning of what was to come, and some observers situate the starting point of the crisis as early as summer 2007. Thus, I define as postcrisis all national elections in the years 2008–2011.[1] I include twenty-nine countries in my analysis: twenty-six of the twenty-seven EU-member states plus the nonmembers Iceland, Norway, and Switzerland.[2] Two countries, Portugal and Latvia, have already held two postcrisis elections, which are both included in this analysis. Thus, my analysis is based on a total of thirty-one cases.

For each country, I consider two distinct definitions of incumbency: the party of the chief executive and the parties forming the government coalition taken as a whole. To characterize the national political context, I distinguish between Western European and Central and Eastern European countries. In addition, I introduce a dummy variable for "clarity of responsibility" to distinguish between "majoritarian democracies" (high clarity) and "consensus democracies" (low clarity) in Western Europe, but not in Central and Eastern Europe (because there are too few cases in that region to make reliable distinctions between majoritarian and consensus systems). On the basis of Lijphart's first ("executives-parties") dimension (1999, 312) and Powell's distinction of proportional, mixed, and majoritarian countries (2000, 41),[3] I classify France, Greece, Ireland, Malta, Spain, the United Kingdom, and Cyprus as majoritarian democracies and all the other Western European countries as consensus democracies.

To measure the gravity of the crisis in each country, I use three economic indicators: the GDP growth rate in the year preceding the election (defined as the quarterly GDP growth rate at the time of the election compared with the corresponding quarter of the previous year),[4] the budget deficit in the year before the election year (as a percentage of GDP),[5] and the unemployment rate in the quarter preceding the election.[6] The sum of these indicators—which I refer to as an "Economic Crisis Index"—provides a rough idea of the extent to which a country has been hit by the crisis.[7] The more negative the value of this index, the more pronounced are the expected grievances in a given country. Table 10.1 provides an overview of these indicators for the thirty-one cases. The countries are ordered according to the Economic Crisis Index, from most to least severe. Overall, the three indicators are only weakly to moderately correlated: GDP growth is weakly correlated with the deficit/surplus (r = .09) and the unemployment rate (r = −.08), while the unemployment rate and the deficit/surplus are moderately correlated (r = −.42). The countries most severely hit by the crisis (through late 2011) were the so-called PIIGS in Western Europe (Portugal, Ireland, Iceland, Greece, and Spain; see Chapter 2 in this volume), and Hungary, Latvia, and Lithuania in Central and Eastern Europe. However, the value of the Economic Crisis Index is quite negative in most countries, indicating widespread grounds for economic discontent across much of Europe. Only Switzerland and Norway have come through the crisis so far virtually unscathed.

In Table 10.2, I begin by analyzing the relationship between postcrisis election results and pre-crisis election results, looking separately at results for the party of the chief executive and for the parties of the governing coalition as a whole in Western Europe and in Central and Eastern Europe. The results point to a key difference in the party systems in the two parts of Europe. In Central and Eastern Europe, there was only a weak relationship between the performance of incumbent parties in successive elections. This high volatility of electoral results in Central and Eastern European countries indicates that, contrary to the party systems in Western Europe, those in Central and Eastern Europe are not yet institutionalized, with new parties entering the competition in every election and significantly altering election outcomes.

More detailed analysis (not shown here) confirms that in Central and Eastern Europe countries, newly created parties without any track record at all were the real winners in the first elections after the crisis, to the detriment of the incumbents, whether from the left or the right. In Western European countries, only the new populist right has benefited from the predicament of governing parties in postcrisis elections. Moreover, this effect for the new populist right holds only for consensus democracies, where electoral access is not constrained by a majoritarian electoral system. These results confirm the general "populist" hypothesis, both for Western European and Central and Eastern European countries.

Table 10.1 Economic Indicators of the Crisis, by Country.

Country	GDP Growth	Unemployment	Deficit-Surplus	Economic Crisis Index[a]
IRE	0.0	19.1	−32.4	−51.5
ICE	−6.0	18.6	−13.5	−38.1
ESP	0.8	28.2	−9.2	−36.6
PT(2)	−0.6	23.9	−10.1	−34.6
PT(1)	−2.0	18.9	−3.5	−24.4
GR	−3.5	11.0	−9.8	−24.3
LAT(2)	5.1	18.4	−8.3	−21.6
LAT(1)	3.4	14.3	−9.7	−20.6
HU	−0.9	14.8	−3.7	−19.4
CY	0.4	12.9	−6.0	−18.5
LIT	−1.8	5.8	−9.5	−17.1
SLK	4.4	13.5	−8.0	−17.1
UK	1.6	7.1	−11.4	−16.9
LUX	−7.3	5.5	−3.7	−16.5
GER	−5.1	10.4	0.1	−15.4
DK	1.7	13.3	−2.9	−14.5
BEL	2.7	10.9	−5.9	−14.1
POL	4.5	9.5	−7.9	−12.9
ITA	0.3	9.1	−1.5	−10.3
CZ	2.3	5.8	−5.9	−9.4
EST	8.6	17.5	0.1	−8.8
NL	2.4	5.5	−5.5	−8.6
BUL	0.0	9.1	1.7	−7.4
AU	2.0	5.8	−0.9	−4.7
ROM	2.9	4.4	−2.6	−4.1
SWE	6.6	9.6	−0.7	−3.7
MAL	5.7	6.9	−2.4	−3.6
SLO	3.4	6.7	−0.1	−3.4
FIN	5.1	5.8	−2.5	−3.2
SWI	2.3	4.6	0.5	−1.8
NOR	−1.4	7.2	19.1	10.5
Average	1.2	11.4	−5.0	−15.2

Note: [a] Economic Crisis Index = GDP Growth − Unemployment + Deficit-Surplus.

Table 10.2 Postcrisis Electoral Support for Incumbent Parties as a Function of Pre-Crisis Support and Clarity of Government Responsibility.

	Western Europe		Central and Eastern Europe	
	Prime Minister's Party	All Cabinet Parties	Prime Minister's Party	All Cabinet Parties
Pre-crisis election result	.992*** (.131)	.972*** (.149)	.435 (.468)	.393 (.328)
Majoritarian	−5.14 (3.54)	−2.64 (3.89)	—	—
Intercept	−3.66 (5.01)	−6.02 (8.72)	8.87 (15.03)	15.34 (17.05)
R^2	.77	.77	.09	.14
N	20	20	11	11

* p = .05, ** p = .01, *** p = .001.

Notes: Ordinary least squares regression coefficients (with standard errors in parentheses).

For Western European countries, the analyses presented in Table 10.2 also include a dummy variable reflecting the presumed greater clarity of responsibility in majoritarian systems. The results show that electoral punishment was indeed greater in majoritarian countries, where responsibility can more clearly be attributed to the party of the chief executive, than in consensus democracies. On average, the party of the chief executive lost roughly 5 percent more of the vote in the first postcrisis election in majoritarian countries than in consensus democracies. If we include all members of the governing coalition in the analysis, the difference in punishment between the two types of democracies diminishes, but there is still more punishment (by 2.6 percent) in majoritarian democracies.

For a more detailed examination of the impact of different aspects of the crisis, I elaborate the basic analysis presented in Table 10.2 by including in turn each of my three indicators of the gravity of the crisis. I begin with the impact of *economic growth*. Figure 10.1 shows the relationship between real GDP growth in the year preceding the election and the change in the electoral support of the parties in the governing coalition. The relationship turns out to be very strong for Central and Eastern European countries, but virtually nonexistent for Western European countries. The correlation between GDP growth and the change in the prime minister's party vote is 0.81 for

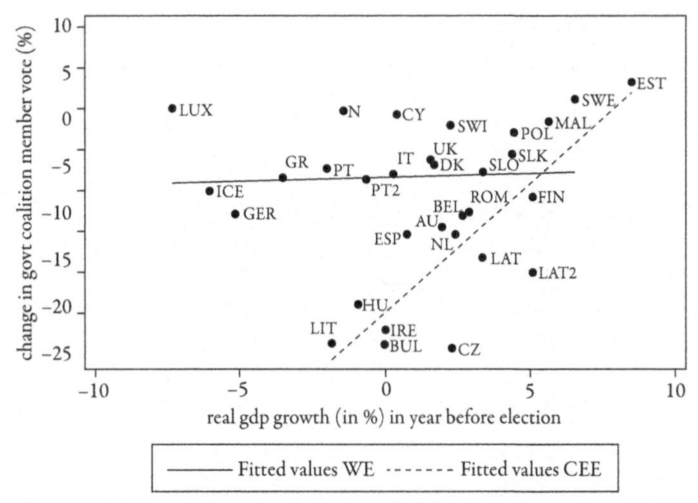

FIGURE 10.1 Election-Year GDP Growth and Change in Electoral Support for the Governing Coalition.

Central and Eastern European countries, but only 0.05 for Western European countries.

The absence of any relationship in Western European countries is quite unexpected. Although Western European countries had, on average, much worse performance than Central and Eastern European countries in terms of economic growth in the years immediately preceding the postcrisis elections (0.3 percent compared to 2.9 percent), government coalitions in these countries were generally less severely punished than government coalitions in Central and Eastern European countries. On average, Western European government coalitions lost 8.3 percent of the vote in the first postcrisis elections, compared to 15.8 percent for government coalitions in the Central and Eastern European countries. In the three countries with the worst overall growth rates in the year preceding the elections—Germany, Iceland, and Luxemburg—the incumbents were only partially punished (in Iceland, the Independence Party, the party of the prime minister, but not its coalition partner, the Social Democrats; in Germany, the Social Democrats, a coalition partner, but not the Christian Democrats and their Chancellor Angela Merkel), or not at all (in Luxemburg).

The regression analyses reported in Table 10.3 confirm these results. In Central and Eastern European countries, a drop in the growth rate of 1 percent led to a drop in the vote for the incumbent parties of almost three percentage points. In Western European countries, only governments in majoritarian

Table 10.3 Postcrisis Electoral Support for Incumbent Parties as a Function of Pre-Crisis Support, Clarity of Government Responsibility, and GDP Growth Rates.

	Western Europe		Central and Eastern Europe	
	Prime Minister's Party	All Cabinet Parties	Prime Minister's Party	All Cabinet Parties
Pre-crisis	.978***	.957***	.458	.529*
Election Result	(.140)	(.156)	(.428)	(.178)
GDP growth	.036	−.079	1.498	2.882**
rate	(.514)	(.527)	(.908)	(.597)
Majoritarian	−5.82	−3.64	—	—
	(3.78)	(4.14)		
Majoritarian ×	.876	1.074	—	—
GDP growth	(1.251)	(1.249)		
Intercept	−3.18	−5.14	3.80	.01
	(5.38)	(9.02)	(14.08)	(9.50)
R^2	.78	.78	.32	.78
N	20	20	11	11

Notes: Ordinary least squares regression coefficients (with standard errors in parentheses).
* p = .05, ** p = .01, *** p = .001.

countries suffered electorally from low economic growth rates, with a drop in the growth rate of 1 percent leading to a drop in support of one percentage point. Table 10.3 also shows that the results for the party of the chief executive are similar, although less pronounced than for the governing coalition as a whole.[8]

For the *unemployment rate*, we find exactly the opposite relationship from the punishment of the governing parties: the electoral implications of high unemployment rates turn out to be rather strong in Western European countries (r = −.53 for prime ministers' parties and r = −.38 for all coalition parties taken together), but nonexistent or even reversed for the Central and Eastern European countries (r = −.01 for prime ministers' parties and r = .29 for all coalition parties). Figure 10.2 illustrates this relationship. Slovakia and Estonia are clear outliers in this regard: in spite of very high unemployment rates, their prime ministers' parties were hardly punished at all. Excluding these two countries from the analysis increases the relationship considerably (r = −.46 for prime ministers' parties and −.04 for all coalition parties). The corresponding analysis presented in Table 10.4 shows that the unemployment

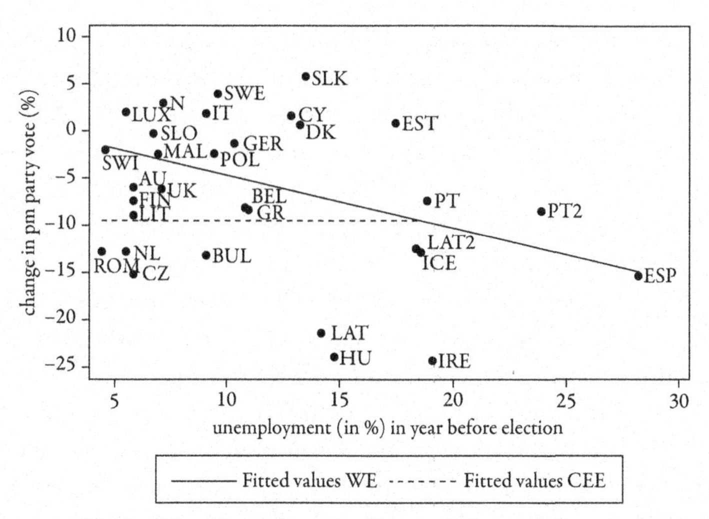

FIGURE 10.2 Election-Year Unemployment Rate and Electoral Support for the Prime Minister's Party.

Table 10.4 Postcrisis Electoral Support for Incumbent Parties as a Function of Pre-Crisis Support, Clarity of Government Responsibility, and Unemployment Rates.

	Western Europe		Central and Eastern Europe	
	Prime Minister's Party	All Cabinet Parties	Prime Minister's Party	All Cabinet Parties
Pre-crisis election result	.990*** (.120)	.943*** (.155)	.437 (.497)	.432 (.340)
Unemployment rate	−.341 (.302)	−.154 (.350)	−.019 .633)	.475 (.679)
Majoritarian	1.59 (6.90)	6.23 (7.69)	—	—
Majoritarian × unemployment	−.388 (.467)	−.608 (.507)	—	—
Intercept	.05 (5.00)	−2.74 (10.94)	9.02 (17.02)	8.15 (20.37)
R^2	.83	.82	.09	.19
N	20	20	11	11

Notes: Ordinary least squares regression coefficients (with standard errors in parentheses).

* p = .05, ** p = .01, *** p = .001.

rate at the time of the elections explains part of the electoral punishment of prime ministers' parties in Western European countries. An unemployment rate of 10 percent, a rather usual rate in these countries at the time of the first postcrisis elections, reduced the support of the prime minister's party by about 3.5 percent in consensus countries, and by about 7 percent in majoritarian countries. For the coalition partners in consensus countries, the punishment turns out to have been less severe.

Third, the gravity of the *budget deficit* in the year preceding the election year is best able to account for incumbents' electoral punishment. The relationship between the government's deficit and the change in electoral support is particularly close for prime ministers' parties and governing coalitions in Western Europe (r = .77 and r = .65, respectively). As is illustrated by Figure 10.3a, this relationship is only partly driven by the outliers Norway (which, thanks to oil, had a record budget surplus of 19.1 percent) and Ireland (with a record budget deficit of −32.4 percent, owing to the government guarantee provided for its failing banks). Without these outliers, the correlation remains high for the prime ministers' parties (r = .64), although not for the governing coalitions (r = .22). In Central and Eastern European countries, the corresponding relationship appears, at first sight, to be virtually nonexistent (r = .12 and r = .15, respectively). However, once we exclude two outliers, Slovakia and Poland, from the analysis, we find that the correlation is more similar to the Western European countries, and quite sizeable for prime ministers' parties (r = .46), though not for broader governing coalitions (r = −.04). Figure 10.3b illustrates these relationships without the outliers.

As far as the Central and Eastern European outliers are concerned, the Polish prime minister was spared punishment in spite of a substantial budget deficit, the Estonian prime minister in spite of high unemployment, and the Slovakian prime minister in spite of both. The clue to these exceptions lies partly with the fact that all three countries experienced sizeable growth rates in the year leading up to the elections (see Table 10.1), and partly with the successful accession of Estonia and Slovakia to the eurozone. Slovakia became the second country in Central Europe to introduce the euro on January 1, 2009, and Estonia joined the eurozone on January 1, 2011, the year of its first postcrisis election. In both cases, this step was perceived by the political elite and citizens as a triumph of economic development and management (see Chapter 11, by Beissinger and Sasse, in this volume).

Table 10.5 reports the results of multivariate analysis for the budget deficit. For Western European countries, the size of the budget deficit has a strong effect on electoral support for the prime minister's party. In Western

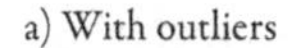

a) With outliers

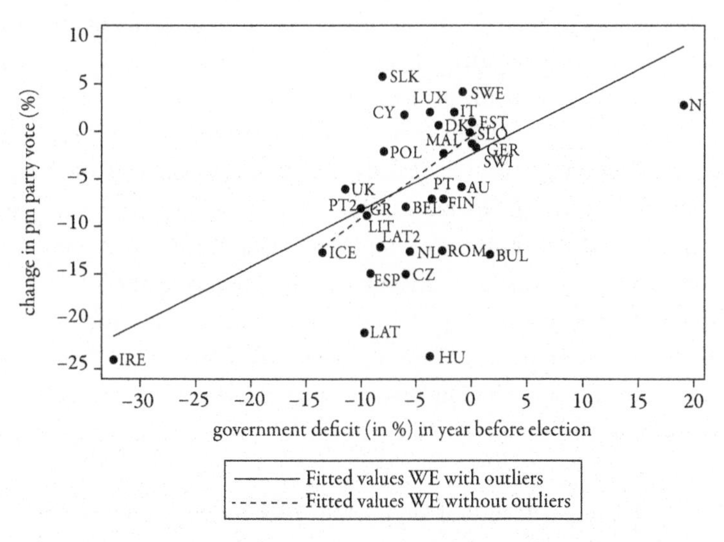

b) Without outliers

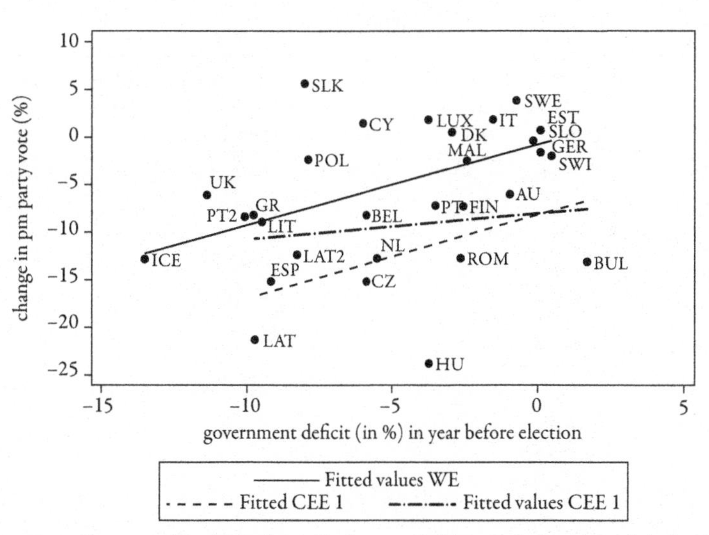

FIGURE 10.3 Previous Year's Budget Deficit and Electoral Support for the Prime Minister's Party.

European consensus countries, electoral support is reduced by 0.5 percent for every 1 percent increase of the deficit; in Western European majoritarian countries the effect is even stronger, with a corresponding 0.75 percent reduction in electoral support. Once we leave Poland and Slovakia aside, however, the increase turns out to be strongest in Central and Eastern European countries, with a one percent reduction in support for the prime minister's party for every 1 percent increase in the deficit. Together with the clarity of government responsibility in majoritarian systems, this effect goes a long way to explain the reduction of support for prime ministers' parties and government coalition parties in all Western European countries. Together with GDP growth (see the last column of Table 10.5), it also goes a long way to explain changes in support for coalition parties, but not for prime ministers' parties specifically, in Central and Eastern European countries (excluding Poland and Slovakia).[9]

Overall, we can conclude this analysis by observing that it has largely confirmed the expectations of the economic voting approach: incumbent parties were severely punished for the negative economic consequences of the crisis, and the punishment was most severe when voters could clearly attribute responsibility, as was the case in Western European majoritarian

Table 10.5 Postcrisis Electoral Support for Incumbent Parties as a Function of Pre-Crisis Support, Clarity of Government Responsibility, and Deficit/ Surplus Rates.

	Western Europe		Central and Eastern Europe			
	Prime Minister's Party	All Cabinet Parties	Prime Minister's Party	(without SLK, POL)	All Cabinet Parties	(without SLK, POL)
Pre-crisis support	.968*** (.092)	.941*** (.108)	.423 (.492)	−.082 (.328)	.401 (.343)	.550** (.122)
Deficit/surplus	.499* (.190)	.332 (.198)	.250 (.735)	1.071 (.456)	.330 (.825)	.606 (.316)
Majoritarian	2.90 (3.52)	6.39 (3.78)	—	—	—	—
Majoritarian × deficit/surplus	.261 (.284)	.519 (.297)	—	—	—	—
GDP growth rate	—	—	—	—	—	2.425** (.432)
Intercept	−1.71 (3.56)	−3.52 (6.28)	10.49 (16.65)	26.61 (10.95)	16.50 (18.13)	1.18 (6.92)
R^2	.90	.89	.10	.48	.16	.91
N	20	20	11	9	11	9

Notes: Ordinary least squares regression coefficients (with standard errors in parentheses).

* p = .05, ** p = .01, *** p = .001.

democracies. The aspect of the crisis that triggered this punishment apparently varied between Western European and Central and Eastern European countries, with unemployment rates being more critical in Western Europe and GDP growth rates more critical in Central and Eastern European countries. However, with the exceptions of Poland and Slovakia, the budgetary balance seems to have played a crucial role in the extent to which parties of the chief executive in particular have been punished by the voters. We now turn to case studies to provide a more detailed account of how this punishment has come about.

The Interaction Between Contention and Electoral Politics: Case Studies

Although available economic and electoral data make it possible to examine the electoral impact of the crisis systematically and statistically, a lack of equally good protest data makes it impossible to be equally systematic in connecting convention and contention, the electoral and the protest arenas. Instead, I shall explore these dynamics in four cases—two in Western Europe and two in Central and Eastern Europe—in order to illustrate how electoral outcomes are embedded in a wider context of political protest. In selecting the cases, I have chosen the countries most severely hit by the crisis (see Table 10.1): Iceland (an example of a consensus democracy) and Ireland (an example of a majoritarian democracy) in Western Europe, and Latvia (a consensus democracy) and Hungary (a majoritarian democracy) in Central and Eastern Europe.

Iceland

Tiny Iceland (population 320,000) is, arguably, the first country to have taken the full hit of the crisis, and one of the countries where the havoc wreaked by the crisis was most far-reaching. As a result of the unfolding international banking crisis, Iceland's three largest banks were collapsing and had to be nationalized in October 2008. At the same time, its economy imploded. In November 2008, the IMF approved a $2.1 billion loan for Iceland, which thus became the first Western European country since 1976 to receive an IMF loan. The country had to take drastic measures, including introduction of capital controls to stop the depreciation of its currency (which had been devalued by up to 70 percent during the crisis), restructuring of its banking system (which included recapitalization of the three successor banks and the refusal to honor bonds and to guarantee the savings of foreign depositors), and adoption of austerity measures to arrive at fiscal consolidation in the medium term.

The extraordinary chain of events that was triggered by the Icelandic crisis illustrates several of the general points raised in this chapter. First, it illustrates the electoral consequences of economic disaster. In this particular case, the electoral consequences were forced on the parties by preceding popular protests, which created a real political crisis and decisively modified the strategic calculus of some of the main parties. In addition, this case shows how direct-democratic institutions may be used in addition to elections to put pressure on the government, and how a popular protest movement may find unexpected allies in the political system. In the Icelandic case, the population had some substantive success with its protest, since it strengthened the hand of the government in negotiations with foreign investors. Nevertheless, this case also illustrates quite well the dynamic scenario in which discontent with the governing parties may first lead voters to turn to established opposition parties, but then to embrace exit strategies once those parties fail to deliver the expected recovery.

Only three months into the crisis, Iceland became the first European country to lose its government to the economic fallout. Prime Minister Geir Haarde announced the resignation of the coalition government of his conservative Independence Party and the Social Democratic Alliance. The announcement came after intensive public protests over the government's role in the economic meltdown in October 2008. As thousands began losing their jobs, public anger grew. Public outcry at the failure of politicians and officials to accept responsibility for the crisis reached its peak in January 2009 when the Parliament (Althingi) assembled after the Christmas holiday. The major demands of the protesters were for the removal of the government and government officials in the Central Bank and Financial Supervisory Authority, new elections as soon as possible, a new constitutional order, and even a new republic to replace the provisional constitution from 1944, when Iceland unilaterally separated from occupied Denmark.

Violence reached a level unprecedented in Icelandic politics (Hardarson and Kristinsson 2010, 1011). On January 20, a mob of riotous protesters pounded on the walls of Iceland's parliament building, denouncing the government for its incompetence. The riot—which involved some two thousand demonstrators who broke windows, banged on pans and drums (the "pots and pans revolution"), and hurled eggs and skyr, a kind of Icelandic yogurt, at parliament and at riot police—seems to have profoundly shaken Icelandic politicians.

The resignation of the coalition government was provoked by the Social Democrats, who had grown increasingly restless. When the protest movement reached well into their own ranks during the mass demonstrations, they forced the conservative prime minister to resign and to call general elections for April 25, two years early. In the meantime, they formed a provisional minority government together with the former opposition left-green movement. All major parties—including the Independence Party and its recent coalition partners, the Progressives (1995–2007) and the Social Democrats (2007–2009)—responded to the popular criticism by changing leadership. A new political party, with strong roots in the pots-and-pans revolution, the Civic Movement, emerged before the election.

In the 2009 spring elections, instead of revolting against the established party system as a whole, Icelandic voters revolted against the crash by punishing the conservative Independence Party and rewarding the Social Democrats (Hardarson and Kristinsson 2010, 1015). The Independence Party lost 12.9 percent of the vote, down to 23.7 percent, the worst result in the party's history. The provisional coalition government won an absolute majority of votes, primarily because of a major swing to the Left-Greens (a gain of 7.4 percent, to a total of 21.7 percent). The Social Democrats also gained some 3 percent, becoming the largest party with a total of 29.8 percent. Turnout was 85.1 percent, up slightly from 83.7 percent in 2007.

As demanded by the pots-and-pans revolution, the postcrash government decided to revise the constitution. A constitutional committee appointed by parliament convened a national assembly consisting of a thousand citizens drawn at random from the national registry.[10] The national assembly discussed constitutional matters for a day or two, concluding that a new constitution was needed. The committee then organized a nationwide election in November 2010, with 522 candidates standing for twenty-five seats in a constitutional assembly. Despite open antagonism from the opposition parties, 84,000 voters showed up, or 37 percent of the electorate. After the Constitutional Court had declared this vote unconstitutional, the parliament then appointed the twenty-five elected candidates to a constitutional council, which delivered its proposed constitution to parliament in July 2011.[11]

In spring 2010, the voters also went to the polls to vote in the first *referendum* in the history of the Republic of Iceland. The object of the vote concerned the terms of repayment for the Icesave debt. The name refers to deposit accounts of the Icelandic Landsbanki in the United Kingdom and the Netherlands. Once Landsbanki had collapsed early in the crisis, these deposit accounts of British and Dutch creditors had to be covered by the state's Depositors' and Investors' Guarantee Fund, formed according to the terms of the EEA (European Economic Act) agreement from 1994. At the end of 2009, the Icelandic parliament had passed a repayment deal worked out in negotiations with British and Dutch authorities. The deal was, however, highly unpopular with the Icelandic public, and over a quarter of the electorate signed a *petition* urging the Icelandic president to veto it. The president heeded the call, sending the Icesave bill to a referendum as stipulated by Icelandic law. In the referendum, no less than 93 percent of the participants voted against the deal. In the meantime, the government had already invited British and Dutch negotiators back to the negotiating table to obtain an improved agreement.

By the time the government arrived at a new deal, however, it had lost most of its popular backing. Polls at the end of 2010 indicated it could count on the support of only 18 percent of the voters.[12] This situation is explained in part by the fact that the Left-Greens were deeply divided over the question of EU membership and the rescue by the IMF. Although the popularity of the Independence Party had increased in opposition, the conservatives were still largely considered to be the culprits of the crash. The voters now increasingly turned to protest parties. But the new Civic Movement, which had polled 7.2 percent in the 2009 elections, proved to be highly unstable; thanks to internal disagreements, its four parliamentarians had left the party after only a few months. In local elections in spring 2010, voters turned to yet other protest parties: in the country's capital, Reykjavik, the "Best Party" of the comic Jon Gunnar Kristinsson became the largest party, with 35 percent of the vote, followed by the conservatives with 33 percent, the Social Democrats with 19 percent, and the Left-Greens with 7 percent. Jon Gnarr had founded the Best Party at the end of 2009 as a parody of traditional politics. Among other things, he asked for a "transparent" handling of corruption and promised to break all campaign promises.[13] The Best Party participated in the elections only in Reykjavik. In Kopavogur, two new lists (one named the "Second Best Party") jointly obtained 24 percent of the votes, while in Akureyri, the fourth largest town of the country, an independent "People's List" came out of nowhere to obtain 45 percent of the vote and the absolute majority in the city council (Hardarson and Kristinsson 2011, 1003).

Finally, the improved deal with the British and Dutch authorities once again was not to the liking of the president. In February 2011, he refused to sign the new Icesave law. Although he acknowledged that the new deal was in many ways more advantageous than the previous one, he considered that the people should be given the right to decide on the issue, especially since the composition of the Parliament had not been changed since the last referendum vote and the people had not had the opportunity to renew their confidence in Parliament. In April 2011, almost 60 percent of Icelandic voters refused once again to accept the Icesave debt deal, to the consternation of the government and the British and Dutch authorities. Half a year later, in October 2011, three years after the breakdown of Iceland's banks, the Supreme Court of the country finally ruled that the remaining assets of the Old Landsbanki (which had been put aside by the government in an emergency law introduced during the 2008 financial crisis), and not the state (as had originally been planned), had to be used to pay off the British and Dutch depositors (while other debtors such as hedge funds, insurance companies, or other banks were not to receive anything), removing the last uncertainty about whether the country could settle its Icesave debt to Britain and the Netherlands. The ruling was binding and could not be appealed.

Ireland

In Ireland, the government's mishandling of the crisis triggered extraordinarily harsh electoral punishments, first in local elections and then at the national level. It is another case of a government being forced to call early elections by a minority partner that got cold feet. More clearly than in Iceland, where the economic crisis provoked a deep political crisis involving the whole population, the Irish case was one in which protest was mainly, though not exclusively, triggered by the government's austerity measures. In Ireland, the government first took such measures on its own initiative; later, it was forced to impose such measures by its international rescuers. In both instances, organizations representing the groups most directly hit by these measures immediately reacted with protest mobilizations. Although not given to protesting in the streets, the Irish population voiced its discontent heavily in demonstrations and strike actions. Contrary to the Icelandic case, however, Ireland illustrates the futility of the protests and the ensuing stoic resignation of the hard-hit population.

Unsurprisingly, the unfolding economic crisis was the main focus of politics in Ireland beginning in late 2008. Fears of a run on the country's banks had led the government to take the fateful decision to guarantee the liabilities of all six Irish financial institutions in late 2008. This decision, whereby all bank creditors were underwritten by the government, opened the Irish state to estimated potential liabilities of €400 billion. Hypothetical at first, the costs of the rescue mounted as the banks' losses grew, creating a gigantic hole in public finances. The banking crisis became a public debt crisis. In November 2010, Ireland became the second country in the eurozone, after Greece, to have to accept a bailout from the EU and the IMF.

It soon became apparent that executives from all the banks had misled the government in the run-up to the decision on the Guarantee Scheme (O'Malley 2009, 2010). This and other scandals related to the government's handling of the banking crisis contributed to mounting anger in the population, anger that had already been rising because of the government's austerity measures. These measures included increased taxes, through an "employment levy," and reduced spending in all areas. In February 2009, the government's announcement of the imposition of a "pension levy" on all public servants as the main plank of its recovery plan triggered the first large-scale protest action. Following the announcement, a one-day strike by thirteen thousand civil servants was organized by the public sector unions (CPSU), the first industrial action of its kind in Ireland in almost twenty years, and a huge demonstration with about a hundred thousand participants took place in Dublin to protest against the pension levy. The Irish Congress of Trade Unions (ICTU), which organized the march, said it was campaigning for "a fairer and better way" of dealing with the economic crisis.

In June 2009, local elections were held against the backdrop of a struggling economy. It was not surprising that the problems besetting the national finances dominated the election campaign, relegating such local government policy issues as planning, housing, and roads to the margins of the debate (Quinlivan and Weeks 2010). With the opposition parties successfully turning the elections into a referendum on the performance of the national government, it was an uphill struggle for the two incumbent parties—Fianna Fail and the Green Party—to keep the focus local. Fianna Fail suffered its worst-ever local election performance (losing 7.8 percentage points, down to 25.4 percent), while its partner in government, the Greens, lost 1.5 percentage points (down to 2.3 percent). Fine Gael emerged as the largest party at the local level with 32.2 percent of the vote, a gain of 3.8 percentage points.

Protesting continued in fall 2009, with thousands of workers around the country taking to the streets in a series of marches in early November to protest against proposed government cuts in pay and services. Rallies organized by the ICTU were held in Dublin, Cork, Dundalk, Galway, Limerick, Sligo, Tullamore, and Waterford. The main march in Dublin was attended by seventy thousand people. In Cork city, between twelve thousand and fifteen thousand took part in the protest. The ICTU opposed the government's economic strategy, insisting it would inflict unfair hardship on working people and the vulnerable in society. November 2009 also saw the largest student protest for a generation taking place outside the Dail in Dublin, with at least twenty-five thousand students voicing their opposition to increased student fees. The president of the Union of Students in Ireland (USI), Gary Redmond, declared, "The sleeping giant that is the student movement has been awoken." According to the *Irish Times*, the protest was "powerful, uplifting—and very peaceful."

One year later, in November 2010, Ireland became the third Western European country after Iceland and Greece to have to accept a rescue package from the EU and the IMF, €85 billion to recapitalize the banks and meet the government's budget. After a humiliating week of denying it needed help, the Dublin government was forced to concede to what were alleged to be ECB demands for an EU/IMF intervention. Strict conditions for a tough austerity program were attached to this support: tax rises and spending cuts worth a cumulative €30 billion, the equivalent of one-fifth of a single year's GDP, were imposed over the years to 2014. The intervention, which the opposition parties pushed hard to frame as a loss of sovereignty for the state, was a severe embarrassment for Fianna Fail and caused the minority partner, the Green Party, to announce its intention to withdraw from the government as soon as the budget measures were passed (O'Malley 2011, 1009).

In reaction to this agreement, one of the largest demonstrations in the history of the Irish Republic brought more than one hundred thousand people onto Dublin's streets in protest over the international bailout and four years of austerity ahead. The huge crowds braved freezing temperatures to demonstrate against the cuts aimed at driving down Ireland's colossal national debt. Among those on the main march there was deep anger that most of the €85 billion from the EU and IMF would be used to shore up Ireland's ailing banks. The terms of the European element of the bailout aroused particular ire. There was something approaching a consensus in Ireland that the country rescued Europe (specifically, German and French investors who had lent heavily to Irish banks), not the other way around.[14] The protests centered on a mile-long march along the banks of central Dublin's River Liffey to the General Post Office building, the iconic site of an historic clash between Irish republican rebels and British troops in the country's long struggle for independence. The choice of venue for the protests by ICTU, coordinating the march through the city, reflected the mood of anger, dismay, and recrimination in the wake of the economic shocks of the past ten days.

Following the collapse of the coalition between Fianna Fail and the Greens, early national elections were scheduled for February 2011. In January, prime minister Brian Cowen stepped down as Fianna Fail's president, hoping to bolster the chances of his party in the upcoming elections, but to no avail. The voters punished the Fianna Fail–led government most severely, marking what the *Economist*[15] called "the most momentous watershed in Irish politics since 1932, when Eamon de Valera first led Fianna Fail, the nationalist party he had founded, into government." The party that had shaped much of modern Ireland was humiliated by the voters, dropping from 41.5 percent to 17.4 percent of the vote, and from seventy-eight seats to twenty. The voters massively chose the opposition parties—Fine Gael (36.1 percent of the vote, up from 23.3 percent) and Labour (19.4 percent, up from 10.1 percent). The Greens, who had been Fianna Fail's coalition partner, lost most of their support (1.8 percent, down from 4.6 percent). For Fine Gael, a center-right party, the election marked its greatest success ever. By preferring Fine Gael over Labour, the voters made a rather traditional choice, replacing one conservative party with another.

The two parties that gained significant support in the election had announced during the campaign that, once elected, they would hold the bond-holders accountable, too; but it was not to be. Having formed a new coalition government, they found they did not have much choice but to continue the austerity program of their predecessors. However much the new government grumbled about the EU/IMF agreement, its room for maneuver was tightly constrained. Actually, things got even worse. In April 2011, new stress tests revealed that the Irish banks needed another €24 billion in capital from the state to survive. The government had no choice but to accept this additional request, raising the overall amount of public support for the Irish banks to no less than €70 billion, a sum roughly equal to the entire yearly government budget. It was the fifth time the Irish state declared that the problem was now solved once and for all. As the *Economist* observed, these painful adjustments have, "so far, been accepted by Irish people with surprising stoicism, despite a rise in unemployment to 14 percent."[16]

Latvia

In Latvia, popular discontent was already running high before the onset of the crisis as a result of the government's incapacity to handle the overheating economy and some high-level corruption scandals (see Beissinger and Sasse's Chapter 11). This case illustrates the amalgamation of general discontent with political corruption predating the economic crisis with new discontent created by the government's austerity measures resulting from the crisis. Latvia is not the only Eastern European country where corruption was a crucial trigger for popular discontent—a fact that may go a long way toward explaining why the austerity measures adopted to manage public deficits did not account for as much of the electoral punishment in Central and Eastern Europe as in Western Europe. Even more than Iceland, the Latvian case also illustrates the interplay between electoral and direct-democratic processes and the role played by institutional allies of the popular movements. In the end, however, both electoral punishment and popular protest seem to have been as ineffectual as in the Irish case.

The economic crisis hit Latvia shortly after the country voted on a proposed amendment to the constitution that would have empowered citizens to dismiss the parliament and call extraordinary elections. The referendum had been initiated by the trade unions in the "umbrella revolution" in 2007—a mass rally in support of the head of the Anti-Corruption Bureau, who had faced several attempts by the ruling coalition to remove him. In a shrewd move, the government scheduled the referendum vote in the midst of the 2008 summer holidays. Although participation fell short of the required 50 percent threshold, 96.8 percent of the voters accepted the proposed amendment. The unexpectedly high turnout and the overwhelming support for the proposed amendment sent a very strong message to the political elite, despite the fact that the constitution remained unaltered (Ikstens 2009).

The global financial crisis brought Latvia's vulnerabilities to a head. Years of unsustainably high growth and large current account deficits coalesced into a financial and balance of payments crisis. In December 2008, the Latvian government had to agree to an IMF rescue deal centered on maintaining the exchange rate peg to the euro; the deal implied the restructuring of the Latvian banking system and the adoption of a series of austerity measures. The latter included severe cuts in public spending that, among other things, reduced salaries in the public sector by some 25 percent over a period of two years in 2009–10. Particularly painful was the issue of old-age pensions, which the IMF believed to be excessively high and in need of trimming down (Ikstens 2011, 1043).

These austerity measures triggered a peaceful rally organized by the opposition and trade unions in Riga, the country's capital, on January 13, 2009. Some twenty thousand participants gathered a few blocks from Parliament to appeal to the president to call new elections. A small minority of protesters began demolishing nearby buildings and looting shops. Unused to violent protest, police were caught off-guard, and order was restored only several hours later. Four more massive protest events followed, as many Latvians felt that the proposed cuts were arbitrary, without any clear vision or planning, and were directed disproportionately at the masses (Ikstens 2010).

Just as in Iceland, this popular mobilization found an unexpected ally in the political elite: the day after the January riot, President Valdis Zatlers, in an extraordinary move, presented an ultimatum to Parliament and the government requiring a number of constitutional changes, including giving citizens a direct right to vote on calling extraordinary parliamentary elections. If the two institutions failed to comply with his request by March 31, the president promised to initiate a call for extraordinary elections himself.

In the meantime, in February 2009, the conservative Prime Minister Ivars Godmanis reshuffled his coalition cabinet in a vain attempt to avoid making the deep public spending cuts required by the IMF. The Godmanis government was soon replaced by a new coalition under the leadership of Valdis Dombrovskis from the liberal "New Era" party, still including ministers from the conservative People's Party of the previous prime minister. Parliament partly accepted the proposed constitutional changes; among other concessions, it granted citizens the right to initiate the calling of extraordinary parliamentary elections. Even if the concessions did not go all the way, Zatlers took advantage of the increased public confidence in the recently established new coalition government to announce that he would not launch the dismissal procedure (Ikstens 2010, 1055).

In early 2010, tensions grew between the two main coalition partners, the conservative People's Party and the liberal New Era Party, as the latter relentlessly blamed the former for the deplorable state of the country. The conservatives ended up leaving the governing coalition in March 2010, denouncing "the uncritical obedience of the Dombrovskis cabinet to the IMF" and promising to come up with an alternative plan of action (Ikstens 2011, 1038). At the same time, they promised to support the "constructive steps" of the government to deal with the crisis—but to no avail. In the first postcrisis national elections, in October 2010, the conservative party suffered a record loss (−21.4 percent), while the liberal New Era Party was rewarded with a large electoral gain (+11.6 percent) for its constitutional concessions and its "brave and responsible leadership" in the stormy waters of the economic crisis.

The new parliament, however, did not last for very long. After it had refused to repeal the immunity of one of its members involved in a corruption case, President Zatlers, under the powers given him by the Constitution, called a referendum for parliamentary dissolution just before the presidential election by Parliament in June 2011. The furious deputies voted in a new president, but the voters supported Zatlers's move by passing the referendum with 94.3 percent of the vote. As a result, new parliamentary elections were held in September 2011, which led to the victory of the pro-Russian Harmony Centre Party with 28.4 percent of the vote. Zatlers' newly founded Reform Party, which had mainly campaigned against graft, came in second (20.8 percent), while the governing New Era Party lost heavily (−12.4 percent, down to 18.8 percent). In spite of its victory, the Harmony Party was excluded from the new governing coalition, which was formed when Zatlers and Dombrovskis agreed to join forces.

Hungary

In Hungary, we find most of the elements of the Latvian case again: the combined impact of domestic corruption and internationally imposed austerity on the mobilization of popular discontent, the important role of the referendum, the minority coalition partners jumping ship, and the extraordinary electoral punishment of the incumbents. As in Latvia, protest mobilization against the government preceded the onset of the global economic crisis. What is particular to the Hungarian case, however, is the deliberate instrumentalization of popular protest mobilization and of the referendum by the opposition. In Hungary, the socialist government had already had to take austerity measures long before the onset of the global crisis. The use of the referendum allowed the conservative opposition, Fidesz, to mobilize permanently against these measures, and to maintain the pressure on the government until the first postcrisis national elections. Hungary is the only country, among the four cases considered here, in which the radical right benefited from the crisis.

Hungary was already in a political crisis when the Great Recession was first felt. In the fall of 2006, the incumbent socialist Prime Minister Ferenc Gyurcsány, whose party had won two national elections in a row, admitted he had lied about the state of the country's economy during his recent election campaign. The reaction was immediate: the conservative opposition and the radical right started protesting and rioting at Parliament Square. Counting on a solid majority in Parliament, the prime minister survived a vote of confidence, but this incited the opposition under the leadership of Victor Orban (Fidesz) to launch a referendum against the government's austerity measures. In October 2006, the opposition launched no less than seven carefully framed referendum proposals. The referendum vote was scheduled for March 2008. Against the background of the government's very unpopular austerity measures, the opposition triumphed in the vote (Pallinger, 2012. The failure of the government in the referendum raised questions about the future of the reforms and about the future of the government. Soon after the referendum, the socialists' coalition partner, the liberal SZDSZ, left the governing coalition and the socialists continued as a minority government.

As the global economic crisis hit the country in fall 2008, the weakness of the Hungarian currency (which was devalued by about 20 percent) and the economy became obvious. Only a €20 billion IMF loan helped the country through its immediate problems in late 2008. Moreover, the crisis severely hit the population not only because the level of popular indebtedness was high but also because a large proportion of the debt was in foreign currency. Thus the devaluation directly affected those who had bought their houses with foreign money. Eventually, the crisis also intensified social conflicts, particularly between Roma and ethnic Hungarians.

Increasing social tensions and ethnic conflict provided the opportunity for the radical right to increase its support (Ilonszki and Kurtán 2009). The Hungarian Guard, a paramilitary organization that frequently appeared in local communities for "demonstration purposes," provided the basis for a new party of the populist right, Jobbik. In the first postcrisis national elections, in April 2010, Jobbik came out of nowhere to obtain 16.7 percent of the vote. In addition to exploiting ethnic tensions, Jobbik played on the general discontent with the incumbent political elite and called for increasing political accountability and an extensive investigation of corruption scandals (Várnagy 2011, 993). Jobbik's success is rather exceptional for Central and Eastern European countries, where the new populist right generally tended to *lose* votes in the aftermath of the crisis.

The first postcrisis elections produced still another great winner: the opposition party Fidesz, in coalition with the Christian-Democrats, gained another 10.7 percent and arrived at an absolute majority of 52.7 percent of the vote and a two-thirds majority of the seats (68.1 percent). The socialists took an unprecedented beating (losing 23.9 percent of the vote). The other main losers of the election were the Liberal Party (SZDSZ) and the Hungarian Democratic Forum (MDF), the two parties that had dominated Hungarian politics in the 1990s; they formed an alliance for the elections but failed to reach the 5 percent threshold needed to be represented in Parliament.

After its election victory, Fidesz immediately launched an ambitious and contentious legislative program. In one of its first legislative acts, the new government granted dual citizenship to all Hungarians living outside of the country's borders who could demonstrate knowledge of the Hungarian language and had some claim to Hungarian ancestry; this measure provoked tensions especially with the Slovakian government. With respect to the management of the economic crisis, the government suspended talks with the IMF about further loans in early July 2010 and decided to follow its own controversial plan of recovery, which included a flat rate personal income tax, reduction of the corporate income tax, and a highly controversial measure to abolish mandatory private pension funds. The government also embarked on rewriting the Hungarian Constitution. Last but not least, it took steps toward putting Hungarian media under closer government control (Várnagy 2011, 995ff.).

For several months, public protests against these measures focused on the government's attempt to curb press freedom. In April, seven thousand people demonstrated against the new constitution pending in Parliament. In June, protests against the austerity measures in particular were organized by "Szolidaritas"—a group that had chosen its name deliberately to connect with the Polish Solidarnosc, and that recruited its adherents among union members, especially policemen, fire fighters, and emergency service workers. Given the weakness of the parliamentary opposition, it is no surprise that protests were mainly organized by unions and social movement organizations.[17]

These protests articulated the increasing disaffection of the Hungarian population with the Orban government. Polls in late 2011 indicate its support had fallen from 52 percent in the last election to 32 percent.[18] Against the background of these developments, the opposition started to reorganize itself. In October 2011, a group around the former Prime Minister Ferenc Gyurcsány split off from the increasingly ineffectual Socialists and formed the Democratic Coalition, a party that positioned itself closer to the center. Finally, in November 2011, given the failure of its economic policies, the Orban government was forced to make a U-turn and to apply to the IMF for another loan.[19]

Conclusion

The political fallout of the current financial and economic crisis cannot yet be definitely assessed. The economic consequences of the crisis have not fully played out yet, which means that the political implications, too, are still open-ended. Nevertheless, my exploration of the political consequences in the electoral arena and in the arenas of interest intermediation in thirty European countries has provided some results worth thinking about.

My analysis of electoral outcomes has confirmed the prediction of the literature on economic voting, that incumbents would be punished for lackluster economic performance. As expected, punishment was most severe in majoritarian countries, where the responsibilities can be clearly attributed to the government. In both Western European and Central and Eastern European countries (except for Poland and Slovakia), budgetary deficits were crucially important for explaining the electoral punishment of incumbents. Unemployment rates at the time of the election also played a significant role in Western European countries, while economic growth rates were of some relevance in Central and Eastern European countries. It seems that in Central and Eastern European countries in particular, the magnitude of the economic crisis mattered mostly in combination with preexisting homemade corruption and political scandals.

Embedding the electoral process in the larger political context, my case studies confirm that popular contention outside of the electoral channel closely interacted with conventional electoral politics. In all four of the countries I studied, protest mobilization was triggered by the government's adoption of austerity measures. These measures provided the link between the budgetary deficits on one hand and protest mobilization and electoral punishment on the other. In all four countries, austerity measures were imposed by deals they were forced to make with the IMF (jointly with EU/IMF in the case of Ireland). In Ireland and Hungary, the governments had already taken such measures before turning to international loans. In each instance, whether the measures were imposed by the international institutions or unilaterally by the national government, their announcement immediately provoked protests in the streets. The importance of austerity measures for triggering such protests is also confirmed by the contribution of Beissinger and Sasse in Chapter 11, and by the cases of Greece and Portugal, which have not been treated here but also had to resort to rescue packages from the IMF. There is, however, an important difference between Iceland and Ireland on one hand and Latvia and Hungary on the other: whereas the financial and economic crisis constituted the trigger of popular protest in the first two cases, this protest was already in full swing when the crisis intervened in Latvia and Hungary, thanks to corruption scandals and the malfunctioning of the party systems. In the two Central and Eastern European countries, the economic crisis served to amplify an already ongoing political crisis, whereas in the two Western European countries it created such a crisis from scratch.

Protest mobilization, in turn, has been shown to have important repercussions for elections and elected officials. In all four countries, cabinets were reshuffled under the pressure of protest mobilizations. In Iceland and Ireland, the withdrawal of support by minority partners under external pressure triggered early elections. In Hungary, the withdrawal of the minority partner led to a weak minority government. In Latvia, the reshuffling was more complicated, but eventually it also led to the withdrawal of the former prime minister's party and to a minority government. Together, the experience of the governments in these four countries indicate that, faced with popular reactions to an economic crisis of extraordinary proportions, government coalitions become highly unstable and suffer from the lack of loyalty of minority partners. This may help to explain why indicators of economic hardship are more closely correlated with the electoral performance of prime ministers' parties than of governing coalitions more broadly.

These case studies also document the close interaction between conventional politics and contentious mobilization in the streets, given that protesters got the support of allies within the established institutional structure. In both Iceland and Latvia, it was the president who provided such support, against the government and the Parliament. In Hungary, the support was mainly forthcoming from the parliamentary opposition, which used all possible means to discredit the government. The case of Hungary also shows that, once the government changed and the opposition was decisively weakened, protesters could no longer rely on government support but had to draw on the support of other organizations such as unions and social movement organizations. This was also the case in Ireland, where public sector unions and student organizations proved to be the main supporters of public protest. The experience of Southern European countries (not discussed here) confirms the importance of unions and professional organizations of groups particularly hard hit by the austerity measures for the mobilization of protest.

Third, the case studies illustrate the importance of direct-democratic instruments for the mobilization of protest, and for enhancing the possible impact of protest on the government's policies. In three of the four countries, referendums imposed constraints on the government's policies (in Iceland and Hungary) or on the political process (imposing early elections in Latvia).

However, as I have argued, the impact of protest mobilization on governments' policies may be severely limited by the constraints imposed on the governments by international pressure. As the governments in the countries hardest hit by the crisis discovered, one after another (the Hungarians later than the others), their maneuvering space did not permit them to make substantial concessions to their citizens' vocal protests. So far, only in tiny Iceland have citizens been able to force the government to resist outside pressure to some extent. With the support of their country's president, and thanks to an institutional mechanism (the referendum) allowing the population to veto the government's decisions, popular protest has been able to prevent the government from giving in to international pressure to expiate the banks' sins with taxpayers' money. Thanks to its citizens' protest, Iceland was able to avoid the fate of Ireland and Latvia. In the case of Iceland, all types of channels were involved in the showdown between the government and the citizens: electoral choices, referendum votes, constitutional assemblies, and protest in the streets mutually reinforced each other and led to an unexpected outcome.

In Latvia, the popular protest achieved at least a procedural success, forcing a constitutional change and early national elections. These elections, however, ended up having a rather ambiguous outcome with respect to the composition of the new government. In Hungary, the change of government led to a profound policy change, but it is unlikely that the ambitious economic program of the new government will be able to avoid the constraints imposed by the international organizations and "the market" in the medium term. Finally, in Ireland, both the old and the new government could not be forced by popular protest to make any concessions at all. The international pressure was simply too strong. Protest has, nevertheless, subsided in Ireland, a sign of resignation and an indication that the "government constraint" hypothesis applies to the protest arena as well.

Even in Iceland, where citizens' protests had some substantive success, their impact was so limited that many voters took the exit option in the secondary, local elections after the postcrisis national vote. In Hungary, too, the "exit" hypothesis found some support, as the governments voted into office in the first postcrisis elections turned out to be unable to deal with the constraints imposed by international organizations and "the markets." More generally, however, participation rates in the first postcrisis elections across Europe did not decline significantly, with changes in turnout ranging from +4.4 percent (in the United Kingdom and Bulgaria) to −19.3 percent (in Romania), and averaging −1.8 percent. According to the scenario sketched in the introduction to this chapter, the critical elections for the "exit" hypothesis will be those following the first postcrisis elections, when voters have come to realize that the parties replacing the punished government were not able to do any better than their predecessors.

Notes

1. In two countries (Italy and Malta), the first postcrisis elections took place in spring 2008, before their economies really went sour. In another three countries (Austria, Lithuania, and Slovenia), the corresponding elections occurred in September or October 2008, at the very time of the crash of Lehman Brothers, but too early for its economic consequences to play out.

2. France is excluded from the analysis because its first postcrisis election was not held until spring 2012.
3. For Cyprus, I use some results based on an analysis of the Democracy Barometer (http://www.democracybarometer.org/).
4. Source: Eurostat (GDP and main components—volumes [namq_gdp_k]).
5. Source: Eurostat (gov_dd_edpt1-Defizit).
6. Source: Eurostat(lfsq_urgan).
7. This index is calculated as the sum of the GDP growth rate and the public deficit, minus the unemployment rate. A few countries ran budget surpluses, and these are *subtracted* from the index rather than *added*.
8. The differences with respect to the effect of GDP growth between my analysis and those presented by Larry Bartels in Chapter 7 largely derive from differences in our selection of cases (for example, he includes 2007 elections) and the distinction I make here between Western European and Central and Eastern European countries.
9. Again, these results deviate to some extent from those in Chapter 7, where Bartels finds that controlling for growth diminishes the effect of budget deficits on electoral support for incumbents. These divergent findings derive from differences in case selection, as noted earlier, plus differences in measurement. Whereas I measure the budget surplus or deficit in the year preceding the election year, Bartels measures the debt accumulated by a government over the three years of the crisis (2008–2010), which provides an imprecise measure for the elections in his dataset held early in the crisis period.
10. Thorvaldur Gylfason, October 11, 2011: "From Crisis to Constitution" (http://www.voxeu.org/index.php?q=node/7077).
11. See Hardarson and Kristinsson (2011, 1001ff.) for more details on this issue.
12. *NZZ*, Nr. 282, December 3, 2010.
13. *Spiegel Online*, May 30, 2010.
14. The *Economist*, February 29, 2011, 23–26.
15. The *Economist*, March 5, 2011, 32.
16. The *Economist*, October 22, 2011, 38.
17. See Charles E. Ritterband, "Wachsendes Potenzial an Protest gegen Orban," *NZZ*, Nr. 279, November 29, 2011, 7.
18. Ibid.
19. The *Economist*, November 26, 2011, 42.

References

Duch, Raymond M., and Randolph T. Stevenson. 2008. *The Economic Vote: How Political and Economic Institutions Condition Election Results*. Cambridge: Cambridge University Press.

Fuchs, Dieter 1991. "The Normalization of the Unconventional: New Forms of Political Action and New Social Movements." In Gerd Meyer and Frantisek Ryszka (eds.),

Political Participation and Democracy in Poland and West Germany, 148–169. Warsaw: Wydaeca.

Gamson, William A., and David S. Meyer. 1996. "Framing Political Opportunity." In Doug McAdam, John D. McCarthy, and Mayer N. Zald (eds.), *Comparative Perspectives on Social Movements: Political Opportunities, Mobilizing Structures, and Cultural Framings*, 275–290. Cambridge: Cambridge University Press.

Goldstone, Jack A. 2003. "Introduction: Bridging Institutionalized and Noninstitutionalized Politics." In Jack A. Goldstone (ed.), *States, Parties, and Social Movements*, 1–24. Cambridge: Cambridge University Press.

Hardarson, Ólafur Th., and Gunnar Helgi Kristinsson. 2010. "Iceland." *European Journal of Political Research* 49: 1009–1016.

Hardarson, Ólafur Th., and Gunnar Helgi Kristinsson. 2011. "Iceland." *European Journal of Political Research* 50: 999–1003.

Hellwig, Timothy, and David Samuels. 2007. "Voting in Open Economies: The Electoral Consequences of Globalization." *Comparative Political Studies* 40, 3: 283–306.

Hirschman, Albert O. 1970. *Exit, Voice and Loyalty: Responses to Decline in Firms, Organizations, and States*. Cambridge, MA: Harvard University Press.

Ikstens, Jánis. 2009. "Latvia." *European Journal of Political Research* 48: 1015–1021.

Ikstens, Jánis. 2010. "Latvia." *European Journal of Political Research* 49: 1049–1057.

Ikstens, Jánis. 2011. "Latvia." *European Journal of Political Research* 50: 1035–1044.

Ilonszki, Gabriella, and Sándor Kurtán. 2009. "Hungary." *European Journal of Political Research* 48: 973–979.

Keeler, John T. S. 1993. "Opening the Window for Reform: Mandates, Crises, and Extraordinary Policy-making." *Comparative Political Studies* 25, 4: 433–486.

Kriesi, Hanspeter, Ruud Koopmans, Jan Willem Duyvendak, and Marco Giugni. 1995. *New Social Movements in Western Europe: A Comparative Analysis*. Minneapolis: University of Minnesota Press.

Lewis-Beck, Michael S., and Mary Stegmaier. 2007. "Economic Models of Voting." In Russell J. Dalton and Hans-Dieter Klingemann (eds.), *The Oxford Handbook of Political Behaviour*, 519–537. Oxford: Oxford University Press.

Mair, Peter. 2009. "Representative Versus Responsible Government." MPIfG Working Paper 09/8. Köln: Max-Planck-Institut für Gesellschaftsforschung.

McAdam, Doug, and Sidney Tarrow. 2010. "Ballots and Barricades: On the Reciprocal Relationship Between Elections and Social Movements." *Perspectives on Politics* 8, 2: 529–542.

Mény, Yves, and Yves Surel. 2002. "The Constitutive Ambiguity of Populism." In Yves Mény and Yves Surel (eds.), *Democracies and the Populist Challenge*, 1–21. Basingstoke: Palgrave.

Meyer, David S., and Sidney Tarrow. 1998. "A Movement Society: Contentious Politics for a New Century." In David S. Meyer and Sidney Tarrow (eds.), *The Social Movement Society*, 1–28. Lanham, MD: Rowman & Littlefield.

O'Malley, Eoin. 2009. "Ireland," *European Journal of Political Research* 48: 986–991.

O'Malley, Eoin. 2010. "Ireland," *European Journal of Political Research* 49: 1017–1024.

O'Malley, Eoin. 2010. "Ireland," *European Journal of Political Research* 50: 1004–1010.

Pallinger, Zoltán Tibor. 2012. "Citizens' Initiative in Hungary: An Additional Opportunity for Power-Sharing in an Extremely Majoritarian System." In Theo Schiller and Maija Setälä (eds.), *Citizens' Initiative in Europe: Procedures and Consequences of Agenda-Setting by the People*. Basingstoke: Palgrave Macmillan.

Piven, Francis Fox, and Richard A. Cloward. 1977. *Poor People's Movements: Why They Succeed, How They Fail.* New York: Vintage Books.

Powell, G. Bingham Jr., and Guy D. Whitten. 1993. "A Cross-National Analysis of Economic Voting: Taking Account of the Political Context." *American Journal of Political Science* 37, 2: 391–414.

Quinlivan, Aodh, and Liam Weeks. 2010. "The 2009 Local Elections in the Republic of Ireland." *Irish Political Studies* 25, 2: 315–324.

Reinhart, Carmen M., and Kenneth S. Rogoff. 2009. *This Time Is Different: Eight Centuries of Financial Folly*. Princeton, NJ: Princeton University Press.

Schattschneider, E. E. 1975 [1960]. *The Semisovereign People.* New York: Wadsworth Thomson Learning.

Schmitt, Hermann. 2005. "The European Parliament Elections of June 2004: Still Second-Order?" *West European Politics* 28, 3: 650–679.

Singer, Matthew M. 2011. "Who Says 'It's the Economy'? Cross-National and Cross-Individual Variation in the Salience of Economic Performance." *Comparative Political Studies* 44, 3: 284–312.

Tucker, Joshua A. 2006. *Regional Economic Voting: Russia, Poland, Hungary, Slovakia and the Czech Republic, 1990–1999*. Cambridge: Cambridge University Press.

Van der Brug, Wouter, Cees van der Eijk, and Mark Franklin. 2007. *The Economy and the Vote: Economic Conditions and Elections in Fifteen Countries.* Cambridge: Cambridge University Press.

Várnagy Réka. 2011. "Hungary." *European Journal of Political Research* 50: 991–998.

Wells, Robin, and Paul Krugman. 2010. "Our Giant Banking Crisis—What to Expect." *New York Review of Books*, May 13: 11–13.

Wolfsfeld, Gadi. 1997. *Media and Political Conflict: News from the Middle East.* Cambridge: Cambridge University Press.

11

An End to "Patience"?

THE GREAT RECESSION AND ECONOMIC PROTEST IN EASTERN EUROPE

Mark R. Beissinger and Gwendolyn Sasse

THIS CHAPTER EXPLORES the dynamics of economic protest across post-communist Eastern Europe in the context of the Great Recession. According to the IMF, as of 2010 the postcommunist countries were the world region worst hit from the Great Recession, experiencing steeper economic declines than any other part of the world (IMF 2010). Major economic contractions occurred in seven postcommunist countries (Croatia, Estonia, Hungary, Latvia, Lithuania, Slovenia, and Ukraine). By 2009 the GDP of Latvia was 22 percent lower than in 2007, while that of Lithuania had declined by 14 percent. From 2007 to 2009 unemployment rose in Hungary from 7.4 percent to 10 percent, in Estonia from 4.7 percent to 13.7 percent, in Lithuania from 4.3 percent to 13.7 percent, and in Latvia from 6.0 percent to 17.1 percent. At the same time, there was considerable variation within the region in the effects of the recession. Four countries (Bulgaria, Czech Republic, Romania, and Russia) experienced economic stagnation rather than negative growth, while seven countries (Albania, Belarus, Macedonia, Moldova, Poland, Serbia, and Slovakia) actually continued to achieve positive growth throughout the years of the global recession.

Note: The authors thank Larry Bartels, Nancy Bermeo, and participants in the Oxford conference on Popular Reactions to the Economic Crisis for their comments on an earlier draft of this chapter, as well as Tiffanee Brown, Lydia Dallett, Susan Divald, Andrea Hudecz, Seongcheol Kim, Jana Pakstaitis, Olga Radchenko, and Bryn Rosenfeld for research assistance connected with this project.

The Great Recession was not the first time in recent memory that postcommunist Europe went through a period of dramatic economic contraction. The 1990s witnessed much more severe economic downturns for most countries of the region, as these societies underwent the transition from socialist to capitalist economic systems. In the three years after 1991, GDP fell by 23 percent in Estonia and 18 percent in Latvia. Yet these two countries weathered the transition to capitalism with less economic pain than many countries in the region; the corresponding declines in GDP were much steeper in Russia (37 percent), Ukraine (55 percent), and Moldova (59 percent). However, as the literature on postcommunist economic transitions emphasizes, for the most part the transition to capitalism, though wrenching, did not produce major waves of protest in many countries, as citizens displayed a surprising degree of "patience" (or at the very least, quiescence) in the midst of massive economic decline. There were, of course, exceptions. Major waves of strikes and labor protest occurred periodically in Russia in the 1990s, particularly over the issue of unpaid wages (Robertson 2010). Poland has routinely been singled out as an exceptional case of labor mobilization under socialism and continued mobilization in the early postcommunist period (Ekiert and Kubik 1998, 1999; Seleny 1999). But in general, and contrary to what many analysts had predicted, "patience" or quiescence is thought to have predominated over protest, particularly in comparison with other regions of the world that also experienced IMF-led structural adjustment programs (Greskovits 1998. See also Przeworski 1991; Agh 1991; Haggard and Kaufman 1992; Walton and Seddon 1994; Howard 2003; Ost 2005; Vanhuysse 2006).

The reaction to the Great Recession in Eastern Europe, however, indicates that, at least in some parts of the region, this period of quiescence in response to economic decline has come to an end. In 1992—a year in which the GDP of Latvia contracted by 32 percent—only three known major demonstrations involving thirty-six hundred participants (and no mass violence) occurred in Latvia over economic conditions.[1] By contrast, in 2009 Latvia experienced thirteen major demonstrations over economic conditions, involving more than fifty thousand participants and including significant violence resulting in forty-three injuries, major property damage, and more than 250 arrests. Indeed, as we will see, the Latvian example is no aberration; in a number of the postcommunist countries the protests touched off by the Great Recession were considerably greater than those that occurred in response to the economic downturn of the early 1990s.

In this chapter we explore the factors that shaped patterns of economic protest across eighteen European postcommunist countries during the

Great Recession. We seek to explain how the Great Recession altered the level and nature of economic protest in the region, and to explore the factors that explain the considerable variation in patterns of economic protest across postcommunist Europe during this period. As we will show, contrary to what one might expect, protest overall in the region declined during the Great Recession. But this is not true of all forms of protest, or of protests over all types of issues. Strikes, protests over ethnic and nationalist issues, and protests for greater economic benefits declined sharply during this period. By contrast, demonstrations assumed greater weight in protest repertoires, and protests against economic cutbacks rose sharply to become the dominant type of protest within the region. In this respect, the Great Recession altered not only protest repertoires but also the character of economic protest, transforming it from a proactive endeavor demanding salary and benefit increases to a more defensive one voicing discontent over austerity measures.

One might logically expect that those countries experiencing more economic pain would also be those experiencing greater economic protest, and indeed we show that countries that continued to grow exhibited lower levels of protest. But we also show that among those countries undergoing significant economic contractions, there was considerable variation in the extent to which economic pain translated into economic protest. Ironically, those countries that were most vulnerable to a high level of economic protest in the late 2000s were those that had been in the forefront of economic reform in the 1990s and most eager to integrate with Europe. This was so, we argue, for two reasons: (1) they were more vulnerable than other countries of the region to a serious economic downturn in the context of global recession, as a result of their high dependence on the global economy; and (2) integration into the EU and the factors that underlay it (as well as relatively successful patterns of economic growth associated with it in the late 1990s) generated expectations about an improving standard of living that were dashed in the context of the Great Recession.

We also show that a number of other factors shaped the extent and nature of protests in those states that experienced economic contractions: (1) level of public sector employment, (2) IMF rescue packages, (3) public trust in government in the run-up to the crisis, and (4) political party mobilization. We illustrate these causal processes through paired comparisons of Latvia and Estonia on the one hand and Hungary and Ukraine on the other. All four countries experienced severe economic downturns in the context of the Great Recession (among the seven most severe economic contractions in our sample). But even though Latvia and Hungary were among the countries exhibiting the highest levels of economic protest (in terms of number of protests, participation rate, and extent of violence) during this period, Estonia and Ukraine remained relatively quiescent. We argue that these variations in outcomes resulted from the countries' differential reform trajectories and how they interacted with varying degrees of trust in government and varying abilities on the part of political actors to instrumentalize and channel political polarization.

Patterns of Economic Protest in Postcommunist Countries

To analyze patterns of protest across European postcommunist states during the global financial crisis, we constructed an event database of major protests and incidents of mass violence throughout the region. Electronic searches were conducted of five leading international newswires (Reuters, Associated Press, Agence France Presse, Deutsche Presse Agentur, and Interfax) for the period from January 2007 through December 2010. All articles that reported on demonstrations, strikes, or mass violent events in any of the eighteen European postcommunist countries examined in this study were saved in monthly media files for subsequent review and coding. (The Appendix provides a more detailed description of our coding procedures.) The utility of using five wire services is clear from the fact that no single wire service covered more than 43 percent of the 967 protest events recorded in this study. Reuters, which is often used in cross-national studies of protest events (as, for instance, in the *World Handbook of Political Indicators*), covered only 17 percent of the protest events in the data. Our use of multiple sources also increased the quality of the coded information for many events, filling in details about individual events that otherwise would have remained unknown had only a single source been available.

Of course, media studies of protest events are known to have significant biases, and those biases are likely to be even more significant in a study based on international wire services. Large numbers of protest events are ignored in international wire service reports (especially small events and events outside capital cities), and any media-based study of protest activity is unlikely to be a fully accurate reproduction of patterns of protest. It may, however, be a representative sample of a certain sort. On the basis of what is known about how the media report on protest events, one would expect that international wire services would tend to report primarily on politically salient events and on events involving violence or taking place in a country's capital. These may actually be the most important events for understanding the impact of economic decline on patterns of protest in any case, since they are the events most likely to affect the political process. For purposes of obtaining a reasonably representative sample across eighteen countries, international wire services are probably the best sources available, since country-level sources have quite different policies on reporting about protest events. It is possible—even likely—that certain international wire services covered particular countries more thoroughly than others. The use of reports from five international wire services can serve to mitigate this selection bias. The sample is right-censored in that both the Great Recession and economic protest in the postcommunist countries continued beyond December 2010, when our data collection ended. But we began sampling in January 2007, well before the onset of the recession in late 2008, in order to be able to identify how the recession itself may have altered patterns of protest.

There is no scholarly consensus over how best to measure trends in protest action. A simple event count can be thought of as representing the frequency of attempts by movements to organize collective action. Often, this is weighted by the number of days over which a protest event occurs, since a one-day protest represents a qualitatively different protest effort from a prolonged, multiweek action.[2] But we are also interested in the resonance of attempts to mobilize—in particular, the number of people who actually participate in a protest event.[3] We assume that the factors shaping movement attempts to mount protests are likely to differ from those that shape the decisions of large numbers of people whether or not to participate in these actions, given the opportunity to do so (Beissinger 2002).

We report all three measures (events, protest days, and protest participation) in Figure 11.1, which provides an overview of the evolution of protest events in the region over time by form of action, as captured by the five international wire services. As is evident from the figure, during the period of the Great Recession (and contrary to what one might expect) there actually was a general decline in protest activity in the postcommunist region—irrespective of whether one measures protest by the number of events, protest days, or participants. The decline began prior to the onset of the Great Recession but continued to deepen in 2009 in the midst of the global financial crisis. In terms of protest repertoires, most acts of protest reported by the wire services during this period (90 percent) involved demonstrations; only 11 percent involved strikes and only 9 percent involved mass violent events. (Protest events in the sample could include more than one action form.) But even

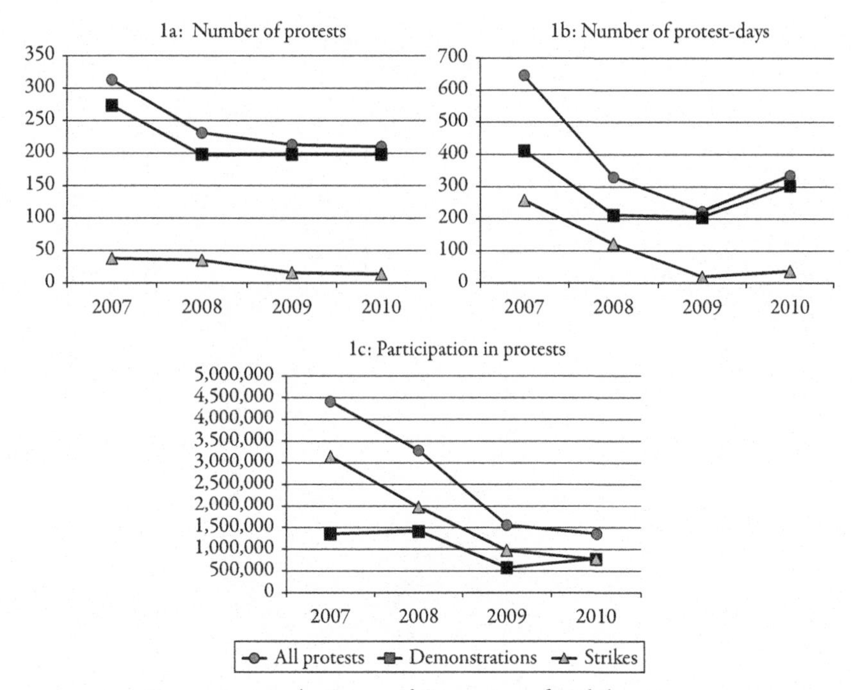

FIGURE 11.1 Protest Activity by Form and Dimension of Mobilization, 2007–2010.

though they constituted a relatively small proportion of protest events overall, strikes accounted for 65 percent of all participants in protest actions during this period.

Over the course of the global financial crisis, the incidence of strikes (both in terms of raw numbers and as a relative proportion of protest events each year) declined sharply, as strikes became a diminishing part (and demonstrations became a larger part) of protest repertoires. Such patterns are in accord with the findings of the scholarly literature on strikes, which has generally found that strikes tend to be more frequent when economies are expanding rather than contracting, since in tough times workers' jobs are at the mercy of employers, and workers have greater difficulty withholding labor when their jobs are under threat. (See, for instance, Tilly and Shorter 1974; Hibbs 1976.)

As Figure 11.2 shows, much of the overall decline in protest activity in the region during the Great Recession was driven by a decline in protests over non-economic issues (in particular, ethnic and nationalist issues). This decline does not appear to have been connected with the recession. In both Russia and Hungary, for instance, 2007 (the year before the onset of the recession) saw unusually intense ethnic and nationalist protest mobilization—in Russia, due primarily to the conflict with Estonia over the removal of a Soviet war memorial

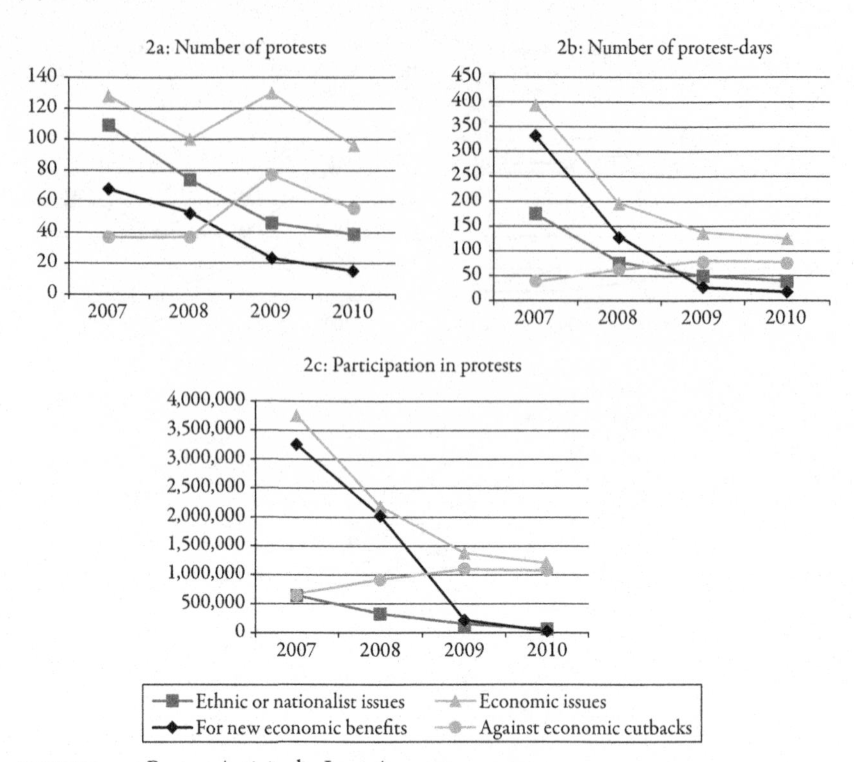

FIGURE 11.2 Protest Activity by Issue Area, 2007–2010.

and activity by extremist right-wing groups; and in Hungary, the result of the activation of Viktor Orbán's Fidesz party and protests by right-wing extremists against the socialist government of Prime Minister Ferenc Gyurcsány. The latter were linked to the domestic economic crisis experienced by Hungary prior to the onset of the global financial crisis and prepared the ground for ongoing mobilization once external economic constraints grew.

Economic protest actually remained at roughly the same level during the Great Recession as prior to the Great Recession, increasing as a proportion of all protests during this period. Yet, the duration of economic protests and the overall number of people who participated in them declined sharply during this period. Even so, economic issues throughout the Great Recession resonated among protestors in ways that protest over other issues simply did not. Thus, although constituting 47 percent of the number of protests and 55 percent of the number of protest days, economic protest accounted for 80 percent of the participants in protest during this period. Particularly in 2009, immediately after the onset of the global financial crisis, the region experienced an increase in the number of economically related acts of protest, amounting to 61 percent of all protests and 89 percent of all participants in protests during that year.

Moreover, the Great Recession was associated with a sharp shift in the nature of the economic issues raised in protests. In 2007, before the onset of the economic crisis, three-fourths of all participants in protest acts in the region mobilized in support of obtaining new economic benefits (increased pay, improved working conditions, or improvements in services). By contrast, in the wake of the global financial crisis, protest aimed at obtaining new benefits fell precipitously (declining to only 14 percent of protest participants in 2009 and 2 percent in 2010), while protest against economic austerity measures (cuts in pay, benefits, or services) came to dominate protest agendas, with protests revolving around these demands mobilizing 71 percent of all protest participants in the region in 2009 and 80 percent in 2010. In short, the global recession fundamentally altered the character of protest politics in the region, transforming protest into a largely defensive set of actions in reaction to austerity measures that cut pay, benefits, and services rather than revolving around gaining new benefits, as had overwhelmingly been the case during more prosperous times.

These overall patterns hide considerable country-level variations, and it is at the country level that one can identify some of the factors differentially shaping protest responses across the region. Table 11.1 provides a general overview of patterns of protest across the eighteen European postcommunist states examined in this study, weighted by their population size.[4] As can be seen, not all countries experienced a high rate of protest over economic issues during this period, and in some countries (Belarus and Estonia, for example) protest over other issues predominated in the agendas. In this study we focus on patterns of protest over economic issues rather than patterns of protest in general, since we are interested specifically in probing the differential protest responses to the Great Recession, and as we have seen, economic protest played the dominant role in the protest repertoires of the region during the Great Recession. It is of course possible that there is an economic component to protest over other types of issues (for instance, democratization or ethnic conflict) that we are bracketing by looking only at protest over economic issues. However, we expect that protest over these other issues is likely to be less directly connected with patterns of economic performance and more likely to be driven by other factors, such as ethnic stratification and diversity and government repression, that are less relevant for understanding the impact of the recession on patterns of protest.

Table 11.1 Country-level Indicators of Patterns of Protest, 2007–2010.

Country	Total Protests	Protests per Million Pop.	Protests Raising Economic Demands	Economic Protests per Million Pop.	Protests Against Economic Cutbacks	Protests Against Cutbacks per Million Pop.	Protest Participation	Protest Participation per 1,000 Pop.	Participation in Economic Protests	Participation in Economic Protests per 1,000 Pop.	Participation in Protests Against Economic Cutbacks	Participation in Protests Against Cutbacks per 1.000 Pop.	Economic Violence index[a]
Albania	9	3.0	2	0.7	0	0.0	54300	18	23000	8	0	0	0
Belarus	30	3.1	10	1.0	5	0.5	46931	5	11185	1	5810	1	0.693147
Bulgaria	69	9.7	48	6.8	13	1.8	2308658	325	2262287	319	23098	3	4.034241
Croatia	29	6.5	14	3.1	7	1.6	204010	45	178660	40	37100	8	0
Czech Rep.	46	4.5	17	1.7	8	0.8	1101484	108	1077742	106	816067	80	0
Estonia	12	9.4	1	0.8	1	0.8	7100	6	3000	2	3000	2	0
Hungary	92	9.2	52	5.2	37	3.7	651453	65	557372	56	402622	40	3.091043
Latvia	33	15.0	16	7.3	13	5.9	74875	34	56175	25	42075	19	4.817617
Lithuania	10	2.8	7	2.0	4	1.1	29500	8	25050	7	14650	4	3.931826
Macedonia	12	5.8	2	1.0	0	0.0	349650	168	310000	149	0	0	0
Moldova	6	1.4	1	0.2	0	0.0	49183	11	100	0	0	0	0
Poland	72	1.9	47	1.2	19	0.5	1210550	31	1184850	31	560800	15	2.197225
Romania	70	3.2	50	2.3	31	1.4	1510955	69	1399905	64	1138400	52	1.791759
Russia	247	1.8	94	0.7	43	0.3	1143226	8	253155	2	48766	0	2.74084
Serbia	43	5.9	14	1.9	2	0.3	292843	40	50000	7	10300	1	2.944439
Slovakia	6	1.1	2	0.4	1	0.2	15948	3	5148	1	4500	1	0
Slovenia	9	4.5	9	4.5	4	2.0	899500	450	899500	450	572100	286	1.098612
Ukraine	172	3.8	68	1.5	18	0.4	654255	14	224580	5	86017	2	1.386294
TOTAL	967		454		206		10604421		8521709		3765305		

Note: [a] Calculated as the natural log of the product of the number of people injured in mass violent events concerning economic issues; * the score on a property

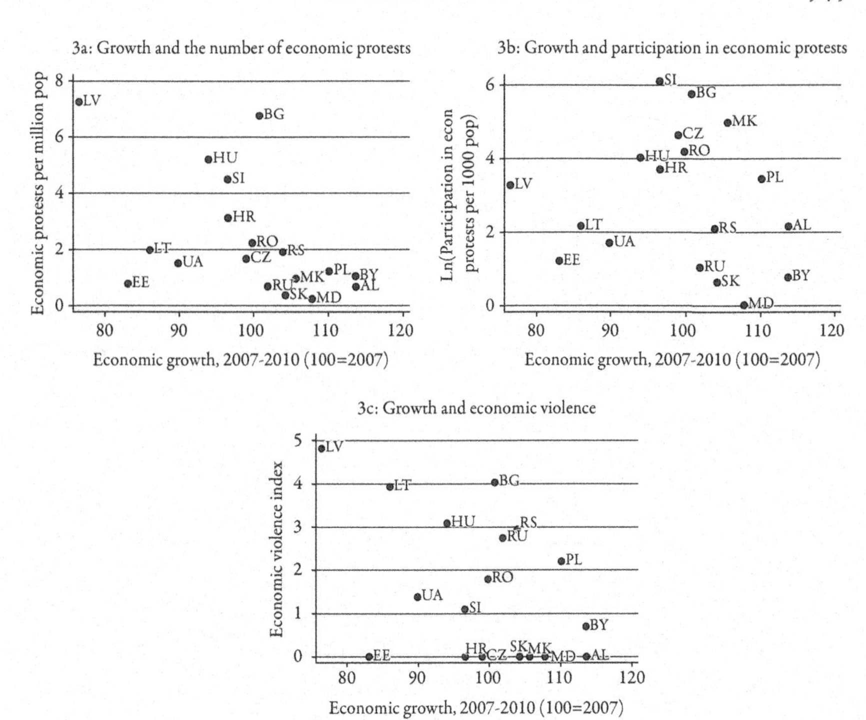

FIGURE 11.3 Economic Growth and Economic Protest, 2007–2010.

In Figure 11.3 we use the population-weighted figures on protest activity to examine the bivariate relationship between rates of economic growth and patterns of protest over economic issues, aggregated over the entire 2007–2010 period. In Figure 11.3a we focus on the number of events, and in Figure 11.3b on the number of participants. In Figure 11.3c we focus on variation in the level of mass violence over economic issues (as measured by an index reflecting the number of people injured in mass violent events and the level of property damage involved in them).[5] In all three figures, there is a negative relationship between economic growth and level of economic protest, and the patterns of variation in all three bear certain similarities. In Figure 11.3a, for instance, those countries that experienced a positive rate of economic growth during the Great Recession (Albania, Belarus, Macedonia, Moldova, Poland, Slovakia, Serbia, and Russia) also had a lower number of economic protests per population. But among countries that experienced zero or negative growth (Bulgaria, Croatia, Czech Republic, Estonia, Hungary, Latvia, Lithuania, Romania, Slovenia, and Ukraine), there was a great deal of heterogeneity in the extent to which they experienced protest over economic issues. Figure 11.3b shows a similar pattern for levels of participation, with a downward trend among those countries that experienced a higher rate of growth, but with significant variation among countries that experienced zero or negative growth. Latvia, Hungary, Bulgaria, Croatia, Slovenia, Lithuania, and Romania exhibited the highest number of economic protests, while Bulgaria, Slovenia, Macedonia, Czech Republic, Romania, Hungary, Poland, and Latvia displayed the highest levels of participation in economic protests. In Figure 11.3c, the overall pattern is again sharply negative, with greater variance in level of violence among countries that experienced zero or negative economic growth. Latvia, Bulgaria, Lithuania, and Hungary stood out for their relatively high levels of economically related violence during this period.

Thus we are left with a puzzle: economic growth may explain why those societies that continued to benefit from growth during the Great Recession did not experience a high level of economic protest, but it cannot explain why, among those societies that experienced significant economic downturns during the Great Recession, some exhibited considerable economic protest while others did not. Countries experiencing similar amounts of economic pain exhibited significantly different degrees of protest over the consequences of economic contraction. We now turn to a multivariate analysis of patterns of economic protest and to two paired case studies to help explain this puzzle.

Multivariate Analysis of Patterns of Protest

In the analysis that follows, we use country-years as the basic unit of analysis and implement a cross-sectional time-series design, focusing on four dependent variables of interest: the number of protests (weighted by their duration) over economic issues, the number of participants in protests over economic issues, the number of protests (weighted by duration) specifically against economic cutbacks, and the number of participants in protests specifically against economic cutbacks.[6] As we saw earlier, economic protest during the 2007–2010 period varied considerably in its goals. In the context of the Great Recession, protest for new economic benefits receded as the predominant form of economic protest, with protest over economic cutbacks instead coming to dominate agendas. By exploring the factors shaping protest over economic issues more broadly and against economic cutbacks more specifically, we can gain a good sense of some of the key drivers during the Great Recession.

For the event-count dependent variables, we use a random effects negative binomial model.[7] For the participation dependent variables we use a tobit model, which addresses the issue of nonrandom selection when a variable is censored or truncated at a certain point. In this case, one cannot have participation in protest without first having a protest, so that a simple regression model confounds the issue of how many people decide to participate in protest with the issue of whether or not a protest is organized in the first place. Participants in protest generally do not decide whether and when an event will occur, but only whether to participate in an event already organized by others. By censoring those observations in which no protests occurred, we can estimate whether a particular independent variable increased or decreased participation, given the availability of an opportunity for people to participate in protest.[8]

We begin with baseline models relating population size and rates of economic growth to the number of economic protests (in Table 11.2) and the number of participants in those protests (in Table 11.3). As reported in Model 1 in Table 11.2a, both variables have statistically significant relationships with the number of protests over economic issues in general. As one would expect, countries with larger populations experienced more economic protest, and economic growth was strongly related to lower levels of economic protest. Controlling for population size, we found that every percentage point of increase in economic growth (relative to the base year of 2006) decreased the expected number of economic protests annually by 5.5 percent. As Model 1 in Table 11.2b indicates, population size and rate of economic growth were also strongly related to protest against economic cutbacks specifically. Every percentage point of economic growth (relative to the base year of 2006) decreased the expected number of protests over economic cutbacks annually by almost 8 percent. Thus, in a country that experienced an economic decline of 14 percent below the 2006 level (as occurred, for instance, in Latvia in 2009), one would expect a 77 percent increase in the rate of economic protest in general and a 109 percent increase in the rate of protest over economic cutbacks, whereas in a country that experienced 14 percent economic growth compared to the 2006 level (as occurred, for example, in Poland in 2009), one would expect equivalent *decreases* in economic protest and protests against economic cutbacks.

Model 1 in Table 11.3a shows that population size had a marginally significant relationship with the number of people who participated, given the opportunity to participate in a protest over economic issues, but economic growth did not. However, as Model 1 in Table 11.3b indicates, given the opportunity to participate in a demonstration against economic cutbacks, both population size and economic growth had statistically significant effects on the number of people who participated. Every percentage point of economic

Table 11.2 Random Effects Negative Binomial Regression of Yearly Economic Protest Events (Weighted by Duration).

Table 11.2a: All Economic Protest Events

All Economic Protest	Model 1		Model 2		Model 3		Model 4		Model 5	
Variable	*IRR*	*z–score*	*IRR*	*z–score*	*IRR*	*z–score*	*IRR*	*z–score*	*IRR*	*z–score*
Ln population	2.051	6.17****	2.136	6.25****	2.046	5.96****	2.260	5.97****	2.056	5.97****
GDP growth (2006 = 100)	0.945	−3.83****	0.949	−3.46****	0.943	−3.57****	0.943	−3.62****	0.941	−3.47****
Freedom House score, 2006			0.952	−0.94			0.878	−1.64		
EBRD economic reform index, 1998					0.847	−0.49	0.528	−1.37	0.825	−0.53
Public sector employment									1.002	0.09
Dummy, IMF standby program									0.897	−0.36
Number of observations	72		72		68		68		68	
Number of groups	18		18		17		17		17	
Wald chi-square	42.17****		44.01****		40.14****		40.82****		40.14****	
Log likelihood	−211.612		−211.180		−200.880		−199.421		−200.811	

Table 11.2b: Protest Events over Economic Cutbacks

Protest Against Economic Cutbacks	Model 1		Model 2		Model 3		Model 4		Model 5	
Variable	*IRR*	*z-score*	*IRR*	*z-score*	*IRR*	*z-score*	*IRR*	*z-score*	*IRR*	*z-score*
Ln population	2.150	5.18****	2.284	5.28****	1.987	6.84****	1.969	5.68****	2.003	7.01****
GDP growth (2006 = 100)	0.922	−4.44****	0.928	−4.00****	0.937	−3.91****	0.937	−3.89****	0.951	−2.85***
Freedom House score, 2006			0.926	−1.15			1.009	0.14		
EBRD economic reform index, 1998					2.128	2.95***	2.192	2.39**	2.376	3.73****
Public sector employment (%), 2005									1.049	2.24**
Dummy, IMF standby program									1.836	2.01**
Number of observations	72		72		68		68		72	
Number of groups	18		18		17		17		18	
Wald chi-square	35.33****		36.20****		51.61****		52.07****		64.08****	
Log likelihood	−140.402		−139.747		−130.397		−130.387		−126.623	

Table 11.3 Tobit Regression of Annual Participation in Economic Protest Events.

Table 11.3a: Participation in All Economic Protest Events

Participation in All Economic Protest	Model 1		Model 2		Model 3		Model 4		Model 5	
Variable	*Coeff.*	*z-score*	*Coeff.*	*z-score*	*Coeff.*	*z-score*	*Coeff.*	*z-score*	*Coeff.*	*z-score*
Ln population	80930.0	1.93*	107930.9	2.91***	80742.5	1.98*	110946.0	2.67***	116529.1	3.02***
GDP growth (2006 = 100)	−7198.3	−1.21	−1597.5	−0.28	−566.4	−0.82	−3699.1	−0.58	−2099.5	−0.34
Freedom House score, 2006			−37700.9	−2.45**			−41059.9	−1.79*	−42684.0	−2.44**
EBRD economic reform index, 1998					83339.4	0.91	−50970.9	−0.44		
Public sector employment (%), 2005									4462.5	0.67
Dummy, IMF standby program									−54181.0	−0.5
Number of observations	72		72		68		68		72	
Number of groups	18		18		17		17		18	
Uncensored observations (censored at 0)	55		55		51		51		55	
Wald chi-square	4.40		11.06**		5.32		9.88**		11.70**	
Log likelihood	−789.385		−787.096		−732.354		−728.499		−786.740	

Table 11.3b: Participation in Protest Events Against Economic Cutbacks

Participation in Protest Against Economic Cutbacks	Model 1		Model 2		Model 3		Model 4		Model 5	
Variable	*Coeff.*	*z-score*	*Coeff.*	*z-score*	*Coeff.*	*z-score*	*Coeff.*	*z-score*	*Coeff.*	*z-score*
Ln population	77431.9	2.58***	95511.3	3.34***	72511.2	2.84***	82651.9	2.92***	100347.9	3.76****
GDP growth (2006 = 100)	−9532.4	−2.48**	−6948.4	−1.81*	−7366.8	−1.96**	−7147.9	−1.90*	−4564.4	−1.22
Freedom House score, 2006			−23604.1	−2.15**			−12698.6	−0.85	−32305.8	−2.79***
EBRD economic reform index, 1998					88745.8	1.60	43037.5	−0.56		
Public sector employment (%), 2005									4794.6	1.07
Dummy, IMF standby program									42953.5	0.68
Number of observations	72		72		68		68		72	
Number of groups	18		18		17		17		18	
Uncensored observations (censored at 0)	42		42		38		38		42	
Wald chi-square	9.87***		14.40***		13.22***		13.90***		18.79***	
Log likelihood	-583.205		-581.149		-523.808		-523.451		-566.496	

growth (relative to 2006) increased the annual number of participants in protests against economic cutbacks by about 9,500 persons, so that an economic decline of 14 percent below the 2006 level (Latvia in 2009) would be associated with more than 130,000 more participants in protests against economic cutbacks, whereas a country with 14 percent growth above the 2006 level (Poland in 2009) would have had 130,000 fewer participants in such protests. In short, the baseline models show that the effect of economic contraction on protest mainly occurred through encouraging movement activists to organize more frequent protests over economic issues (and over economic cutbacks in particular). But even if we take this into account, the belt-tightening effects of the recession did encourage greater numbers to participate in protests against economic cutbacks in those countries that experienced contractions.[9]

In Models 2, 3, and 4 we introduce two other independent variables that we expect to affect the level of economic protest in the context of economic contraction: (1) a country's Freedom House score (ranging from 2 to 14, with a score of 2 representing full democracy and 14 representing full autocracy) for 2006, on the eve of the Great Recession[10] ; and (2) the EBRD Economic Transition Index for 1998, measuring the extent to which a country had made the transition to capitalist forms of economy in the 1990s.[11] We expect a negative relationship between the Freedom House score and economic protest, as more authoritarian polities should be less tolerant of attempts to organize protests in general, and individuals living in more autocratic countries should be less willing to risk participation in the face of negative incentives.

There are also a number of reasons one might expect prior patterns of economic transformation to affect economic protest in the context of the Great Recession. Those countries that were more progressive in terms of transforming their economies into market economies in the 1990s were the very countries that earlier had demonstrated "patience" in the midst of economic contraction. This might have led one to expect similarly quiescent responses to the Great Recession. However, there are also some reasons to believe the opposite would be true: those countries that had been in the forefront of economic reform in the 1990s would experience a higher level of protest during the Great Recession. "Patience" in the 1990s had been closely intertwined with the promise that rapid economic transition and the additional pain that countries underwent for the sake of integration with the European Union would eventually bring a higher standard of living.[12] Indeed, the decade prior to the Great Recession had been one of remarkable economic growth throughout the region, reinforcing these expectations. But for many living in the region, the sharp economic decline of the Great Recession shattered those dreams, undermining the implicit economic contract between state and society on which European integration was built.

It could also be that countries that had reformed themselves more thoroughly in the 1990s were more vulnerable to the effects of the Great Recession in the late 2000s because of the consequences of economic reform for their economies. The EBRD Economic Transition Index is strongly correlated with the proportion of a country's GDP comprising imports and exports, and with the role of foreign direct investment in a country's economy—both factors that would likely make a country more vulnerable to a global economic downturn. However, these factors would not be expected to operate directly on protest, but indirectly through their effect on economic decline, so that we are in essence already controlling for their effects by controlling for the influence of economic growth on protest.

Still, in interpreting the effects of democratization and the transition to capitalism on economic protest during the Great Recession, we need to proceed with caution; as is well known, there was a close relationship between democratization and economic reform in the 1990s, and indeed the level of autocracy in a postcommunist country in 2006 was still strongly negatively correlated ($r = -.73$) with the extent to which it had engaged in economic reform in the 1990s. Therefore, in Models 2 through 4 we test for the effects of each of these two variables separately and jointly, exploring which provides better explanatory power, if either. Surprisingly, the findings show that, if we control for population size and economic growth, a country's level of democracy had no independent effect on the frequency with which movements organized economic protests or protests against economic cutbacks. Level of democratization did, however, have an independent effect on the willingness of people to participate in these protests assuming the availability of an opportunity to participate. Every one-point increase toward autocracy on the Freedom House scale resulted in about 38,000 fewer protestors per year over economic issues in general and about 24,000 fewer protestors against economic cutbacks. Thus a country such as Russia, which is relatively high on the Freedom House scale (i.e., more autocratic) would be expected to have about 340,000 fewer participants in economic protests in general during this period and 216,000 fewer participants in protests against economic cutbacks than a country such as Latvia, which is relatively low (i.e., more democratic) on the Freedom House scale.

By contrast, we found that the EBRD Economic Transition Index, despite having no relationship with the frequency of economic protest in general or with participation in economic protests or in protests against economic cutbacks, was strongly associated with a significant increase in the frequency of protest against economic cutbacks (with every point on the EBRD index more than doubling the rate of protest on these issues, controlling for the effects of population size and economic growth). Thus, one would expect three times as many protests over economic cutbacks in a country such as Hungary (on the cutting edge of economic reform in the 1990s) than in a country such as Ukraine (a perennial laggard), even though the two countries experienced similar levels of economic contraction during the Great Recession. In short, the very countries that had led the transition from socialism to the market in the 1990s with relatively little protest were in the forefront of protest over the effects of the Great Recession in the late 2000s.

Finally, in Model 5 we add two additional factors that might also be associated with economic protest in the midst of economic decline: (1) public sector employment as a percentage of total employment, and (2) whether a country adopted an IMF Standby Arrangement in order to deal with the financial fallout from the recession. High public employment could affect economic protest during recession in several ways. Countries with large public bureaucracies that had failed to contain public spending were highly exposed to the impact of the financial collapse at a time when funds no longer flowed as easily into public coffers. Public employees and their benefits are likely to be the first targets of cuts when governments are forced to rein in spending during difficult times. Moreover, public employees tend to be highly unionized and organized, and therefore relatively more easily mobilized in the face of threats to their standard of living. Highly visible and easily politicized as both domestic political failure and foreign interference in domestic affairs, IMF rescue arrangements have often served as pretexts for protest waves around the world, as they typically require the adoption of austerity measures aimed at bringing the borrower's economy back into balance. The IMF played a major role in extending loans to postcommunist countries during the transition from socialism without eliciting much protest reaction. However, if the Great Recession brought a climate of diminished "patience," we might expect that the effect of IMF rescue packages in postcommunist Eastern Europe would be no different in the rest of the world, where they are often associated with protest.

As Model 5 indicates, every additional percentage point of total employment that resided in the public sector increased the frequency of protest against economic cutbacks by about 5 percent. Thus, a country such as Latvia (which had a proportion of public sector employment of almost 35 percent) would be expected to experience nearly 50 percent more protests against economic cutbacks compared to Estonia (whose public sector employment was only 24.5 percent of total employment). The adoption of an IMF Standby Arrangement increased protest against economic cutbacks by 84 percent. Those postcommunist countries that experienced the highest levels of economic protest and violence associated with the Great Recession were indeed those that relied on IMF loans to prop them up, and they were also early seekers of entrance into the EU (Hungary, Latvia, and Romania). By contrast, postcommunist countries that borrowed heavily from the IMF during this period but were not EU members (Belarus and Ukraine) experienced little protest associated with their adoption of Standby Arrangements.[13] Neither public employment nor IMF loans had any independent effect on economic protest overall or on level of protest participation.

These findings held up to a number of robustness checks.[14] Next we explore them in more detail through two paired case studies (Estonia-Latvia and Hungary-Ukraine) that illustrate some of the causal mechanisms involved and identify a number of additional processes that are not easily incorporated within a quantitative framework.

Latvia and Estonia: A Paired Case Comparison

Latvia and Estonia have similar economic and political reform records; both experienced similar EU integration processes; their economies have similar sectoral structures; both enjoyed buoyant pre-crisis economic growth,[15] followed by severe economic contractions in 2008 and sharp rises in unemployment in 2008–09. In light of these similarities, the stark contrast between Latvia's high number of economic protests and participation rates and Estonia's quiescence throws into sharper relief more fine-grained differences between the two countries that help to explain these differing protest outcomes. Latvia's higher level of public sector employment (34.7 percent in 2005, compared to 24.5 percent in Estonia)[16] and the IMF rescue package in Latvia are obvious differences, but other factors contributed to the contrasting patterns of protest as well.

One might have expected both Latvia and Estonia to exhibit significant protest mobilizations in the early 1990s. Protest for independence in the late Soviet era had created a powerful precedent, and the economic reform process was radical and imposed significant social costs. However, the absence of protests organized by ethnic Estonians and Latvians may be at least partly explained by the shared drive to build an independent state and "return to Europe." For their part, the sizeable Russophone populations in both countries were initially politically disenfranchised and encountered persistent obstacles to full social and political integration. Moreover, Russophones are a diverse group with a shared language rather than clear social or ethnic markers; many had opportunities to migrate to Russia or work in Europe; Russophone parties lacked organizational coherence, and the mainstream political discourse was skewed to the center-right and right, tending to crowd out minority views. These factors may go some way toward explaining the relative quiescence of Russophone populations in both Latvia and Estonia.

In the absence of systematic data on the participation of specific ethnic groups in economic protests during the Great Recession, we cannot address this cleavage systematically. However, very few economic protests in Estonia or Latvia during the Great Recession seem to have had a distinct ethno-linguistic dimension to them, at least as reported in the media. Public sector employment is higher among ethnic Latvians, and outmigration (within the EU) has been higher among the Russophones, suggesting that ethnic Latvians might have accounted for a significant (if not the main) share of economic protesters during the crisis. In Estonia, neither Estonians nor Russophones mobilized over economic conditions during the Great Recession in significant numbers.

Although Estonia and Latvia tend to be discussed as variations of the same case in terms of economic and political reforms, a closer look reveals important differences that shaped how they experienced the boom and bust cycle of the 2000s and the strict austerity measures both countries imposed on their populations. One crucial difference is that Estonia consistently pursued a balanced budget and generated a budget surplus since 2002, which it used to build up a Stabilization Reserve Fund precisely for emergency situations (Kraan, Wehner, and Richter 2008, 10; Martin 2010). By contrast, Latvia did not secure its reserves but instead spent its growth proceeds (Kraan et al. 2009, 190). As a result, Estonia's austerity measures could concentrate on cutting other expenditures than social transfers, whereas Latvia's IMF-overseen austerity program introduced cuts across the board. By softening the blow of austerity cuts, Estonia's balanced budget and financial reserves helped the government maintain a public reputation for effectiveness. (On the importance of budget deficits for protest mobilization, see Kriesi's Chapter 10 in this volume.)

Similarly, different degrees of corruption led to variation in levels of public trust in government in the two countries. Indeed, on a number of corruption measures Latvia has performed consistently worse than Estonia.[17] Latvia entered the financial crisis with the issue of corruption conspicuous on the public agenda after a number of high-level corruption allegations against party and government officials and controversial government decisions aimed at restraining its Anti-Corruption Bureau, which had been investigating several prominent businessmen with political influence. Several demonstrations over these issues had mobilized sections of society already prior to the onset of the Great Recession (in particular, a rally in October 2007, at which several thousand protesters called for the resignation of Prime Minister Aigars Kalvitis of the People's Party over his decision to dismiss the head of the Anti-Corruption Bureau) and opened the way for a series of protests driven by economic demands once the implications of the crisis became more tangible. The prime minister was forced to step down in early December 2007 after President Zatlers called for his resignation. Corruption issues remained high on the political agenda, with the chief of the Anti-Corruption Bureau eventually dismissed in June 2008 in yet another controversial decision, leaving the bureau without a new head until early 2009.

Estonia's transition from communism has been less conflictual than Latvia's, and the quality of formal and informal institutions has been higher (Kuokstis and Vilpisauskas 2010; Pettai and Mölder 2010). Ironically, when the Latvian Prime Minister Kalvitis resigned in late 2007 in the wake of corruption scandals after three years in office, he had become the longest-serving prime minister in Latvian politics since 1991. The political volatility in Latvia (compared to government stability in Estonia) underpinned perceptions of a lack of government effectiveness. This volatility was only partially masked by a repeated pattern of keeping the government in place while replacing its members (a pattern that continued during the financial crisis).

The link between perceptions of government ineffectiveness or corruption and protest is an indirect but important one. These perceptions undermined public trust in government, which in turn helped to politicize society in the context of a crisis situation. In Latvia public trust in the government was low (20 percent in spring 2007, and still only 13 percent by spring 2010). By contrast, even in the midst of severe economic contraction it remained high in Estonia (66 percent in spring 2007, and 53 percent in spring 2010)—significantly higher than the EU average of 41 percent for 2007 and 29 percent for 2010 (Eurobarometer 67, 2007; Eurobarometer 73, 2010).

On the eve of the Great Recession, recognition of past economic progress and expectations of continued economic improvement were high in the Baltic states. When asked in spring 2007 if their situation had changed in the last five years, 75 percent of Estonians said their situation had improved, 16 percent said it was unchanged, and only 8 percent thought their situation had worsened. Latvians were somewhat less positive but still well above the EU average at the time: 58 percent thought their situation had improved, 23 percent saw it as unchanged, and

18 percent said it had worsened (Eurobarometer 67, 2007, 265). The outlook for the next five years was similarly optimistic: 66 percent of Estonians and 58 percent of Latvians expected their situation to improve in the next five years (well above the 43 percent average for the EU as a whole; Eurobarometer 67, 2007, 266). The impact of the crisis would have thus come as a shock to populations in both countries, but Estonia's policy track record and its stable and trusted government provided it with a buffer that was lacking in Latvia.

Latvia's large public sector also played an important role in spurring protest in response to the economic crisis. In September 2008 health workers, teachers, and police demonstrated in Riga to demand higher salaries (*Telegraf*, September 19, 2010). Soon afterward, on October 30, about a thousand doctors and nurses began a two-day strike while the Saeima (the Latvian legislature) was debating an austerity budget envisaging job and health expenditure cuts. In December the Latvian government agreed to an IMF rescue deal (involving the EU) of €7.5 billion (of which €600 million was immediately disbursed, with further tranches earmarked for 2009–10). As a result, a range of austerity measures were put in place to bring the budget deficit under control, including job cuts and an average public salary cut of 25 percent. The IMF deal proved the crucial catalyst for mobilizing the public sector at large. On January 13, 2009, large-scale antigovernment protests involving about ten thousand people turned violent when hundreds of youths (apparently a mixture of Russian speakers and Latvians) overturned cars, looted shops, and threw cobblestones ripped from the streets of the old city into the windows of Saeima's building (Reuters, January 13, 2009). This was the worst violence in Latvia since 1991, and it triggered a swift political response by President Zatlers, who openly criticized the coalition government for having lost touch with voters. Following the Trade Union Federation's call for a constitutional referendum, he asked the Saeima to strengthen his constitutional powers to initiate new elections in the event of legislative gridlock and to give the public the right to seek early elections via a referendum. Zatlers also urged the government to facilitate a turnover in government posts and bring opposition parties into the cabinet (Reuters News, January 14, 2009). Prime Minister Godmanis survived a vote of no confidence in early February, but his position became untenable when two of his coalition partners left the government. In March 2009, Valdis Dombrovskis of the New Era Party took over as prime minister. Throughout 2009—in the run-up to and after the Saeima's approval of further budget cuts to qualify for a tranche of the IMF package (AP, June 18, 2009)—smaller and medium-size anti-austerity protests, led by public sector workers, continued. Dombrovskis temporarily oversaw a minority government, but he won a narrowly contested election in October 2011 against the Harmony Center, the center-left party associated with the Russophone electorate. Early parliamentary elections held in September 2011, after a referendum on the dissolution of parliament, kept Dombrovskis in office as part of a coalition government, although his party had actually come in third, after Harmony Center and the new Reform Party set up by former President Zatlers.

Estonia's government stability and relative quiescence in the midst of an analogous economic decline make for a marked contrast. Prime Minister Andrus Ansip (Reform Party) was appointed in 2005 to replace Juhan Parts and managed to see out an entire elected term in office from 2007, surviving a vote of no-confidence over austerity measures in February 2009 and overseeing a minority government after his coalition partner, the Social Democrats, left in May 2009. He was reelected (albeit narrowly) in March 2011, again as part of a coalition of center-right parties (with Pro Patria and Res Publica Union; *European Voice*, February 24, 2011).

Estonia's entrance into the eurozone on January 1, 2011, also set Estonia apart from Latvia (although Latvia maintained its currency peg against the euro). After EU membership, the adoption of the euro had become the next big international test of new member states' economic and financial credentials. Estonia's commitment to staying on target for euro membership despite the financial crisis provided an external and domestic anchor and reinforced its image of policy coherence. Because Estonia did not need to be bailed out with the help of an IMF loan, the government could present itself as strong, providing an additional societal buffer against protests in the midst of severe economic pain.

The comparison between Latvia and Estonia confirms that a large public sector hit particularly hard by austerity measures played an important role in evoking economic protest, and that IMF rescue packages also acted as an important lightning rod for protest. The comparison also brings out the importance of domestic differences related to the public's trust in transparent and effective government, the existence of financial reserves, and external reform anchors (such as the adoption of the euro) for explaining differential protest responses to the economic disaster.

Hungary and Ukraine: A Paired Case Comparison

Hungary and Ukraine varied greatly in the type and comprehensiveness of their economic and political reforms in the 1990s,[18] but in the middle to late

2000s both countries experienced a deep financial and economic crisis that required the help of the IMF. In Hungary a severe domestic crisis after many years of expectations tied to the country's reform success was reinforced by the global financial crisis; in Ukraine external shocks abruptly ended a short period of strong economic growth and plunged the country back into its long accustomed crisis. Hungary saw sustained large-scale protest mobilization, whereas Ukraine continued to experience only small-scale protests on a wide range of economic and political issues. These differing trajectories and Hungary's larger public sector (31.5 percent in 2005, compared to 21.6 percent in Ukraine) go some way toward explaining why protest activity was more significant in Hungary than in Ukraine. But the disparate political landscapes of these countries also provide some critical clues to the dynamics involved in producing differing protest responses to the Great Recession. Indeed, they point to the fact that economic conditions, a sizeable public sector, and a catalyst such as an IMF loan and accompanying austerity programs need to be activated by social movements or political parties in order to translate into significant protest. Hungary and Ukraine share an extremely polarized political environment—arguably a conducive starting-point for protest. But they are polarized differently, and the nature of this polarization, combined with differing expectations within their respective publics about government, played important roles in producing contrasting protest outcomes. Hungary belonged to the frontrunners of reform in the region, and after more than two decades since the start of comprehensive economic reforms and several years into EU membership, a domestic financial crisis and the immediate austerity program hit society hard, further polarized it, and fed into party-led mobilization. Ukraine's extremely drawn out political and economic reform process since 1991 and the disillusionment that enveloped Ukrainian society after the enormous mass mobilizations of the Orange Revolution in 2004 made the new financial and economic crisis less of a rallying point for political parties and for society at large.

In 2006 Hungary had the largest budget deficit in the EU. Austerity measures, including an envisaged 10 percent cut to the public sector, were introduced before the onset of the Great Recession in response to the country's economic problems. The domestic economic crisis unfolded against an extreme and growing political polarization between the Socialist Party (MSZP) and the center-right party Fidesz under Viktor Orbán. A leaked "secret speech" by Socialist Prime Minister Ferenc Gyurcsány in autumn 2006 in which he admitted that he had lied about the state of the economy before the elections provided the trigger for a long series of antigovernment protests, culminating in Fidesz's landslide victory in the April 2010 elections, when the political center/center-left was practically obliterated and democratic checks and balances came unhinged.

From early 2007, there were repeated antigovernment protests of varying magnitude (several hundred to several thousand) in Budapest and cities across Hungary demanding the prime minister's resignation over the government's plan to raise taxes, cut subsidies, and dismiss thousands of public sector employees (AP, January 20, 2007). In February antigovernment protesters staged road closures in a hundred locations across the country in protest against the austerity package. In addition, there were sector-specific protests and local issue-specific protests tied to the austerity measures.

During these first protests Fidesz still appeared "weak and divided" (*New York Times*, March 11, 2007). However, Fidesz gradually stepped up the pressure on the coalition of Socialists and liberal Free Democrats (SZDSZ) by actively shaping the public discourse and organizing protests (some deliberately coinciding with national holidays), using the social unrest over austerity measures to boost its own electoral support. Antigovernment protests increasingly acquired nationalist overtones, as Fidesz faced growing competition from the extreme right in Jobbik, a right-wing youth movement transformed into a party in 2003 that was gradually increasing its support base. In September 2007 antigovernment protests marked the first anniversary of the leaked prime minister's speech, with mass protests against anti-austerity measures mobilizing an estimated ten thousand people.

In late October and early November, train drivers staged warning strikes across the country against government plans to close various rail routes. This was followed by about half of Budapest's bus drivers and about four thousand bus drivers across Hungary, who protested against planned layoffs. In March 2008 a Fidesz-initiated referendum, approved by the Constitutional Court, put three questions to the public: on the introduction of doctors' fees, hospital charges, and university tuition. More than 80 percent of those who participated voted against all of the proposals.

Hungary narrowly averted a financial crisis with the help of an International Monetary Fund–led $25.1 billion rescue package put in place in November 2008. It involved the EU and was tied to strict austerity measures aimed at controlling the budget deficit. Hungary's currency fell to an all-time low against the euro, as investors fled amidst concerns over the country's high budget deficit, public sector debt, and heavy reliance on external financing (Reuters, November 29, 2008). Large-scale foreign borrowing had allowed the country to run a sizeable current account deficit (7.5 percent of GDP in

2006, and 6.4 percent in 2007) and a large fiscal deficit in 2006 (Cordero 2009). Access to cheap international credit saw the private sector and households exposed to high debts, often held in foreign currencies. When external capital inflows dried up in connection with the global financial crisis, the Hungarian economy imploded. The presence of the IMF mission further fueled the ongoing protests. In late November 2008 they built into large-scale anti-government actions against pay and pension cuts, with about ten thousand workers across Hungary going on strike at train stations, manufacturing plants, schools, pharmacies, and electricity plants. Several thousand public sector workers represented by thirty unions also protested outside the Hungarian National Assembly against pay cuts (Reuters, November 28, 2008). On December 15 the budget tabled by the prime minister, including a slight upward revision of the fiscal deficit targets that was sanctioned by the IMF, passed the National Assembly. Immediately, rail worker strikes started up again, and public sector unions announced a new series of strikes for early 2009 (Reuters News, December 15, 2008).

The momentum of regular Sunday demonstrations against the government gradually picked up throughout the spring of 2009. In March Prime Minister Gyurcsány resigned in the hope of enabling the Socialist Party to catch up in the polls before the elections scheduled for early 2010. In mid-April Gordon Bajnai (MSZP) was sworn in as the new prime minister. In Hungary's highly politicized setting, this internal turnover triggered further demonstrations, strikes, and clashes with the police. The extremist party Jobbik achieved a breakthrough in the European Parliament Elections in June 2009 (gaining three representatives) and continued to position itself in anticipation of the 2010 elections. Large-scale anti-austerity protests by public sector workers continued until the elections in April 2010, which saw Fidesz win a landslide victory and Viktor Orbán become prime minister, commanding a two-thirds (constitutional) majority in the National Assembly without an effective opposition. Jobbik gained parliamentary representation (twenty-six seats) as Hungary's third-strongest party. It had played an important role in the mobilization of sustained protest and affected a significant shift of Hungary's party system to the right.

Compared to Hungary, Ukraine's transition in the 1990s proved considerably more complex. This was due to the country's integration into the Soviet economy, the need to build a new independent state alongside fundamental political and economic reforms, and the existence of strong regional cleavages not only around language and identity issues but also including differences in economic structures and domestic and international political preferences (Sasse 2010). In addition to the post-Soviet output collapse, soft budget constraints saw the country slide into hyperinflation by late 1993 and only gradually recover through monetary stabilization in 1996. The privatization process was slow and gathered speed only in the late 1990s (D'Anieri, Krawchuk, and Kuzio 1999, 166–205). And it was not until the early to mid-2000s that Ukraine began to experience significant positive economic growth. Presidential policy wavered continually during these years to appease certain regional constituencies, numerous governments collapsed, and the constitutional division of power between the president and the prime minister became politicized (and remains ambiguous even today).

The authoritarian drift of the scandal-ridden Kuchma regime ended abruptly with the Orange Revolution in late 2004, a moment of massive protest mobilizations (centered on Kyiv and the western regions) against electoral fraud in the presidential elections. The protests led to a rerun of the elections and brought to power a reform coalition of President Viktor Yushchenko and Prime Minister Yuliya Tymoshenko. After many years of economic crisis, corruption, and an uncertain foreign policy course, public expectations for domestic reform and Ukraine's European integration were high, at least in western and central Ukraine. However, these expectations were soon dashed by the growing policy disagreements and personal rivalry between Yushchenko and Tymoshenko and by repeated government changes that saw the return of Yushchenko's 2004 electoral rival Viktor Yanukovych as prime minister in 2006 (and eventually, in 2010, as president). Corruption remained rampant, further undermining societal trust in government.[19] Opinion polls showed that throughout 2007 around 40 percent of respondents did not support the activities of the government; this proportion rose throughout 2008, peaking in March 2009 at 63.7 percent (Opinion Polls for 2007–2009, from the Razumkov Centre). Even after the presidential elections in 2010 that were won by Yanukovych, 30 percent immediately disapproved of his new government, and opposition steadily rose to 45 percent by the end of 2010 and to 62.6 percent in 2011 (Razumkov Centre, Opinion Polls, 2010–2011). In response to the question of whether Ukraine was developing in the right or wrong direction, there was only a brief period in early 2005, immediately after the Orange Revolution, when more than 50 percent of Ukrainians responded positively, dropping to about 20 percent by the end of 2007, and even lower by 2009 (Razumkov Centre, Public Opinion, 2004–2008). Such widespread disillusionment with Ukrainian politics that cut across the political spectrum and across the country's regional divide limited the ability of any political actor to mobilize public support around a tangible political alternative. It would be misleading to characterize Ukrainian society as apolitical; there was persistent low-level protest mobilization (at times reaching several thousand protesters) in Kyiv and regional cities over a wide range of political issues, such as opposition to NATO membership, Crimean Tatar mobilization, protest over economic issues, and pre-election rallies orchestrated by the two main parties (Yanukovych's Party of Regions and Tymoshenko's Bloc). But these scattered protests have not jelled into larger campaigns or events. None of the dominant political actors had the credibility or vision to formulate a tangible political alternative that would tap into the alienation accompanying the economic crisis, not even for parts of the country.

Ukraine's brief period of impressive economic growth in the mid-2000s (GDP grew by more than 12 percent in 2004 and by more than 7 percent in 2006 and 2007) was driven by the steel sector benefiting from high global steel prices and was accompanied by property and credit booms. All this came to a halt as a result of the external shock of the global financial crisis. However, even the IMF rescue package of $16.4 billion, agreed on in late October 2008, sparked only a few medium-sized protests and no sustained protest campaigns. The last installment of the IMF loan was frozen in late 2009 when the Ukrainian government raised minimum wages and pensions. The involvement of the IMF—against a backdrop of earlier IMF loans in the late 1990s—failed to act as a catalyst for large-scale protests like those in Latvia or Hungary. Ukraine's biggest anti-austerity protests (up to five thousand protesters) occurred in December 2008; the implications of the IMF deal for jobs and social transfers were singled out by the protesters (mostly coal miners from state-run mines and pensioners) at the time (DPA, December 23, 2008). In February 2009 several thousand people protested against the austerity budget of the city of Kyiv. The protests brought together representatives of the Ukrainian Trade Union Federation, workers of state-run companies, public sector employees, and political activists from both Yanukovych's and Tymoshenko's parties (Ukraine General Newswire, February 12, 2009). The biggest protest since the legislative elections in 2007 took place in April 2009—estimates vary between twenty thousand and fifty thousand participants—at a pre-election rally by Yanukovych supporters demanding the resignation of the president and prime minister for their failure to resolve the economic crisis (Reuters, April 3, 2009; dpa, April 3, 2009). This event occurred a week after the legislature passed two bills restoring the flow of IMF credits. In July 2010 a new IMF loan of $15.2 billion was agreed on, directly linked to a significant hike in household gas and utility prices. The period October–December 2010 also saw a series of medium-sized protests (involving several thousand people) by small business owners and employees against the new tax code, resulting in President Yanukovych vetoing the provisions on higher taxes for small businesses (AFP, November 30, 2010). Though effective on their own terms, the interests represented were issue-specific and failed to mobilize a wider societal concern about the economic crisis.

For a country the size of Ukraine and with the depth of economic contraction that Ukraine experienced during the Great Recession, economic protest was decidedly small. The Ukrainian case illustrates that economic crisis, an IMF program, the precedent of recent massive mobilization, and a high level of political polarization need not translate into large-scale mass protest without parties mobilizing along this cleavage and without the public believing in the prospect of a credible alternative. In Ukraine's postrevolutionary political landscape, disillusionment with all the key actors prevails. A series of elections in close succession provided sufficient opportunities for the main political parties to mobilize around the fallout from the economic crisis; however, they chose instead to tap into familiar regional identity cleavages without extensively activating the issues of profound economic hurt that Ukraine has experienced as a result of the Great Recession. By contrast, in Hungary the political landscape was polarized between left- and right-wing parties. Given that the homegrown financial crisis prior to the Great Recession was associated with the Socialist Party, the combined effect of domestic and international crises gave the right-wing party Fidesz an opportunity to stoke and channel public discontent into electoral support. Growing support for the extreme right party Jobbik moved Fidesz further to the right. Ukraine's political scene is similarly polarized between two political parties and their leaders (Yanukovych and Tymoshenko), but they represent regional constituencies rather than clear ideological programs. Having rotated in and out of office, both leaders failed to articulate a credible alternative amidst the widespread disillusionment of Ukrainians across regional and political affiliations.

Conclusion

It is hardly surprising to find that in the region of the world hit hardest by the Great Recession in the 2007–2010 period, significant outbursts of protest occurred. However, the story of the end of "patience" in Eastern Europe is not quite that simple. As we have seen, countries in the region weathered the economic crisis differentially, with some continuing to experience economic growth and others undergoing severe contraction. In Tolstoyan fashion, those "happy" countries that continued to experience economic growth in the midst of global crisis were all little affected by protest, while those "unhappy" countries that experienced significant economic contractions were all "unhappy" in their own ways, displaying quite varied protest responses to economic decline. We showed that those countries that were most vulnerable to a high level of economic protest during the Great Recession were precisely those that had been in the vanguard of economic and political reform in the 1990s, in part because they were more vulnerable to economic downturn as a result of their high dependence on the global economy, in part because they had generated huge expectations surrounding their track records of reform and EU integration, which were dashed in the context of the Great Recession. But a number of other factors also shaped differential protest responses to economic crisis. Countries with high levels of public sector employment experienced greater protest, as austerity measures targeted public employees in particular, and public employee unions provided the mobilizing capacity for generating large and sustained protest campaigns. IMF rescue packages yielded both an opportunity and a grievance for accelerating protest, through the cutbacks they mandated and in how they demonstrated government incapacity. Governments that, prior to the onset of the crisis, already lacked public trust or a reputation for effectiveness were more likely to see sustained and significant protest. We also showed the importance of political context and the key role that political parties and public expectations play in politicizing the cleavages born out of economic crisis. (For further analysis of the link between electoral politics and protest mobilization in response to the crisis, see Kriesi's Chapter 10 in this volume.) If parties lack the credibility or desire to mobilize citizens around the issues of economic pain that they are experiencing, and if citizens are disillusioned and incapable of imagining that collective action might be an effective remedy to their plight, then even a severe economic contraction, an IMF austerity program, and a past history of mobilization will not produce significant or sustained waves of protest.

Thus the protest response to the Great Recession in postcommunist East Europe shows that there is certainly a relationship between deprivation and protest. But it also shows that this relationship is hardly a simple one and depends on the presence of particular facilitating structural conditions, opportunities, and mobilizing structures. The stark contrast between the relatively more "patient" or quiescent protest responses in Eastern Europe during the transition to capitalism in the 1990s and the more contentious protest responses to the Great Recession (even though they both involved deep economic pain) raises broader questions about the conditions under which individuals mobilize collectively against economic hardship. "Patience," it seems, is much harder to sustain the second time around.

Appendix: Procedures for Coding of Event Data

For the purposes of this study, a *demonstration* was defined as an event (1) that was a voluntary gathering of persons with the purpose of engaging in a public collective display of sentiment for or against public policies, (2) that involved a minimum of one hundred persons, and (3) in which the number of participants was not restricted by the organizers of the event (i.e., it was not a conference, convention, or other restricted organized meeting). A *strike* was defined as a work stoppage with the aim of protesting the policies of government, enterprise management, or some other authority (with a minimum size of one hundred participants). For both demonstrations and strikes, a minimum of one hundred participants was required for an event to be included in the sample, since events with fewer participants than that are usually not reported in media sources. A *mass violent event* was defined as collective violence against people or property, with a minimum size of fifteen participants. For ease of coding, any protest act that lasted for a portion of a day was counted as having lasted for an entire day.

Searches of Reuters were conducted using Factiva, while searches of AP, Agence France Presse, Deutsche Press Agentur, and Interfax were conducted using LexisNexis. To ensure that the use of index terms and relevancy filters on searches undertaken in LexisNexis did not bias the results, the list of article headlines returned using the narrow search criteria was systematically compared for a period of six months with the list of article headlines generated by an unfiltered, traditional subject search. No biases were found. As a further check on the coverage of the five international wire services, searches of national newswire services for seventeen of the eighteen countries were undertaken for a period of three months to see whether local coverage of protest events differed systematically from international coverage. The results suggested that coverage of events in Hungary, the Czech Republic, and Lithuania by the international newswires likely underestimated the extent of politically salient protest in these countries. Between January 1 and March 31, 2009, national newswires reported on nine events in Hungary, eight events in the Czech Republic, and seven events in Lithuania that were not covered by the five international wire services. In all other cases, however, coverage of events was roughly identical. At the same time, the results suggested that national wire services had their own substantial lapses in coverage, as a number of the events captured by the international newswires went unreported by the national outlets examined.

Once the media reports were collected, they were examined in detail by one of three members of the coding team and coded using a common coding protocol and detailed set of instructions into a relational database. Information on fifty-five fields was collected, including data on the location of the event, the type of event, the duration of the event, the number of participants, the specific demands made and the targets of protest, the types of participants and the organizers of protest, the police response and the number of arrested or injured, and the extent of civilian-led violence and the degree of damage it caused. All sources used to code each record were hyperlinked to the individual record, thereby allowing the use of this rich body of reports on protest activity as part of the parallel qualitative analysis in the second half of this essay. In order to ensure inter-coder reliability, coders met weekly to resolve questions jointly (and with participation of the principal investigators). A sample check on inter-coder reliability for a sixth of the coded cases revealed an inter-coder reliability of approximately 95 percent. The coding of all events was also reviewed by the principal investigators to further ensure accuracy and consistency.

Notes

1. Data comes from Beissinger (2002).
2. In our sample, the duration of protest events varied from a portion of a day to a high of 134 days, with more than 90 percent of events lasting for a day or less.
3. The number of participants in the events we recorded ranged from a minimum of 100 to approximately 800,000, with a median of 738.
4. In the scholarly literature on cross-national patterns of protest, population size is normally related to the amount of protest in a society (for example, Hibbs 1973, 25). This well-researched pattern accords with the assumptions of critical mass theory, which argues that the larger and more variegated a population, the more likely it is that groups will find a sufficient number of participants to overcome collective action problems (Marwell and Oliver 1993). Indeed, as we will show, across the eighteen postcommunist countries examined here population size was systematically related both to the frequency of protest events and to the level of participation in them.
5. Property damage was coded as follows: those events that involved no violence were coded as 0; those involving violence but no property damage as 1; those involving minor property damage as 2; those involving sporadic looting or arson as 3; those involving widespread looting or arson as 4; and those involving major property destruction as 5.
6. We use event counts weighted by duration, as is common practice in event-count analyses, since this better reflects protest effort than simple event counts.
7. Since this is a short panel (only four years), and some of the independent variables to be tested are time-invariant, a fixed-effects model would not be appropriate. See Cameron and Trivedi (1998, 287–292). For robustness checks, we tested these results against a pooled sample with standard errors adjusted for clustering by country.
8. On cross-sectional time-series tobit models, see Arellano and Honoré (1998).
9. For all four models we tested for the presence of any lagged effects of economic growth on protest and found none.

10. By using 2006 (the year prior to our first measurements of protest), we seek to avoid potential issues of endogeneity, as protest itself (and reactions to it on the part of regimes) could affect the measurement of democracy.
11. The EBRD Transition Index includes thirteen measures of economic reform on issues of privatization, enterprise governance and restructuring, price liberalization, trade and foreign exchange, competition policy, banking reform, securities markets, and infrastructure reform, each ranging in score from 1 (little reform) to 4.33 (the level typical of advanced industrial economies). The measure used here represents an average of the thirteen measures. Data for the Czech Republic are missing from the EBRD data.
12. On the stereotypes about the West associated with EU accession among Hungarians, for instance, see Fölsz and Tóka (2006).
13. Essentially, this factor is controlled for in the protest event models in Table 11.2 by the EBRD Economic Transition Index, which is highly correlated with EU membership.
14. We tested the event models and the tobit models using a pooled sample with standard errors adjusted for clustering at the country level, with no major changes in the substantive results. (The pooled model for economic protest in general, however, did indicate very weak statistical significance for the EBRD Transition Index and IMF Standby Arrangements.) We also tested for the inclusion of a series of other independent variables to see if they changed the results in any way (with no effect): the degree of fractionalization of government parties in the legislature, the degree of fractionalization of opposition parties in the legislature, the seat difference between the largest government party and the largest opposition party in the legislature, the difference in vote share between government parties and opposition parties, the percentage of unemployed, and gross debt as a percentage of GDP. We did find some additional effects from a yearly change in unemployment variable, which in the event count models soaked up much of the effect of our GDP growth variable (as one might expect) but had no effect on the findings overall or on their interpretation.
15. According to the World Bank (2006), Latvia recorded the fastest economic growth in the EU in 2006 (12.2 percent GDP growth), with Estonia not far behind (10.6 percent).
16. Figures are computed from EBRD Structural and Institutional Change Indicators data, using the share of the private sector in total employment in order to estimate the share of public sector employment as a percentage of total employment. The data are available at http://www.ebrd.com/pages/research/economics/data/macro.shtml.
17. According to Transparency International's Corruption Perceptions Index (CPI), ranking more than two hundred countries worldwide, Latvia scored 4.8 (out of 10) in 2007 and came in thirty-ninth out of the countries included, compared to Estonia scoring 6.5 and being ranked twenty-eighth. See Transparency International, CPI (2007).

18. Hungary had an EBRD economic reform index of 3.92—significantly higher than Estonia and Latvia.
19. According to Transparency International's CPI, Ukraine scored 2.7 out of 10 in 2007 and ranked 118th out of about 200 countries; see Transparency International, CPI (2007).

References

Ágh, Attila. 1991. "Transformations to Democracy in East Central Europe: A Comparative View." In György Szoboszlai, ed., *Democracy and Political Transformation*, 103–122. Budapest: Hungarian Political Science Association.

Arellano, Manuel, and Bo Honoré. 1998. "Panel Data Models: Some Recent Developments." In James J. Heckman and Edward Leamer, eds., *Handbook of Econometrics*, Vol. 5, 3230–3296. Amsterdam: Elsevier Science.

Beissinger, Mark R. 2002. *Nationalist Mobilization and the Collapse of the Soviet State*. Cambridge: Cambridge University Press.

Cameron, A. Colin, and Pravin K. Trivedi. 1998. *Regression Analysis of Count Data*. Cambridge: Cambridge University Press.

Cordero, Jose Antonio. 2009. *The IMF's Stand-by Arrangements and the Economic Downturn in Eastern Europe: The Cases of Hungary, Latvia, and Ukraine*. Washington: Center for Economic and Policy Research, September.

D'Anieri, Paul, Robert Krawchuk, and Taras Kuzio. 1999. *Politics and Society in Ukraine*. Boulder, CO: Westview Press.

Ekiert, Grzegorz, and Jan Kubik. 1998. "Contentious Politics in New Democracies: East Germany, Hungary, Poland, and Slovakia, 1989–93." *World Politics* 50 (4), 547–581.

Ekiert, Grzegorz, and Jan Kubik. 1999. *Rebellious Civil Society Popular Protest and Democratic Consolidation in Poland, 1989–1993*. Ann Arbor: University of Michigan Press.

Eurobarometer. 2007. *Standard Eurobarometer 63*, Spring. http://ec.europa.eu/public_opinion/archives/eb/eb67/eb67_en.htm.

Eurobarometer. 2010. *Standard Eurobarometer 73*, Spring. http://ec.europa.eu/public_opinion/archives/eb/eb73/eb73_en.htm.

Fölsz, Attila, and Gábor Tóka. 2006. "Determinants of Support for EU-Membership in Hungary." In Robert Rohrschneider and Stephen Whitefield, eds., *Public Opinion, Party Competition, and European Union in Post-Communist Europe*, 145–164. Houndsmills, Basingstoke: Palgrave Macmillan.

Greskovits, Béla. 1998. *The Political Economy of Protest and Patience: East European and Latin American Transformations Compared*. Budapest: Central European University Press.

Howard, Marc Morjé. 2003. *The Weakness of Postcommunist Civil Society*. Cambridge: Cambridge University Press.

Haggard, Stephan, and Robert Kaufman, eds. 1992. *The Politics of Economic Adjustment: International Constraints, Distributive Conflicts, and the State.* Princeton, NJ: Princeton University Press.

Hibbs, Douglas A. 1973. *Mass Political Violence.* New York: Wiley.

Hibbs, Douglas A. 1976. "Industrial Conflict in Advanced Industrial Societies." *American Political Science Review 70* (4), 1033–1058.

IMF. 2010. "World Economic Outlook," January 26, at http://www.imf.org/external/pubs/ft/weo/2010/update/01/pdf/0110.pdf (accessed on May 17, 2013).

Kraan, Dirk-Jan, Joachim Wehner, and Kirsten Richter. 2008. "Budgeting in Estonia." *OECD Journal on Budgeting 8* (2), 1–40, http://www.oecd.org/dataoecd/59/23/42007202.pdf.

Kraan, Dirk-Jan, Joachim Wehner, James Sheppard, Valentina Kostyleva, and Barbara Duzler. 2009. "Budgeting in Latvia." *OECD Journal on Budgeting 9* (3), 1–43.

Kuokstis, Vytautas, and Ramūnas Vilpisauskas. 2010. "Economic Adjustment to the Crisis in the Baltic States in Comparative Perspective." Paper presented at the Seventh Pan-European International Relations Conference, Stockholm, September, http://stockholm.sgir.eu/uploads/Economic%20Adjustment%20to%20the%20Crisis%20in%20the%20Baltic%20States%20in%20Comparative%20Perspective.pdf.

Martin, Reiner. 2010. "Boom and Bust in the Baltic Countries—Lessons to Be Learnt." *Intereconomics 4*, 220–226.

Marwell, Gerald, and Pamela Oliver. 1993. *The Critical Mass in Collective Action.* Cambridge: Cambridge University Press.

Ost, David. 2005. *The Defeat of Solidarity: Anger and Politics in Postcommunist Europe.* Ithaca, NY: Cornell University Press.

Pettai, Vello, and Martin Mölder. 2010. "Freedom House: Nations in Transit—Estonia." June, 29. http://www.unhcr.org/refworld/docid/4d53f0220.html.

Przeworski, Adam. 1991. *Democracy and the Market. Political and Economic Reforms in Eastern Europe and Latin America.* Cambridge: Cambridge University Press.

Razumkov Centre. 2004–2011. *Public Opinion Polls.* http://www.razumkov.org.ua/eng/poll.php?poll_id=75; http://www.razumkov.org.ua/eng/poll.php?poll_id=67; http://www.razumkov.org.ua/eng/poll.php?poll_id=66.

Robertson, Graeme B. 2010. *The Politics of Protest in Hybrid Regimes: Managing Dissent in Post-Communist Russia.* Cambridge: Cambridge University Press.

Sasse, Gwendolyn. 2010. "Ukraine: The Role of Regionalism." *Journal of Democracy, 21* (3), 99–106.

Seleny, Anna. 1999. "Old Political Rationalities and New Democracies: Compromise and Confrontation in Hungary and Poland." *World Politics 51* (4), 484–519.

Tilly, Charles, and Edward Shorter. 1974. *Strikes in France, 1830–1968.* Cambridge: Cambridge University Press.

Transparency International. 2006, 2007. *Corruption Perceptions Index (CPI)*, http://www.transparency.org/policy_research/surveys_indices/cpi.

Vanhuysse, Pieter. 2006. *Divide and Pacify: Strategic Social Policies and Political Protests in Post-Communist Democracies*. Budapest: Central European University Press.

Walton, John, and David Seddon, eds. 1994. *Free Markets and Food Riots. The Politics of Global Adjustment*. London: Blackwell.

World Bank. 2006. *Economic Policy and External Debt Data*. http://data.worldbank.org/indicator/NY.GDP.MKTP.KD.ZG.

Index

CPSIA information can be obtained
at www.ICGtesting.com
Printed in the USA
BVOW04s2040261116
468980BV00002B/9/P